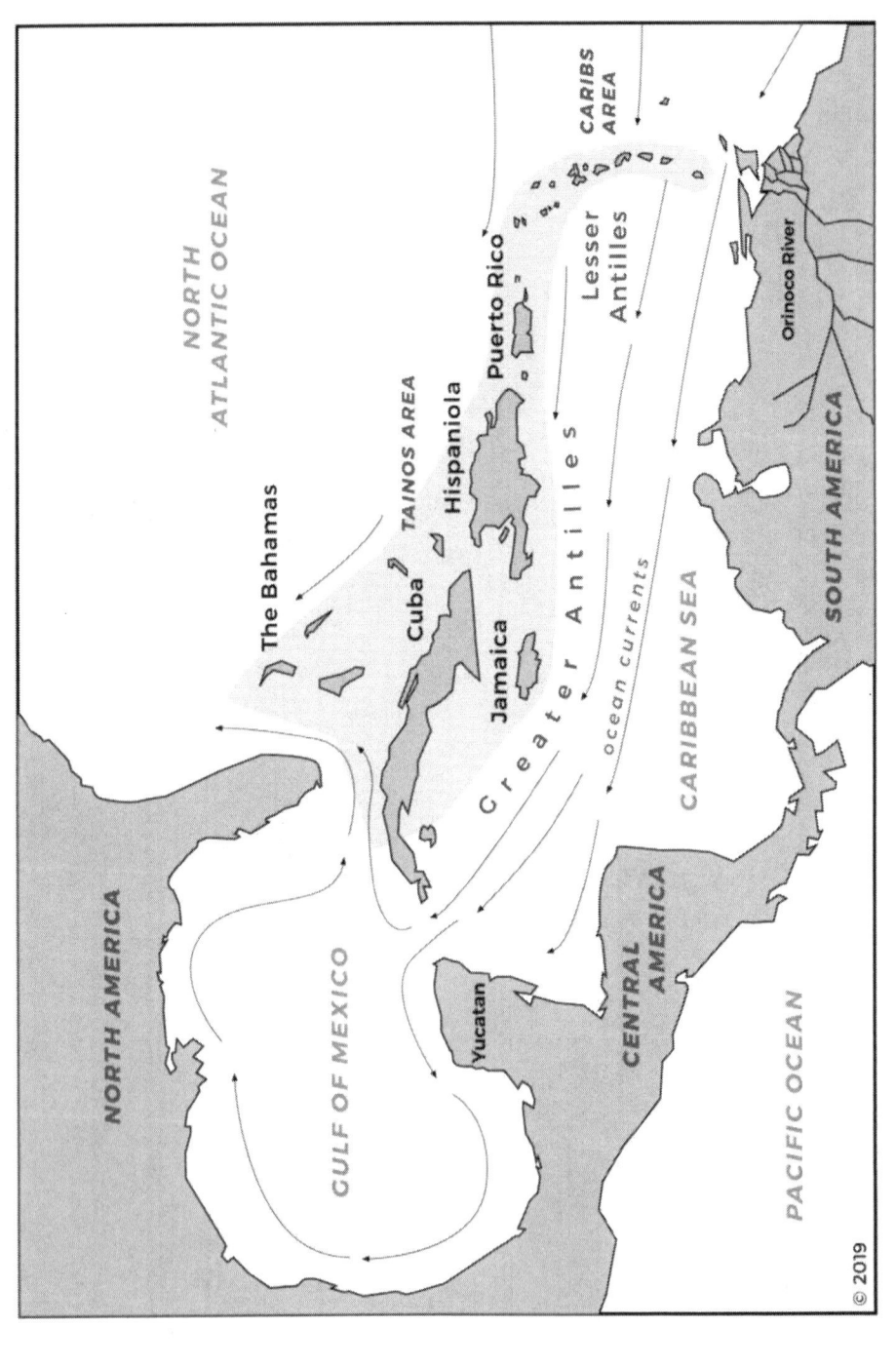

TAINOS and CARIBS
The Aboriginal Cultures of the Antilles

Sebastián Robiou Lamarche

Translation by
Grace M. Robiou Ramírez de Arellano

Editorial Punto y Coma
San Juan, Puerto Rico
2019

To my grandchildren

Tainos and Caribs:
The Aboriginal Cultures of the Antilles

© 2019 Sebastián Robiou Lamarche, Ph. D.
All rights reserved
Translation from Spanish: Grace M. Robiou Ramírez de Arellano
Design: Claudia Robiou Ramírez de Arellano

Editorial Punto y Coma
P.O. Box 9403
San Juan, Puerto Rico, 00908

puntoycomasrl@gmail.com

ISBN 9781796741322

CONTENTS

FIRST PART
THE BEGINNING OF THE END

CHAPTER 1
The clash of two worlds   22
The pre-Columbian vision of the New World   22
The fascinating New World   26
The search for Matininó   29
The first Tainos in Europe   32

CHAPTER 2
Why the colonization?   36
Matininó fades   37
La Isabela, the first factory   40
A frustrated exodus   43
The end of two seamen   46

SECOND PART
THE ANTILLEAN PRE-COLUMBIAN CULTURES

CHAPTER 3
The origin of the true discoverers   50
Regarding ethnohistory and archeology   51
Historical development pre-Columbus   53
The genetic connection   57

CHAPTER 4
A necessary compendium   59
The Archaics. The discoverers of the Antilles   61
The Agro-Ceramics: the first pottery-making farmers   65
The Ostionoids: the precursors to the Tainos   71

THIRD PART
TAINOS: HISTORY AND SOCIETY

CHAPTER 5
Five centuries is nothing...   78
A Renaissance quartet   78

A parenthesis in time	81
The rediscovery of the Taino	83
The pioneers of the 20th century	87

CHAPTER 6

The idealization of the Tainos	90
The origin of the chiefdom	91
Antillean chiefdoms	93
The *cacique*, center of power	95
Regarding *nitaínos*, *behiques* and *naborías*	100

FOURTH PART
TAINOS: MYTHOLOGY AND COSMOLOGY

CHAPTER 7

Beyond Guanín...	104
Myth, time and space	104
The time of the origins	106
The creation of the universe	110
The formation of society	113
The omen of the end	116

CHAPTER 8

Areíto or to remember is to live	119
Space and social structure	122
Taino geomancy	125
Chacuey: a possible astronomical calendar	129

FIFTH PART
TAINOS: FROM AGRICULTURE TO ART

CHAPTER 9

Cycle of the Eternal Return	134
The magic of the stars and the agricultural cycle	135
The *cemíes*, the power behind agriculture	136
Iguanaboína: governess of climatological balance	142
Agricultural technology	147
Mythical plants: *digo*, *güeyo* and *cohoba*	149
The *cohoba* ceremony	150
Magical-medicinal plants	155

CHAPTER 10
The mythical origin of art	158
Taino navigation	160
Regarding Taino artists and their work	163
Artistic manifestations	165
Beyond Coaybay	177

SIXTH PART
CARIBS: HISTORY AND SOCIETY

CHAPTER 11
Fable and reality	182
The origin of the dichotomy	183
A long century of confrontations	185
The French chroniclers	188
In the footsteps of the Caribs	191
The unknown Igneri	195

CHAPTER 12
Two societies in one	197
The woman: force of production and reproduction	198
The *raison d'être* of men	201
Time of peace or how to prepare for war	204

SEVENTH PART
CARIBS: FROM SLAVERY TO ANTHROPOPHAGY

CHAPTER 13
A slave society	212
Etiquette and protocol	213
A chiefdom in gestation?	214
The spirit world	216
The nautical warriors	219
Round trip to dry land	221

CHAPTER 14
The cannibalistic ritual	226
Why anthropophagy?	227
Acáyouman: the father of the lineage	231

EIGHTH PART
CARIBS: MYTHOLOGY AND COSMOLOGY

CHAPTER 15
Carib Myth-Astronomy — 236
The creation of the world and the stars — 237
The stellar kinship system — 238
The Big Dipper: the heron's canoe — 241
Isúla, the celestial barbecue — 243
Coulúmon, the celestial lobster — 244
Bakámo, the Great Serpent — 247
The Milky Way: the path of the turtle — 250

CHAPTER 16
Lost wisdom — 253
Moon, Sun, comets and planets — 253
Eclipses and cosmic chaos — 256
The Carib stellar calendar — 259
The Carib worldview — 261

NINTH PART
DISINTEGRATION AND LEGACY

CHAPTER 17
An imminent end — 266
The apparition at Santo Cerro — 267
The Moon and the Taino rebellion — 269
Xaragua, genocide in action — 271
Expansion to Puerto Rico, Cuba and Jamaica — 273

CHAPTER 18
The rebellion of the Dominicans — 277
The demographic catastrophe — 278
Caribs: between war and peace — 281
The rediscovery of the Carib — 283
The aboriginal patrimony — 285
Professing the indigenous heritage — 289

REFERENCES AND BIBLIOGRAPHY — 293

Author's Note

This book was published originally in Spanish under the title *Taínos y caribes, las culturas aborígenes antillanas*. Since its publication in 2003, it has been recognized as having contributed to a better understanding among the general public of the history of the Antillean cultures before, during and after the arrival of the Europeans.

Over the years, I have received a considerable number of requests from people around the world expressing their desire that the book be made available in English. *Tainos and Caribs: The Aboriginal Cultures of the Antilles* was inspired by those demands. I hope that the English edition broadens the reach of knowledge from anthropologists, historians, archeologists, linguists, artists and others about the Tainos and the Caribs, two cultures that have captivated my interest and imagination for over 25 years.

The original design of the book was made with great care by my daughter Claudia. This English edition reviews and updates the original text and bibliography. The complete translation from Spanish was carried out meticulously by my daughter Grace, whose great effort and enthusiasm makes this edition possible. [1]

I thank both of them for their wholehearted commitment and devotion in the publication and dissemination of this work.

Sebastián Robiou Lamarche
San Juan of Puerto Rico
March 2019

---

[1] Unless otherwise noted, the translation of primary source content was done based on the original Spanish publication of this book in 2003.

Foreword

It is with great honor and privilege that I write this foreword to the English version of *Tainos and Caribs: The Aboriginal Cultures of the Antilles*. I knew this book would become a classic from the moment I read it in 2004. Its publication in English is a testament to the many fine qualities that this book possesses, among which I wish to highlight a few that distinguishes it from other publications on the ancient Caribbean. I also wish to address why the revision and English version of this work surfaces at an opportune time in the histography of the Caribbean. In many ways, the original version of this book foreshadowed our current understanding of the Caribbean archipelago as a heterogenous and complex mosaic. Recent scientific findings support this view of the human past.

From an academic perspective, this book is based on solid research. I cannot think of another popular publication on the subject of the Tainos and Caribs that describes all periods of historical development and all forms of academic inquiry. This book makes use of ethnohistoric documents, archeological evidence and information obtained from osteological and genetic analysis of human remains. The analysis is carried out methodologically and relies on the author's extensive knowledge of mythology, religion, and astronomy. The discussions are appropriately situated geographically, chronologically and culturally and cover the history of the entire Caribbean basin. In short, Robiou does not hold anything back yet is able to present a coherent story that is also impressively enjoyable!

As a field archaeologist and curator, I find that one of the greater traits of this book is that it overcomes a common communication barrier that exists between those of us who conduct the research and the non-specialists who are interested in reading about our findings. It has been estimated that new findings or corrections in the general sciences take ten years or longer to reach school textbooks. In many cases, the findings do not make it to the readers at all. The statistics are worse in the specialized field of Caribbean archaeology.

Remarkably, this book defies the odds because it neither oversimplifies the content nor underestimates the capabilities of the reader. Unlike other publications written for the public, Robiou does not treat the audience as an ignorant or under-educated entity. Instead, he promotes an active conversation and reminds researchers who are busy talking to one another that their audience should be much larger and include the actual "owners" of the cultural heritage they purport to study.

Notably, Robiou recognizes that Taino and Carib societies were not simple. Quite the opposite, he describes their cultures as vibrant and sophisticated. This is in contrast to many publications on the ancient history of the Caribbean that describe the past in a childish manner. Perhaps this is because early archeologists did not have enough information to create more than a fragmented picture of the past. Or, maybe, we tend to view ancient native peoples through the lens of 17th and 18th century Europeans who perceived the indigenous as innocent groups that relied on nature for their sustenance and lived in an idyllic world. Not surprisingly, this view persists today, also assisted by the prejudice with which modern, contemporary and highly technological societies view the unsophisticated past. Robiou thoughtfully presents a different view, opposing the trends I describe, and this is best exemplified in the author's discussions on mythology and cosmology. The approach taken in this book is refreshing and most needed in Caribbean archeology and anthropology.

Finally, the revision and English edition of *Tainos and Caribs* is well-timed because recent developments reaffirm the composite view of the Caribbean presented in the original publication. A social movement led by people who claim to descend from the original indigenous groups has gained some academic recognition since the original version of this book was published. In parallel, recent research points to a more complex and multi-linear historical development than we imagined previously. Advanced archeological research is generating new theories regarding the extent to which different ethnic groups overlapped or co-inhabited the islands. Genetic research is augmenting the questions being asked and requiring that assumptions regarding traditional homogeneous conceptions about who we call Taino and Carib be questioned.

For these reasons, this new edition commands as much attention as the original publication and motivates us to continue to ask ourselves who these indigenous peoples were that lived in our beautiful islands hundreds of years ago, where did they come from and what made their lives meaningful. I trust that you will enjoy this edition as much as I did.

L. Antonio Curet
Curator, National Museum of the American Indian
Smithsonian Institution, Washington D.C.
March 2019

Foreword to the Original Edition

Ricardo E. Alegría

The Taino Indians of the Greater Antilles, as well as the Caribs of the Lesser Antilles, were the first aboriginal inhabitants of the New World to establish relations with European conquerors.

Laws and norms had not yet been established in the last years of the 15th century and the first decade of the 16th century to try to defend the native inhabitants from the abuse and the pushing and shoving that came with their interaction with the European conquerors and colonizers. The result was the rapid disintegration of Taino society, which disappeared within a century.

In Puerto Rico, where the indigenous population at the time of the conquest was not large, the results were even more dramatic than in Hispaniola and Cuba. In 1543, when Bishop Rodrigo de Bastidas arrived on the island of San Juan (Puerto Rico) with the purpose of promulgating the royal decree granting freedom to the Tainos, who from the beginning of the colonization had been "entrusted" in Hispaniola, Cuba and Puerto Rico, he informed the King that he had found only 60 Taino inhabitants. In the other Greater Antilles, the Taino population did not subsist for much longer. Although it is true that as a society the Tainos disappeared, it is no less true that their biological and cultural heritage, together with that of the Europeans and Africans, continues to survive in the current Antillean population.

The rapid disappearance of the Taino society did not permit its study in the manner that other indigenous cultures have been investigated, like in Mexico and Peru. Only limited descriptions are available to contribute to our knowledge of the Taino culture in the Greater Antilles at the time; namely, texts by Christopher Columbus, Diego Álvarez Chanca, Ramón Pané, Bartolomé de las Casas, Gonzalo Fernández de Oviedo, Girolamo Benzoni, Pedro Mártir de Anglería. Other, less important, shallow accounts narrated by explorers and colonizers are available also. In addition, an abundant body of documentary evidence from the colonization process that is still not known in its totality, has enriched what we know about the Taino culture during the Spanish colonization. In contrast to the manner in which Sahagun documented the Mexica and Guaman Poma the Inca, the Taino lacked a person who documented their indigenous worldview and culture.

The situation was not very different for the Caribs of the Lesser Antilles. Despite the fact that the Caribs managed to survive longer in some of the islands, their culture had undergone a transformation by the time it was described by the French chroniclers. This was due to their close interactions with the Taino culture and the African slaves they captured from Spanish colonies and slave ships. The African influence began to manifest itself in the 16th century when in some documents the chroniclers refer to them as "black Caribs." The Caribs had already suffered the influence of the French and English colonists on their islands. The main sources for the study of their society were written several decades after their initial contact with the Europeans.

Fortunately, Columbus, Las Casas and Oviedo made early, although brief, descriptions of the Carib society during the first decades of the 16th century. However, it is the French missionaries and colonizers and, to some extent, the English, who will contribute the main information we rely on today to recognize various aspects of the Carib culture. The writings of César de Rochefort, Juan Baptiste Dutertre, La Borde, Jean Baptiste Labat and others, are essential to distinguish aspects of Carib society. Despite their extremely transformed culture, the Caribs are the only indigenous people of the Antilles who survived the European conquest and colonization; their descendants today live in the island of Dominica. In the Central American coasts there are also the Garifunas that originate from the Caribs mixed with African blacks on the island of St. Vincent, which the English settlers evicted to the island of Roatan, off the coast of Belize, at the end of the 18th century.

The archaeological investigations that, since the last decades of the 19th century have been carried out in the Greater Antilles and have extended into the 20th century, have enriched our knowledge of important aspects of the history and culture of the Tainos. Today, we know how their predecessors, as well as the cultures that preceded them, migrated from the coasts of South America, from the countries we now recognize as Venezuela and Guiana, more than 2,500 years ago. Archeology also allows us to learn cultural aspects that had disappeared at the time of the encounter with the Europeans.

In the case of the Caribs, archeology has not had the same importance as in the Greater Antilles. Due to the fact that the Caribs were the last indigenous people to inhabit the Lesser Antilles, living on the islands a few centuries before their discovery by Columbus, their archaeological sites were recent and superficial, thus destroyed by intensive agriculture promoted by the French and English colonizers. In light of this situation and the aggravating circumstance that not many archaeological excavations were carried out by professionals, the archeology of the islands inhabited by the Caribs has not been fully studied and understood.

Scholars of the aboriginals of the Greater Antilles, making use of the limited historical and archaeological information that was available, have contributed to the knowledge of the Taino culture since the last decades of the 19th century. Numerous studies on individual cultural aspects stand out, however few are those that tried to offer a vision of the aboriginal culture as a whole. Among those works to highlight is that of Agustín Stahl, *Los indios borinqueños* (1889); that of Nicolás Font Roldán, *Cuba indígena* (1881) and that of Antonio Bachiller y Morales, *Cuba primitiva* (1881). Another work of those years was that of Frederick Ober, *Aborigenes of the West Indies* (1895).

During the first decades of the 20th century when, after the Spanish-Cuban-American War, the archaeologists of the United States became interested in the research and study of the Antillean indigenous peoples, works such as those of Jesse Walter Fewkes, *Aborigenes of Porto Rico and Neighboring Islands* (1907) and *A Prehistoric Island Culture-Area in America* (1922) were produced. An interesting synthesis about Antillean archeology and ethnography is that of Thomas Joyce, *Central America and West Indian Archeology* (1916).

In Puerto Rico, the work of Cayetano Coll y Toste, *Prehistoria de Puerto Rico* (1907) stands out, while in Santo Domingo Narciso Alberti y Bosch writes *Apuntes para la prehistoria de Quisqueya* (1912). In Cuba, Mark Harrington stands out with *Cuba Before Columbus* (1921) and J.A. Cosculluela, who contributes *La prehistoria de Cuba* (1922). Meanwhile, in Hispaniola, Herbert Krieger wrote *Aborigenes of the Ancient Island of Hispaniola* (1930).

It was during the 1930s that Yale University's Department of Anthropology became interested in the archeology of the Greater Antilles. Some of its most outstanding scholars carried out important excavations in several of the islands. Among Yale's main contributions are the work of Froelich Rainey, *Porto Rican Archeology* (1935, 1942); Cornelious Osgood's *The Ciboney Culture* (1942) and Irving Rouse's *Porto Rican Prehistory: West and South* (1952) and *Porto Rican Prehistory: South and East* (1952). In 1992, Rouse published a magnificent synthesis of Taino culture based on his archaeological and ethno-historical research in the Caribbean islands: *The Taíno, Rise and Decline of the People Who Greated Columbus*. An important work of investigation about the ceremonial plazas used in Utuado to play ball was published in 1941 by John Alden Mason: *A Large Archaeological Site at Capá, Puerto Rico*.

A seminal study on Antillean cultures is the work of the Swedish scholar, Sven Loven, entitled *Origins of the Tainan Culture* (1935). In Puerto Rico, Adolfo de Hostos stood out as the author of several important essays on Taino archeology during the first half of the 20th century.

Archaeological and ethno-historical studies have gained great popularity in the Antilles in the last decades. Numerous valuable essays have been published about various aspects of the indigenous cultures that populated the islands. These essays have enriched our knowledge of Antillean archeology. Nevertheless, not many studies have tried to provide a picture of the Antillean cultures as a whole. In Cuba, we can point to the works of Pichardo Moya (1956), Manuel Rivero de la Calle (1966), Fernando Ortiz (1943), José Juan Arrom (1967), Ernesto Tabío and Estrella Rey (1966), Lourdes Domínguez (1978), J.M. Guarch (1978). In the Dominican Republic, we find the works of Joaquín Priego (1967), Luis Padilla de Onis (1943), Roberto Cassá (1974), Manuel García Arévalo (1977) and Marcio Veloz Maggiolo (1992). This last one contributes with two works where he makes a synthesis of the indigenous cultures of Hispaniola and the Caribbean.

In Puerto Rico, various attempts to offer a general synthesis of the indigenous cultures that populated the island are embodied in the work of Pablo Morales Cabrera with *Puerto Rico indígena* (1932), Labor Gómez and Manuel Ballesteros with *Vida y cultura precolombina de Puerto Rico* (1980). There is also Ricardo E. Alegría's book for children, *Historia de nuestros indios* (1950).

None of the above works could have been written without considering numerous and valuable monothematic studies that various investigators from Cuba, the Dominican Republic and Puerto

Rico carried out. These essays are cited in the extensive bibliography of this book.

In Jamaica, attempts to provide us with a synthesis of the aboriginal cultures are rare. There are also not many studies in Haiti aimed at presenting a general picture; the work of Michel Aubourg, *Haiti Prehistorique* (1951), stands out.

In the case of the Lesser Antilles, few works exist as well. There are, however, excellent archeological studies. Among these, I highlight that of J. Ballet, *Les Caraïbes* (1875) and that of Father Robert Pinchon, *Les peuples precolombiens dans le Petites Antilles* (1952). Douglas Taylor, the main scholar of the Carib language, is the author of several essays on linguistics and *The Caribs of Dominica* (1938). The Puerto Rican Jalil Sued Badillo has contributed with the work *Los caribes: realidad o fábula* (1978). The Centro de Estudios Avanzados de Puerto Rico y el Caribe published *French Chronicles of the Carib Indians* (1981), translated by Manuel Cárdenas with an Introduction entitled "The first news about the Carib Indians" by Ricardo E. Alegría.

The Proceedings of gatherings of the International Association of Caribbean Archeology which have been, since 1964, carried out in the region, have contributed notably to the study of Antillean cultures.

Today, thanks to Sebastián Robiou Lamarche, the study of the indigenous cultures of the Antilles is enriched by the valuable historical, ethnographic and archaeological information presented in this book. In describing the culture of the Tainos and Caribs, the author provides us a magnificent summary of the results of the most recent archaeological investigations that have been carried out in the Antilles.

The author holds a master's degree from the Centro de Estudios Avanzados de Puerto Rico y el Caribe, in Puerto Rican and Caribbean Studies. He is currently studying for his doctorate [Ph. D., 2008]. He has also taken courses in archeology, anthropology and history. He has participated in archaeological research both in the Dominican Republic and in Puerto Rico, and attended several international congresses. In his research, he has manifested great preference for and has distinguished himself for his work on astronomy and the worldview of the indigenous people of the Antilles, a subject in which he is the author of several important essays.

The work prefaced today has been written, as the author indicates, for the general public. This book provides the most relevant information from the latest research conducted by anthropologists, historians, archaeologists and linguists. These findings, disseminated in books and magazines, are often not available to the general public. *Taínos y caribes, las culturas aborígenes antillanas* is significant because it synthesizes the available documentation on the two indigenous cultures of the region. In general, existing studies only cover one of the two cultures, the Tainos or the Caribs. By discussing both, the author has the opportunity to describe the similarities and differences that existed between them. His careful and comprehensive reading of ethno-historical sources, to include the Spanish, English and French chroniclers, enhances the work. His knowledge of English and French allows him to refer to the extensive and important bibliography written in these languages, without whose knowledge a complete understanding of the Antillean inhabitants can not be acquired.

Robiou Lamarche also offers us an overview of some controversial topics related to the ancient cultures of the Antilles. He evaluates the diverse opinions with gravity and professional ability, offering his own with objectivity and without offending personally those with whom he disagrees. He does this without insisting that only his dictum is valid. The author strengthens the book with important and numerous illustrations of archaeological and ethnographic objects, as well as engravings from historical sources, that his daughter Claudia has artistically integrated into the text.

The copious bibliography is another valuable contribution made by the author to the general public, students and scholars interested in the subject of the archeology and ethno-history of the Antilles. The author has maintained his professional character and has not censored those works that offer a different interpretation to his, but which are always valuable contributions to the study of the indigenous inhabitants of the Antilles.

We wish success to the work of Robiou Lamarche and we can anticipate that it will be received with interest in the Antilles and among scholars of the aboriginal cultures of our America.

San Juan of Puerto Rico
August 2003

Introduction to the Original Edition

The purpose of *Taínos y Caribes, las culturas aborígenes antillanas* is to synthesize, both for the general public and for the specialist, the accounts written by Spanish and French chroniclers and the most recent historical, anthropological, linguistic, archaeological and even genetic research on our ancient settlers. Likewise, the objective is to offer the reader a summary view of the process that Antillean cultures experienced before, during and after the European discovery. In other words, to describe in a succinct manner the origin, peak, decline and legacy of the Taínos and Island-Caribs, commonly called Caribs.

To this end, I have managed to consult over the years almost 400 specialized books and articles written from the 15th century to the present day. As it is, this compilation has allowed me to prepare a vast bibliography (included in the tenth and last part of the book), that will be of great value for those who wish to revisit the original sources.

Excluding the bibliography, the book is divided into nine parts, each with two chapters. In the first part, I quote the valuable impressions written by the pioneering chroniclers, including Columbus himself, regarding the characteristics of the indigenous peoples and the wonderful natural world they found. And how that idyllic and fanciful new world began to fade with the beginnings of colonization. In the second part, going back in time through archaeological research, I present the distinctive features of the cultures that occupied the Greater Antilles chronologically before the arrival of the European: the *arcaicos*, the first farmers and pottery makers, and the precursors of the Taínos.

Then, based on both ethnohistorical and archaeological documentation, in the next three parts of the book, I present a broad exposition of Taino culture, emphasizing details of their historiography, mythology, cosmology, social organization, agriculture and art. Similarly, in the following three parts, I analyze the Carib culture of the Lesser Antilles, highlighting their unknown and often distorted features.

In the ninth part, I return to the first years of the European conquest to explain how, for various reasons, in a relatively short time, the indigenous cultures of the Antilles practically disappeared.

Then, I synthesize the extensive and rich cultural heritage left by the Tainos and the Caribs in the societies of the region. In doing this, I intend to position both cultures in their righteous place in the history of the Antilles.

Even as I kept the book at the summary level, I still examine in it several topics traditionally treated by specialists: the origin of the archiacs (*arcaicos*), the origin of the first farmers and pottery markers, the enigma of the *ciguayos*, the formation of chiefdoms, the dichotomy of the Carib society, the parallels and the differences between the Tainos and the Caribs, as well as the cannibalism of the latter.

In the light of the most recent research, I try to rectify certain concepts about these and other issues that persist. At the same time, based on my research of recent years, I aspire to provide certain comparative interpretations between the Taino and Carib cultures in aspects such as their social structure, worldview, myth-based astronomy, symbology and their knowledge of navigation and medicinal plants.

The book also has a meticulous selection of illustrations that will allow for a better appreciation of the text. I thank my daughter Claudia for her resolute cooperation in the design of this publication.

I wish to express my gratitude to Mr. Ricardo E. Alegría, founder of the Instituto de Cultura Puertorriqueña and the Centro de Estudios Avanzados de Puerto Rico y el Caribe, for his wise advice over the years and for having written the Prologue to this book. I also thank Francisco Moscoso, professor at the University of Puerto Rico, Manuel A. García Arévalo, member of the Academia Dominicana de la Historia in the Dominican Republic, and Lourdes S. Domínguez, archaeologist at the Oficina del Historiador de la Ciudad de La Habana, Cuba, for their motivaton and comments.

I wish for this book to serve for pleasant and educational reading.

Sebastián Robiou Lamarche
August 2003

FIRST PART

THE BEGINNING OF THE END

CHAPTER 1

The clash of two worlds

One can make sense of the European discovery of the continent originally called the Indies, at a later time known as the New World, and eventually named America, from different perspectives.

For the European, the discovery represented the beginning of a new era in which novel cosmographic and philosophical conceptions were forged. Chronicler López de Gómara once said that the discovery was "the greatest thing after the creation of the world." The discovery represented the translocation to the new continent of the imperial borders and economic interests of Europe. In later centuries, the struggles for power in Europe would be mirrored in America, while the colonies produced goods and services for the exclusive benefit of the metropolis.

For the aboriginals in America, who were the true discoverers of the continent, the arrival of the European meant the beginning, in the short- or long-term, of the collapse of their societies, which were at different levels of development at the time of Columbus' arrival. The inhabitants of the Greater Antilles, who believed initially that the Spanish were celestial beings and welcomed them with legendary hospitality, drastically changed their minds and began to treat the colonizers with resolute hostility when their true intentions were revealed. It was in the Greater Antilles where the blunt first contact between the two worlds occurred and it was most likely the coveted gold the main factor that incited the beginning of the end for the Tainos.

The pre-Columbian vision of the New World

It is principally through Christopher Columbus' *Diary* that we know of his impressions of the inhabitants and the islands he discovered. Those islands would be later called Antilles because of the fable of Antilia or Antilla, an island that was believed part of the ancient Atlantis. Columbus' *Diary* is lost today, but we know of it thanks to the opportune transcriptions made by his son, Ferdinand, and Father Bartolomé de Las Casas.

In the first voyage, Columbus was fascinated and in awe by what he saw. Believing he had arrived in the Eastern empire of the Great Khan cited by the famous Marco Polo, Columbus sailed from the Lucayas (Bahamas) to the north coast of Cuba (Juana), and from there to Bohío (Hispaniola), where decides to return to Spain.

Day after day, island after island, he writes his thoughts with admiration, while at the same time assessing and glorifying everything that is revealed to him. In no time at all and as a man of his time, he projects on the local inhabitants and the natural surroundings his European worldview. It is worth reproducing his very first impressions:

Friday, October 12, 1492 [2]:

At two hours after midnight the land was sighted [...] they arrived at a small island of the Lucayos [Bahamas], called, in the language of the Indians, Guanahani [San Salvador]. Then came naked people [...]

I, that we might form great friendship, for I knew that they were a people who could be more easily freed and converted to our holy faith by love than by force, gave to some of them red caps, and glass beads to put round their necks, and many other things of little value, which gave them great pleasure, and made them so much our friends that it was a marvel to see.

They afterwards came to the ship's boats where we were, swimming and bringing us parrots, cotton threads in skeins, darts, and any other things; and we exchanged them for other thing that we gave them, such

---

[2] The contents of Columbus' diary during his first voyage were first made known to the public in the epitome incorporated in Ferdinand Columbus' book, which has come down to use only in the Italian translation of Alfonso Ulloa, as *Historie del S.D. Fernando Colombo nelle quali s'ha particolare e vera relazione della vita e de' jatti dell' Ammiraglio D. Christoforo Colombo suo padre*, etc. (*The life of the Admiral Chrisopher Columbus by his son Ferdinand*) (Vince, 1571). The English translation given here is that of Sir Clements R. Markham in 1893 with slight revisions by Grace M. Robiou Ramírez de Arellano in 2019.

Columbus in Hispaniola exchanges gifts with the Tainos.
Great Travels, Book IV (Theodor de Bry, 1594).

as glass beads and small bells. In fine, they took all, and gave what they had with good will. [...]

They go as naked as when their mothers bore them, and so do the woman, although I did not see more than one young girl. All I saw were youths, none more than thirty years of age. They are well very well made, with very handsome bodies, and very good countenances. Their hair is short and coarse, almost like the hairs of a horse's tail. [...]

They paint themselves black, and they are [...] neither black nor white. Some paint themselves white, others red [...]. Some paint their faces, others the whole body, some only round the eyes, others only on the nose.

They neither carry nor know anything of arms, for I showed them swords, and they took them by the blade and cut themselves through ignorance. [...]

I saw some with marks of wounds on their bodies, and I made signs to ask what it was, and they gave me to understand that people from other adjacent islands came with the intention of seizing them, and that they defended themselves. [...]

Saturday, October 13:

As soon as dawn broke many of these people came to the beach [...] Their legs are very straight, all in one line, and no belly, but very well formed. They came to the ship in small canoes, made out of the trunk of a tree like a long boat, and all of one piece, and wonderfully worked, according to their land. They are large, some of them holding 40 to 45 men, others smaller, and some only large enough to hold one man. They are propelled with a paddle like a baker's shovel, and go at a marvelous rate. If the canoe capsizes, they all promptly begin to swim, and to bail it out with calabashes that they take with them. [...]
I was attentive, and took trouble to ascertain if there was gold. I saw that some of them had a small piece fastened in a hole they have in the nose, and by signs I was able to make out that to the south, or going from the island to the south, there was a king who had great cups full, and who possessed a great quantity.

Sunday, October 14:

Some of them brought us water, others came with food, and when they saw that I did not want to land, they got into the sea, and came swimming to us. We understood that they asked us if we had come from heaven. One old man came into the boat, and others cried out, in loud voices, to all the men and women, to come and see the men who had come from heaven, and to bring them to eat and drink. Many came, including women, each bringing something, giving thanks to God, throwing themselves on the ground and shouting to us to come on shore. [...]
Close to the above peninsula there are gardens of the most beautiful trees I ever saw, and with leaves as green [...] I saw so many islands that I hardly knew how to determine which I should go first. Those natives I had with me said, by signs, that there were so many that they could not be numbered, and they gave the names of more than a hundred.

In those first three days, Columbus had already forged what José Juan Arrom, Cuban scholar of Taino culture and emeritus professor at Yale University, called the "Columbian vision" of the new lands: naked and innocent (the natural man), good servers and

Engraving where the fantasy of the Old World
is mixed with the reality of the new lands.

well-trained (the economic man), clever and willing (the social man), and easy to convert (the religious man). This was the manner in which the foundation for the future conquest and colonization of the New World was established.

The fascinating New World

On Friday, October 26, Columbus records for the first time in his *Diary* the word *canoa* (canoe), the first Taino word to appear in the Spanish language. He began little by little to comprehend the meaning of other words. Guided by skilled aboriginals he apprehended, among which was possibly the one who would later be baptized as "Diego Colón," on October 28 Columbus arrives in the north coast of the island of Cuba. He baptized Cuba with the name of Juana. He declares that it is "the most beautiful that eyes have seen." He reports finding large canoes and towns of "fifty houses, where he said there were a thousand neighbors because many live in a house." In one of them, the indigenous inhabitants "touched […] and kissed […] hands and feet, marveling and believing that [my people] came from heaven."

Along the coast of Cuba, he searches and searches for the island of Baneque, which his fanatical imagination makes him believe has beaches covered in gold.

It is in Cuba that the Admiral first documents the indigenous people's fear towards cannibals. Perhaps mixing medieval European fables with the information being provided by his guides, on Friday, November 23, Columbus writes that on the nearby island of Bohío, east of Cuba, "there were people who had an eye on their foreheads, and others who were cannibals, and of whom they were much afraid." Days later, on Monday, November 26, he notes that "all the people he has hitherto met with have very great fear of those of Caniba or Canima," adding that "they live on the island of Bohío, which must be very large [...] and they believe that they are going to take people from their homes." Columbus, however, was not inclined to believe them. Rather, he was "inclined to believe that it was people from the dominions of the Gran Khan who took them into captivity."

Columbus' descriptions are likely evidence of the warrior expeditions carried out by the Caribs, who occupied part of the Lesser Antilles at the time, to Taino territory in the Greater Antilles. As it turns out, it was precisely in the direction of the Lesser Antilles, to the east, where the aboriginal guides always pointed out that gold was to be found. Columbus had yet to find gold, but as we shall soon see, in experiencing and documenting the Taino beliefs regarding where gold was to be found and their fears of man-eating people, Columbus and his men were unveiling - unknowingly - the Taino mythology.

On December 6, Columbus navigates to Bohío, an island he called La Española (today formed by Haiti and the Dominican Republic, which we refer to as Hispaniola). He calls Hispaniola "the most beautiful thing in the world." While navigating along its north coast in an easterly direction, he praises its natural beauty, the mighty rivers, the wide bays and the high mountains that seem to reach the sky. He sees immense sown fields and mentions the existence of towns with a central square of "a thousand houses and more than a thousand men." The houses "were made in the manner of *alfaneques*, very large" and were "well swept and clean." He says that his men "saw two women as white as they could be in Spain."

Importantly, Columbus observes that the inhabitants of Hispaniola constitute a more organized society. He recounts the exchange of food and gifts he held with a "king," who he would later, on December 18, learn to call *cacique*. "The *cacique* was a youth of about 21 years of age, and he had with him an aged tutor, and other councilors who advised and answered him, but he uttered very few words. [...] They sat at his feet [...] and they were all of fine presence [...]" Days later, Columbus understands that the word *nitaíno* meant "grande" (large or important), although he "did not know if they said it for a nobleman or governor or judge."

As if summarizing, Columbus writes on Monday, December 24:

> *[...] I have spoken in a superlative degree of the country and people of Juana, which they call Cuba, but there is as much difference between them and this island [La Española] and people as between day and night [...] the things and the great villages of this island, which they call Bohío, are wonderful. All here have a long manner and gentle speech, unlike the others, who seem to be menacing when they speak. Both men and women are of good statute [...] and their houses and villages are pretty, each with a chief, who acts as their judge, and who is obeyed by them. All these lords use few words, and have excellent manners. Most of their orders are given by a sign with the hand, which is understood with surprising quickness.*

Columbus points in this paragraph to some differences that chroniclers and contemporary archaeologists would later corroborate: the maximum development of Taino culture was achieved in Hispaniola and on another island later discovered, San Juan Bautista, now Puerto Rico.

Meanwhile, the Admiral does not cease in his quest to find gold. By now he has managed to learn that the precious mineral is found in an inner region of Hispaniola called Cibao, which he believes is the Cipango mentioned by Marco Polo. But misfortune prevents him from his search. That night, a well-known story takes place: La Santa María crashes against a reef and a fort is built using its remains. The fort becomes known as the Nativity Fort and was the first Spanish settlement in the new lands. In the same account, Columbus reports meeting Guacanagarí, the first *cacique* of Hispaniola whose name is documented. Columbus describes

Guacanagarí as approximately 23 years old and, like his peers, no more than 1.58 meters tall (about 5'-2"). According to studies of physical anthropology, only 3% of Taino people reached 50 years of age.

In that first meeting, Guacanagarí tells Columbus, who he believed to have "come from heaven," of his fear "of the Caniba, who they call the Caribs, who come to take them, and bring arches and arrows without iron," and a peculiar, mutually beneficial relationship arises between them. Columbus entrusts to Guacanagarí the 39 men in the Nativity Fort.[3] In exchange, Columbus offers Guacanagarí protection against the Caribs. Guacanagarí, who "does not understand what weapons are, because they do not own or use them," is impressed. As it turns out, Columbus would return from his second voyage to find the fort burnt and its occupants dead.

The search for Matininó

Continuing his navigation in La Niña, the Admiral meets Martín Alonso Pinzón, who had separated from the fleet in his light ship La Pinta before La Santa María rans aground. Pinzón exposes his reasons for his separation from the group, claiming to have reached the island of Baneque, where "he found nothing of gold." Columbus doubts Pinzón. Some historians believe that Baneque was the island Burenquen or Boriquén (today Puerto Rico), while others believe that these are rash conjectures.

On Sunday, January 6, 1493, Columbus documents in his *Diary* having heard that there is an island with a large amount of gold to the south of Juana (Cuba). This island was called Yamaque, an apparent reference to Jamaica. He also learns something that he would be told often: that to the east "there was an island where there were only women, and this many people knew." By this moment in time, Columbus' interest in the fantastic golden island of Baneque had dissipated; from now on, he would search for this new island inhabited by women only that will turn out to be the mythical Matininó.

---

[3] Chronicler Fernández de Navarrete lists the names of forty men, including two Englishmen.

Days later, in front of what he would later name Río de Oro, an old European legend emerges. The Admiral claims to see "three mermaids that came clearly out of the sea, but they were not as beautiful as they are painted, that in some way they had the shape of a man in the face." Undoubtedly, three dolphins that his imagination turned into sirens.

Columbus continues his journey and after several days arrives in the northeastern peninsula of Hispaniola. This is Samaná Bay at present. The following excerpt illustrates how he reaffirms the aboriginal beliefs that he had heard on several occasions to date.

Sunday, January 13, 1943:

He sent the boat on shore to a beautiful beach [...] They found some men with bows and arrows [...] They asked one of them to come on board the caravel and see the Admiral [...] He was very ugly of countenance, more so than the others that he had seen. [...] He wore his hair very long, brought together and fastened behind, and put into a small net of parrots' feathers.

Due to the differences he observed in their looks and use of weapons, Columbus quickly thought that these people must belong "to the Caribs, who eat men." He then asks about the Caribs and one of the men "pointed to the east." Then, Columbus reports that "he called gold *tuob*, and did not understand *caona*, as they call it in the first part of the island that was visited, nor *nozay*, the name in San Salvador [...]" And that was because, as Columbus himself realized, although there was a common language, there was also "a difference in the words owing to the great distance between the various islands."

In asking about the island of Matininó, Columbus is told that it "was peopled by women without men, and that in it there is much *tuob*, which is gold or copper, and that it is more to the east of Carib." Then, a new island emerges: "the island of Goanin, where there was much *tuob*." Later, we will see that Matininó and Guanín were two islands of Taino mythology linked to the cultural hero's canoe trip and his obtaining of *guanín*, the valued alloy of gold and copper brought to the Antillean arch from South America. It seems that Columbus and his men, held as celestial beings, acted out for the Taino the mythical feat of the nautical hero who obtains cultural goods for his people.

Shortly thereafter, the first confrontation between the Spanish and those men with large bows and arrows and "a kind of club [*macana*]"takes place. It is described as "a piece of a pole, which is like very heavy instead of a sword." When the aboriginal men allegedly attempted to apprehend the Christian men who had disembarked, these defended themselves with their weapons, killing several aboriginals. When the Admiral was informed, he confirmed his original impression: they were "those Carib, who ate men." Also, he writes that "even if they are not Caribs, they are a neighboring people, with similar habits, and fearless, unlike the other inhabitants of the island, who are timid, and without arms." At this point, the Admiral ponders that these people may attack the Nativity Fort and the men he had left there.

It has been a controversial topic to establish whether those aboriginal people located in the region attributed to the so-called *cigüayos* were of another ethnicity, although their features (belligerent attitude, long hair and weapons) are consistent with the description that both Spanish and French chroniclers would give years later to the Caribs of the Eastern Antilles. It is feasible, then, to say that these warriors were Caribs and that by conquering the Arawak women of the area, they would not leave archaeological evidence of their presence, as it happened in the Lesser Antilles. However, the peculiarities and dissemination of the *cigüayos* in Hispaniola continues to be disputed.

The Admiral decides at this time to depart from what he called the Gulf of Arrows. His decision was motivated by the abundance of gold that he was told existed in Matininó, the "island entirely peopled by women, without men" that evoked for him a European legend about the existence of Amazon women. Before departing, however, he captures four young people for "giving such a good account of all those islands that were towards the east." On January 16, 1493, he steers his new course, pointing to "the fourth quarter of the northeast" in the direction shown by "some Indians […] taken yesterday."

Nevertheless, the bad condition of the caravels forces the Admiral to abandon his endeavor and return to his Old World with samples of what was found: Indians, objects of gold and other materials, plants and birds.

The first Tainos in Europe

The trip back was not easy. A storm almost capsized the two battered caravels. Had the vessels failed, history would not have registered the success of the daring Genoese who discovered the route from Europe to America.

Aboard the ship, Columbus manages to write a letter to the Queen and King transmitted via Luis de Santangel, a court official, where he tells them of his discovery. In this letter he summarizes his diary, without abandoning his fantastic realism tone. This letter confirms that Columbus believed, without reservation, to have reached the East, the lands of Great Khan, Catay, the Chinese province of which Marco Polo spoke.[4]

Columbus writes that "in these islands, so far I have found no monsters, as some expected." However, he mentions that in the Cibao province of Hispaniola "people with tail are born" and that there is another island "where the natives have no hair." Convinced of the existence "of people considered in all the isles as most ferocious, who eat human flesh" and of people who, in canoes "overrun all the isles of India [West Indies], stealing and seizing all they can," Columbus does not avoid associating them with the island of Matininó: "These are those who exchanged the women of Matininó [...], in which there is no man whatsoever."

As for the indigenous people that he calls Indians, he writes:

> *They have no religion not idolatry, except that they all believe power and goodness to be in heaven. They firmly believed that I, with my ships and men, came from heaven, and with this idea I have been received everywhere, since they lost fear of me.*

We will see that this would not be exactly the case. Years later, the humble Father Ramón Pané would collect part of the

---

[4] This translation of Christopher Columbus's letter of March 14, 1493, is from *Select Letters of Christopher Columbus with Other Original Documents Relating to His Four Voyages to the New World*, translated and edited by R. H. Major (London: The Hakluyt Society, 1847) with slight revisions by Grace M. Robiou Ramírez de Arellano in 2019.

beliefs that constituted Taino religious thought. And not long after that, the Spaniards' own behavior would convince the Taino inhabitants that Columbus was not a divine being.

As a navigator, he recognizes and emphasizes the nautical capability of the indigenous people:

> *In these isles there are a great many canoes, something like rowing boats, of all sizes, [...] a galley could not keep up with them in rowing, because they go with incredible speed, and with these they row about among all these islands, which are innumerable, and carry on their commerce. I have seen these canoes with seventy and eighty men in them, and each had an oar.*

It was precisely two of these indigenous seamen who were knowledgeable about the geography of the Antilles, who convinced King John II of Portugal that Columbus had indeed reached a new continent. It turns out that the Admiral arrived first at Lisbon in March 1494. As Las Casas would write, the Portuguese monarch demanded proof of the veracity of the Admiral's allegations:

> *Hence the king [...] brought a bowl of beans and placed them on a table [...] and by signs he sent an Indian to draw or point to those so many islands [...] that the Admiral claimed to have discovered; the Indian, very confidently and quickly, pointed to the island La Española and the island of Cuba and the islands of the Lucayos and the others he knew.*

Surprised, the King discreetly undid with his hand the pattern traced by the Taino man. He then called another Taino to repeat the test:

> *[...] the Indian, with diligence and as if what he was being ask to do was mindless, organized the beans in the same pattern as the previous Indian, and by chance added many more islands and lands, explaining with reason in his language [...] all that he had drawn and its meaning.*

These two Taino geographers were amongst the indigenous people that Columbus adopted as guides and interpreters during his voyage. Obviously, he knew who to choose. Only seven of these guides and interpreters survived the trip back to Europe, according to Las Casas. Chronicler Gonzalo Fernández de Oviedo, for his part, reported that he witnessed the baptism of six indigenous at Court.

Of these, we know that a relative of Guacanagarí was christianized by King Ferdinand himself, who gave him his name. Prince John welcomed another as "Juan de Castilla." In the two years that "Juan de Castilla" lived, he resided in the palace, was taught and learned Spanish. Another was sponsored by the Admiral giving him the name of his brother and son, Diego Colón.

There is no doubt that "Diego Colón" was one of the two geographers who amazed the Portuguese king. Diego travelled again with the Admiral on his second voyage. Perhaps for this reason, Columbus managed to reach the new world through the eastern Antilles, where he had been told that the fabulous island of Matininó was located.

First known representation of the Antillean aboriginals.
Insula Hyspana (Hispaniola). Basel (1493).

CHAPTER 2

Why the colonization?

While news of the first voyage spread in Europe and the letter written by Columbus to the Queen and King enjoyed wide circulation thanks to the printing press, a fleet of 17 ships with more than 1,200 crew members would depart to the new world at the end of September of 1493 under the command of the Admiral.

If the purpose of the first voyage was to explore, the goal of the second voyage was primarily to colonize. Spain wanted to mimic in the new world what Portugal had established on the Atlantic coast of Africa: colonies that produced for their benefit. It was the period in history when European empires began to expand to distant lands by means of navigation, sponsored by mercantilist capitalism. That is, the accumulation of wealth based on the acquisition of precious metals controlled by the merchants of the metropolises. The Spanish monarchs, in need of the essential gold and of new sources of income, would support and regulate this type of enterprise that was compatible with the Church doctrine of evangelization and expansionism.

For these reasons, Christopher Columbus had signed the Capitulations of Santa Fe with Queen Isabella before his first voyage. The Capitulations granted Columbus and his heirs the titles of Admiral of the Ocean Sea (the best known), Viceroy, Governor-General of the islands discovered, and also gave him the tenth part of all riches to be discovered in or produced from the voyage. Such was the Admiral's tenacity to return to the Indies and reach the Nativity Fort.

Juan Ponce de León was likely among Columbus' companions on the second voyage. Ponce de León was a veteran of the wars against the Moors and the future colonizer of Puerto Rico. Undoubtedly among Columbus's crew this second time were three important characters: Ramón Pané, who would compile the Taino mythology known to us today, and two dissimilar chroniclers of this trip, the Sevillian doctor Diego Álvarez Chanca and the Italian Michele de Cuneo.

Encounter with Carib canoes during Columbus' second voyage, according to Cronau (1892).

Matininó fades

The second voyage was not a riddle. Columbus studies his notes and also, most likely, the reports of the indigenous seaman "Diego Colón," and plots a new route to arrive the islands that he could not reach on his first trip.

Taking advantage of the winds and currents from equatorial Africa, Columbus establishes the shortest route between the two continents. This is the route that will be used by European navigators for centuries. Years later, this route would facilitate also the crossing to the Antilles of ships full of African slaves.

After sailing for 39 days, the fleet arrives in Dominica, an island in the Lesser Antilles. He named it Dominica because it was Sunday and "domingo" is the Spanish word for Sunday. The fleet continues towards Hispaniola discovering left and right dozens of islands of the Antillean arch.

The fleet then stops on the island called Santa María de Guadalupe. (Upon becoming a French colony, the Spanish name was retained though altered to French ortography and phonology, hence this island is known today as Guadeloupe.) Las Casas mentions a curious detail: in a house they found pieces of a shipwreck "that the sailors called *quodaste*, at which all marveled and could not imagine how it would have arrived there, if it were not for the winds and the seas." Indeed, it was shipwreck from a vessel that sunk between the Canary Islands and the coasts of Africa, and that had arrived in the Antilles following the same ocean current used by the Admiral when navigating between Europe and America.

In Guadeloupe, Columbus and his men find objects that they interpret as proof of cannibalism by the Caribs. Chronicler Diego Álvarez Chanca, in his letter to the Mayor and Town Council of Seville, reports that they found in a house "a lot of spun cotton and cotton for spinning, and things related to its maintenance [...] he specially brought four or five bones belonging to the arms and legs of men. It was then that we suspected that those islands were those inhabited by the Caribs, the people who eat human flesh [...]" A few days later, Chanca would confirm the finding: "We asked the women who were captives on this island, what these people were: they answered that they were Caribs."

The polemical dichotomy between Caribs and Tainos was present also in Guadeloupe. When a small boat with Spaniards on board arrives at the beach, a group of awed aboriginals exclaim "tayno, tayno, which means good." The Spanish "[rescued] more than 20 women who had been held captive [by the Caribs], and some of the young men that had been taken captive came fleeing as well."

Chanca shares other experiences as well:

We went ashore many times to walk around their towns and dwellings [...] we found an infinite number of bones of men and also the upper part of the skull, which they hung in their homes as pots to keep their belongings.

For Chanca, this Carib practice had traces of cannibalism. However, Las Casas glimpsed another possibility:

They must be from men or people they loved, because it is not likely [the bones] are from the people they ate; the reason being that if they consume that many humans as some say, the bones and skulls would not fit in their homes.

Chanca would come to think similarly to Las Casas when, in a town north of Hispaniola, they found a very well-guarded skull:

We decided [...] that it was the skull of the father or mother, or of someone whom they loved very much.

Later, we will learn that this ritual was part of a Taino myth related to the origin of the sea and of fish.

While in Guadeloupe, Chanca writes that "many men did not appear, and the cause was that, as the women told us, 10 canoes had left to rob other islands." It is possible that this Carib custom was the origin of the Taino belief in the mythical Matininó, an island allegedly inhabited only by women. In this manner, the mystery of Matininó, of which Columbus had heard about insistently during his first voyage while discovering the north coast of Hispaniola, would be unveiled slowly.

Chanca also underlines the difference between Carib women and Taino women held captive:

> *[...] The Carib women had in each leg two woven cotton rings. One next to the knee and the other along the ankle, in a manner that the calves are made to look large. The two rings are tight-fitting, and they consider this attractive, and it is because of this difference that we differentiate one from the other.*

Later on, he points out a distinctive feature of Carib men:

> *The difference from these to the other Indians in their custom, is that the Caribs have the hair very long, and the other [the Taino] have their hair cut in thousands of different ways, and they wear paint in their bodies in diverse ways [...]"*

Both observations would be corroborated years later by the French chroniclers who lived on the islands inhabited by the Caribs.

Continuing in their journey from island to island, the fleet then arrives on November 14, 1493, on the island called Santa Cruz. (Today, this island is called St. Croix and is the largest island in the unincorporated territory of the U.S. Virgin Islands.) It was here that the first clash between the Caribs and Spaniards took place. A canoe with "four men and two women and a boy" was chased by a boat with 25 Spaniards. When they saw themselves attacked, "the Caribs [...] daringly put their hands to the arches, the women as well as the men." As a result, two Spaniards were injured, one fatally. Even with a capsized canoe, the Caribs continued firing their arrows. One of them continued swimming despite being wounded by a spear. According to Michele de Cuneo, who claims to have been on the boat, the only option left was "to bring him to the edge of the boat and we cut off his head."

In his letter to an Italian nobleman, Cuneo narrates that he took for himself "a beautiful cannibal" who he saw naked and "I wanted to take pleasure with her." She objected, so he whipped her and finally achieved his purpose: "Suffice it to say that she really seemed trained as a whore." This would be the first documented interracial sexual encounter in the New World.

La Isabela, the first factory

On November 19, 1493, the fleet arrives on the island that the Admiral called San Juan Bautista, in honor of Prince Juan. The Taino women rescued in Guadeloupe called this island Burenquen, as heard and noted by Chanca. According to a linguistic analysis performed by José Juan Arrom, the word Burenquen was composed of *burén*, the clay plate where cassava (*casabe, cazabe*) was cooked, and the intensive suffix *-ken*, that would in effect be equivalent to saying "burenquísima" in Spanish or "very *burén*" in English; that is, "optimal land for cultivation of *yuca* [manioc, *Manihot esculenta*] and the manufacture of cassava."

As soon as the Spaniards approached the island, some of the Taino women aboard the caravels dove to the sea to return to their homeland, an act that Ricardo E. Alegría, the Puerto Rican anthropologist and historian, called "the first example of ardent love for one's country that is recorded in our history."

A letter written by Columbus discovered years ago seems to demonstrate that the fleet traversed the island by the north coast - not by the south, as had been favored traditionally - stopping two days for the crew to rest in what was probably the bay of Aguada-Aguadilla. Or, according to the most recent theory, somewhere near the Río Grande de Añasco.

Continuing the journey towards the west, they see in the distance an island that "was not big." It was probably the current islet of Desecheo. Navigating now the shores of Hispaniola westward - in the opposite direction to the first voyage - Columbus searches for the Nativity Fort. Chanca writes that the inhabitants called the first segment "Hayti, and then the other province together they called Xamaná, and the other Bohío."

According to Las Casas, on the coast of Samaná the Admiral releases from captivity one of the aboriginals that he had taken during his first voyage. This aboriginal was one of the seamen that Columbus brought to and back from Spain with the purpose of telling others upon his return to the Antilles of the greatness of the kingdom of Castile. It would be interesting to know what this man told others about the country of the "men from heaven." One night during this part of the voyage, six of the ten Taino women, "the most beautiful of Boriquen," who the Spaniards still kept captive on their ships, managed to escape by swimming.

Arriving at the Nativity Fort, Columbus discovers that it has been burnt down and that the men he had left behind have been killed. Guacanagarí, *cacique* of Marién and friend of the Admiral in his first voyage, blames Caonabo, the powerful *cacique* of Maguana, for the incident. Over time, many historians will regard the destruction of the Nativity Fort as a symbol of the first indigenous rebellion against the Spanish and their allies. It is also likely that there existed a struggle between the two *caciques* to integrate and consolidate power in the hands of Caonabo.

By this time, Columbus is convinced that gold is to be found in Hispaniola and not in the small islands to the east. For this reason, he decides to found a settlement in the eastern part of Hispaniola, closer to the mines in Cibao. He called the new city La Isabela, in honor of his queen. Soldiers, sailors, friars, doctors, pharmacists, cartographers, craftsmen and farmers formed this first factory of the New World with their production of plants (wheat, barley, lemon, orange, sugar cane) and animals (horses, cows, pigs, sheep, goats, chickens) brought for the first time from Europe to the Indies.

In his account, Chanca describes some of the flora, fauna and certain customs of the indigenous people of the area of La Isabela. He believes that they want to be Christians, "since they are worshippers, because in their homes there are figures in many ways." When asked, the indigenous people tell Chanca that these figures are "things of Turey, which means heaven." In his chronicles, however, Chanca begins to demystify the Columbian vision of the aboriginal: "it seems to me that their bestiality is greater than that of any beast of the world." Cuneo, similarly, writes: the indigenous people "live like animals" and "they are sodomites." These observations by Chanca and Cuneo foreshadow the theological and philosophical controversies pertaining to the humanity or the bestiality of the indigenous people of the New World that will dominate later discourse.

Engraving of La Isabela, first European city in America.
Insula Hyspana (Hispaniola). Basel (1493).

Neither is Cuneo optimistic about the natural environment in the New World. He considers that many of the fruits "only serve for the pigs." Among his observations, he mentions in passing an important detail: "The cannibals and Indians [referring to the Taino] speak the same language." To some extent, he was right. Centuries later, in the middle of the 20th century, ethnologist Douglas Taylor would demonstrate that the language of the Caribs of the islands was fundamentally that of their Arawak women; that is, from the same origin as the Taino language.

Once established in La Isabela, Columbus begins the conquest of the central region of Hispaniola in search of gold. We will return to this topic later in the book. For now, we sum up Columbus' stay in La Isabela by remembering that the Admiral, recognizing that he was a navigator at heart and not a colonizer, names his brother Diego as governor and raises the sails of the three caravels on April 25, 1494, to continue his journey.

A frustrated exodus

The Admiral then heads west, sailing this time along the south coast of Cuba. As in the first voyage, the inhabitants of the area think that Columbus and his ships "had descended from the sky."

Columbus continues his search for gold and relies on his godson, "Diego Colón," to interpret the signals of the aboriginals, who point him in the direction of Jamaica. Columbus and his men are attacked with stones as they arrive and attempt to disembark in Jamaica, according to Cuneo. Father Andrés Bernáldez, a chronicler of the Catholic Monarchs and in whose house Columbus stayed when he returned from his second voyage, also reports a confrontational arrival when he writes that the fleet was attacked by "seventy canoes, all loaded with people and rods as weapons."

Bernáldez adds that the Admiral responded by pulling out his weapon and "caused all the Indians to flee." From one of the ships the Spaniards also released a dog that "followed [the Tainos] and bit them, and [the dog] did them great harm, because a dog is worth against the Indians like ten men." Used as a weapon in

Jamaica for the first time, the dog would become a valuable instrument of combat in the next few years of conquest.

Columbus continues his journey and sails along part of the north coast of Jamaica. At this time, he decides to return to Cuba in his quest to find the continent. He navigates the south coast of Cuba seeing an endless number of small islands. On one occasion, the aboriginals mention a province where "all the people have tails." On another occasion, a crew member informed him that he had seen a group of aboriginals, one of whom had a "white tunic down to his feet." Later, two men approached him "in white robes that reached below the knees, who were as white as men of Castile." Accustomed by now to the nudity of the indigenous inhabitants, in this instance it was the Spaniards who, surprised, fled.

Separately, in reaching the opposite, westernmost corner of the long island of Cuba, "Diego Colón" finds himself unable to communicate with the inhabitants. This detail from the written accounts of the second voyage suggests that the Admiral had arrived in Guanahatabey, the western region of Cuba that, apparently, was still populated by the *arcaicos*, the first inhabitants of the Antilles.

Believing still that Cuba was a peninsula of China, Columbus returns to Jamaica. In the southern coast, the Admiral has a memorable encounter with a *cacique* and his entourage. The explanation of this encounter was documented by Bernáldez based on Columbus' story as told to him. It shows the variety of ornaments and objects used by the Jamaican Taino.

The story goes like this: After receiving a cordial visit from the *cacique* of the region, to whom the interpreter "Diego Colón" recounted his unforgettable experience visiting Europe, the Admiral decides to leave the next day. As the Admiral and his men begin to sail, three large canoes managed to reach the ships. In the larger, well-painted canoe, came the *cacique* with his wife, two daughters, two sons, five brothers and other assistants.

Imagine now what Columbus and his men witnessed, based on this account by Bernáldez:

> *He brought in his canoe a man that served as a midshipman, this one alone stood in the bow with a colored feathered smock [...] and on his*

head a large plumage that looked very well, and he held in his hand a white flag without any sign.

Two or three men came with their faces painted in colors in the same way, and each had on their head a large, well-tailored plumage, and on the forehead a round tablet as big as a plate [...] and in their hand a toy with which they made sound;

There were two other men painted in another form; these brought two wood trumpets very well carved with birds and other details [...] each brought a very beautiful hat made of very thick green feathers, of the finest workmanship; six others wore white-feathered hats and came together to guard the belongings of the Cacique.

The Cacique had a jewel made of wire around his neck, from an island that is called Guanique [Guanín], it is very fine, so much so that it appears to be eight-carat gold, was in the shape of a fleur de lis, the size of a plate, attached to the neck with a thread of fat marble stone beads [...] and on the head a large garland of small green and red stones placed in order [...] and he also brought a jewel that hung from his forehead, to his ears hung two big golden tablets with very small green beads; he brought a belt, although he was naked [...]

The *cacique*'s wife was only adorned with pieces of cotton in her intimate part, in her arms and legs; the eldest daughter, also naked, had a cord of very black stones tied around her and from which hung a piece of cotton woven with green and red stones.

Once the *cacique* boarded the ship, he expressed his intention to the Admiral: "I want to go with you with my house in your ships to see the great King and Queen of your Lords and see the most abundant and richest land in the world, where they are, and to see the wonders of Castile, which are many, according to what your Indian told me."

The Admiral, says the royal chronicler, had compassion for the *cacique* and his family. He told him that he received him as a vassal of the monarchs, but that they would stay. Columbus had still much to discover and there would be "time for another opportunity to fulfill his wish."

This was how the first Antillean attempt to emigrate to other lands was frustrated.

The end of two seamen

Columbus's second voyage ended with the exploration of the southern coast of Hispaniola and the return to La Isabela. The third and fourth voyages add relatively little to the knowledge of the indigenous people of the Antilles.

The fourth voyage, nevertheless, took the Admiral back to Jamaica, but not to look for the *cacique* to whom he had promised to return. Given that his vessels were ruined, Columbus decides to run them aground on the beach in the north of Jamaica. Stranded there, the Jamaicans refused to supply him with provisions. Consequently, Columbus appealed to his audacity.

Relying on astronomical charts he carried with him, Columbus noticed that a lunar eclipse was predicted to occur on February 29, 1504. He then summoned the indigenous rebels and told them that the moon would come out very "angry and blood-colored," since their God was angry about their behavior. When the expected eclipse began, "the Indians began to fear, and fear grew so much that they came crying greatly, shouting, laden with food for the ships [...]," writes Las Casas.

Old engraving of the eclipse of 1504 in Jamaica.

The Admiral then entered his cabin and, claiming that he was going to speak with his God, came out a short while later to say that he had obtained forgiveness and that, as a sign, "they would see that [their God's] rage would pass and the light of the moon would return." It happened as Columbus predicted and the issue of lack of food and provisions was resolved to his satisfaction.

Clearly, the Admiral needed to be rescued from Jamaica. To that end, the loyal Diego Méndez and other companions would depart in two canoes to Santo Domingo, the new capital of the colony of Hispaniola, with the sole purpose of obtaining a caravel to rescue Columbus and his men. This would be "one of the most risky and glorious expeditions that any man has ever undertaken," according to the historian Washington Irving. Many of the members of this expedition would later be colonizers of Puerto Rico. Two years later, in 1506, Christopher Columbus would die in Valladolid unaware that the new lands he discovered were truly a new continent.

By this moment in time, "Diego Colón" - the seaman and geographer, the Taino interpreter who was instrumental in helping Columbus - lived in Hispaniola. Just as Columbus was frugal in providing details about "Diego Colón's" life, little is also known about the end of his life.

His biography can be condensed as follows: he was probably a native of Guanahani (San Salvador), where Columbus recruited him because of his intelligence and seaman skills; he served as a guide and began to learn Spanish during the first voyage; in Lisbon, he astonishes the Portuguese king with his description of the geography of the islands; he was baptized by the Admiral and served as the official interpreter during the second voyage.

Father Bartolomé de Las Casas claims to have met "Diego Colón," perhaps as a way to document the Admiral's experiences: "he lived on this island for many years, talking with us." Las Casas documents Diego's name several times as entrusted to the service of Spaniards. A document from 1517 alludes to him and another Taino declaring that, "although they were not *caciques*, they were always servants to the Spaniards and great interpreters of the language and they seemed very inclined to live as Christians."

Hence, "Diego Colón," whose aboriginal name is unknown to us, was instrumental and can be considered the first guide and interpreter of the New World.

By 1496, the La Isabela settlement project had failed. Settlers moved to the south coast led by Bartolomé Colón and founded Nueva Isabela, later called Santo Domingo, a city that would be for years the colonial center and the main port of departure for expeditions to new lands. In the streets of the abandoned La Isabela, writes Las Casas, a strange group of noble men were seen, well dressed and with tight-fitting swords. When these men were asked where they came from, they did not respond, but, taking off their hats to say hello, "they removed the heads of their bodies together with the hats, leaving them beheaded, and then disappeared."

This alleged ghostly apparition, the first known in America, could be considered a symbol of the end of an era; it is symbolic of the explorers' failure to establish meaningful ties with their conquered aboriginals.

The settlement of Santo Domingo marked the beginning of a new era. We now proceed to ask ourselves the origin of those indigenous people who inhabited the Antillean islands at the time of European discovery.

Sebastián Robiou Lamarche

SECOND PART

THE ANTILLEAN PRE-COLUMBIAN CULTURES

CHAPTER 3

The origin of the true discoverers

The origin of humans in America has long been a controversial subject. Despite the existence of various theories that point to the Pacific, Europe, Africa or places like the legendary Atlantis as birthplaces, specialists generally agree today that the first settlers in America came from Asia through the Bering Strait (Beringia) that separates Alaska from the Asian continent.

It should be noted that this theory is not new entirely. The idea was pioneered by the chronicler Father José de Acosta in 1590, when he foresaw that the new land "that we call the Indias, is not completely different from the other world [...] than the one portion of earth and the other come together somewhere [...] or at least they come close to and move up to each other."

In addition to the archaeological studies, one of the most recent contributions to the theory of the Asian origin of the true discoverers of the new continent is the linguistics work by Johanna Nichols from the University of California. She estimated the time necessary for the 150 families of indigenous languages existing in America to emerge. Nichols' analysis posits three population waves:

- 30,000 - 40,000 years ago, when the first settlers crossed the Bering Strait and populated the southern cone, at a time when ice sheets covered much of North America;
- 11,000 - 12,000 years ago, when, given the changing climate, some of the first immigrants returned northward, spreading from the Gulf Coast of Mexico or from Central America to North America, while another group crossed the Bering Strait, expanding their reach along the Pacific coastline;
- 5,000 years ago, when the last wave settled in Alaska, Canada and Greenland.

The most recent studies that inform the period of time when movements occurred are based on human mitochondrial DNA haplogroups. These studies point to an initial movement of people along Beringia approximately 25,000 years ago. These human migrations may have occurred along coasts or across the seasonal sea ice.

The Antilles were one of the last regions of America to be inhabited. Archeological records indicate that the first settlers arrived from the continent to the islands about 6,000 years before the caravels of Columbus came ashore.

Regarding ethnohistory and archeology

For years, scholars have used the term 'prehistory' to refer to events belonging to the era before recorded history. We should warn, however, that the term has fallen into disuse due to its arbitrariness. In every culture, with or without recorded history, humans are the protagonists, the forgers of history. History, in this sense, evolves to be the social development of humans in time and space.

Similarly, the word 'culture,' often used as a synonym for civilization, has been tied wrongfully to scientific development and material progress. Culture is what every human group develops when they are provided with a common set of social relations, knowledge, beliefs, artistic ideas and characteristics of their own. As such, there is no such thing as a primitive culture, much less one culture that is superior or inferior to another. Rather, there are degrees in the historical development of each culture.

To summarize the history of the aboriginals from the Antilles, we will review the role of two fundamental sources of information: ethnohistory and archeology.

The ethnohistory (from ethno: ethnic group, people, nation) refers to the documentation compiled mainly by chroniclers - conquerors, colonizers and evangelists - about a culture. In the first part of this book, we cited the writings of several chroniclers to learn about the first impressions of the Europeans upon arriving in the Antilles. Archeology, on the other hand, is the scientific study of material remains of past human life and the activity of those individuals. Archeology's purpose is to reconstruct the cultural characteristics of a population. In this second part, we will review the archaeological evidence to help us understand the cultures that inhabited the Antilles before the discovery. The European conqueror would never know these cultures.

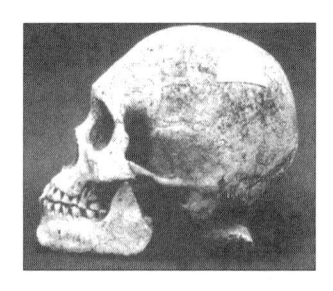

Taino burial in fetal position; skull with frontal deformation.
La Caleta, Dominican Republic (Morbán Laucer, 1979).

Ethnohistory and archeology are disciplines that complement each other. Thus, in the next chapters we will use the ethnohistorical and archaeological bibliography when describing the Taino and Carib cultures.

Importantly, researchers use several other sciences to study history: anthropology (the study of human beings and their ancestors in relation to physical character, environmental and social relations); physical anthropology (the comparative study of the evolution of physical peculiarities of the human body); ethnology (the study of psychological aspects of a culture, as well as race and relations); ethnobotany and ethnozoology (the study of plants and animals used by a human group); ethnolinguistics (the study of the relations between linguistic and non-linguistic cultural behaviors); mythology (the study of myths and rituals); ethnoastronomy and archaeoastronomy (the study of astronomical knowledge and of cosmogonic beliefs); genetics (the comparative study of genetics and variation among organisms).

In an archaeological site, the oldest culture will occupy the deepest position while the most recent will be the most superficial. That is to say, the material evidence found by archaeologists will typically occupy horizontal strata of lower to higher antiquity. This stratification allows for the establishment of a relative chronology of events experienced by several human groups that have occupied the same place.

But, archeologists must rely on other scientific evidence to determine the age of a culture. The most common and accepted method of dating is called radiocarbon chronometry. This method is based on the fact that, when an organism dies, so begins a constant disintegration of its carbon-14 molecules. By determining in a specialized laboratory the amount of disintegration per minute of the sample, one can establish the time when the organism died. Typically, the average dates obtained are organized into an event having occurred before Christ (BC), after Christ (AD), or before and after our common era.

The carbon-14 method will allow us to establish, in general, the historical chronology of the Antillean cultures. Columbus never even suspected that those cultures that pre-dated the Indians he encountered had existed.

Historical development pre-Columbus

Ricardo E. Alegría grouped the cultures of the aboriginals in the Antilles into three Cultural Complexes: Archaic, Arawak and Carib. A cultural complex is a unit that gathers cultural expressions, has an apparent common origin, occupies an extensive and determined geographical area for a long time, and maintains its own characteristics. Alegría named the regional variations of cultural complexes "phases" and he further subdivided them into "manifestations" that represent small local cultural units. In Puerto Rico, for example, he divided the Arawak Cultural Complex chronologically into the Saladoid Phase (with its Hacienda Grande and Cuevas Manifestations) and the Tainoid Phase (with its Ostionoid and Taino Manifestations).

Cultural complexes are the synthesis of multiple population movements, and the outcome of a process of colonization or immigration toward and between the Antilles. Irving Rouse, emeritus professor of anthropology at Yale University and former director of the Peabody Museum of Natural History at the same institution, studied pre-Columbian Antillean cultures for more than half a century and proposed the definitions for colonization and immigration that follow.

Colonization and immigration differ only in degree and respond to a process of territorial occupation over time. Rouse proposed that population movement occurs when a new cultural group controls a geographic area, replacing the societies that occupied the area previously. In contrast, colonization is when the original group survives along with the new settlers. The first Antillean settlers - the Archaics - experienced both colonization and immigration in several occasions during their history.

Immigration distinguishes itself from colonization in that immigrants - invaders or not - integrate into the existing society, contributing their cultural elements to it. Immigrants may end up losing their original identity. Such seems to be the case of the continental Carib invaders to the Lesser Antilles years before the European discovery. By killing the men and keeping their women, the Caribs adopted the existing Island-Arawak culture, hence creating over time the Island-Carib culture regularly called Carib. To some extent, this is equivalent to the term "interaction" used more recently by archaeologists.

Two other mechanisms allow for the diffusion of certain cultural features beyond the established cultural boundaries: emigration and commercial exchange. Rouse called those areas of cultural interconnection "spheres of interaction." In the Antilles, spheres of interaction are typically configured around the channels that separate one island from another, instead of occurring on the same island, given that for the indigenous inhabitant it was easier to navigate than to travel by land. A key example of a sphere of cultural interaction is the Mona Channel; the east coast of Hispaniola and the west coast of Puerto Rico show common archaeological features from a certain period. Briefly, traditional archeological research points to two major cultural stages in the Antilles: Archaic and Agro-Ceramic. In each stage, several migrations or cultural interactions may have occurred from the continent to the Antilles.

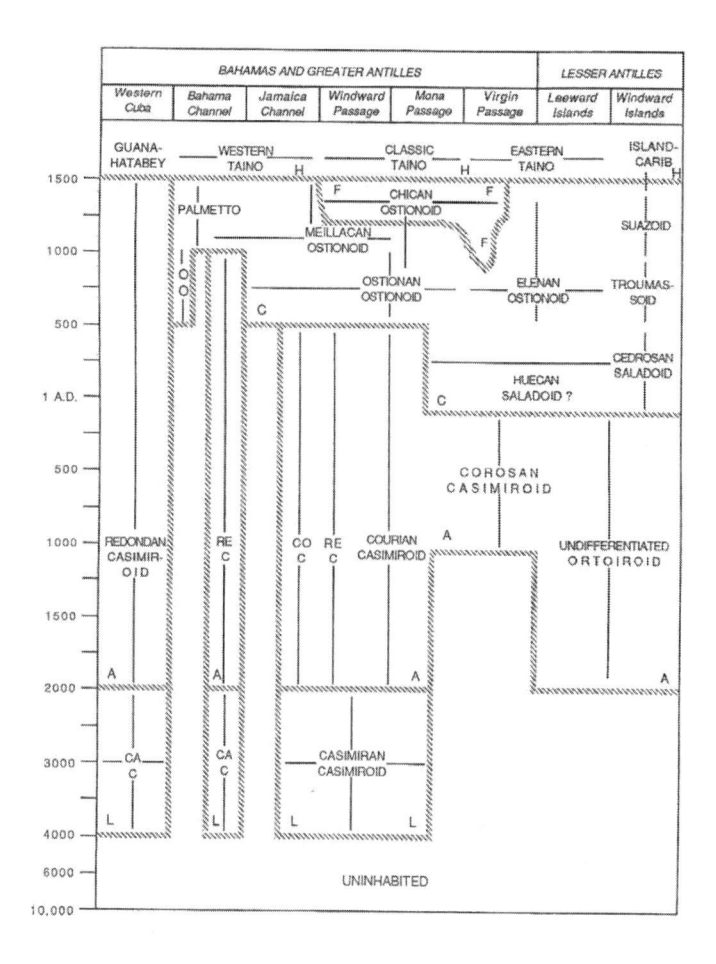

	BAHAMAS AND GREATER ANTILLES					LESSER ANTILLES	
	Western Cuba	Bahama Channel	Jamaica Channel	Windward Passage	Mona Passage	Virgin Passage	Leeward Islands	Windward Islands

Chronology of the series and subseries of cultures in the West Indies (Rouse, 1992).

In the Archaic stage, two groups of settlers are known to have arrived in the area. The first group probably came from Central America; the second group is believed to have ascended from South America through the arch of the Lesser Antilles. In the Agro-Ceramic stage, the settlers came from the South American coast. According to Rouse, the population movement represented by the Agro-Ceramic stage led to the practical disappearance of the Archaic people in the Antilles. Rouse believed that the Agro-Ceramic stage saw the development of the Saladoids, which later would give origin to the Ostionoids and these, finally, to the Chicans or Tainos. In other words, that cultural development in the Antilles was unilinear.

More recently, however, this theory is not considered to be correct necessarily. It is believed that some kind of interaction occurred between the Archaic and the Agro-Ceramic people.

Beginning in the 1980s, Luis Chanlatte and Yvonne Narganes, both from the University of Puerto Rico's Archaeological Research Center, offered a different perspective and postulated a new scheme of cultural development in the Antilles. Based on excavations carried out over the years in La Hueca and Sorcé, on the island of Vieques, Chanlatte and Narganes proposed that the Agro-Ceramic period is constituted chronologically not by one, but by two, successive migrations. First, the La Hueca Cultural Complex, referenced to as Huecan or Agro-I; then, the Saladoid-Igneris or Agro-II, also reported in Sorcé.

The main difference between the archeological theories of Chanlatte and Narganes and other archaeologists is that the former insist that there are clear differences between the Huecan and the Saladoid-Igneris sites, while the latter believe that the Huecan are derived from the Saladoid culturally.

Contrary to Rouse, Chanlatte and Narganes believe that the Archaic populations that existed on the islands for thousands of years did not disappear, but rather assimilated the cultural features of the Agro-Ceramic. They believe some form of cultural fusion occurred. Hence, the Ostionoids (Agro-III) resulted from the slow transformation of the Archaics in Agro-Ceramics, yielding the first properly Antillean pottery. In turn, the Taino phase (Agro-IV) becomes the sum of all previous cultural stages in the later stage of their development.

In 2015, Ivonne Narganes presented her doctoral thesis entitled "Sorcé, history of a fishing village." Her broad and innovative documentation regarding the indigenous people's diet is based on archeological digs performed over many years in the island of Vieques.

In recent years, Reniel Rodríguez Ramos, a post-doctoral researcher from Leiden University currently at the University of Puerto Rico, proposed in his studies of the Puerto Rico and Caribbean archaeological data that a dynamic cultural and economic interaction existed in the region and, as a result, a more active relationship between Puerto Rico and the north coast of South America, perhaps going as far as the Isthmo-Colombian region.

The genetic connection

The South American origin of the Agro-Ceramic culture has been established mainly by comparative studies in the fields of archeology, physical anthropology, linguistics, mythology and cosmology. More recently, genetics has played a decisive role.

Around 1999, Juan C. Martínez Cruzado, professor of genetics at the University of Puerto Rico in Mayagüez, together with a group of collaborators, developed an innovative research study on mitochondrial DNA (mtDNA) found in Puerto Rican hair roots. As it is known that female mtDNA is transmitted intact, without being combined, over generations, if indigenous mtDNA was present on a study subject, then it meant that an aboriginal existed in the subject's female lineage. Further, Martínez Cruzado classified the genetic characteristics of his subjects into the existing large ethnic groups, the so-called haplogroups, of continental origin. For example, most New World aboriginals are known to belong to four haplogroups (A, B, C, D). From these haplogroups arise haplotypes, which can be identified with specific tribes.

From a representative sample of 804 Puerto Ricans, Martínez Cruzado found that 97 percent of those with indigenous female mtDNA belonged to haplogroups A (52%), C (36%) and B (9%). It is known that haplogroup A originates primarily in the area of Mexico and Central America, thus it is likely that subjects in this group have descendants that reached "Puerto Rico from the Yucatan peninsula through the Greater Antilles." Because of its genetic properties, haplotype A suggests that these groups of inhabitants were "always part of a small population, such as that associated with nomadic cultures without agriculture." In other words, probably the Archaic. However, the fact that two other haplotypes with mutations have been also identified suggests that other Archaic groups arrived in Puerto Rico as well, as archeological research demonstrates.

Both haplogroups B and C are of Amazon origin. Among those subjects classified into haplogroup C - which seems to have arrived in the Antilles about 1000 years before haplogroup B, research by Mayra Troche Matos established that 60 percent was of type AM79, a haplotype found with great frequency among the current Yanomami of South America. Hence, genetically, a substantial part of the Taino would have female common ancestors with the Yanomami. And, consequently, the AM79 could belong to "the pottery culture that emigrated to Puerto Rico about 2,000 years ago." One possible explanation for this connection is to consider that the ancient women of the Yanomami belonged to the same Agro-Ceramic groups that emigrated to the Antilles and that, after several generations living on the islands, those people gave rise to the Taino culture. Moreover, what is most interesting about this genetic research is that another female haplotype, the AM32, associated with other Amazonian tribes other than the Yanomami, seems to have arrived in Puerto Rico together or after AM79. And, curiously, while the AM79 is dispersed throughout the island, the AM32 tends to be found in the northern region, which suggests that AM32 comes from a small, yet different, South American tribal group that settled in that area. If that is true, we could speculate whether in pottery, being a function of women, the stylistic differences between these tribal groups resulted in the differences seen between the Saladoid and the Huecan styles in Puerto Rico or, should these groups had arrived centuries later, if it could have influenced the beginning of the Ostionoid style.

According to Martínez Cruzado, "the predominant haplogroup (A) would belong to the original population of Puerto Rico, the pre Agro-Ceramic [...] the minor haplogroup (C) would belong to the Agro-Ceramic culture that later arrived from Venezuela." That is to say, "the Tainos would be the product of a mixture between at least two ancestral indigenous cultures." Martínez Cruzado's investigations have been expanded to the neighboring Dominican Republic. It is interesting to compare the results of the general composition of mtDNA in Puerto Rico (61.3% indigenous, 27.2% African, 11.5 European) and the Dominican Republic (70% African, 15% indigenous, 15% European), which demonstrates the social changes and biological events that occurred in these islands throughout history. More recent research on nuclear DNA (nDNA), genetic instructions with information coming from both parents rather than from the mother only, shed light on a more complex panorama.

Undoubtedly, the history of the development of Antillean cultures still awaits more interdisciplinary research, the time being, let us transport ourselves through time and get to know the cultures that began to occupy the Antilles more than 6,000 years before the European discovery.

CHAPTER 4

A necessary compendium

The history of Antillean cultures can be summarized in the following paragraphs, which will serve as the basis of our study. In it, we consider the main archeological investigations yet leave aside the scientific nomenclature with the goal of facilitating a better understanding by the reader.

- *The first Antillean settlers: about 6,000 BC*

They came probably from Central America and settled in Cuba and Hispaniola. They were mainly hunters, settling inland and fabricating objects made of flint or flint stone.

- *The fishermen - gatherers: about 4,000 BC*

They were natives of South America and became the first humans to populate the Lesser Antilles and Puerto Rico. They made objects using polished stones and, contrary to the previous settlers, exhibited a preference to live in the coasts, where they fished. As with the previous settlers, they were gatherers and did not develop agricultural techniques or pottery, although there is evidence that certain groups could have initiated these practices. Generally, both the first settlers and the fishermen are called Archaic. The Mona channel that separates Hispaniola and Puerto Rico seems to have constituted a common border between these groups.

- *The Agro-Ceramics: from 500 BC to 600 AD*

They were natives of the coast of South America and probably settled in the Antilles in several migration waves. Traditionally, it is believed that they were the first to introduce the manioc and the confection of cassava to the Antilles. Unquestionably, they introduced a developed agricultural experience and the fabrication of sophiscated ceramic objects, spreading their practice up the arch of islands in the western Antilles, to Puerto Rico and possibly part of the eastern coast of Hispaniola. These groups were of Arawak origin and their culture is traditionally referred to as Saladoid because of the archeological findings at Saladero, in Venezuela.

- *The precursors of the Taino: from 600 to 1,200 AD*

This group is the result of either the Agro-Ceramics adapting to the island ecosystem, or of new migrations and influences from South America, or of the Archaic adopting the techniques of the Arawak. They are characterized by new techniques in agricultural production, a change in pottery style, an increase in the population, and a progressive spread of their culture to Hispaniola, Cuba, Jamaica and the Bahamas, either displacing or interacting with the Archaic in those islands. This group is traditionally referred to as Ostionoid, despite its regional variations, because of the original archeological findings at Punta Ostiones, in Puerto Rico.

- *The pinnacle of the Taino: from 1200 to 1500 AD*

The pinnacle of the historic process is reached before the arrival of the European in the Antilles and is characterized by the formation of a more complex society, where the societal hierarchy is expressed in the role of the *cacique*, and where there are such things as ideology, technique and art. Hispaniola and Puerto Rico are at the center of this apogee in native Antillean culture.

- *Carib emigrants: from 1000 to 1500 AD*

This phase is best described by the invasion or migration by the Kalinagos (the continental Caribs) to part of the Lesser Antilles from the coasts of South America. This group took possession of the Arawak women and adopted mainly their language and others cultural traits, constituting the Island-Carib culture, or simply Carib culture.

This compendium of Antillean cultures is not intended to be absolute or final and is only intended as a guide to our presentation. In the balance of this chapter we will analyze the presence of the Archaic and the first Agro-Ceramic in the Antilles, and the emergence of the Ostionoids (or pre-Taino) in Puerto Rico.

The Archaics: the discoverers of the Antilles

The general consensus among archaeologists today is that the Archaic, the first settlers of the Antilles, arrived in at least two migratory waves via rafts or canoes from distant areas of the continent.

The first migration occurred approximately 6,000 years before Christ (BC), from the Central American region of Belize to Cuba and extending then to Hispaniola and perhaps, to some extent, Puerto Rico. Given that the sea level was lower than it is today, the migrants used the islets that existed at that time between the continent and the islands, to facilitate their movement. The fact that the coasts of that time period are today under water prevents us from determining if other migrations took place previously.

The second migration occurred some 2,000 years later when another cultural group, this time from the island of Trinidad, located off the coast of South America, arrived in the Lesser Antilles on their way to Puerto Rico. Again, the Mona channel impeded their further expansion as the water segment served as a natural frontier between Archaic groups of the time. There is also the possibility, which cannot be ruled out, that a migration from Florida took place around this time as well, although it has not been proven by archeological evidence.

The names assigned to these first settlers of the Antilles have varied over time. When their archaeological remains began to be studied in the middle of the 20th century, they were called Ciboney or pre-Agro-Ceramic. Later, when classified according to two major cultural periods, the first group was called Lithic, Paleo-Indian or Paleo-Archaic, and the second was called Archaic or Meso-Indian. Since then, they have been renamed taking into consideration the name of the guiding archaeological site where evidence of their culture was found. Thus, Irving Rouse grouped them into two major cultural series: the Casimiroid (also known as Barreroid, Mordanoid or Seboruco-Mordán) and the Ortoiroid or Banwaroid, each with its corresponding subseries that responds perhaps to a process of adaptation, interaction or Antillean hybridization.

Some authors believe that the first reference to the Archaic appears in the chronicles by the Spanish discoverers. Father Las Casas, for example, mentions the Guanahatabey people who lived in the extreme west of Cuba, in the province of Pinar del Río, the area where interpreter "Diego Colón" reported having problems communicating with the indigenous population. On the other hand, Oviedo and Anglería refer to other inhabitants of the Guacayarima Peninsula, in the southwest of Hispaniola. The evidence of these groups tend to demonstrate that in the Greater Antilles there was no homogeneous level of social development and that even the Taino, as we shall see, had regional variations.

As stated before, the first Antillean Archaics, probably of Central American origin, are reported in Cuba and Hispaniola. One of the oldest archaeological sites is located in Levisa, in the vicinity of Seboruco, Cuba, with carbon-14 testing indicating it is older than 5,000 years BC. On the Barrera-Mordán sites in the Dominican Republic, the date is c. 4,000 BC. The main characteristic of the Lithic is the use of flint or flint stone flakes for the manufacture, among other objects, of scrapers, burins, blades and spearheads. In the Cuban site of Guayabo Blanco, the use of gouges made of shell is typical.

These pioneer settlers inhabited mainly the interior of the islands where they hunted large mammals now extinct. It seems, however, that during certain times they moved to the coast in search of other resources. From the abundant nature that surrounded them, they collected fruits, seeds and plants.

The second migratory wave of Archaic settlers came from South America and progressively occupied the eastern part of the Antilles, reaching then Puerto Rico and Mona Island. They have been called Banwaroid because they came from the Banwari-Trace deposit on the island of Trinidad, where the oldest date is about 6,500 years BC.

In Puerto Rico, among the oldest Archaic evidence occurs in Puerto Ferro, Vieques, with an approximate date of 4,000 BP. There are also the excavations performed in the 1990s by archaeologists Carlos M. Ayes in Angostura, Manatí River, and by Miguel Rodríguez and Juan González in Maruca, Ponce (2,700 BC).

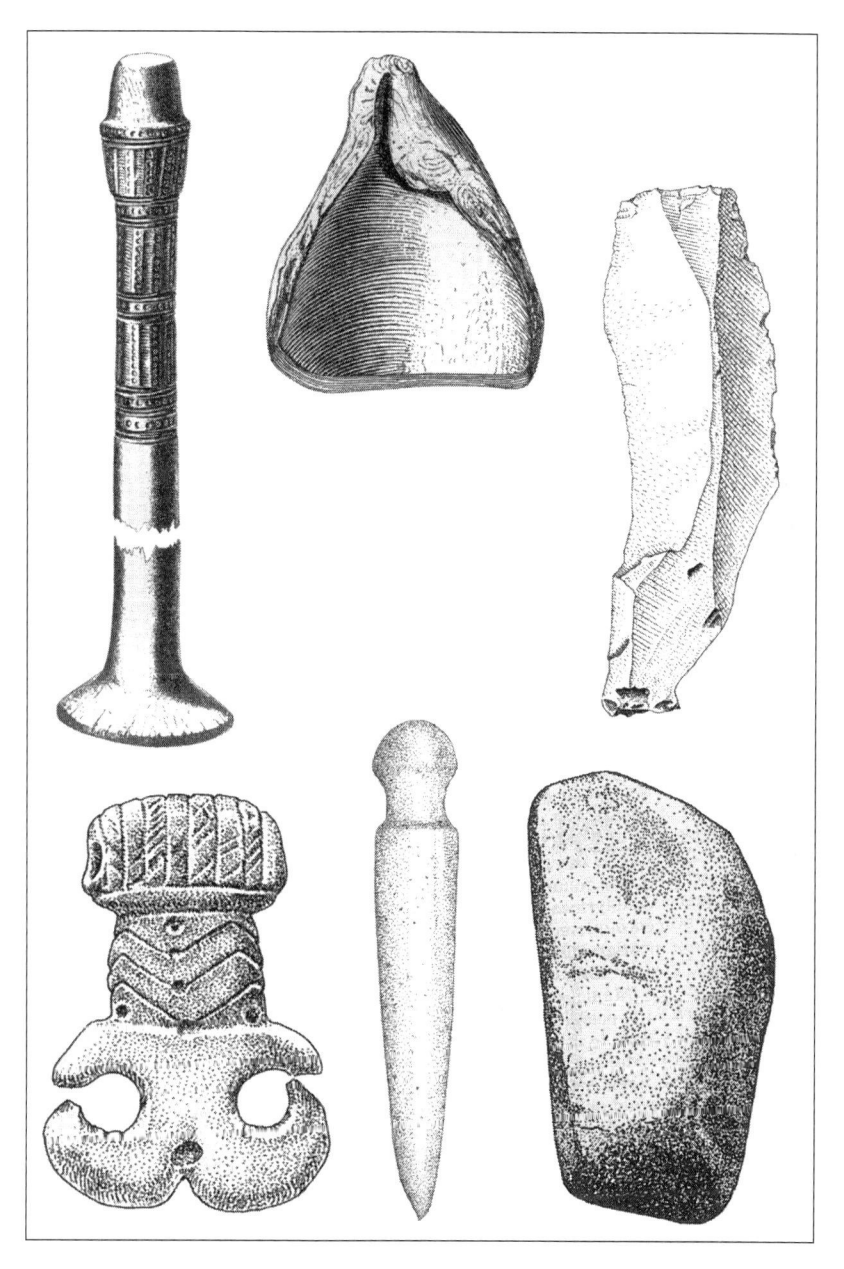

Archaic people in the Greater Antilles. Above, from left to right: wood carving and shell artifact, both from Pinar del Río, Cuba (Harrington, 1921); stone tool, Rancho Casimira, Dominican Republic. Below, from left to right: stone carvings, Ile à Vache, Haiti, and stone instrument, María de la Cruz cave, Loíza, Puerto Rico (Rouse, 1992).

The Archaics of South American origin are also foragers but, contrary to the Lithic ones of Central American origin, their settlements occur preferably along the coast and in swampy areas, which indicates that they exploited the marine resources. They are characterized by the confection of artifacts in seashells and polished stone, including the *majadores* and grinders that they used to crush shells, seeds and roots.

Some archaeologists believe that after 1,500 BC a process of hybridization - the exchange of artifacts and techniques - took place between the Casimiroid and the Banwaroid who had arrived in Hispaniola. Several centuries before Christ some groups of Antillean Archaic owned an incipient pottery, such as that of the El Caimito deposit in the Dominican Republic, yet they also developed the processing of the tuber of the *guáyiga* or *marunguey* (*Zamia* sp.), a practice that has endured in the eastern region of the country until our days.

It is generally considered that the Archaic society was formed by bands, which are groups probably united by family ties that anthropologists estimate had between 30 and 40 individuals. They were semi-nomadic because they had sufficient natural resources both inland and on the coast. Maybe they did not know the bow and arrow, but they used spears and various types of stone axes. Their skull was not deformed, as would be the case with that of the future Saladoid Agro-Ceramic people and, contrary to these, who usually buried the dead in a fetal position, the Archaic people usually buried their dead with the body extended.

The findings of certain pieces of symbolic type (gladioliths, polished stone balls, stone and shells pendants, wooden staff) allow us to think that they possessed definite religious beliefs.

Some pictographs (drawings with pigments on stone) of concentric circles that are found in the Isle of Youth in Cuba and that have been linked to the lunar and solar cycles, are believed to be of Archaic origin. If this is true, it is possible that the stars had mythical meaning to the inhabitants of the Antilles at the time, in a manner similar to other ancient cultures, and that they had begun to correlate the astronomical cycles with the seasons for hunting, fishing and gathering.

The Agro-Ceramics: the first pottery-making farmers

Around 500 BC, groups of people of Arawak origin who inhabited the north coast of South America began to arrive in the Antilles using their skills in canoe navigation.

Although Richard T. Callaghan has theoretically demonstrated in a computerized study of pre-Columbian navigation patterns that direct contact may have existed in a casual manner between the populations of the South American coast and the Antilles, it is unquestionable that population movements from the region of the Guianas used the arc of islands of the eastern Antilles to connect the two areas, establishing a route that was serve as a bridge over the years.

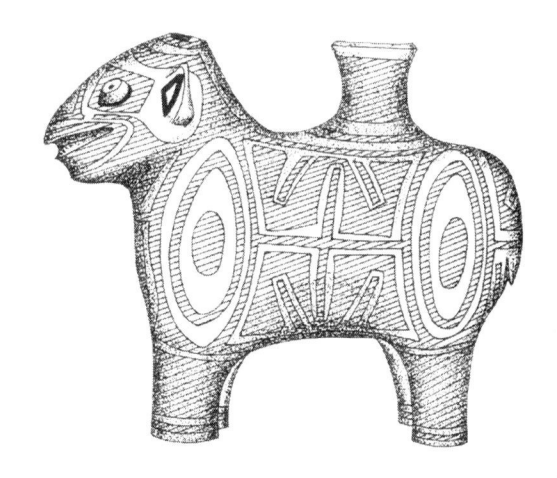

Ceramic effigy. Hacienda Grande, P.R. Drawing by Peter Roe.

The people of Arawak origin practiced slash-and-burn agriculture, which required a periodic movement to new segments of land. For this reason, the small islands of the eastern Antilles did not meet their needs fully. Hence, they relied on the surrounding marine resources to support their livelihoods. It is possible that the impact of the hurricanes, a phenomenon practically unknown in the South American coast, was another factor that contributed to their instability in these islands. For these reasons and perhaps others, the Awaraks reached Puerto Rico in about a hundred years. Puerto Rico, which afforded a greater size, better protection and abundant resources for fishing and gathering, became their hub for centuries.

Because the pottery of the Arawaks is believed to be inspired by that found at the Saladero archeological site in Venezuela, these ancient Antillean settlers have traditionally been called Saladoids. Other authors called them Agro-Ceramics because of the technical knowledge they possessed in both agriculture and pottery.

According to the aforementioned hypothesis of Chanlatte and Narganes, the Huecans (Agro-I) and then the Saladoids (Agro-II) would be the first Agro-Ceramic inhabitants of the Antilles. They have also been called Island-Arawak, Island Saladoid or Igneri, which is the same name that the Carib immigrants from South America would give to the inhabitants of the Lesser Antilles centuries later.

The archeological evidence tells us that the Agro-Ceramic inhabitants lived in coastal towns they established near coral reefs, mangroves and sources of drinking water. In this ecosystem, they were able to find crabs and, to some extent, conch like the *burgao* (*Cittarium pica*). Due to the large quantity of crustaceous found in the Saladoid deposits excavated in 1935, the American archeologist Frolich Rainey named them the Culture of the Crab. In the same fashion, however, these communities fed themselves by hunting or capturing iguanas, snakes, birds, fish, turtles, manatees and *hutias*, this last one being a rodent that lived in the forests. They collected also various fruits, roots and seeds.

Although for years archeologists believed that the Agro-Ceramic people were the first to introduce to the Antilles the cultivation of manioc, Jaime Pagán Jiménez's research in the 2000s found microscopic starch residues of manioc, maíz and other cultivable plants on lithic artifacts from Archaic periods. This means that agriculture was present in the Antilles previously than traditionally believed.

The manioc (*yuca, Manihot esculenta*), a tuber, was turned into cakes of cassava after shredding, squeezing, and cooking in the *burén*, a thick and round clay griddles buttressed by three clay cylinders (*topias*) that allowed it to be placed over fire. From this point forward, cassava became the food staple of all Antillean aboriginal cultures. Even the European conqueror adopted cassava and used it in his maritime expeditions, where it became known as the "bread of conquest."

The uniqueness of the Agro-Ceramic culture is the excellence of their pottery. They mastered every step of its fabrication: they knew how to properly select the clay, add to it the precise proportion of degreaser so that it would not crack, make - using the rolling method - objects of fine thickness, and cook them at high temperatures to obtain pottery that would not be surpassed by any later Antillean culture.

Among the Saladoids, the decoration of the objects was carried out by painting, molding, creating incisions, or combinations of these methods. The paint was of mineral and vegetable origin and was used on the outer surface of bowls and on the inside of plates and trays. The decoration of the bowls was mostly based on geometric motifs and was made using white paint on a red or polychromatic background; the handles were molded to simulate animals (zoomorphic), among which we find primarily South American species such as monkeys, caymans, tapirs or human-animal mythical beings (anthropozoomorphic) that responded to their beliefs. In this regard, Mela Pons Alegría has conducted revealing iconographic studies of the period.

A large part of the Saladoid containers are characterized by their inverted bell shape and by the presence of handles in the shape of the letter "D" that do not exceed the edge of the bowl and in the upper part of which there is a small perforated hook to hang the object. They also made bottles with several handles, small masks, incense burners, large hollow figurines. They also worked on a smaller scale the stone (mortars, petaloid axes and rectangular flat-convex axes), shell and quartz, jadeite and amethyst for corporal adornments.

In Puerto Rico, the most important site of this cultural group, Hacienda Grande in Loíza, achieves its peak around 200 BC. Four hundred years later, around 250 AD, this group would cross the Mona Channel and reach some places in eastern Hispaniola, where it seems that they influenced certain Archaic populations with their pottery.

Tainos and Caribs. The Aboriginal Cultures of the Antilles

Agro-Ceramic people in Puerto Rico.
Above image: Saladoid vessel, Sorcé, Vieques (Chanlatte and Narganes, 2002); above and to the right: effigy vessel (Rouse, 1992) and amulet in jadeite from La Hueca, Vieques (University of Puerto Rico). Below: designs on vessels from Hacienda Grande, Loíza (Pons-Alegría, 1993).

According to Chanlatte and Narganes, the Huecans differ from the Saladoids because a high percentage of the pottery of the former is decorated with a unique design (crosshatched pattern) devoid of paint but occasionally filled with white or red paste. In addition to a utilitarian pottery, the Huecans developed pottery for their ceremonies that included inhalers and effigy vases, although their decorative techniques seem to be less varied than that of the Saladoids. Their principal artisan manifestation was the awe-inspiring confection of amulets - mainly zoomorphic - carved in semiprecious stones (agate, jade, jadeite, serpentinite, malachite, amethyst, topaz), nacre, shell, bone and wood.

Among these, their distinctive "Andean condor" stands out. It depicts a bird with a trophy head held between its claws, a reason that these archaeologists have interpreted it as having traces of Andean influence. However, Peter G. Roe, an anthropologist at the University of Delaware, believes that the "trophy head" is not an artistic motif exclusive of the Andes and that the bird in question corresponds rather to the vulture king of the Guianas, the area from where, in any case, the Huecans came from.

The fact that the Agro-Ceramic people - be them Huecan or Saladoid - shared with the Archaic the same coastal habitat serves as the foundation for the two prevailing hypotheses regarding Antillean cultural development: either the Archaic that lived in the islands were displaced or exterminated by the new population movement of South American origin or, on the contrary, the Archaic adopted from the new groups the new agricultural-pottery techniques, creating several local manifestations over time.

Agro-Ceramics were tribal people organized in independent villages composed of up to 200 individuals. This lifestyle was characterized by slash agriculture for the cultivation of tubers; a productive society ruled by domestic activity and relationships based on kinship; common property; dwellings of oblong shape occupied by extended family members (constituted by father, mother, children and several generations of the same) forming semicircular settlements with a central communal plaza; the absence of centralized power (chiefs were temporarily chosen only for certain activities) and the presence of the shaman or healer.

Regarding the funeral practice, the Saladoid usually buried their dead in a squatting position. That is, with their legs flexed and with very few or no offerings. However, skeletons of a kind of domesticated dog held in great esteem have been found next to human remains, such as occurs at the Punta Candelero deposit, in Humacao, studied by the archaeologist Miguel Rodríguez López.

Interestingly, certain objects associated with the Agro-Ceramic culture persisted through the centuries and developed fully among the Tainos. For instance, the trigonolite or three-pointed stone. In the old deposits, this object is reported as being of a small size and lacking decorative features; however, it will achieve its maximum expression in Puerto Rico and eastern Hispaniola, regions that were occupied by the Saladoids or where Saladoid influence was significant, during the Taino era. The trigonolite must have had religious significance, for its form is inspired by the apex of a gastropod shell, or by the mountains that impressed newcomers to the islands, or by a prototype from the continent. Perhaps it represents the mountain from which valued water arose and was linked to the principle of agricultural fertility that evolved along with the object's design.

There are also bowls fabricated by the Agro-Ceramic people with two small tubes that seem to have been used to inhale hallucinogenic powders. These inhalation objects track well with the hallucinatory ritual of South American origin in which aboriginals believed to communicate with their superior beings. If that is the case, then it is probably that the use of the seed of the *cohoba* tree (*Anadenanthera peregrina*), whose hallucinogenic effect would serve as the basis for the main religious ceremony of the Tainos, was also originally introduced by these immigrants.

In Puerto Rico, about 100 years AD, pottery began to reflect certain changes: it lost its exquisiteness and became coarser and thicker. Gone is the polychromatic designs and the elaborate decorations; the use of shell carvings and semiprecious stones also declines. This period, corresponding to the Cuevas style (100-600 AD) found by Rouse in the district of Trujillo Alto, has been interpreted as "the decadence of the Saladoid," a "pottery de-evolution," a "final ripping apart of the Saladoid," perhaps resulting from the social process underway at the time (perhaps women had less time for the confection of pottery) or due to the colonization of the interior sections of the island. It appears that this new pottery style emerged in parallel to that which will be common during a new and important era in Antillean culture.

The Ostionoids: the precursors to the Tainos

Ostionoid pottery was first reported in 1919 by Dominican-Puerto Rican historian and archeologist Adolfo de Hostos in Punta Ostiones, Cabo Rojo, in the south-west coast of Puerto Rico. Upon study, it came to reflect a period of decisive social change that took place in Puerto Rico around 600 AD.

Divergent hypotheses exist to interpret this change in pottery. Rouse and others understand it as the local evolution of the Saladoid; further, Chanlatte and Narganes describe it as the transformation experimented by the Archaics as the result of Agro-Ceramic influences. In turn, Veloz Maggiolo sees it as South American influences not necessarily resulting from migration patterns, creating a new island mode of thinking. Roe bases it on a break of the continuous exchange sustained by continental groups, while Curet interprets is as the outcome of an emerging elite.

In general, archaeologists are inclined to agree that the Ostionoids were the result of an island process, although they differ in how it occurred: whether by local evolution, by acculturation or by novel external influences.

Be that as it may, there is no doubt that the new cultural group exhibited different socioeconomic behaviors than the previous Agro-Ceramic group. In Puerto Rico, for example, archaeological research indicates that the agricultural techniques employed by the Ostionoids began to undergo radical change, while at the same time the group sought other sources of food in rivers and in the interior of the island. While it is true that slash-and-burn agriculture did not disappear, archeological deposits such as those in Collores, Puerto Rico, indicate the emergence of the "montones" or mound technique (planting on a mound of earth with remains of vegetative material that offers greater fertility), a method that would allow a significant increase in production and, consequently, population.

Although the cassava continued to be the main source of carbohydrates, there is a dietary shift: the consumption of crabs and conch ("burgao", *Cittarium pica*) decreased and the number of fish and large marine conch such as the "carrucho", "lambí" or "cobo" (*Strombus gigas*) increased. Due to the abundance of the marine conch, archaeologist Froelich Rainey originally called it the

Culture of the Conch. There is evidence that in some areas the hunting of wild birds, perhaps through traps, also developed. The presence of stone mortars has made it possible to suggest that corn (*maíz, Zea mayz*) was probably milled and consumption of it increased. Doubtlessly, the Ostionoids achieved an advanced domain of their environment at multiple levels.

The cited conditions in which food resources were produced abundantly and agriculture was exploited favored a parallel development in society and population growth. The communal space began to be defined with greater precision with respect to its use: housing, cultivation, ritual, burial. The dwelling maintained its oblong shape but was reduced in size, suggesting a societal change towards the nuclear family. It is also the time period that evidenced the first Antillean constructions of the *batey* or ball game (Tibes, El Bronce, Las Flores) in Puerto Rico, a step in the transformation of the previous communal space that culminated in the great ceremonial plazas of the Tainos.

These developments demonstrate that an organized labor force existed; hence, the principle of established authority. In sum, these findings have made it possible to declare that the Ostionoids represent the first step in the evolution from a tribal to a chiefdom society in the Antilles. Indeed, the Puerto Rican historian Francisco Moscoso, from the University of Puerto Rico, concluded that the Ostionoids were proper Taino at tribal level and that the denominated Taino found by the Europeans, were the same culture but at the level of chiefdom.

Archaeological evidence indicates that these Taino precursors used stone more often; they carved amulets, grinders, axes. The evidence also points to an increase in the quantity and size of three pointed *cemíes* and certain objects related to the ritual of the *cohoba*, a practice that would achieve its maximum expression with the Taino chiefdoms that existed at the time of the European discovery.

With regards to pottery, two series can be established for this pre-Taino period in Puerto Rico: the Elenoid in the eastern half of the island and the Ostionoid in the west. Over time, these two styles will be reported in the east zone as well, in Monserrate (600-900 AD) and Santa Elena (900-1,200 AD), and in the west the Ostiones Puro and the Modificado (900-1,200 AD).

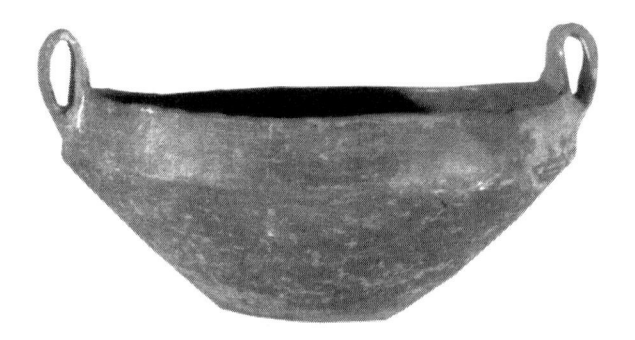

In general terms, Ostionoid bowls are of navicular and ovoid forms; the handles form loops that protrude the edge of the vessel; the use of white paint disappears, while reddish and, in some cases, black paint dominates; decoration is less frequent, limited to simple incisions or overlapping molded ornaments.

Among the ornaments, the decoration of bowls with faces is unique to Ostionoid pottery. These were originally called "monkey-face," but they have been interpreted more recently as bat heads. The French archaeologist Henry Petitjan Roget has shown that the chiropteran (mammal) motif was transmitted from the continental to the island Saladoid. Broadly speaking, where the Saladoids maintained a certain representation of the South American fauna, the Ostionoids or Taino began to reproduce the island fauna.

In this manner, when the bat motif reappears in the Ostionoid period, the traits reflected do not seem to correspond to a South American bat as it did in the Saladoid. We believe that in the Ostionoid period the characteristics are rather those of the abundant *Artibeus jamaicensis*, a bat that is native to Central America and whose entrance to the Greater Antilles occurred through Jamaica, perhaps following the same route as the first Archaic migrations.

This island species has the characteristic of having a cutaneous projection that gives it the appearance of having a raised or raised nose, a detail that clearly appears on the Ostionoid faces. If so, the hypothesis that the Ostionoid is an island style is reinforced, since the iconography reflects the Antillean fauna.

Clay pot resembling bat figure. Aguas Buenas, P.R.
(Based on Fewkes, 1907).

Indeed, the bat - sometimes stylized, sometimes humanized - is also present in other forms of bowls, in ornaments and in shell carvings, which demonstrates the important ideological status occupied by this flying mammal. The fact that the bat also had a relevant position in Taino art (perhaps representing *Maquetaurie Guayaba*, the "Cacique de los Muertos", or a "totem clánico"), demonstrates, in our opinion, that an island worldview had been forged by the Ostionoid or Taino periods. Thus, the myths natural to South America - which hundreds of years prior had arrived with the first Agro-Ceramics - must have progressively been transformed and adapted to the environment of the islands, creating what we have called an *island eco-mythology*.

As such, the material changes of the Ostionoids detected by the archeology from the 7th century AD forward correspond to a new island mentality, to an emerging Antillean ideology that will achieve its maximum expression in the Taino chiefdoms.

This new socio-cultural movement did not remain in Puerto Rico exclusively. Towards the year 700 of our era, its archaeological manifestations are reported in the eastern part of Hispaniola. There, displacing or interacting with existing groups of

Archaics or former Agro-Ceramics, it seems that these migrations took two routes: one towards the south-east of the island and another towards the north-central zone. According to Rouse, this last branch expanded to Haiti, Jamaica, eastern Cuba and the archipelago of the Bahamas. In the south-eastern region of Hispaniola, the Ostionoid style will persist with regional variations from 900 to 1,200 AD; while, on the south coast, a similar process will culminate in the Boca Chica or Chican style, whose pottery is related to the Taino.

In particular, in the central Valley of the Cibao, the Meillacan style arose, perhaps due to the influence of Archaic elements rather than by alleged migrations from the South American coast. This style will spread through the north of the island to the former inhabitants of Jamaica and Cuba, giving rise in the Bahamas to the Palmetto style.

The diversity of natural resources and the implementation of new agricultural production methods allowed the Ostionoids to reach, in Hispaniola, the maximum expression of the cultural process that had started in Puerto Rico around 600 BC. As Veloz Maggiolo underlines, they adopted, in the east and from the late Archaics, the processing of the root of the *guáyiga* or *marunguey* plant (*Zamia* sp.), perhaps by reducing the manioc crop or exploiting the rich mangrove fauna; in the north coast, they relied more on fishing, the collection of conch and turtle eggs; in the central and fertile valley of the Cibao, the cultivation in mounds achieved great expansion, at the same time that the *várzea* system, the cultivation in limestone silts in the margins of rivers, emerged. In general, the island inhabitants at this time captured iguanas (*Cyclura* sp.), rodents such as *hutía* or *jutía* (*Plagiodontia aedium*), as well as various birds, although hunting was not a highly developed activity.

It seems that, beginning on the year 1,200 of our era, the Chican style that emerged in the south-east of Hispaniola and that was linked to the Taino chiefdoms, managed to spread to the rest of the island. To the west, it reached the Meillacan zone and, to the east, Puerto Rico. There, it influenced the Elenan and Ostionoid styles, forging the creation of the regional styles Esperanza and Capá, respectively.

In sum, it is possible to ascertain that it was the development of the Ostionoids for a range of about 600 years, first in Puerto Rico and then in Hispaniola, that produced the Taino culture. In the following chapters, we will learn the most relevant characteristics of the Taino culture, based on the documents produced by chroniclers as well as the main archaeological investigations of recent times.

THIRD PART

TAINOS:
HISTORY AND SOCIETY

CHAPTER 5

Five centuries is nothing...

The fifth centenary of the "encounter between two worlds" conmemorated in 1992 was the cause of both celebrations and protests. Some people called for a celebration of Spanish culture and the Christianization of the New World; others protested the destruction and exploitation suffered at the time and ever since by the aboriginal peoples of the Americas. Two positions that responded to two ancient historical realities.

Amidst new caravels and fireworks, the interest in the subject of the indigenous history and culture of the Antilles resurfaced on both sides of the Atlantic. For example, the official committees formed to plan these controversial celebrations in the Dominican Republic and Puerto Rico organized various activities pertaining to the aboriginal subject. In Guadeloupe, the exhibition "Presents Caraïbes: 500 Ans d'Histoire Amérindienne" took place in 1993. The next year, Taino art was the subject of an extraordinary exhibition held at the Musée du Petit Palais in Paris. In 1997 and 2000, the Museo del Barrio in New York offered other excellent exhibits along with lectures on Taino art and culture. Various other competitions, conclaves, exhibitions and publications were held in different latitudes.

Five centuries of documented history about the Taino had been achieved. Let us look briefly at the historiography.

A Renaissance quartet

In addition to the writings of Colón, Chanca and Cuneo that were cited in the first part of this book, it is necessary to review the later chroniclers to make use of all the available sources and acquaint ourselves fully with the subject of Taino culture.

Columbus's great achievement - which quickly spread throughout Europe thanks to the printing press - coincided with the transition from the Middle Ages to the Renaissance, a period that saw the blooming of the arts, music and knowledge. The 16th century was a decisive driver of intellectual change in Europe: together with the mercantile capitalism that sought to expand into new lands, Renaissance humanist thought motivated the study of the various facets of the human being.

It is within this Renaissance context that we find the four main chroniclers of the Tainos. The two most renowned were Father Bartolomé de Las Casas (1474-1566), otherwise known as the Protector of the Indians because of his resolute defense of the rights of the indigenous people, and Gonzalo Fernández de Oviedo (1478-1557), who, on the contrary, became the apologist of the conquest. They arrived in the Antilles in 1502 and 1514, respectively. They rolled in "when the Taino society was already mortally wounded." Las Casas arrived years after the conquest began in Hispaniola and Oviedo came to settle in Santo Domingo in 1523 when the Taino culture was in marked disintegration. But their works, not often disparate, are fundamental ethnohistorical sources.

Las Casas, who was ordained as priest in Hispaniola, seems to have begun writing his *Historia de las Indias* in 1527 perhaps as a reaction to the publication, the previous year, of *Sumario de la natural historia de las Indias* by Oviedo, a work that would precede Oviedo's *Historia general y natural de las Indias* published in 1535. In this valuable and extensive work, Oviedo describes the Antillean flora, fauna and geography; records important details about the dissociated Taino culture, collects information from Puerto Rico and, as a glorifier of the conquest, cites to facts and names of characters that only he records.

Witness to many acts of brutality against the indigenous people, Las Casas, on the other hand, criticized Oviedo for justifying the conquest. As a result, Las Casas managed to publish his *Brevísima relación de la destrucción de las Indias* in 1552, a harsh criticism against the atrocities committed against the indigenous people that would be the basis of the "Black Legend" of the Spanish conquest in America. *Brevísima* would be the only major work of Las Casas printed during his lifetime, as his most important *Historia de las Indias* would not be published until 1875, hundreds of years after it was written. Something similar happened with his extensive *Apologética* that would see the light of day in 1909.

In spite of the lack of objectivity attributed to Oviedo by his critics, his works are a compulsory reference because of how well they document the disappearance of the Taino culture. Further, Las

Casas reproduced passages from the lost *Diary* by Christopher Columbus and extracted paragraphs from the missing *Relación* by Ramón Pané that we will examine later. The third member of the quartet never came to America. However, he noticed while at the Spanish court that a New World had been discovered and dedicated himself to interviewing the protagonists of the American drama, including the Admiral himself. Pedro Mártir de Anglería (1459-1526), a learned Italian Renaissance man living in the Spanish court, wrote important letters in Latin - sometimes accompanied by indigenous objects - that he sent to influential European personalities. He narrated details of the aboriginals, of the conquest, and of the history of Spain. The compilation of his writings was edited as *Décadas del Nuevo Mundo*, published in Spanish for the first time in 1892. It is significant that Anglería included a short, but the first ever, Taino vocabulary and a compendium of Pané's manuscript.

The character that culminates the quartet of chroniclers is Hernando (Fernando) Colón (1488-1539), the natural son of the Admiral who accompanied him during the fateful fourth voyage. He was a cosmographer and possessed the most important library of his time. His *Historia del Almirante* - published in Italian in 1571 before the Spanish manuscript was lost - is based on the diaries and narrations of his father. To a large degree, the fundamental value of his work is that it completely transcribes the text of the aforementioned *Relación* by Pané, thanks to which we know today of the existence of this primary source regarding Taino beliefs.

Beyond Colón, Oviedo, Las Casas and Anglería, other writers who partially provide information about the Tainos are Diego Álvarez Chanca, Father Andrés Bernáldez, Francisco López de Gómara, Antonio de Herrera and Girolamo Benzoni. In addition, the documents deposited in the Spanish archives are important reference materials: royal charters, letters, legal disputes, as well as the contracts and interrogations related to *encomiendas (*colonial grants of land and native inhabitants).

Influenced by the European descriptions provided by the chroniclers, publications arose primarily during the 16th and 17th century with engravings that depicted aboriginal life as a fantasy that was far from the reality experienced in the New World. An example is the engravings of the Belgian Theodor de Bry, published between 1590 and 1634, in which he represents an imaginary Taino ritual with figures most commonly found in Satanic iconography.

Religion and divine cult of the Indians. *Great Travelers*, Book IV
(Theodor de Bry, 1594).

A parenthesis in time

During the 17th century, the great continental civilizations of America monopolized the attention of European historians, displacing what was left of the Tainos. Curiously, the beginning of French colonization in the Lesser Antilles meant that the French chroniclers wrote about the Caribs during this century.

In the 18th century, Father Pierre François Xavier de Charlevoix published *Histoire de l'Isle Espagnole ou de S. Domingue* (1730), a comprehensive study based on the manuscripts of Father Jean Baptiste le Pers - who lived on the French side of Hispaniola - and of original documents in the French archives. On one of the maps included in this voluminous work are the drawings of three aboriginal artworks, most likely the first reproduction of Antillean archaeological objects. The following page depicts a map of Hispaniola showing, for the first time, various aboriginal objects (Charlevoix, 1730).

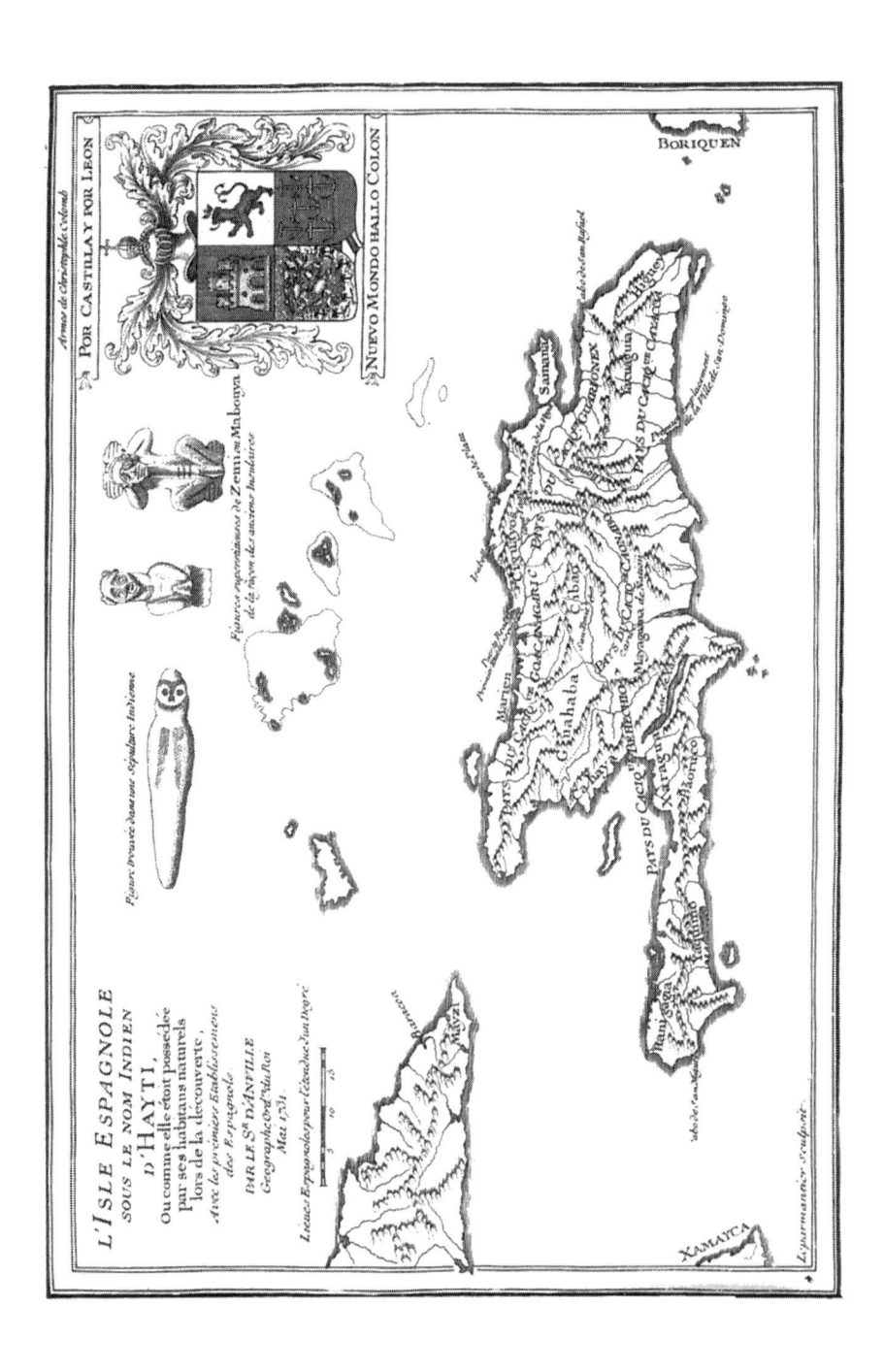

Tainos and Caribs. The Aboriginal Cultures of the Antilles

Years later, Father Juan de Talamanco described and illustrated in Madrid "four idols that were brought to me from Hispaniola at the end of 1749." In 1762, Luis José Peguero compiled *Historia de la conquista de la isla Española de Santo Domingo*, a manuscript based mainly on Herrera and Oviedo that was printed in 1975. In books like *Essai Sur L'Histoire Naturelle de St. Domingue* (Paris, 1776) by Father Louis Nicolson, indigenous pieces found in the then-French colony were analyzed.

In his *Historia geográfica, civil y natural de la isla de San Juan Bautista de Puerto Rico* published in 1788, Father Agustín Iñigo Abbad y Lasierra, who was a Benedictine monk and precursor of Puerto Rican historiography, exposed plainly the characteristics of the Tainos using the accounts of several chroniclers and historians, including Charlevoix.

During the next 19th century, the body of knowledge and objects collected over the centuries by explorers, priests and colonizers in the Americas, Africa, the East and Oceania, provoked an interest in the understanding of the origin of man and the historical processes that build a culture. This enthusiasm was not free of West ethnocentrism. The new sciences of anthropology, ethnography and archeology emerged in this century.

The rediscovery of the Taino

The subject of the original inhabitants of the Antilles remained active for two centuries due in large measure to the existence of historical documentation for its study. In the 19th century, the ethnographic information was completed by archeological findings of significance.

In what appears to be the first historical report of an aboriginal piece of art from the Antilles, Thomas Ryder wrote a letter in which he described a necklace of beads and carved figures. He included the necklace with the missive. The letter appears in volume XIII of *Archaeologia*, the annals of the Society of Antiques of London. The objects had been found years before by a fugitive slave in a cave located near Cabo Nicolás, in the western part of Hispaniola.

In March of 1851, Sir Robert Schomburgk wrote a letter to an English nobleman that would become the first archeological report of Antillean findings.

In it, Schomburgh, a German scientist who explored English Guiana before settling in Santo Domingo as a British consul, described with considerable accuracy the plaza of Indian of San Juan de la Maguana and the pictographs of the caves of El Pommier (now Borbón). These were sites that he discovered during his travels through Hispaniola. He believed, consistent with a fashionable hypothesis at the time, that the Antillean findings "belong to a race infinitely superior in intelligence to that which Columbus found... from the northern parts of Mexico."

During the same time, Andrés Poey and Miguel Rodríguez Ferrer performed the first archaeological excavations in Cuba. In June of 1854, Puerto Rico hosted the first formal fair or exhibition intended to showcase the commercial and cultural development of the island. The archaeological collections of José Julián Acosta and George Latimer were exhibited.

That same year, Haitian Emile Nau published *Histoire des Caciques d'Haiti*, an account of Carib history based on French historians. Nau made a mistake in this publication by attributing to the Taino certain beliefs of the Caribs; among them, that Louquo was the supreme being who lived in heaven. These errors were transmitted on by several influential Dominican historians, such as José Gabriel García and Bernardo Pichardo.

Then, in 1868, the American Daniel G. Brinton published *The Myths of the New World*, an innovative treatise on continental indigenous symbolism and mythology. Despite mentioning them only in passing, Taino and Carib mythology did not escape Brinton's attention. Three years later, Brinton became the first to establish a linguistic link between the Tainos (who he called Island-Arawak) and the Lokono or Arawak of the Guianas. In 1898, he published an article on Cuban archeology in *American Archaeologist* and the following year, in *Races and Peoples*, he attempted to distinguish the different ethnic groups of the Antilles, suggesting the separation of Arawak and Carib.

In Havana, in 1876, Enrique Dumont published a pioneering work on Puerto Rican archeology entitled *Investigación acerca de las antiguedades de la isla de Puerto Rico*. Concurrently, the German Leopold Krug printed in Berlin a report on a large rock with petroglyphs located near Gurabo, Puerto Rico, which he refused to declare had calendrical connotations, as the locals believed, because "the indigenous people lacked astronomical knowledge."

The Frenchman Louis Alphone Pinart carried out two important works between 1881 and 1890: an official archaeological site finding in the Dominican province of Samaná (where he is known to have prepared the first Antillean report on physical anthropology) and his original article on the petroglyphs of the Antilles. In 1883, Antonio Bachiller y Morales edited *Cuba primitiva*, a sketch of Cuban prehistory. The following year, *La fábula de los caribes* was published in Havana. In his book, Juan Ignacio de Armas stated that the cannibalistic ritual of the Caribs did not exist and, being rather an invention by the conqueror, did not differ from the Taino ritual.

Agustín Stahl, a well-known Puerto Rican doctor and pioneer naturalist, published *Los indios borinqueños* in 1889, an interesting work that nevertheless perpetuates errors; he rejects, for example, that the Tainos had religious ideas because he believed that "they were unable in their poor intelligence and narrow judgement, to formulate speculations of a metaphysical order." In 1891, the Dominican Alejandro Llenas published in Paris his study of an aboriginal skull.

That same year, on account of the international fair that took place in Chicago on the occasion of the fourth centenary of the discovery of the New World, a Special Commissioner for the event visited the Antilles. His name was Frederick A. Ober, an adventurer, zoologist and prolific writer who would carry back with him numerous relics of historical value. Among his numerous and varied works, Ober published *Camps in the Caribbees* (1880), *In the Wake of Columbus* (1893), where he makes reference to his visit, and *Aborigins of the West Indies* (1894).

Father José María Nazario Cancel published *Guayanilla y la historia de Puerto Rico* in 1893. In this work he reported that, since 1880, he had owned "over 800 anthropoglyphites," stones with strange engravings that came "from the library of Agüeybana," according to an old, dying woman who he said confided in him and had kept the secret of the stone's location as a family tradition. Father Nazario's stones have provoked a long and controversial archeological debate. Most of the stones are kept under the custody of the Instituto de Cultura Puertorriqueña in Puerto Rico. Later, in the 1990s, historian Aurelio Tió upheld their authenticity and affirmed that the stones, based on certain epigraphic analyses, demonstrated that "the indigenous people of Puerto Rico knew how to read and write […] utilizing a Basque syllabary."

New and hopeful investigations have been carried out in recent years by the Puerto Rican archaeologist Reniel Rodríguez Ramos. Meanwhile, the mystery continues.

Some of the polemic stones found in 1880 by Father Nazario near Yauco, P.R. (Based on Tió, 1990).

Before the end of the century, in 1897, Cayetano Coll y Toste received an award for the manuscript *Prehistoria de Puerto Rico* (published in 1907), which constituted a serious attempt to interpret Taino culture. During the 19th century, several private collectors of Antillean "antiquities" emerged. In Cuba, Colonel Federico Rasco, Eduardo García Feria and R.S. O'Fallon; in the Dominican Republic,

Archbishop Arturo de Meriño, Alberto Llenas, Ramón A. Imbert and Edward Hall; in Puerto Rico, Father José María Nazario, José Julián Acosta, George Latimer, Eduardo Neumann Gandía and Agustín Stahl; in Guadeloupe, Louis Guesde (who was born in 1844 in Humacao, Puerto Rico).

As archaeologist Paola A. Schiappacasse Rubio has investigated, most of these collections went to international museums or became part of local museums founded in the next century.

The pioneers of the 20th century

The new century began with the critical and systematic publications by the American Jesse Walter Fewkes. His historical, ethnological and archaeological method led him to look for a cultural area, an Antillean cultural unit. As a result of having studied over 1,200 pieces, Fewkes produced a typological classification of objects, that established the foundations for Antillean archeology. Among his many writings, his books *The Aborigines of Porto Rico and Neighboring Islands* (1907) and *A Prehistoric Island Culture Area of America* (1922) stand out.

In parallel to Fewkes' work, it is necessary to mention the partial investigations carried out by Luis Montané and Juan Cosculluela in Cuba, William L. Abbott in the Domincan Republic, and Thomas Joyce in the British Museum's collection.

Further, Narciso Alberti Bosch, a Dominican doctor and tireless explorer and pioneer archaeologist, published between 1908 and 1932 over 15 articles and a book, *Apuntes para la prehistoria de Quisqueya* (1912). His book was a titanic editorial effort and described unexplored places. However, he postulated a Mediterranean origin to the original cultures of Quisqueya (Hispaniola), in tune with the theories popular at the time. Alberti Bosch never finished editing *Clave para descifrar el simbolismo de los cemís antillanos y el significado esotérico de los signos míticos que tienen grabados* (1922). We consulted this work at the Museo del Hombre Dominicano in the Dominican Republic and opine that, despite its subjectivity, it constitutes an interpretation of great value to the origins of the universe present in Taino art.

The U.S. military occupation of Santo Domingo (1916-1924) brought archaeologist Theodoor de Booy, who took with him about 2,000 pieces of art to the Heye Foundation Museum in New York.

Other researchers or archaeologists, sent primarily by institutions, museums or private collectors from the U.S. and Europe, also travelled to the Antilles in the first decades of the 20th century.

Such was the case of research conducted by the New York Academy of Sciences that gave rise to J. Alden Mason's excavations in Capá and other sites in Puerto Rico in 1914 and 1915; Froelich G. Rainey's archaeological survey in the Bahamas, Haiti, Dominican Republic, Puerto Rico and the Virgin Islands in 1934 and 1935, and Irving Rouse's study of Puerto Rican sites during the summers from 1936 to 1938.

From 1919 and onward, the important work of historian Adolfo de Hostos on Antillean ethnology and archeology was carried out and disseminated partially in *Anthropological Papers* (1941). In 1955, his valuable archaeological collection containing numerous Dominican pieces, became part of the Museo de la Universidad de Puerto Rico. Mark R. Harrington's archeological research on the island was published in the book *Cuba Before Columbus* in 1921. This book is the first to distinguish the Archaic and Agro-Ceramics cultures, and also coined the term "Taino culture."

In 1924, Sven Lovén's thesis was printed in German and revised and translated into English as *Origins of the Tainan Culture* (1935). In this book, Lovén synthesizes the ethnohistorical documents and the archaeological investigations conducted to date by Jesse W. Fewkes and H.W. Krieger in the Antilles. Lovén does not question the link between the Tainos and the continental Arawaks, and defines terms that are still valid today, such as "Island-Arawak," "Igneris," and "sub-Taino culture." In 1937, the pathfinding publication of Irving Rouse's work on the pre-history of Puerto Rico strengthened his continuous dedication to the archeology of the Caribbean basin. In what amounted to an endeavor of over 50 years, Rouse published countless articles on island archeology, summarizing his hypothesis in *The Tainos: Rise and Decline of the People Who Greeted Columbus*, published in 1992.

Beginning in the 1940s, several influential local researchers emerged. Among them: Fernando Ortiz in Cuba, Jean Prince-Mars in Haiti, Emile de Boyrie Moya in the Dominican Republic, and Ricardo E. Alegría in Puerto Rico. Thus, when in 1950 the first Round Table of Archaeologists of the Caribbean was held in Havana, Cuba, the Antillean archeology had already achieved its maturity.

Fernando Ortiz (Cuba), Emile de Boyrie Moya (Dominican Republic), Ricardo E. Alegría (Puerto Rico).

Since then, there have been significant advancements by trained new archaeologists, anthropologists and research institutions in the Caribbean and elsewhere. Among these it is worth mentioning in Cuba the Gabinete de Aqueología (Archeology Cabinet) and *Cuba Arqueológica*, a digital magazine; in the Dominican Republic, the Fundación García Arévalo and the Museo del Hombre Dominicano with the publication, *Boletín* (Bulletin); in Puerto Rico, the Universidad de Puerto Rico and the Centro de Estudios Avanzados de Puerto Rico y el Caribe, where a master's degree in archeology is offered. In recent years, Leiden University (Netherlands) has sponsored important research in the Caribbean.

An example of this academic progress is the International Congress of Archeology of the Caribbean, organized in 1961 by Father Robert Pichon and Jacques Petitjean Roget in Martinique. These prestigious events have continued to be held every two years in a different host country in the Caribbean.

CHAPTER 6

The idealization of the Tainos

Antillean writers and artists influenced by 19th century romanticism adopted the indigenous theme in their work as a symbol of national identity. This is why Cuban patriot and poet José Martí advised on prioritizing the study of American aboriginal cultures over the study of classical Greece.

Motivated perhaps by the desire to embrace and value that which is autochthonous, the Tainos came to be idealized as a "the noble savage" who lived in wholesome happiness in an "affable and peaceful" town on a group of paradise islands until the arrival of the European. To this end, the Tainos were pictured as a homogenous culture of people, a depiction that is not necessarily true to the facts.

From the archaeological perspective, the Tainos were classified by Rouse into three groups: "classic Taino" (Hispaniola, Puerto Rico and eastern Cuba), "western Taino" (Jamaica, central Cuba, Bahamas and the extreme southwest of Hispaniola) and "eastern Taino" (Lesser Antilles not occupied by the Caribs). Previously, Lovén had classified only the inhabitants of Hispaniola and Puerto Rico as Tainos. To these, Alegría added the inhabitants of Jamaica. Rouse's distribution, however, should not be considered absolute because the Chicoid pottery associated with the Tainos is not a definite reflection of cultural homogeneity.

Archeology itself reveals differences between the Tainos in Puerto Rico and Hispaniola with regards to their artistic creations and megalithic constructions. These variations could be an index that help explain the different levels of development reached by the distinct chiefdoms. Uneven artistic manifestations occurred regionally in Hispaniola, as noted by Manuel García Arévalo. In fact, ethnohistorical sources confirm these variations: in Hispaniola, very similar ethnic groups (Tainos, *cigüayos* and *macorijes*) have been reported, all with a general, common language and, apparently, two distinct dialects.

It is possible that the *cigüayos* and *macorijes* were sub-divisions of the Taino ethnic group or, on the contrary, that they came to

Hispaniola as a result of other South American migrations (including Carib), but that they were enveloped in an extensive process of sociocultural, political and economic integration led by the Taino chiefdoms.

In sum, the historical process that occurred in and between the Antillean islands and the continent was neither parallel nor the result of unilinear evolution. For this reason, when bearded strangers arrived "from heaven," the Greater Antilles were inhabited by various ethnics groups that employed diverse ways of life and who coexisted under the Taino chiefdom political system.

The origin of the chiefdom

In the second part of this book we saw that the archaeological evidence suggests that in the Antilles the aboriginal societies manifested themselves - throughout time and space - in the levels established traditionally by anthropologists: bands, tribes, chiefdoms.

The ethnohistorical evidence, in turn, shows that the Caribs of the eastern Antilles were tribal, even though there is evidence of chiefdoms in development. In the Greater Antilles, it is permissible to think that, if the European found chiefdoms on the islands, the group of people archeologically called Ostionoids must have been Tainos at the tribal level.

How the transition from the tribal level to chiefdoms occurs has long been a matter of controversy. From a socio-economic perspective, some people believe that the emergence of surplus in production processes at the tribal level leads to a transformation in the division of labor and social relationships. Consequently, the individuals and groups of kinship that enjoyed prestige and rank previously, begin to occupy the hierarchical position that would give way to chiefdom. According to leading anthropologists on chiefdoms such as Robert Carneiro and Elsa Redmond, this system is fundamentally the result of a tribal warrior leader establishing his authority. To explain it, we will refer briefly to the society of the Caribs, who we will discuss in greater depth in future chapters.

The French chronicles ascertain that there was no established authority among the Caribs. The "captains" were selected only in time of war and their authority ceased as soon as war ended.

However, the authority of these tribal leaders increased as their prestige as successful warriors grew. Thus, once an individual was elected war chief in a village, he may become the head of an alliance of several villages or even neighboring islands. Over time, his authority would be more continuous and, with the help of polygamy, constitute a predominant social group. It seems that this was the case of Ukalé and Kalamiena, two powerful Carib "captains" of Dominica referenced by the French chroniclers. Indeed, these two characters could be conceived as protagonists in the unfolding of a leadership framework among the Caribs of the 17th century.

We could envision a similar development process unfolding among the precursors of the Tainos. Chiefdoms could have arisen as a result of the progressive control of a particular leader and group of warriors that imposed themselves either through prestige or by force within their own group, towns and even neighboring islands. It is permissible to think that this was the case with Caonabo, a native of the Lucayas (Bahamas) according to Las Casas, who became one of the principal chiefs of Hispaniola due to his courage.

These groups of power would, in turn, gain control gradually over the production forces. But, as the French anthropologist Maurice Godelier has pointed out, to achieve social control, force is not enough; it is necessary for the leader to gain prestige by giving of himself so that his fellow men, in reciprocity, recognize and accept his authority. For this reason, the revolutionary agricultural practice of growing crops by heaping them into a raised mass of soil ("montones"), which emerged with the Ostionoids in Puerto Rico, resulted from the practices established by certain groups of kin who were linked to a means of production that exercised authority over others. In this manner, the resulting surplus production, rather than being the cause of subsequent socio-economic changes, was itself the novel change implemented by Taino tribal leaders in the process of consolidating power that brought technical innovation and new ideological ways of thinking.

Similarly, the dissemination of the Ostionoids from Puerto Rico to Hispaniola and their subsequent expansion within Hispaniola was the consequence of organized groups commanded by leaders who, one way or another, succeeded in instituting their cultural preferences amongst other groups of people.

Accordingly, the emergence of chiefdoms was the result of a complex historical process in which warrior prestige played an important role. It was a process by which several tribal groups on each island imposed themselves on others such that over time, and by 1492, they achieved the formation of chiefdoms that lived in relative peace, that which we call *"pax* Taina." In other words, the pre-Columbian history of the Caribbean was probably not peaceful.

Antillean chiefdoms

By and large, the Tainos in the Greater Antilles reached the anthropological level of chiefdom. Briefly, chiefdom is defined as a complex society in which an intermediary political, economic and ideological system exists between the tribe and the state.

By being in development, the Taino society manifested transition elements that are distinctive of both the proceeding and the prospective social stages. Power was centralized in the figure of the chief (*cacique*) and in his group of kin, considered by some as members of an emerging social class. The individuals in the dominant group acted as controllers of the means of production and probably imposed certain types of taxes on the rest of the population. The property continued to be communal, although there was clear social stratification and work specialization. There was a greater knowledge of climatological cycles and of agricultural technique, which allowed for greater productivity that resulted in a greater concentration of power. The population increased and large towns and ceremonial plazas were built. The social hierarchy corresponded to the hierarchical structure and human qualities attributed to the divinities, with religion reaching a higher degree of sophistication that was reflected in complex ceremonies and in the creation and proliferation of artistic objects.

The kinship groups resulting from the aforementioned historical process formed distinct chiefdoms that were geographically distributed on each island. In Hispaniola, according to Las Casas and Oviedo, there were five chiefdoms with their respective chiefs (in parentheses): Marién (Guacanagarix), Maguana (Caonabo), Maguá (Guarionex), Xaragua (Behechío), Higüey (Cayacoa or Cotubanamá). Further, Dominican historian Bernardo Vega, considering the description of Anglería and ancient documents, concluded that these chiefdoms (and perhaps others) were part of five large indigenous provinces: Caizcimú, Cahiabo, Huhabo, Bainoa and Guaccayarima.

In Puerto Rico, no determination was made about the quantity of existing chiefdoms, but Oviedo cites to six main rebel chiefs: Agüeybana, Aymamon, Mabodomoca, Urayoan, Guarionex and Luisa, that perhaps corresponded to a similar number of chiefdoms. Coll y Toste identified 19 chiefdoms in Puerto Rico. Alegría, meanwhile, documents the names of dozens of chiefs who had varying degrees of authority. But, contrary to what others have said, he believed that "there is no definitive evidence that, before the arrival of the conquerors, there were women exercising the functions of chiefs." Taino people were patriarchal: males held primary power and dominated in roles of leadership. But it also seems that chiefs were chosen primarily through the female line, indicating that Taino people were a matrilineal society, where individuals were considered to belong to the same lineage group as their mother.

In Cuba, the number of chiefdoms - which some people believe did not exist as such - cannot be specified, even though the names of several towns, regions and chiefs are known. The known chief names were: Habaguanex, Guayacayex, Yacahuey, Yaguacayeo. In Jamaica, thanks to Diego Méndez, the loyal servant to Columbus, we know the names of several chiefs: Huareo, Ameyro, Aoamaquique.

Interestingly, some chiefs exchanged their name with the Spaniards in an act of brotherhood, becoming *guatiaos*. We know of Cotubanamá and Esquivel, in Hispaniola; Agüeybana and Ponce de León, in Puerto Rico; Ameyro and Diego Méndez, in Jamaica.

As we have said, the development of the chiefdoms was not simultaneous or similar between islands, not even on the same island. We know that Columbus noticed certain differences: he was surprised by the large canoes in northern Cuba and Jamaica, while noting greater social development in Hispaniola. Unfortunately, Columbus did not learn of the chiefdom of Xaragua, headed by Behechío, brother of the beautiful Anacaona. According to Las Casas, the Xaragua chiefdom was "almost the royal court of this entire island, because they exceeded all others in the policing and in the language and in the conversation and in the beauty of the people."

In contrast, we have already mentioned the marginalized groups who could not communicate with "Diego Colón" and who lived in the eastern end of the same chiefdom of Xaragua, in

Guacayarima. And, in the northeast, at the opposite north-east end of the island, on whose coast the Admiral had reported seeing warlike Indians with features that were similar to that of the Caribs, the *ciguayo* chief Mayobanex thanked the powerful *cacique* Guarionex for having taught him the songs and dances of the ceremonial *areíto*. In other words, for initiating him in Taino beliefs. In sum, the Taino chiefdom system consolidated the political, linguistic and religious unity of the Antilles.

The cacique, center of power

Spanish chroniclers mention that Taino society was composed of *caciques*, *nitaínos*, *behiques* and *naborías*. The *cacique* - from "ka-siqua, in reference to house, that is, head of house or houses"- was, for the European, synonym of king. As early as Columbus' first voyage, chroniclers distinguished the *cacique* from other indigenous inhabitants due to their behavior and adornments. The *cacique* was the highest authority in Taino society. Las Casas later described what seemed to be the most essential occupation of the *cacique*:

> *Their office was to be [...] steward of all, they were in charge of ordering that fields be planted for the bread, that they go to hunt and fish; they brought everything to him and he distributed to each house what was enough to sustain it. He did the same in all things that were necessary, ordering each person or set of persons to do what they had to do and what role they were to have.*

Thus, the *cacique*'s main function was to direct and manage the production process. The Spanish colonizers would take advantage of this situation when they established the *encomienda*, a system that fixed the Spanish conquistadors' entitlement to labor and taxes from indigenous communities. Although the Taino people theoretically remained free subjects of the Spanish Crown, in practice they were enslaved to the *encomendero* (those having encomienda rights). As applied to the Taino society, the *encomendero* would govern their assigned people through their *cacique* and *nitaíno*.

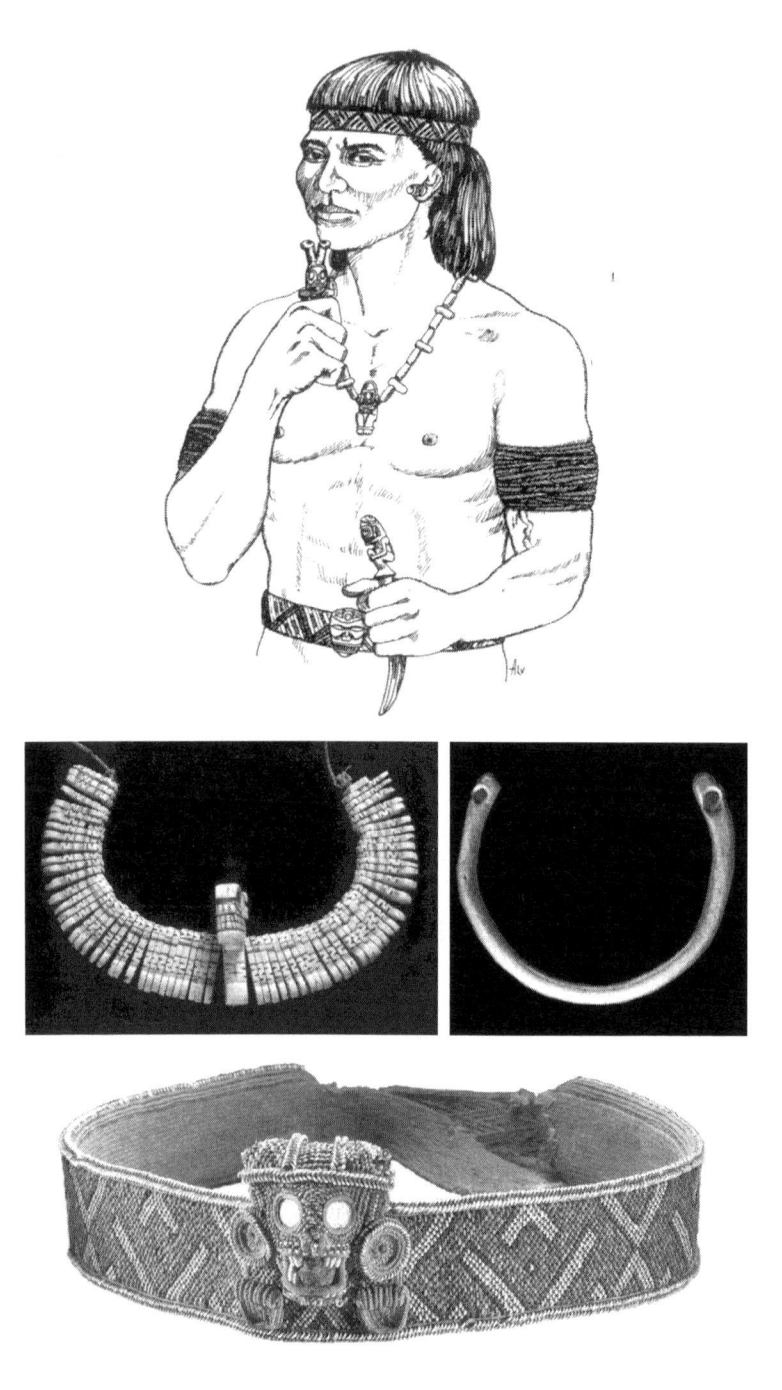

Tainos and Caribs. The Aboriginal Cultures of the Antilles

The ornaments used by the Taino hierarchy included necklace, gold nose piece, woven belt and *guanín*.

Some Spanish chroniclers described seeing three levels of *caciques* (supreme chief, secondary chief and village chief), based on "how pronounced was the degree and dignity or status of the lords," as Las Casas wrote. Las Casas reported the names Matunherí ("Your Highness [...] to only the supreme kings"), Baharí ("Your Honor") and Guaoxerí ("Your Mercy [...] as we say to the knights"). Another name of well-known distinction was Guamiquina ("Great Lord"), which was granted to Columbus during the first voyage and was perhaps also conferred to some *caciques*.

To a large extent, the power of the *cacique* was proportionate to the number of nearby and distant towns that he controlled. The practice of polygamy allowed the *cacique* to have women in different localities; consequently, kinship relationships integrated separate communities into a single chiefdom. We know, for instance, that the *cacique* Behechío of Xaragua had 30 "wives," no doubt an indication of his great power and prestige.

Both the number of names and their meaning gave hierarchy to a *cacique*. Many of the names used associated the *cacique* with the concepts of the center, the height, the brightness or brilliance of the gold or, even more, of the precious *guanín*, the jewel of South American origin that was the alloy of gold and copper and that became the symbol of the Sun. In fact, we will see that the name of the first mythical Taino *cacique*, Anacacuya, was equivalent to Star of the Center or Central Spirit, and that, as such, it would be idealized in the night sky in the Polar Star, the immobile center of the universe, the cosmic Center.

The name of the powerful Caonabo, a *cacique* in Hispaniola, has been interpreted as "Lord of the House of Gold" and the name of his wife, Anacaona, as "Center or Heart of the Celestially Valuable." Of the 40 names held by the aforementioned Behechío of Xaragua, the majority of those registered have the connotations indicated: Tureygua Hobin, translated as "dazzling as the *guanín*," or "Celestial Brightness of the Reddish Metal;" Huibo, translated as "Altitude" or "wiwa," equivalent to "Star;" Starei, synonymous with "splendid, luminous, brilliant." In Puerto Rico, the name of the great *cacique* Agüeybana has been interpreted as "the great sun."

Next to the *guanín*, the *caciques* used other distinctive ornaments that reaffirmed their hierarchy and prestige: cotton tunics and feathers; crowns and masks or *guaizas* of cotton with feathers, colored stones, shells or gold; cotton-woven belts and necklaces made of shell beads or stones, with small masks made of gold or other materials. It is worth remembering the description offered by Father Andrés Bernáldez in chapter 2 of the jewels and objects used by the Jamaican *cacique* who, together with his family, tried to emigrate with the Admiral.

The use of *guanín* by the *cacique* explains a connection to the sky, known among the Taino people as *turey*. The *cacique* served as a religious leader and mediator with the supreme beings that inhabited the sky. Las Casas stated that there were no temples in Hispaniola (and thus in the rest of the islands), "but the same houses of the *caciques* and those who were older than the others... *caney* was the house of the principal gentleman... they made in those houses, especially the *cohobas*," the main Taino religious ritual. Thus, the *caney* served as both the dwelling of the *cacique* and as a temple. Besides hosting the *cohoba* ritual, the *caney* was the place where the *cacique* guarded the *cemíes*, the sculptural objects that are the fundamental symbol in the Taino religion. The *cacique* used the *cemíes* to maintain a direct and exclusive connection with ancestral spirits. And, in front of the *caney*, was the ceremonial plaza, the delineated space where the *areítos* (a type of religious song and dance) were celebrated.

As such, it was believed that the social hierarchy established by the *cacique* emanated from the divine hierarchy, which legitimized all the functions that he exercised. At the same time, a humanization of the supreme deities occurred and was represented in *cemíes* with anthropomorphic features. Consequently, the Taino social structure intended to reflect the model society of the gods. Of course, the most important *caciques* owned the *cemíes* considered to be the most powerful, those that other *caciques* attempted to usurp, believing in this way that they obtained greater authority.

Moreover, the Tainos believed that, since the divine order should not be altered, neither should terrestrial order be disrupted. Hence, the identification of the *cacique* with the sacred justified the establishment of a hereditary power that would ensure the continuation of the cosmic balance achieved.

According to Antonio Curet, the ambiguous rules of Taino descent and succession could be manipulated by the *caciques* to consolidate and stabilize power. However, it seems that, by and large, power was transmitted through the maternal line: the position was inherited by the first son of the *cacique*'s elder sister, thus guaranteeing the same lineage. In this regard, Martyr de Anglería wrote: "They select as the heir of the kingdom the firstborn of the elder sister, if there is one; in his absence, the firstborn of the second sister; and, if the latter does not have children, the firstborn of the third sister, because he considers that there is certainty of that offspring coming from his blood." If there were no heirs from the sisters, then the inheritance passes to the "kingdom of the brothers, and if they do not live, to their children." In the last instance, they appointed as *cacique* the person "who is esteemed throughout the island as most powerful."

Taking into account all of the above, it is likely that in certain chiefdoms a solar cult existed by the end of the 15th century, promoted and centralized in the figure of the *cacique*. The principle of deifying human authority after making divinities more human, culminated in the formation of a sacred solar lineage among several societies of the Americas. The best example is the Inca, the son of the Sun.

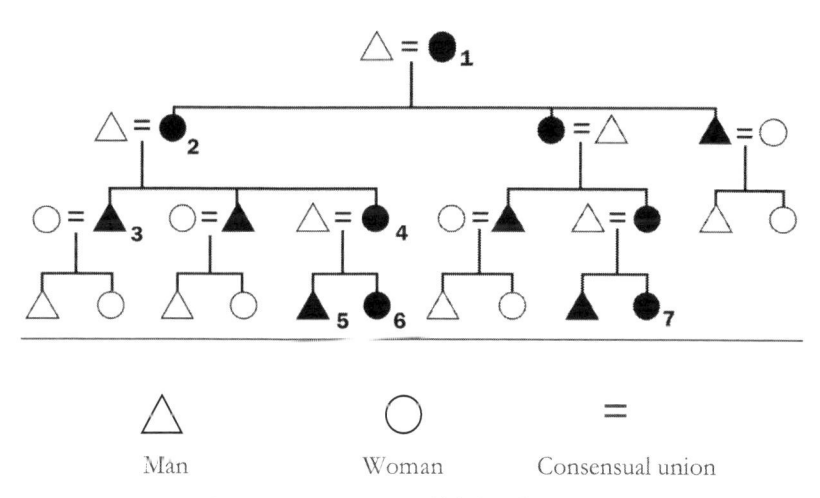

Probable Matrilineal Taino System (in black)

The Cacique **(5)** inherits by being the first-born of her mother **(4)**, who is the eldest or only sister of the former Cacique **(3)**. This former Cacique **(3)**, who was uncle of the Cacique through his mother, had been his foster father. The Cacique's sister **(6)** or his cousin-sister through the matrilineal side **(7)**, will transmit the chiefdom, just as his maternal grandmother **(2)** and her great-grandmother **(1)** did.

Regarding *nitaínos, behiques* and *naborías*

The term *nitaíno* was originally considered by Columbus equivalent to "great [...] nobleman, governor or judge." Subsequently, Las Casas defined it as "knight and principal lord [...], noble and esteemed by better blood, having authority over others." Anglería also related the term to the nobility, "they are unskilled cosmographers of their homeland."

These viewpoints illustrate that the *nitaíno* were closely related to the *caciques*. Perhaps they belonged to their own family or maybe they watched over the territorial limits of the chiefdom. Regardless, there is no doubt that *nitaínos* represented the *cacique* in the management of the production processes. Proof of this is that during the regime of the *encomienda*, *nitaínos* were used as captains or foremen of the indigenous groups. Undoubtedly, the *nitaínos* were part of the power structure of the *cacique*, either because they had ties of kinship with the *cacique* or because they were lords of an emergent ruling class.

The *behiques*, on the other hand, were defined by the chronicler Oviedo as the "great herbalists" who "had knowledge of the properties of many trees and plants and herbs, and as they healed many by such art, they were venerated and respected, like saints [...]" Las Casas added: "They made themselves *behiques* or sorcerers, doctors, and healed by blowing and by doing other external acts and muttering some words." The *behique* or shaman for the Tainos came from the ancient continental tradition of healer or doctor-sorcerer and, as such, enjoyed a respectable social position. In fact, it was in **Hispaniola** where the European first met a shaman.

Although at the tribal level the shaman performed religious functions, it seems that among the Tainos the *cacique* was also influential with the *behique*. The ceremony carried out by the *behique* that is described in detail by Ramón Pané, is a magical ritual of healing by means of medicinal plants, songs and by the action of "sucking" the body of the patient in the affected part to extract the spirit that causes the disease. The *behique* had to fast to perform the healings. However, even if the *behique* participated with the principals in the *cohoba* ritual and the purpose of the ceremony was to consult the *cemíes* to make certain decisions or to know the future, the event was still under the control of the *cacique*.

Contrary to being associated with all things solar, as was the case with the *cacique*, the *behique* was associated with the Moon and with humidity. Mythically, the *behique* is related to the Mother of the Waters, the Great Serpent, the origin of food and medicinal plants and, probably, the production of *cemíes*. Later on, we will study the mythical hero Guahayona who was the First *Behique*, the one who, in the beginning, acquired *guanín* and the secret of magical stones and medicinal plants.

Finally, the *naborías* constitute the working majority of Taino society. "*Naboría* means servant or helper," insisted Las Casas. Oviedo added an apparently contradictory definition: "an Indian who is not a slave, but who is obliged to serve even if he does not want to." It is possible that the *naborías* were originally people enslaved by the Tainos during their consolidation of power in conquered territories and that were integrated into the Taino society over time.

According to the historian Francisco Moscoso, the concept of the *naborías* is clarified when one considers that Pané originally registered the term with an adjective: *yahu naboriu*, "naboria de casa," meaning not a housing unit, but the set of families that together constitute a clan. "The houses of the chiefs were the socio-economic unit in which the Tainos began to experience the dissolution of kinship relations and the emergence of class relations," writes the historian. If so, *naborías* would be part of the "houses" of both *caciques* and *nitaínos*, the emerging Taino ruling class.

Apparently, jobs were divided according to gender and age. The women were in charge of agricultural and domestic activities (cultivation of food and medicinal plants, preparation of the cassava and other foods, manufacture of pottery, raising of children), while the men built the houses, prepared and sowed the plots, hunted, fished and carved objects in wood and stone. The children were responsible for keeping the birds away from the fields. However, as a consequence of the rapid disintegration of Taino society, today we know little or nothing about other details of their daily life or the important rituals that were celebrated to mark births, deaths, passages to puberty, consensual unions or the consecration of a *behique* or a *cacique*.

It is thanks mainly to hermit Pané that we know at least part of the beliefs of the *caciques, nitaínos, behiques* and *naborías* of this Antillean society.

Extracting gold from a river; indian in canoe.
Drawings by Gonzalo Fernández de Oviedo (1535)

FOURTH PART

TAINOS: MYTHOLOGY AND COSMOLOGY

CHAPTER 7

Beyond Guanín...

In addition to discovering a fascinating new material world, Europeans found in Taino society an entirely different mental and ideological experience; a complex system of religious belief that reflected itself in unique myths of origins, strange rituals, and exotic art that they had never known before.

"Everything I write is narrated by them, as I write it" because "this is absolutely true for those people" and "everyone believes it in general, both young and old," wrote Ramón Pané when compiling the beliefs of the Tainos upon the request of the Admiral. To that end, Pané, who had arrived on the second voyage, moved to a region of Hispaniola where, unwittingly or knowingly, he would become the first European to learn an American language, the first to write a book in the New World, and the first American ethnologist, upon finishing his manuscript *Relación acerca de las antigüedades de los indios* in 1498.

In the 26 short chapters that comprise his work, Pané wrote with honest objectivity what he understood of what they told him about the oral literature that was Taino mythology. To this primary limitation we must add that, having lost the original manuscript, what we know today comes from references to his work made by several chroniclers and, mainly, from the translation of a translation made by scholars as the Cuban José Juan Arrom.

Faced with this situation, it is necessary to study the well-known Taino myths comparatively and structurally vis-a-vis the continental myths, to read and reread between the lines, to then believe that we comprehend and can synthesize the scaffolding of the Taino religious world.

Myth, time and space

A myth has been defined as "a symbolic legend of a religious nature" or, even worse, a "thing that exists only in someone's fantasy." Contrary to these definitions, a myth is part of the "ideal realities" of a culture. The myth is, therefore, a sacred truth, a supreme reality. And the mythology of a culture becomes its sacred history.

From an anthropological perspective, no mythology is false or superior or inferior to another. Neither are the beliefs nor the sacred books of religions. There are concepts, however, that in their essence cross cultural barriers. Such is the case of time and space, terms that are closely linked to mythical thought.

"In the beginning God created heaven and earth," reads the Bible. Time (beginning) and space (sky and earth) are two inseparable, juxtaposed and subjective conceptualizations that have existed in all cultures. Cosmogony, the study of the formation of the world, integrates both principles into an ordered whole that transcends beyond the physical universe to make way for cosmology, the philosophical cosmos.

Undoubtedly, the concept of time was born as a result of observing the cyclical movement of the stars in the celestial vault. Sunrise and sunset gave rise to the days; the phases of the Moon allowed us to measure a longer time, the lunar cycle, the origin of our months. With the passage of time it was noted that the Sun moved on the horizon from one end to the other. This is how the solar year was conceived: as the time it takes for the Sun to occupy the same extreme position on the horizon.

In the same manner, the astronomical cycles were soon related to the cycles of nature. It was observed that certain stars or group of stars occupied a certain position in the sky during the rainy or drought season and that other stars, for example, were related to the season when the turtles spawned on the beaches, when certain fruit was collected, or when an animal was abundant. For this reason, the stars were idealized with the shape and name of characters, plants, animals or objects. Consequently, the stars were made into myths because it was believed that beings of origins lived in them, those who in a remote past, in mythical times, had lived on earth and now lived in heaven. To a large extent, from these ideas arose astrology, the belief that the stars influence human beings and nature.

The marking of astro-ecological cycles is, therefore, the basis of the first calendars that defined social time and the moment to carry out economic or ideological activities.

Something similar happened with space. It was generally believed that the structure of the universe was made up of three basic levels: the sky, the earth, and the underworld. Human being inhabited the intermediate plane, a place where the beings from the higher and lower planes manifested themselves. It can be said that almost all cultures have thought that their town or city was the center of the world, the *axis mundi* or center of creation. For that reason, the village, the communal house, the central square, the burials, were regularly oriented astronomically, around a center.

As such, the concept of sacred space-time arose from the celebration of rituals within a demarcated area and during a specific period of time. In that space, at a specific time, vertical communication was established between supernatural beings and human beings. It was thought that this encounter happened when man ascended or descended to the levels of the divinities or when divinities appeared in the human space.

Considering the concepts expressed in the previous paragraphs, we will analyze now the function of time and space in Taino myths, the first known oral literature of the Antilles. In the eighth part of this book, we will discuss these topics as they relate to the Caribs.

The time of the origins

The Tainos believed that the creation of the universe occurred over several eras. This can be discerned from the study of the myths collected by Ramón Pané. In our *Mitología y religión de los taínos*, a book that summarizes and illustrates Taino mythology, the different stages of creation are organized into four cycles.

The first cycle starts when, in the beginning, in the times of the origins, Yaya existed. According to the often - quoted José Juan Arrom, the word Yaya becomes the superlative duplication of "Ia," which in Arawak means "spirit, cause, essence of life." Thus, Yaya was a Supreme Spirit, "whose name is unknown," equivalent to the First Cause for the continental Arawaks.

According to Mircea Eliade, a renowned scholar of comparative religions, the original supreme beings tend to be forgotten and transform over time into an atmospheric-fertilizing god or god of vegetation, becoming the husband or son or an inferior person to a Great Telluric-lunar-vegetable Mother. This process takes place preferentially in agricultural societies, where having an operating divinity that responds to economic needs is paramount.

It seems that this was the case among the Tainos. Yaya, the unattainable High Spirit, perhaps evolved to the practical name Yúcahu Bagua Maórocoti ("Being of the Yuca, Sea, Without Male Predecessor"). As the Tainos told Pané, this deity "is in heaven and is immortal, and no one can see him, and he has a mother, but he has no beginning... his mother is called Atabey, Yermao, Guacar, Apito y Zuimaco, which are five names."

Atabey has been interpreted as Mother of the Waters. Perhaps it came from Aluberi, the First Female Cause for the continental Arawaks. The other names also appear to have a lunar-aquatic connotation. These five names established the hierarchy of this powerful feminine deity in the Taino pantheon. By being mother to Yúcahu, the divine order was projected in Taino society through matrilineality.

Yaya, in turn, had a son named Yayael. The passing of time brings about the first conflict involving Taino kinship, which recalls the famous Oedipus complex: Yayael, the Son of Yaya, wants to kill his father. For this reason, his father banishes Yayael for four "months" and kills him when he returns. Yayael's bones are placed inside an *higüero* recipient and hung from the roof of the hut by Yaya. [The *higüero* is the Calabash tree (*Crescentia cujete*), a variety of gourd. Its fruit is also called *higüero*, "calabaza" or "jícara", and is used as a small cup or bowl for eathing or drinking.] Yayael's bones magically become fish. Yayael, therefore, becomes the First Victim; his death proving that all creation is preceded by a sacrifice. Perhaps this myth also represents a first funerary rite, the basis of the cult of the ancestors, because we know that indigenous inhabitants of the Antilles hung baskets with the bones of their ancestors.

It was then that the four twin sons of Itiba Cahubaba, the Great Birthing Mother or Mother Earth, who had died in childbirth, arrived in Yaya's *bohío*. Perhaps these four twins are a superlative duplication of the two twins of so many other American mythologies and, as such, represent the expansion of space in the four directions. In the absence of Yaya, the twins lower the *higüero* and eat the fish. But, in a hurried attempt at hanging the gourd back, they break it. The Tainos believed that the sea and its creatures originated from the expansion of the contents of the broken magical container.

Probably Itiba Cahubaba, archetype of Mother Earth. Museo del Hombre Dominicano, Santo Domingo, D.R. The four mythical twins taking the *higüero* that contained the remains of Yayael, origin of the sea and fish.
Illustration by Claudia Robiou.

In a separate mythical story, the twins manage to obtain the fire, the manioc and the *cohoba* belonging to Bayamanaco, the God of Fire. In reacting, Bayamanaco spits on the back of Deminán Caracaracol with *cohoba* in his mouth. Deminán Caracaracol was the mangy leader of the twins. His skin was already rough, perhaps as a result of pre-Columbian syphilis. Unfortunately, the phlegm produces painful and progressive swelling, from which his brothers finally manage to extract a "living, female turtle, and so they built their house and raised the turtle." As suggested, this "female turtle" could be an allegory of the first female of aboriginal lineage, or a totem. According to anthropologist Antonio M. Stevens-Arroyo, the adventures of the Taino twins evoke a canoe trip from heaven to earth that occurs in certain South American myths.

Ceramic effigy vase from Dominican Republic, National Museum of the American Indian, N.Y. Possible representation of the mythical twin Deminán Caracaracol with the turtle on his back.

Or, on the contrary, perhaps the stories of the twins recall the descent to the underworld that twins in continental mythologies experience. In those stories, twins manage to obtain food for humans after facing certain underground deities.

In any case, the passages outlined here are a clear allusion to the widespread South American myths of the tree of food, universal flooding, and a hero that is sacrificed, mutilated, amputated or dismembered by a conflict of kinship. These myths are typically depicted in the sky using the Orion constellation and are related to the origin of fish and to the dry season, as Claude Lévi-Strauss studied. This ends the first stage of Taino creation, the time of the demiurges. This cycle could be understood as reminiscent of life prior to the existence of Tainos.

The creation of the universe

The second mythical cycle corresponds to the creation of the Taino universe in the mythical geography of the Antilles.

The Tainos had an island worldview and thought that their ancestors had emerged from Haiti, an island also called Bohío (because *bohío* means home) and which the Spaniards called Hispaniola. The Tainos believed that the island was a female living being, part of a world created before time whose existence they took for granted. They considered the caves a kind of uterus, the portal of entry and exit to the underworld, a cold, damp, dark place, from where creation had arisen. At least three caves were considered by the Tainos as locations where this living organism became an external entity.

The first cave was called Iguanaboína. It was located to the east, in the region of the *cacique* Mautiatihuel ("Lord of the Sunrise Region"). This was the cave of the Great Serpent, a complex underground entity of great importance in the Taino worldview. They believed that the Sun and the Moon, the stars that established cyclical time, had emerged from this cave. Cyclical time was the first step in the spatial creation of the world. In this cave, they worshiped the twin sons of the Great Iguanaboína Serpent: Boínayel ("Son of the Brown Serpent," the God of Rain) and Márohu ("Spirit of Clear Weather," the God of Good Weather). It is possible to think that Iguanaboína, helped by Boínayel and Márohu, formed a triad of good and lucky *cemíes* that controlled the climatological balance in nature.

In contrast, if there was an imbalance between these *cemíes*, the destructive triad of Guabancex (the feminine *cemí* that caused hurricanes), assisted by two others, according to Pané, namely Guataubá (preacher of bad weather, the winds and the rains) and Coatrisquie (responsible for collecting and grouping the waters in the valleys between the mountains), would manifest itself.

It is possible that both three-part manifestations, one set controlling good water (Iguanaboína, Boínayel, Márohu) and the other destructive water (Guabancex, Coatrisquie, Guataubá), were diverse revelations of the powerful Mother of the Waters. We will return to this point later.

The second cave was in Cauta, a mountain with two caves located in the center of Hispaniola. According to Pané, they believed that Tainos emerged from one cave, called Cacibajagua ("Cave of Jagua"). From the other cave, called Amayaúna, the non-Tainos or those "without merit" emerged.

The Taino people were certain that the Cacibajagua cave was the origin of the world. For this reason, this cave was their cosmic Center, the *axis mundi* or axis of creation that communicated with the lower and higher levels of Creation. The Tainos affirmed that avatar beings, or beings from the origins who could not be exposed to solar rays, lived a long time ago in the depth of this cave. We think that they were a type of bat-beings, which would explain the broad chiropteran motif in Taino art, probably a representation of a totem.

The Tainos believed that three of these avatar beings were transformed in different occasions by the Sun into stone, tree and bird upon leaving the underworld through this cave. And that they did so due to either carelessness or destiny. Although Pané does not describe so, we also think that on a fourth occasion, the remaining avatar beings exited the cave and were transformed into the first Tainos. Accordingly, the Sun was the transformer *par excellence* of the beings that inhabited the Taino underworld.

The third cave was called Guacayarima. It was located at the western end of Hispaniola and considered to be the back of the island, that is, the part of living beings that expelled excrement. Perhaps this was the entrance of the Sun to the Taino underworld.

If that was the case, the Sun moved as a nocturnal sun in the underworld to emerge the next day through Iguanaboína, the cave in the eastern end called "Lord of the Sunrise Region" and discussed earlier in this chapter. It is possible that Coaybay was located in the Guacayarima region. Coaybay is the house and room of the dead, the Taino paradise governed by the mythical *cacique* Maquetaurie Guayaba, probable God of the Dead, and possibly represented in art by the typical figures of humanized bats.

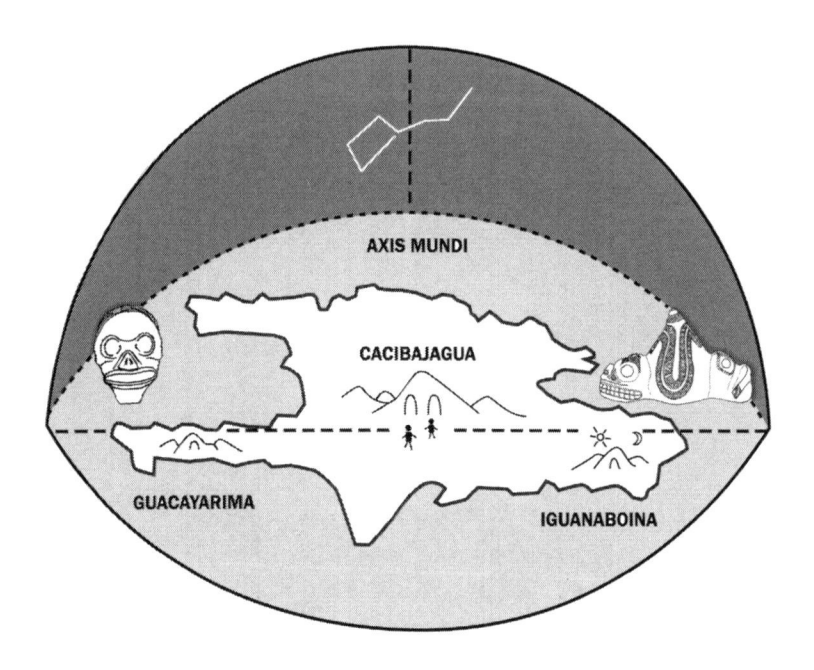

Taino cosmos with the three mythical caves and the figures of the *cacique* of *Coaybay* (the Taino Afterlife), *Anacacuya* (Big Dipper or Ursa Major) and *Iguanaboína* (Great Serpent).

In conclusion, the caves of Iguanaboína, Cacibajagua and Guacayarima, located in the east, center and west of Hispaniola, respectively, were aligned in an axis that projected the movement of the stars. This mythological geography of Hispaniola constitutes the second cycle of creation, according to the Tainos.

The formation of society

The third cycle corresponds to the formation of Taino society in time and space. Guahayona and Anacacuya were among the first Tainos to emerge from the Cacibajagua cave, from the Center of creation. Guahayona and Anacacuya are two important characters in the Taino mythical kinship system to who Pané dedicated a long explanaton.

Guahayona, after sending someone out to look for two magical plants (*digo* and *güeyo*), summons the women so that they abandon their men and go with him to other islands. To do this, he must rid of his brother-in-law Anacacuya, the mythical First *Cacique*. From a canoe, Guahayona shows Anacacuya a conch that lies under the waters - most likely a "lambí," "guamo" or "cobo" (*Strombus gigas*) - and, taking him by the feet, pushes him into the sea. The immersion of Anacacuya to the underwater world has great symbolic importance.

Namely: according to the linguistic analysis conducted by Arrom, Anacacuya means "Central Spirit" or "Star of the Center." This interpretation has allowed us to identify the mythical *cacique* with the Polaris (North Star or Polar Star), which is the star that remains motionless in the sky and, consequently, becomes the Spirit of the Center, as in the Center of the Universe. The Polaris is, then, a symbol of the Center, of the Essential, the point of origin around which everything created revolves. In turn, the observation of the Polaris in the sky is a mandatory reference for navigation, since, in addition to pointing to the celestial north, its height above the horizon corresponds to the latitude of the observer. Therefore, the transmutation of Anacacuya into the Polaris was a landmark in Taino navigation.

Similarly, the Polaris is linked to the Big Dipper (Ursa Major), a constellation that has the shape of a being with one leg. In the latitude of the Antilles, the Big Dipper seems to submerge itself at sea (as Anacacuya did) before dawn during March and April. Its disappearance under the sea lasts about four months and coincides with the main rainy season. But, more importantly: its morning rise over the horizon in August-September coincides with the hurricane season in the Antilles. As a result of this conjecture, we have postulated that the observation of the annual morning cycle of the

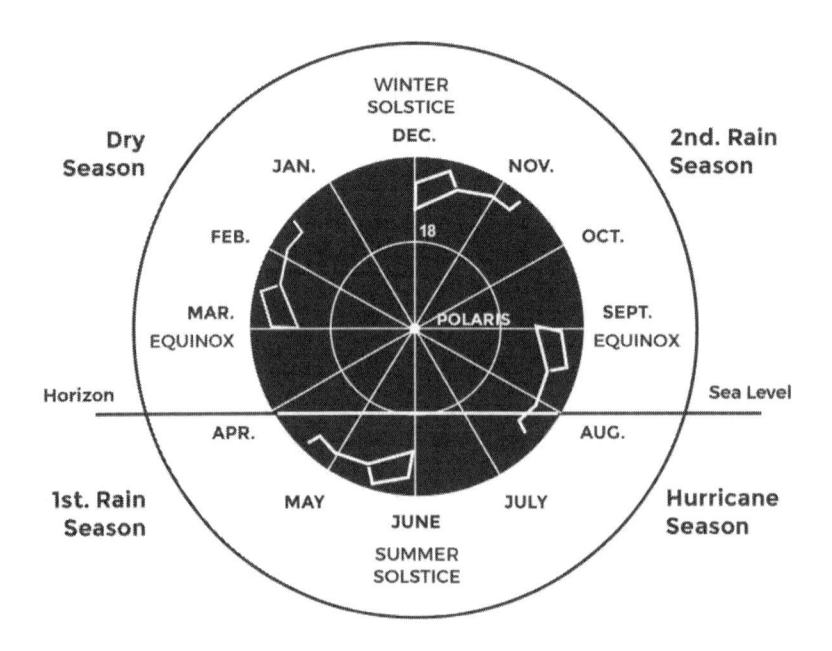

Tainos and Caribs. The Aboriginal Cultures of the Antilles

[Diagram: circular chart showing the morning cycle of the Big Dipper around Polaris, with months labeled around the circle (JAN-DEC), seasons marked on the outside (Dry Season, 2nd. Rain Season, Hurricane Season, 1st. Rain Season), and Winter Solstice, Summer Solstice, March Equinox, September Equinox positions indicated. Horizon and Sea Level marked on a horizontal line through the middle.]

Morning cycle of the Big Dipper (Ursa Major) around Polaris, a possible Antillean climatological calendar, according to the author.

Big Dipper around the Polaris could have served as a climatological-maritime calendar.

Now, before proceeding, it must be added that the mythical voyage in canoe by Guahayona combines two spatial planes in time: one horizontal, one vertical. In the horizontal plane, Guahayona acts as the First Navigator when he makes a round trip that connects his island of origin with distant islands; that is to say, his trip unites the near with the distant, the east with the west. In the vertical plane, Guahayona becomes the First *Behique* or Taino shaman when, due to his ritualistic experience in the remote island of Guanín, he makes a round trip to the upper levels, linking the earthly plane with the celestial one, that which is low with that which is high.

In short, his mythical action will make him the cultural hero, the mediator and unifier of opposites. Without Anacacuya but with all the other women in his canoe, Guahayona arrives at the island of Matininó. He leaves the women there, an action that has been interpreted as the origin of the separation of the sexes with the purpose of prohibiting incest and eliminating inbreeding among the first Tainos. This myth would give way to the belief, heard by Columbus himself, that Matininó was inhabited by women exclusively. Finally, Guahayona arrives at the remote island of Guanín.

In Guanín, Guahayona contracts syphilis (the same disease that was mentioned in reference to the twin Deminán Caracaracol). In a secluded place and helped by a woman called Guabonito, Guahayona overcomes the illness, perhaps thanks to the use of a balm made from the *guayacán* tree (*Guaiacum* sp.). As a result, he takes a new name: Albeborael Guahayona. Before returning to his island of origin, Guabonito gives Guahayona the *cibas* (the magical stones) and the *guanines* (the South American alloy composed of gold and copper, of solar symbolism). With these jewels, Guahayona obtains the secret powers of nature.

There are two aspects to discuss pertaining to this story. Above all, Guahayona's experience in Guanín recalls the death and symbolic rebirth that all processes of initiation imply, as occurs in shamanism. Guabonito could well be the "woman-spirit guide" or the "celestial wife" who, according to Mircea Eliade in his study of shamanism, always accompanies the future shaman in his initiatory journey. At the same time, the apparent disappearance of Guahayona and his reappearance as Albeborael Guahayona simulates the cycle of Venus. This planet, because of its closeness to the Sun, is invisible for several weeks between its appearance as Sunset Star and its reappearance as Morning Star. Venus, like the process of shamanic initiation, offers us a symbolic cycle of life, death and resurrection.

We believe that Guahayona ("He Who Shines by Himself") is identified with Venus in the evening (west) and that Albeborael Guahayona is related to the morning Venus (east). In this way, our mythical character was idealized in reference to this bright star that is only visible in the direction of the sunset or sunrise and, therefore, linked to the solar elements.

Let us return to Cauta, the magical mountain of origin, to find out what happened while the journey of the cultural hero took place.

The omen of the end

While Guahayona took all the women away, the children were left without their mothers next to a stream. Inconsolable, they began to cry due to hunger. And they cried so, so much, that they were slowly transfigured into a kind of frog called *tona*.

Undoubtedly, this Taino belief is a metaphor for a series of South American myths originally studied by Lévi-Strauss. In those myths, the hungry-weeping children become the Pleiades. An extensive ethnohistorical documentation demonstrates that, at the same time, this set of stars are associated with the beginning of the year and the rainy season. The Taino myth is, therefore, an analogy. The frogs in the Taino myth are the equivalent of the Pleiades in the South American myth, although in both symbols the same structural center persists: the celestial water or rainwater. This may explain why the frog is so recurrent in Taino art. It is very possible that the annual cycle of the Pleiades marked the main rainy season for the Tainos and was also the origin of a possible agricultural-ceremonial calendar.

Meanwhile, the myth continues, the men who had been left womenless see in the middle of the rain four slippery asexual beings coming down through the *jobo* tree (*Spondias mombin*). The men are assisted by four other men with rough skin (*caracaracoles* men) in holding and tying the feet and arms of the asexual beings. Then the men look for the *Inriri* bird, also known as the woodpecker. The woodpecker, believing that the asexual beings were trees, carved the sex of women onto them. "And in this way the indigenous people say they have women, according to the elders," wrote Pané. The red spot on the head or chest of the West Indian woodpecker (*Melanerpes sp.*) was believed to be the blood shed by the woman while they were carved.

This myth consists of a mixture of two documented South American myths: the descent to our plane of beings from the sky by means of a tree and the origin of the woman from the trunk of a *jobo* tree. As such, the ancestors of Taino women are androgynous celestial beings.

The new women mark the beginning of the fourth mythical cycle of creation. This fourth and last cycle is the stage of growth, development, expansion and consolidation of the Taino people. In short, the *guanín* era of Taino culture.

The number four is symbolic in the study of Taino mythology: the exile of Yayael lasted four "moons," there were four creators of the twins, the creation of the Sun culminated after four stages, Guayahona's journey lasted perhaps four "moons" (the time that the Big Dipper disappears in the horizon), there were four asexual beings held by four men of rough skin so that the woodpecker could carve four women. Indeed, according to Las Casas, the Tainos counted up to twenty - a multiple of four - using all fingers and toes. Each number had its name; unfortunately, we only know the first four: *hequetí, yamocá, canucum, yamoncobre*.

This constant in the Taino worldview is not the exception; the number four appears in the mythical, religious and esoteric symbology of all cultures worldwide. The explanation is beyond the scope of this book. Carl Jung, the famous Swiss psychologist, said that such unconscious processes are found in the depths of the human psyche.

As it turns out, the arrival of the caravels changed the course of history. A new era was approaching. It was during the celebration of an *areíto* that Pané learned from *caciques* Guamanacoel and Cacibaquel that *cacique* Cáicihu, after a long fast, had received a prophetic message from *cemí* Yucahuguamá, a message that would constitute the first known foresight in America:

> *[...] that those that remain alive after his death would enjoy power for a short time of power, because clothed people would arrive that would rule and kill, and they would die of hunger. But they thought first that these were the cannibals; but later, considering that the cannibals steal and then flee, they believed that the cemí spoke of other people coming. People that came from where now they think the Admiral and his people came.*

The *cemí* prophecy was the story of the future.

The bird *Inriri* (woodpecker) carving four women according to Taino myth.
Illustration by Claudia Robiou.

CHAPTER 8

Areíto or to remember is to live

The *areíto* was the ritual through which the Tainos remembered and transmitted from generation to generation their song and dance traditions, oral literature, beliefs about the origins, feats of the past, *cacique* genealogies, and memories of good and bad times. In the *areíto*, the real and the imaginary merged into a new, ideal reality.

The *areíto* ceremony was carried out by people belonging to both sexes or separately amongst people of the same sex, and perhaps between clans. The participants held each other's hands or interlaced their arms and followed a guide who took steps in a row or circle synchronized to the rhythm of the *mayohabao* (a large drum made of a hollow trunk), *maracas*, flutes and other instruments that evoked the harmony and the rhythm of the cosmos. Everyone drank and danced for long hours until exhaustion, repeating the verses that the guide sang by rote. The Tainos developed an extraordinary memory. Las Casas was amazed that 20 to 30 sheets of Christian doctrine were memorized and recited by the Tainos "with few stumbles and without pain or glory."

In the *areíto*, the Tainos made reference to the experiences of Yayael, Itiba Cahubaba, Deminán Caracaracol, Mácocael, Yahubaba, Anacacuya, and Guahayona. These were the mythical characters whose sacrifice gave way to the various stages of creation. During the ceremony, they referred to the transformation of the mutilated and idealized hero's bones into fish and its idealization in the Orion constellation. They remembered the wanderings of the four twins who obtained fire, cassava and *cohoba*, and caused the great flood. They reminisced about how the Sun and the Moon emerged from the underworld through the cave of the Great Serpent and how the Solar Star transformed the bat-beings that emerged from the cave of the origins in four successive stages.

The Tainos narrated the canoe trip of the first *cacique* and the first *behique*, and at night contemplated them in the sky in the Big Dipper and Venus; they recalled how the woodpecker carved Taino women from asexual beings, and how the whining children turned into frogs that later croaked to the Pleiades to produce rain. They evoked Coaybay, the region of the dead where the Sun disappeared giving way to night and to beings from the underworld like the bat and the owl.

In the *areítos*, the Tainos remembered historic events, past or recent. For instance, they remembered how the *cemí* Baibrama that was burned during a war, grew arms, eyes and a body after being washed with manioc juice. Singing and dancing, the Tainos mentioned *cemí* Corocote of *cacique* Guamorete, who had two crowns on his head and dwelled on top of the *caney*, from where he came down at night to lie with women. One day, when some enemies of the *cacique* burnt the house, the *cemí* escaped to a body of water.

The *cemí* Baraguabael exhibited a similar behavior, for it belonged to the important *cacique* Guarionex, son of Cacibaquel, and came from a species of animal that transformed itself to become a trunk. Hence, it slipped away even when they tied it. The *cemí* Opiyelguobirán of *cacique* Sabananiobabo completed the trio, as it was made of wood and had four feet, like a dog. Even when tied, it always escaped to the jungle.

Cemí Opiyelguobirán (Mason, 1884).
Museo del Hombre Dominicano, D.R.

Areíto ceremony. Illustration from Museo Arqueológico Regional Altos de Chavón, La Romana, D.R. Observe the Taino drum. Detail: Maracas in *guayacán* wood (*Guaiacum* sp.), Museo del Hombre Dominicano, D.R.

In later *areítos*, Tainos told the story of how the evasive *cemí* Opiyelguobirán fled upon the arrival of the Spaniards and submerged itself in a lagoon, never to appear again. In this manner, it escaped the fateful future that awaited the Taino people, according to the aforementioned revelation received years before by *cacique* Cáicihu.

In sum, by reciting the myths in rituals like the *areíto*, the Tainos relived the time of the origins and recreated the most significant moments in the life of their gods and heroes. In other words, the *areíto* allowed Tainos to return to a sacred time. Yet that repetition had to take place in a sacred space, the place where the sky, the earth and the underworld converged. That ceremonial space was the *batey*, the central plaza of the village. The main rituals of Taino society were celebrated in the ceremonial plazas at certain times of the year.

In the previous chapter we explained the mythical function of time and space. Let us now see its social function among the Tainos.

Space and social structure

Generally, anthropologists believe that the social organization of many cultures is projected in the space of the village, which is divided based on clans and where each of the clans is assocated with a totem, a color, a star, a cardinal point and even a particular sound.

Unfortunately, very little ethnohistorical and archaeological evidence exists about the Tainos and the Caribs of the Antilles with regards to their villages. As for the Tainos, Las Casas mentions an arrangement of space in the Higüey region, in Hispaniola, as follows:

> *Within those flat terrains, they cut down the trees they needed to make a plaza, depending on whether it was small or large; and once they had made the plaza, in the middle they cut and made four broad streets in the form of a cross. These streets were made to fight, because without them they could not move, as the mountains are thick, and the rocks and stones are also very rough, although flat.*

Despite this limited description by Las Casas, the division of space into four streets in the form of a cross, whose vertex crossed the central plaza and divided into four the area of the village, suggests that the village space was ruled by symbolic and social organizational elements, rather than by a war-driven purpose. The streets in the form of a cross are, in this sense, a projection of the symbol of the Center. This organization is consistent also with the dualistic division of space that predominated in South America at the time, yet in this case we suppose a spatial distribution between two social groups, each with two clans.

Whether or not this interpretation is correct, we know that both the *caney* (the *cacique*'s dwelling and a temple) and the plaza occupied a central place of prominence in the village, as Las Casas emphasized: "in the best place and position, and in front of the royal house was, in every one of these villages, a large plaza that was the better kept and flattest ground, longer than a square, that they called in their language *batey*... which means ball game." We do not know which part of the village was occupied by the *nitaínos*, *behiques* and *naborías*; undoubtedly, however, there must have been a hierarchy of space, starting out from where the *cacique* lived.

Both the *bohío* and the *caney* were circular, for, as researcher Sven Lovén opined, the rectangular *caney* reported by Oviedo after 1514 was probably the result of European influence. Both constructions were made "of wood and straw, in the shape of a bell ... very high." The *caney* "must have in the middle a post or masthead." No doubt the *bohío* structure was very similar to the round and bell-shaped dwelling of the South American Yekuana people.

If the South American tradition where housing was a reflection of cosmology is maintained, then it is likely that the hut was made in the image and likeness of the Taino cosmos. As such, the circular form of the *bohío* idealized the shape of the celestial vault and probably was oriented on an east-west axis; the central post symbolized the central axis or Sacred Center that communicated the three levels of the universe.

Each Taino village or *yucayeque* ("cassava deposit") could have been constituted by "one hundred and two hundred and five hundred... houses, in each of which ten and fifteen neighbors with their wives and children dwelled," wrote Las Casas. This ratio would establish villages that ranged from 1,000, to an average of 2,000 to 3,000, and up to more than 5,000, inhabitants. The most conservative estimates of the Antillean population at the time of the European discovery - a controversial subject historically - confers around 60,000 inhabitants in Cuba, Puerto Rico and Jamaica, respectively, and about 350,000 in Hispaniola.

Archeology tells us about the changes in the shape and size of a Taino house as it evolved from the tribal to the chiefdom stage of development. Luis A. Curet Salim postulated that, during the early Saladoid and Ostionoid periods (300-900 AD), a house in Puerto Rico was oblong and large in size, suggesting community housing for extended families. In the late Ostionoid and Elenoid periods (900-1200 AD), the house maintained the oblong shape but appeared to be reduced in size, suggesting a change towards the family nucleus. Finally, during the Taino period (1200-1500 AD), the house became of a size comparable to the previous one but circular, such as that reported by the chroniclers. In this sense, Virginia Rivera Calderón's work in Luján (Vieques) demonstrates the changes that occurred in a *yucayeque* over time.

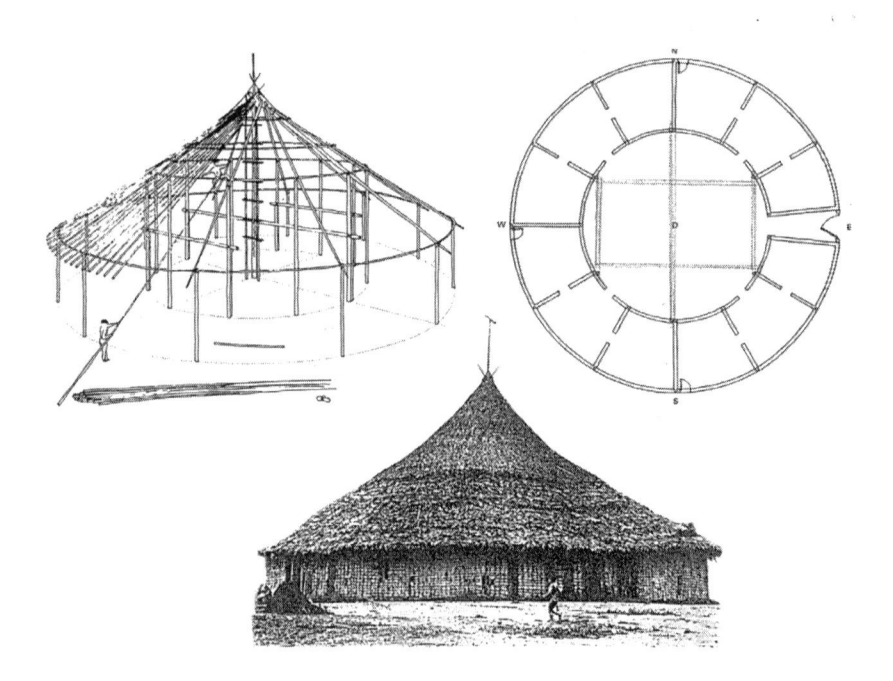

Current Yekuana house from South America (Wilbert, 1981), similar to the Taino *bohío*. The dwelling was a representation of the aboriginal cosmos.

In 2010, Alice V. M. Samson, member of the Caribbean Research Group (Leiden University), published the results of an archaeological excavation in El Cabo, Higüey, at the extreme east of the Dominican Republic. The research, covering seven centuries (800-1504 AD) of the *yucayeque* with 50 different domestic structures (30 houses), concluded that the "Inhabitants rebuilt the same house in the same spot over the course of centuries so that a particular house was just one stage in a long process of renewal." In general, the houses can be classified in four types, all circular (from 6 to 10 meters in diameter) and oriented in a dominant westerly direction.

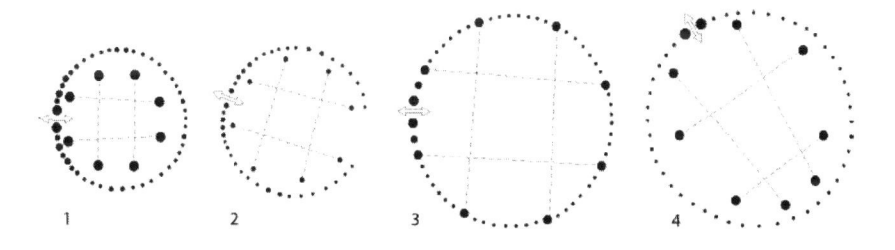

Taino geomancy

Taino society used geomancy: a method of divination that interprets markings on the ground or patters formed, to select the location of villages and ceremonial centers to be in harmony with the cosmic forces of nature.

Although we do not know the norms used to locate *yucayeques*, Oviedo mentioned that Tainos chose locations in "the coasts of the rivers or near the sea or in the areas that pleased them more or were more for their purposes..." It appears that the location of the *batey* or ceremonial plaza evolved from an area in the center of the village during the tribal stage, to a more complex construction selected for its symbolic value, during the chiefdom stage. This process is reflected in archeological findings. The first ceremonial plaza found in the south of Puerto Rico dates to the year 600 AD. From there, we find complex ceremonial plazas at Tibes and Caguana, also in Puerto Rico, and the plazas of San Juan de la Maguana and Chacuey in the Dominican Republic, built a few years before the European discovery.

Indeed, these ceremonial plazas (rectangular, circular or elliptical) are commonly located on a plateau near a river or stream and, generally, they have a mountain or a nearby mountain in the background. Symbolically, we suppose that ceremonial plazas, as the central axis of the world, maintained a relationship with Cauta, the central axis of creation. It follows that the location near a water source (that may come from the nearby mountain) may have had both a practical and symbolic purpose: to evoke the origin of the celestial water, the place where the children were transformed into frogs and where the strange slippery creatures became women. In short, the *batey* may be symbolically linked with the *axis mundi*, the Center, the magical mountain, and the essential water.

We must remember that the word *batey*, in addition to signifying a ceremonial plaza "that is longer than a square," also refers to the "ball game" that took place in this space. The ball game came from a tradition scattered widely throughout South America long before the arrival of the European. It was likely introduced in the Antilles during the first migrations of Agro-Ceramic people. Anonymous of Carpentras, a pioneer French chronicler of the Lesser Antilles, is the only person to document that the ball game was practiced among the Caribs in the village plaza.

Among the Tainos, the ball game was played with two teams with variable numbers of people. The teams were composed of men, women, or both. It is possible teams were made up of clans. The ball, made of vegetable resins, had to be kept in the air by hitting it with knees, buttocks, elbows, hips or shoulders, but no hands. The game required great agility and physical dexterity.

It is possible to think that the ball game had - as in other parts of the South American continent - a cosmological connotation that was hidden or escaped the attention of the chroniclers. This theory is supported by the fact that certain ceremonial plazas are astronomically oriented. Further, we cannot reject that on some occasions the game served to make an important decision, as in the life or death of a prisoner.

Contrary to the alleged direct Mayan influence suggested by some researchers, we believe that the Taino ball game is the culmination of an Antillean historical process. As Francisco Moscoso emphasized, it is rather a process of convergence with Mesoamerica, that is, a similar practice that occurs in independent and historically separated cultures, as archeology shows.

While in Puerto Rico ceremonial plazas demarcated by vertical stones are most common, in Hispaniola this style prevails in the southeast part of the island only. In the central part of Hispaniola, ceremonial plazas were built with ridges of soil and stone, a feature that is reflected in the Cuban ones. In terms of size, ceremonial plazas reached their maximum dimension in Hispaniola. The largest plaza reported in Puerto Rico (Sabana, in Orocovis) is almost 4,100 square meters, while plaza A, the largest in Caguana, also in Puerto Rico, is 1,730 square meters. In contrast, the circular plaza of San Juan de la Maguana in the Dominican Republic is 125,016 square meters and the ellipsoidal plaza in Chacuey measures 35,721 square meters.

Samuel M. Wilson emphasized in his study of the Taino chiefdoms that ceremonial plazas in the Dominican Republic had ten times the average area of those in Puerto Rico (6,605 vs. 642 square meters). This observation allowed him to suggest that "there were significant differences between the Taino society of Puerto Rico and that of Hispaniola." Since the ball game required a limited amount of space, the grandeur of these plazas - which do not seem to have been known to the conquerors - points to another use.

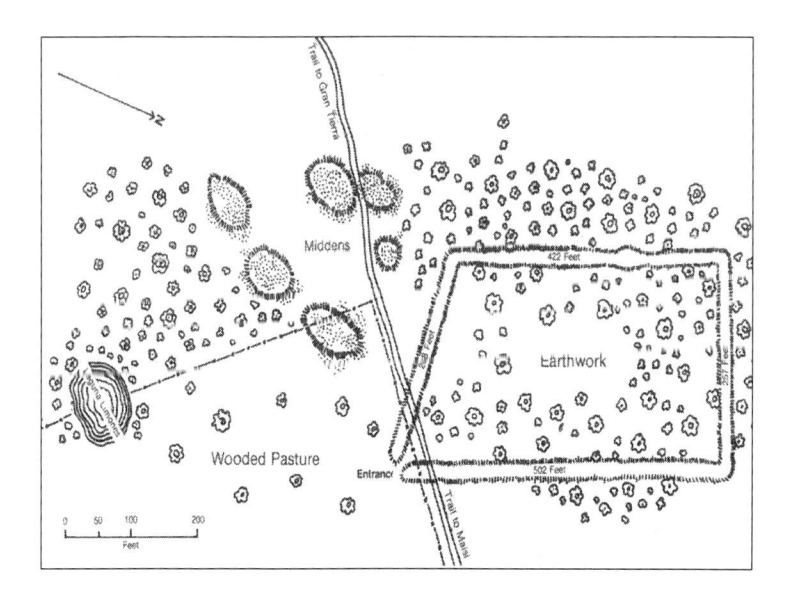

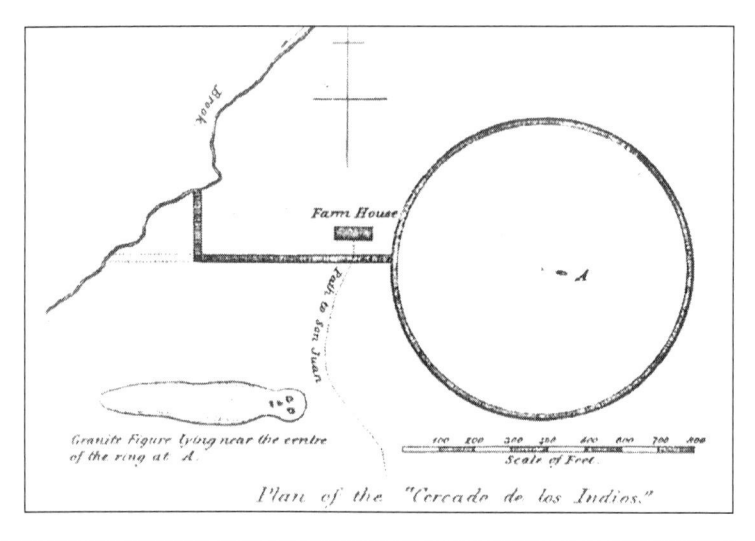

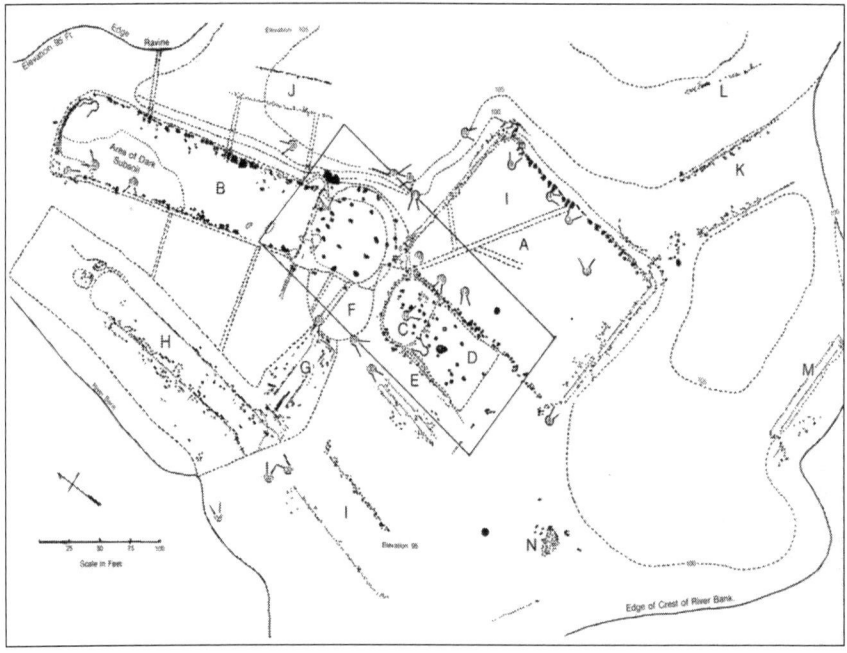

Tainos and Caribs. The Aboriginal Cultures of the Antilles

Bateyes or ceremonial plazas.
Previous page: Laguna Limones, Cuba (Harrington, 1921). On this page:
San Juan de la Maguana, D.R. (Pagán Perdomo, 1985);
Caguana, Utuado, P. R. (Alegría, 1983).

Chacuey: a possible astronomical calendar

Since 1980 we have argued that the great ceremonial plaza in Chacuey, located in the province of Dajabón, Dominican Republic, may have been a place of astronomical observations and cosmogonic rituals. In Puerto Rico, Osvaldo García Goyco was the first to suggest astronomical orientations in the ceremonial plazas in Tibes (Ponce) and Caguana (Utuado).

In Chacuey, the ellipsoidal construction (243 meters x 147 meters in its axes) formed by a ridge of earth and stone about 5 meters wide and interrupted only by an eastern and a western portal, results from the application of the geomancy method. The plaza is located on a plateau on the eastern margin of the Chacuey River, a waterbody that flows from a majestic hill (810 metters high) of the same name located southwest of the plaza. A pile of large stones is located in the northeast area of the plaza. A double road begins from the western portal of the plaza and goes down to the Charco de la Caritas, where a set of important petroglyphs or engravings in stone have been found.

The western portal seems to have been the center of astronomical observations since the rise of the Sun and the ascent of several constellations can be seen from here to correspond with the eastern-facing outline of the plaza.

The main astronomical alignments studied in Chacuey follow:

- The axis of the portals has an astronomical azimuth of 115 degrees; in other words, it is oriented towards the sunrise in the winter solstice (December 21) and the rise of Scorpio in that month, a constellation that probably configured the Great Serpent, Iguanaboína.
- The first section of the road that goes down to the river is oriented towards the equinoxes (March 21, September 21), which is also the direction that Orion emerges, a constellation that probably configured the mythical Yayael.
- Three important astronomical events occur in the direction of the pile of large stones:
    - sunrise in the summer solstice (June 21) with an azimuth of 65 degrees.

- heliacal rise of the Pleiades (June 5) with an azimuth of 67 degrees.
- sunrise on the days of the Sun's passage through the zenith of Chacuey (May 19, July 25) with an azimuth of 69 degrees.

Observe that these azimuths differ by a maximum of only four degrees.

In Chacuey, the rise of the Pleiades and of the Sun in the summer solstice occurs in days that are close to one another and have practically the same orientation. In other words, time and space coincides in both events. This suggests that the beginning of the year - originally signaled by the Pleiades - may have begun to be seen as a privileged time of year in Taino society. This observation resonates with a finding that was discussed earlier: the Sun plays an important role in societies in the chiefdom stage of development, as were the Tainos.

Further, in Chacuey, the path of the Sun through the zenith (that is, when this star transits the vertical axis of the location) is within the range of time in which the Pleiades rise (June 5) and the Sun rises in the summer solstice (June 21). Therefore, it is permissible to think that the 67-day period between the two zenith dates (May 19-July 25) was related to the beginning of the solar year and marked days of special significance in the Taino worldview. The days in which the Sun passes through the zenith would also be significant: it is only on those days that sun rays fall perpendicular in Chacuey at noon.

Similarly, the sunrise at the winter solstice coincides, in time and space, with the heliacal rise of Scorpio in December, a constellation linked to the start of the drought season (January to March) in the Antilles. This explains why Chacuey's portals are oriented towards that important solar date. According to Las Casas, manioc cuttings were planted in the months of drought, before the onset of rains. Therefore, the sunrise at the winter solstice (December 21) probably signaled to the Tainos to begin to prepare the land and to plant manioc, marking the start of the agricultural cycle.

Other complex relationships between the astronomical and climatological cycles may have been observed by the Tainos. Places like Chacuey are the basis of a possible agricultural-ceremonial calendar. This organization of time and space regulated social activities, from the economic output to the few rituals we know about today.

In fact, a ritual other than the *areíto* was celebrated once a year, perhaps towards the beginning of the year or at the start of the agricultural cycle. During this communal activity the distribution of a species of sacred cassava occurred. According to Anglería, the *cacique* summoned everyone to the *caney*. They first sat in a labyrinthine manner; then, they pranced and danced. At a given moment, each participant received a portion of cassava that "was brought intact to his house... and kept there all year as a sacred thing," because they believed "that they would have bad luck and their dwelling would be exposed to various dangers such as fire and hurricane winds, if they lacked the aforementioned portions." This significant ceremony was interpreted by Fewkes as a fertility rite; for Fernando Ortiz, it was magical protection against hurricanes.

The megalithic monument at Chacuey was perhaps a place of great festivities at certain times of the year or a venerated site of pilgrimage. Above all, however, its study reveals something more momentous: the degree of development reached by certain Taino chiefdoms demanded that they have specialists in geometry and astronomy.

Our analysis of monuments such as those found in Chacuey require the conceptual integraton of the principles of time and space. As such, the main stars can be analyzed in their spatial dimension, projecting their position in space and onto the megalithic constructions, and correlating them with the solar cycle.

In sum, the ceremonial plazas could have integrated the conceptualizations of space and time. Should these constructions be aligned towards the main stars at significant points in time, they would represent celestial time in a physical plane. Tainos would have found a way to project cosmic time and the time of the gods onto a space constructed by human beings.

That is, the divine and the human linked in the same space-time.

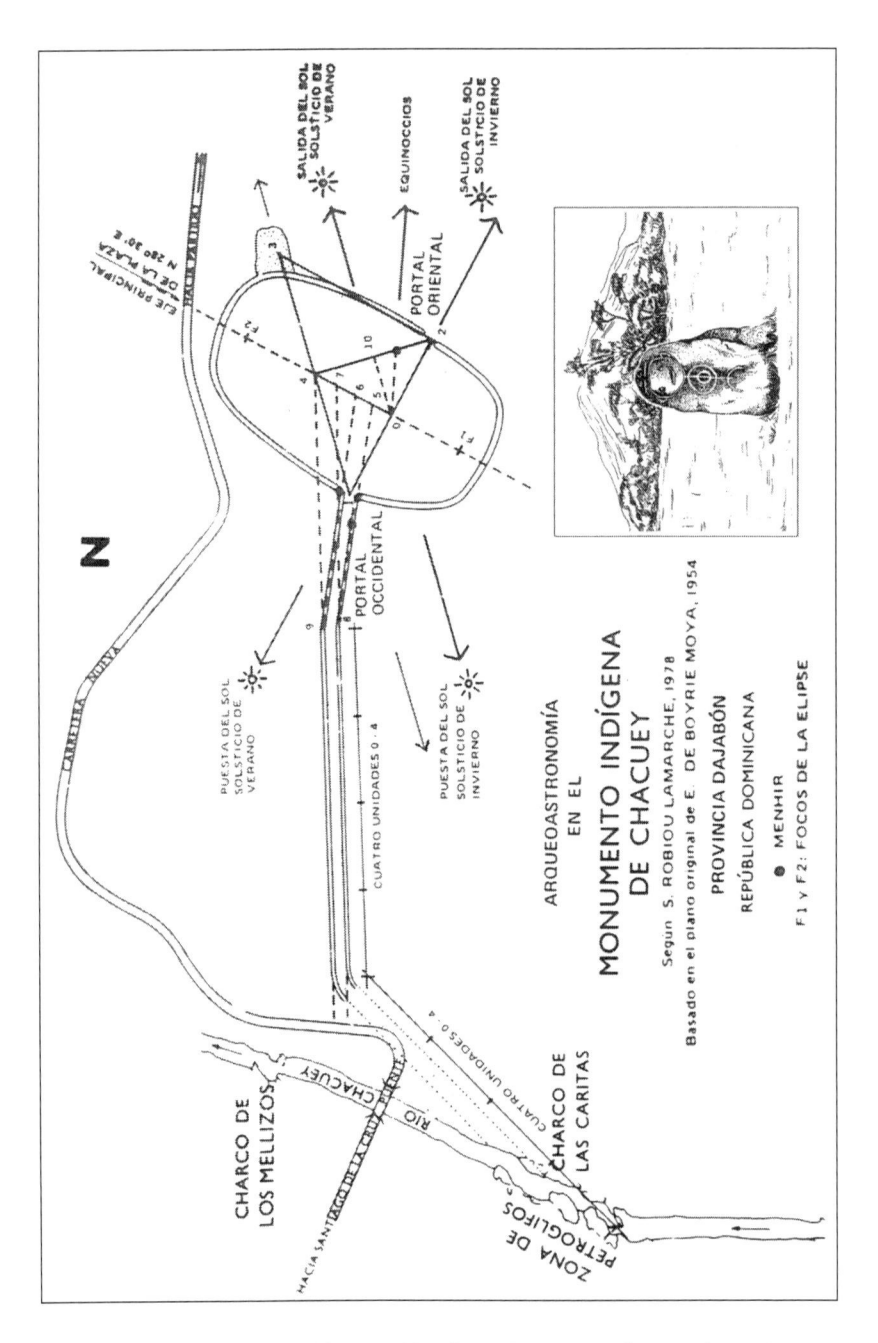

Archaeoastronomy in Chacuey, Dajabón, D.R., according to the author. Detail: menhir with anthropomorphic figure with Chacuey hill in the background.

FIFTH PART

TAINOS: FROM AGRICULTURE TO ART

CHAPTER 9

Cycle of Eternal Return

Beyond believing that the creation had been completed in four stages, Tainos conceptualized time as cyclical or circular in a manner that resembled nature's annual cycles. Tainos reiterated their myths and rituals as well as their social and economic activities in the same fashion that nature repeats its cycles during the stellar or solar year. This interaction between the natural and social cycles codified an annual calendar with mythical-astronomical-seasonal convergences. This calendar - understood as a measure of ecological time - framed the worldview of the indigenous people of the Antilles.

For the Tainos, the morning rise of the Pleiades in the summer solstice probably announced the beginning of the year, the start of agricultural production and the rainy season (May-July). This period tracked with the time when weeping children became frogs. The morning reappearance over the sea of the mythical *cacique* (Big Dipper) coincided with the hurricane season (August-September). The evening presence of the mutilated hero (Orion) presaged the end of the rains and the beginning of the fishing season (October-January).

Later, the morning rise of the Great Serpent (Scorpion) in the winter solstice corresponded with the advent of the dry season, the time to prepare the soil, plant manioc or initiate the agricultural cycle (December-March). The immersion at sea of the mythical *cacique* (Big Dipper) marked the beginning of the nautical hero's (Venus) journey, which was associated with the abundance of the "cobo" (*Strombus gigas*) in shallow waters, the navigation season, the arrival of the rains (April-July), and a new year.

This cycle of "eternal return" that does not claim to be complete or absolute, serves as the basis for the fifth part of this book. We will describe and discuss how various different aspects of Taino culture were intimately intertwined with the artistic manifestations evidenced in Taino art.

The magic of the stars and the agricultural cycle

As we have discussed, the Sun was the creator *par excellence* for the Tainos because it transformed those avatars who emerged four times from the Cacibajagua cave into stone, tree, bird, and Tainos. Sunlight was, therefore, a force of creation, fertility, and life.

The Moon was, in contrast, subject to apparent death and resurrection. This observation highlights, as Mircea Eliade said, "that death is the first condition of all mystic regeneration." Hence, its close link to the rebirth of nature and the agricultural cycle. Tainos used the phases of the moon to count time periods or "months," as reported by Anglería, and also to schedule future activities, such as the rebellion against the conquistador in Hispaniola, as Fernando Colón wrote.

Similar to many other cultures, it can be presumed that the lunar cycle was the basis for an ancient Antillean calendar that began to be replaced by a solar calendar.

But it was the crescent moon that had a magical role in agriculture. Oviedo documented that corn (*maíz*, *Zea mays*) was always planted "at the beginning of the moon, because they have the opinion that, just as she grows, so does the thing that is sown." In the same manner, the manioc (*yuca*, *Manihot esculenta*) "is to always be planted after the moon is or looks new, and as soon as possible in the days that it grows until it is full, but never as it wanes." In other words, the growth of the moon was believed to make plants grow by imitative magic.

Agricultural production was probably limited because planting could only occur on the days of a crescent moon. Based on this restriction, there were about 180 days available for planting each year. The Dominican historian Roberto Cassá estimated that the planting of manioc in heaps required about 60 days of work per year for men and about the same or more for women. This is because in a tribal society the man prepared the land, hunted and fished, while the woman sowed, built homes, made pottery and performed housework. Francisco Moscoso, however, believes that in the Taino chiefdom stage of historical development, men had a more prominent role in agricultural tasks.

If, elsewhere, when we studied the ceremonial plazas and their astronomical orientations, we stated that the agricultural cycle began with the planting of manioc during the drought season that announced the winter solstice (December 21), then we can now add that it ended before the rains arrived, towards the spring equinox (March 21). As manioc was harvested at least a year after planted, yet consumed all year round, it is obvious that Tainos ate manioc that had been sowed more than a year prior. They replenished their eaten manioc with new plants on an ongoing basis.

During the remaining days of the crescent moon, Tainos sowed other agricultural products. They must have known the time of planting and harvesting for each tree and food crop. With a new moon, however, Tainos continued to carry out activities related to the same agricultural cycle.

Oviedo emphasized that *maíz*, contrary to manioc, was sown "when a stick could go into the soil three or four fingers deep with a small blow." He was referring to the days of the new moon, after the morning rise of the Pleiades and around the summer solstice, at the beginning of the year, when rain prevail.

We know that corncobs take approximately four "months" or moons to grow. Their harvest therefore took place when the Pleiades began to descend in the west before dawn, towards the end of October. The second planting of corn took place in the subsequent crescent moon, on the rainy days in November-December, and the harvest would take place around March-April, when said group of stars began to disappear in the west after sunset. The new cycle began, as has been proposed, towards the beginning of June.

In other words, the planting of *maíz* - always on days of crescent moon and humid terrain - was done with the morning or evening presence of the Pleiades (the stars of the rain and of agricultural productivity) and the harvest would take place when they began to disappear in the west before or after sunset.

The cemíes, the power behind agriculture

Taino agriculture was part of a comprehensive ideological framework in which plants and trees had a mythical origin, but their fertilization and growth was the result of the power of the Sun, the Moon and the intervention of supernatural forces and entities embodied in the *cemíes*.

As a result of the historical process that took place in the Antilles, the venerated *cemíes* were figures that mixed features of both animals (zoomorphs) and humans (anthropomorphs), blended various different belief constructs (myth, religion, magic, ritual), and perhaps served as symbols of the union between the iconographic heritage of the Taino ancestors and the humanization of the Taino gods.

So particular was the emphasis on *cemíes* that Jesse W. Fewkes introduced the term "Ceminism" to characterize the Taino religion, which was theocratic, sophisticated and institutional, and in practice accompanied by ceremonies that responded to the social complexity of the chiefdom. The Taino pantheon responded to the hierarchy of the gods just as Taino's hierarchical society did.

Basing himself on Taino myths, Stevens-Arroyo described the existence of twelve spirits, which he divides "into two groups of six, with a main male and female spirit, each served by twin forces." The classification process "produces four triads, one masculine and one feminine for each two contradictory orders." Those spirits related to plant and food life are referred to as "Spirits of Fertility" while all others are called "Spirits of Reversal" because they try to "reverse the ordinary order instead of destroying it."

In our opinion, two opposing but complementary supreme beings or deities, one feminine-lunar, another masculine-solar, prevail in Taino religious thought. These beings could manifest themselves in different planes of the universe through deities responsible for certain functions, not always benign. Unlike the Christian conception that establishes a clear separation between god-good and the devil-evil, a Taino divinity could simultaneously represent the benevolent and the malicious, the essential components of the cosmos that allow - as in all mythology - that after death or destruction, life arises.

The Great Mother, the First Female Cause, was the principle of greater hierarchy. For that reason, five names were attributed to her: Atabey, Apito, Guacar, Yermao and Zuimaco, which have been interpreted to mean "Mother of the Waters, Lady of the Moon, the Tides and Maternity, Universal Mother" by Arrom. One of its various representations may have been Itiba Cahubaba, the Great Birth Mother Earth, from whom emerged the four demiurge twins, a deity perhaps idealized in a series of effigy vases representing a heavy female figure. Another important representation was probably Iguanaboína, whose dual characteristics we will discuss later.

As a curiosity, we refer to a case of syncretism between the Great Mother and the Christian Virgin Mary. (Syncretism is the combining of different beliefs, while blending practices of various schools of thought. Syncretism involves the merging or assimilation of several originally discrete traditions, especially in theology and mythology of religion, thus asserting an underlying unity and allowing an inclusive approach to other faiths.) In Cuba, the conqueror Alonso de Ojeda gave the *cacique* of Cueíba an image of the Virgin Mary and told him that she was the Mother of God. Years later, when he tried to recover the image, the *cacique*, afraid of losing it, escaped with it to the depths of the forest. Undoubtedly, the image of the Spanish Mother of God had already been identified with Atabey, the Great Mother.

On the masculine side, the Supreme Being was idealized in Yúcahu Bagua Maórocoti, a trinity name that has been interpreted to mean "Being of Yuca, Sea, Without Male Antecedent." The Taino people understood him to be the son of the Great Mother. "They believe that he is in heaven and immortal, and no one can see him, and that he has a mother, but he has no beginning," wrote Ramón Pané. He was also called Yucahuguamá. Some believe he was the Yuca God. As we have said, he was probably a deity resulting from a transformation over time of Yaya, the Supreme Spirit, the First Male Cause, the First Father. The name Yúcahu can come from *yawahu* or *yáwaho*, the generic term for the spirits of the forest among the Arawaks of the Guianas.

Cemíes, as a conceptualization of the Taino deities, were worshiped. Each of these cult images had its own iconographic peculiarities. Yúcahu, for example, corresponded with the *cemíes* that, according to Pané, had "three points, and believe that they make manioc [*yuca*] grow." This type of *cemí* with three points carved in stone and whose characteristics have been studied originally by Jesse W. Fewkes, Adolfo de Hostos, José Juan Arrom and others, was ritually buried in the *conucos* (or gardens) with the purpose of fertilizing what was sown. It was, in effect, a *cemí* that promoted fertility, a God of Fecundity. In this regard, Ramón Pané narrated a revealing anecdote. On one occasion, six Tainos stole several Christian images and, throwing them on the ground, "covered them with earth and then urinated on them, saying: 'Now your fruits will be good and great.' And this is because they were buried in a farm field, saying that the fruit that had been planted there would be good."

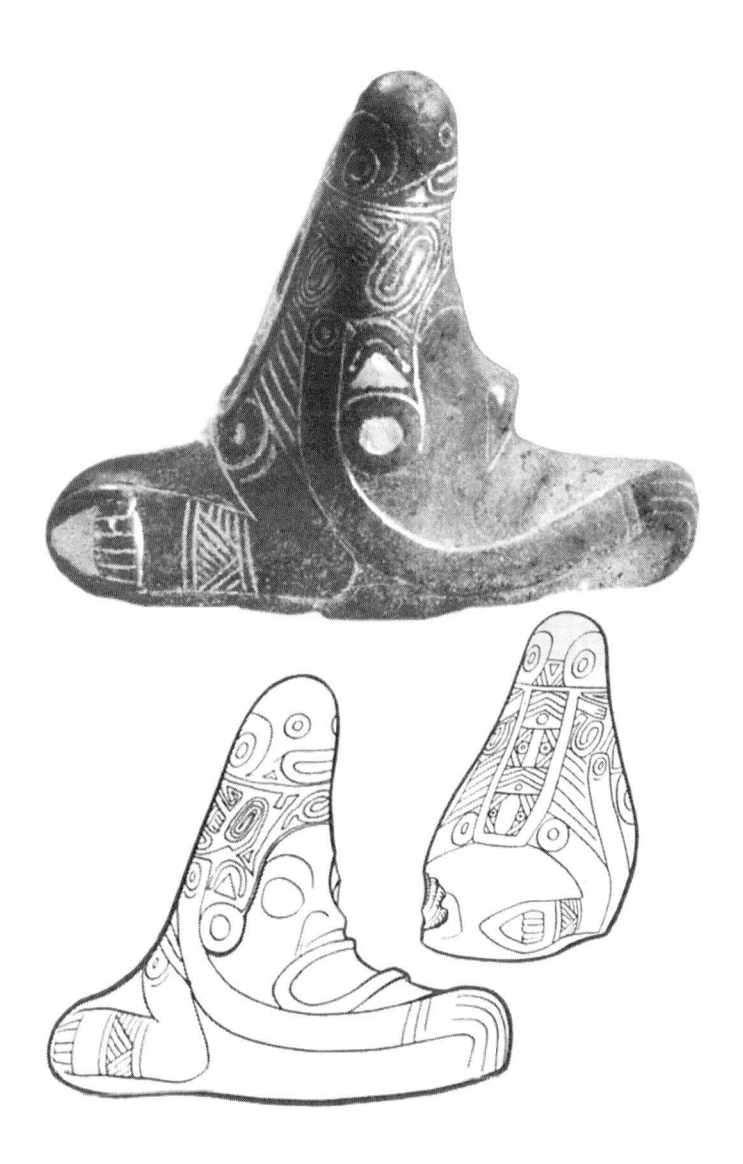

Prototype of three-pointer *cemí*, identified with Yúcahu, God of Fertility. Museo de Antropología, Historia y Arte, Universidad de Puerto Rico.

The fertility ritual performed by these Tainos with Christian images (perhaps thinking that they were more powerful than their own *cemíes*) was branded as offensive and the astonished Tainos were burned alive in public. This is how "the war of images" began, as Serge Gruzinski said.

Another important deity closely linked to agriculture was Baibrama. As we saw earlier, this deity was once burnt, but manioc juice made it possible for his arms, eyes and body to magically grow back. Since that time, the root of manioc grew and grew in size. When this *cemí* was not fed manioc (*yuca*, *Manihot esculenta*), he would get angry and let diseases loose. Since Arrom identified Yúcahu with the Yuca God, he assumes that Baibrama was perhaps a "guardian god related to the home and the domestication and exploitation of manioc." We believe that the opposite is true: Baibrama was the generator of manioc, the probable Yuca God, while Yúcahu Bagua Maórocoti was a deity linked to agricultural fertility in general, to the God of Fertility.

Columbus and Las Casas reported the existence of three "stones" of great devotion that most *caciques* possessed: one "for women to give birth without pain," another "good for cereals and vegetables that have been sown," and the third "for water and the sun when necessary." Arrom suggests that the first "stone" corresponds to some small female effigies carved in bone and shell or clay figures with a bulging belly. Others have speculated that monolithic ball belts, also called stone collars (a possible adaptation of a model originally in wood), may have had a certain role in women's labor.

With regards to the stone collars, the most accepted hypothesis is that they were paraphernalia used in the *batey* or ball game along with elbow stones and masks. Fewkes was probably the first investigator to suggest that the monolithic rings or stone collars were a representation of the mythical serpent, an idea that would later be held by other authors. For example, the pioneering Dominican archaeologist Alberti Bosch, in the unpublished work of 1922 that we mentioned, proposed that stone collars symbolized the coiled sacred serpent and he considered them a distinctive feature of the hierarchical power from which emanated wisdom, immortality and *cacique* force. Years later, Eugenio Fernández Méndez suggested that the rings represented the goddess-serpent identified with Guabancex. More recently, José R. Oliver proposed that these stone collars, carriers of supernatural powers, "were curated and maintained in circulation [...] and formed part of a reciprocal exchange system involving foreign *caciques*" between Hispaniola and Puerto Rico.

Monolithic rings or stone collars of Puerto Rico, an enigmatic object associated with the ball game. (Based on Fewkes, 1907, 1922).

Rather than this feminine *cemí* being the cause of hurricanes and destructive waters, the monolithic rings were probably a conceptualization of the Great Mother of Waters. If this is the case, then we suppose that the ball game could have been, at least in a historical stage, a cosmic fertility ritual. Hence the relationship of the ceremonial plazas with a mountain and a nearby river, a reminder of the mountain and the waters of origin.

The second stone, which was believed to be good for cereals and legumes, also had three points carved in stone (three-pointer) and seems to represent Yúcahu, the God of Fertility. This is how Arrom describes its characteristics: "Disproportionate face located on one of the sides of the triangle, eye dug in so that only the empty basins remain, mouth broadly relaxed, ears with pierced lobes." In some specimens, the arms are extended towards the front, and the legs are flexed on the opposite side. In general, this type of object has at its upper vertex a "striking protuberance that may have wanted to symbolize the bud already filled, next to germinate in a new plant."

Las Casas said that, in gratitude to the generous agricultural deities, the Tainos "gave a certain part as a gift, almost thanking for the benefits received" during the harvest season. They placed offerings of the fruits obtained "in the house of the lords and *caciques*, that they call *caney*, offering it and dedicating it to the *cemí*." In this way, the Tainos redistributed the gifts received from and to the *cemíes*.

Iguanaboína: the governess of the climatological balance

There is, among the stones with three points, a prototype that is unique and could be the aforementioned third "stone," which is "for water and the sun when necessary" and is associated with the Antillean worldview of Iguanaboína, the Great Taino Serpent, the mother of the twins that produced beneficial water, the deity to whom good weather is attributed and who was worshiped in the cave that carries her name.

Among the Tainos, the Great Serpent was linked to the shaman. The relationship between the shaman and the serpent is a constant in the study of continental indigenous societies, as explained by Eliade and other authors. Indeed, Pané wrote that when the relatives of a dead patient decided to take revenge on the *behique*, they gave him so many blows that they left him almost dead. Then, at night, *cemíes* in the form of serpent in "white, black and green, and many other colors" came, and they magically brought the *behique* back to life by licking his face and body. In this manner, the serpent - which every so often is reborn when it changes its skin - becomes a symbol of cyclic renewal. Later, we will learn about the role of the Great Serpent among the Caribs. In South America, the serpent is a mytheme that appeared as the anaconda, the gigantic river serpent. In other instances, the serpent is depicted in South America as the Great Cayman and underwater beings studied by Peter Roe and related to the Spirit of the Waters.

(In the study of mythology, a mytheme is a fundamental generic unit of narrative structure, typically involving a relationship between a character, an event, and a theme, from which myths are thought to be constructed. It is a minimal unit that is always found shared with others, related mythemes and reassembled in various ways or linked in more complicated relationships.)

Arrom, on the other hand, suggested that the third "stone" could be a series of amulets that reproduce two siamese twins joined together on one side and squatting together, a possible representation of Boínayel, the God of Rain (equally represented in individual idols with furrows that descend from the eyes resembling tears) and of Márohu, the God of Clear Weather, according to the myth narrated by Pané. Despite this convergence between myth and iconography, it can be suggested that the third propitiatory "stone" of water and sun was a *cemí* that was superior to the others, that regulated and integrated the above-mentioned twin deities that produced rain and good weather. In such a case, the role corresponds to their mother, the Great Iguanaboína Serpent. Considering this hypothesis, let us analyze the three-pointed *cemí* prototype.

In this prototype, one end represents the head of a mythical being that is a blend of two types of reptiles, one that lacks extremities and another that has four legs and a tail. This end is perhaps an Antillean symbiosis of the South American myths of the anaconda and the cayman. From this great head arises the carved body of a serpent, which coils in or passes through the central part of the idol, evoking the image of the Great Serpent. The central part, higher as in all three-pointed stones, resembles a voluminous breast or a mountain; perhaps it is a symbol of the mountain of origins and the essential water. Undoubtedly, it is an allegory of female fertility.

The Great Iguanaboína Serpent, the governess of climatological balance.
Museo Arqueológico Regional Altos de Chavón, La Romana, D.R.

The third and last end of the stone, similar to the *cemí* model that represents Yúcahu, displays two flexed or crouched legs, a recurring motif of Taino art called by archaeologists "frog legs."

In fact, the frog is one of the most abundant themes of Antillean pre-Columbian art. Cuban researchers Pedro Godo and Miriam Celaya suggest that the frog symbol may represent the South American myth about the origin of fire, the *burén* (a clay griddle on top of wich cassava bread was cooked) and agriculture. Henry Petitjean-Roget, a French historian and archaeologist from Guadeloupe, investigated the presence of the frog in the Antillean aborigine art. Undoubtedly, the batrachian motif is a metaphor for rainwater, associated with the myth of children who were hungry and weepy and turned into frogs.

There are variations in the typology of the three-pointed *cemí*. In some, the head of the Great Serpent is on one side and the frog legs on the opposite side, yet the body of the serpent is not carved. In others, the head of the reptile without extremities is replaced with an anthropomorphic head crowned with a diadem of geometric design. In some, both ends of the three-pointed stone carry anthropomorphic heads, united or separated by the body of the serpent. In this last case, the *cemí* resembles a kind of two-headed serpent. These last versions could be a combined idealization of Boínayel and Márohu, the twin sons of the Great Serpent, gods of rain and clear weather.

In sum, it is possible to postulate that the unique three-pointed stone prototype analyzed corresponded to the third "stone" mentioned by the chroniclers and that it represented Iguanaboína, the female deity that integrates the duality-opposition of rain and the good weather produced by the twins. That is to say, the Great Iguanaboína Serpent would be the governess of climatological balance, the maximum regulator of the constructive water cycle favorable for agriculture.

Its destructive aspect would be manifested in another feminine *cemí*, Guabancex, who, assisted by Coatrisquie and Guataúba (maybe twins), composed the triad of *cemíes* associated with hurricanes, wind and devastating water, according to Pané. These entities operated mainly in the months of August and September, when the reappearance of the Big Dipper over the horizon presaged the hurricane season in the Caribbean Sea.

Contrary to popular belief, the hurricane itself was not a Taino deity. Rather, hurricanes were the manifestation of the *cemíes*. Both Iguanaboína with Boínayel and Márohu, and Guabancex with Coatrtisquie and Guataúba, constituted two triads of opposite but complementary *cemíes*. As such, they could have been the benevolent and malevolent expression of the Great Mother.

Frog representations. Left column, from top to bottom: Holguín, Cuba; Goddess of Caguana (Woman-Frog) petroglyph, Utuado, P.R.; clay seal, P.R.; ornament in shell, Sorcé, Vieques, P.R.
"Llora-lluvia" (cry-rain), possible representations of Boínayel, God of Rain. Clockwise from center: wood *cohoba* idol, Jamaica; Charco de las Caritas petroglyph, Chacuey, D.R.; ceramic vase, Cuba.

Agricultural technology

Protected by the power of the *cemíes* and after centuries of accumulating extensive knowledge about the natural resources and the climatological cycles, the Taino chiefdoms achieved progress in agricultural technology.

By the time the European arrived, the Tainos had perfected several agricultural systems adapted to a variety of tropical ecosystems. Following Moscoso's description, we can summarize them as follows: slash and burn (farming of land using the old South American method); várzea (farming in the flood banks of rivers to take advantage of fertile deposits); *xagüeyes* (farming in hollows of rocks or limestone soil to plant mainly the *guáyiga* or *marunguey*, *Zamia sp.*, from whose root a kind of bread was made that is today called "chola" in the Dominican Republic); acequias (farming with rudimentary irrigation canals, reported mainly in the chiefdom of Xaragua, in Hispaniola); *conucos* (name of the farming field near the village that is also used to refer to crops planted in heaps or earth embankments); terraces (farming on terraces built on the slopes of mountains).

Of these techniques, farming in heaps or mounds ("montones") was most commonly used, mainly for the planting of tubers such as manioc. The mound, consisting of a hump of loose earth, became an ideal medium for cultivation because it conserves moisture and nutrients from the ground. Las Casas reported that Tainos made mounds of the same height as a rod (three feet) with a contour of 9 to 12 feet, separated by two or three feet from each other. In Hispaniola, he described *conucos* of "twenty or thirty thousand heaps in length and five or ten thousand heaps in width." In Puerto Rico, farms of 50,000 and up to 80,000 mounds were reported. According to the Dominican economist and historian Bernardo Vega, the mound system was used by the colonizers to establish a measure of the Antillean land surface: two hundred thousand mounds were equivalent to a "caballería de tierra" (a cavalry of land).

The manioc (*yuca*, *Manihot esculenta*), the plant they called *yacubia*, was the name of the primary tuber cultivated and the main source of carbohydrates in the Taino diet. Six varieties were known: *ipotex*, *diacanan*, *nubaga*, *tubaga*, *coro* and *tabacan*. Oviedo noted that manioc could be harvested at ten months, but Las Casas wrote that "from one year onwards they can get it and make bread, but better than a year and a half past, and better than two, and last up to three, because it can to be under the earth without getting damaged." This property allowed the *conucos* to be real underground manioc stores, because "even though it rains or blows, it does not harm it."

"Guayo" in stone with frog heads used to grate manioc.
Museo del Hombre Dominicano, Santo Domingo, D.R.

The making of cassava (*casabe, cazabe*) entailed a process carried out by women exclusively: after grating the manioc tuber with a stone over the *guariquitén* (which was made of *yagua*, a fiber from the royal palm), the dough was placed inside the *cibucán*, a long and woven cylinder that was twisted to squeeze out the toxic juice from the manioc. Then, they prepared the cassava cakes and cooked them over a *burén* (clay griddle) placed over the fire on three stones. The process ended by exposing the cassava to the sun. The social hierarchy of the Tainos required the elaboration of the *xauxau*, a finer white cassava only for consumption by the *caciques* or principals. Las Casas noted that five or six women could produce between 50 and 70 "arrobas" (about 1,265 to 1,770 pounds) of cassava per day, enough for more than a thousand people.

In addition to manioc and corn, other important crops were the *yautía* (*Xanthosoma* sp.) or *diahutía* (it is alleged that perhaps there were up to ten varieties); *maní* or peanuts (*Arachis hypogaea*); *batata* or sweet potato (*Ipomoea batatas*), perhaps also called *aje* (Las Casas collected the name *yucaba* for the plant, noting that it was edible in 4 to 5 months, while Oviedo identified five varieties, *aniguamar* being the most desired); *yerén*, *lirén* or *lerén* (*Calathea allouia*); *axí* or *ají* (*Capsicum* sp.), which was a seasoning used daily and of which Las Casas reported three species. *Algodón* or cotton (*Gossypium barbadense*), *maguey*, *henequén* or agave (*Agave* sp.), and the *cabuya* or pita cord (*Furcraea tuberosa*), were planted for the manufacture of cloth and fibers.

The following fruits are reported as either farmed or harvested: *ananas* or pineapple (*Ananas* sp.), with the *yayama* being the sweetest variety, but also reported are the *boniama* and *yayagua* varieties; *guayaba* or guava (*Psidium guajava*); *hicaco* (*Chrysbalanus icaco*); *guanábana* or soursop (*Annona muricata*); "lechosa", "fruta bomba" or *papaya* (*Carica papaya*); *jagua* (*Genipa americana*), whose black dye they used to dye their body; *caimito* (*Chrysophyllum cainito*), whose wood was used to make bows; *jobo* (*Spondias mombin*); *corazón*, *mamón*, *chirimoya* or custard apple (*Annona reticulata*); *mamey* (*Mammea americana*); *higüero* (*Crescentia cujete*), a type of gourd, whose fruit they used to make small utensils and maracas; *achiote*, *bija* (*Bixa orellana*), which they used to paint the body red and as an insect repellent.

Among the trees they used were the *ausubo* or *balata* (*Manilkara bidentata*); *caoba* or mahogany (*Swietenia mahogany*); *capá* (*Cordia alliodora*); *ceiba* (*Ceiba pentandra*); *guayacán* (*Guaiacum offuinale*).

Other than the stone axe, the main known agricultural instrument was the *coa*, a long wooden stick with the tip hardened by the fire with which they sowed.

Mythical plants: digo, güeyo and cohoba

In addition to food plants, the **Tainos** had magical and medicinal plants. In Taino mythology, Guahayona as First *Behique* is associated with three magical plants.

As for the *digo* ("with which they cleanse the body when they go to wash," and was also used in initiation rites, funerals and fasts), opinions vary concerning its identity. Some people believe that it corresponds to the fragrant herb "Y" mentioned by Las Casas and Oviedo that served as a purgative and produced a foamy sap used for bathing. However, the Dominican botanist Rafael Moscoso Puello associates the *digo* with the "Flor de la Y" in Cuba and the Dominican "Gloria de la Mañana," which corresponds to the Puerto Rican "Bejuco de Luna" (*Ipomoea macrantha* or *violacea*). This climber plant also has purgative properties; the infusion of its flowers is used to treat cutaneous diseases and its seed contains hallucinatory substances, which tends to reinforce its identification with the mythical *digo*. In fact, a variety of this plant was used by the Caribs in a medicinal bath against diseases of the skin and syphilis.

The *güeyo*, probably tobacco (*tabaco*, *Nicotiana tabacum*), was an herb that after crushing and kneading "they put it in their mouths to vomit what they have eaten" before the *behique* began a healing ceremony. The *güeyo* juice was also given to a dead patient, mixed with his own nails and hair, to "speak" and tell if the *behique* was responsible for his death. Pané reports that the *güeyo* had "the leaves similar to the basil, thick and long, and for another name it is to be called zacón." On the other hand, Sven Lovén, following Las Casas, thought that it was "coca" from the continent. The word reminded Fernando Ortiz of the *huya* or *weya*, a salty seaweed that, mixed with tobacco in the Guianas, was used to appease hunger. But Haitian researcher Jacques Roumain has suggested that *güeyo* could be an Antillean aromatic plant with medicinal properties called *atiayo* or "albahaca cimarrona o de vaca" (*Ocimum gratissimum*) because of its similarity with this plant. Its lanceolate leaves can reach up to 12 cm in length.

The cohoba ceremony

The *cohoba* or *cojoba* is mentioned by all the principal chroniclers. Although in Taino mythology the *cohoba* is alluded to in the *guanguayo* or spit that Bayamanaco (God of Fire) threw to the twin Deminán, perhaps its ritual use was also learned by Guahayona in his shamanic initiation journey. Judging by the chroniclers, the *cohoba* came from "certain herbs that were well grounded, cinnamon in color…" that "the Indians had for a very precious thing, and they raised it in their gardens and crops." For this reason, Lovén insisted that the *cohoba* did not come from a tree, but consisted of pulverized tobacco (*Nicotiana tabacum*).

However, more recently, it is thought that the *cohoba* is equivalent to the *ñopo, yopo, vilca* or *aiuku* in South America, the powder with hallucinogenic properties that comes from the seed of a variety of *acacia* tree called "cojóbana" or "cojobo" in Puerto Rico, and "tamarindo de teta" (*Anadenanthera peregrina*) in the Domnican Republic, identified by William E. Safford in 1916. The tree must have been introduced during the South American migrations to the Antilles. Recalling the mangy skin of the mythical heroes Guahayona and Deminán, the bark of the tree is rough, with deep cracks and prominent warts. And, even more significant: the pod that contains the seeds, resembles the ripples that show in the back of many Taino idols associated with the *cohoba*.

Representation of the *cohoba* ceremony.
Museo Arqueológico Regional Altos de Chavón, La Romana, D.R.

The *cohoba* ceremony was the main religious ritual of the Tainos. It was probably the *behique* who prepared the magical powder by perhaps adding other herbs and crushed shells to increase its effects. On a few occasions, the main participants performed a long fast for six or seven days by ingesting only the juice of the *digo*, with which they also washed.

At the beginning of the ritual an internal cleaning was carried out, causing vomiting with long spatulas designed for that purpose. Once inside the *caney* (house) and sitting in his *duho* (a bench usually made of wood), the *cacique* breathed in the power by means of inhalers in the form of Y. The powder was placed on a kind of dish that crowned a wooden idol. Then, the other participants followed. "There they spoke as if they were in chatter… confusingly, I do not know what things and words," wrote Las Casas. Soon, the drug produced a kind of hallucinatory trance through which the *cacique* believed he communicated with the *cemíes* to learn "good times or adverse times, or who was to have children, or who would die, or who was going to have some control or war with their neighbors."

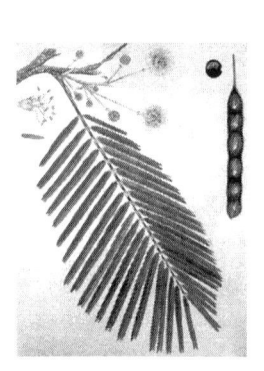

Illustration of the *cohoba* (*Anadenathera peregrina*), according to A. Stahl.

Wood carving of the mythical twins with a top dish to place the hallucinogenic powder. Museo del Hombre Dominicano, D.R. Spatula in manatee bone. Fundación García Arévalo, D.R.

Cohoba inhaler carved in manatee bone. Fundación García Arévalo, D.R.

We believe that the *cemí*, in embodying the spirit of the ancestors, manifested the dichotomy between the two types of time: the mythical and distant time when the Creation occurred and the historical and present time when, by means of rites like the *cohoba*, the past is made present. The *cemí* established, therefore, a peculiar diachronic-synchronic link between both types of time. The *cemí* intertwined the sacred era of the origins controlled by the supernatural beings with the present time ruled by the *cacique*. Hence, the *cemí* unified the imaginary with the real. In such a way that when the *cohoba* ceremony was celebrated, a mythical present was established that allowed the *cacique* to communicate with the divinities of the origins contained in the figures of the *cemíes*. Therefore, the *cacique* became the powerful intermediary between the Tainos and the mythical past. In other words, the triad conformed by *cemíes-cohoba-cacique* was the power that legitimized the Taino religion.

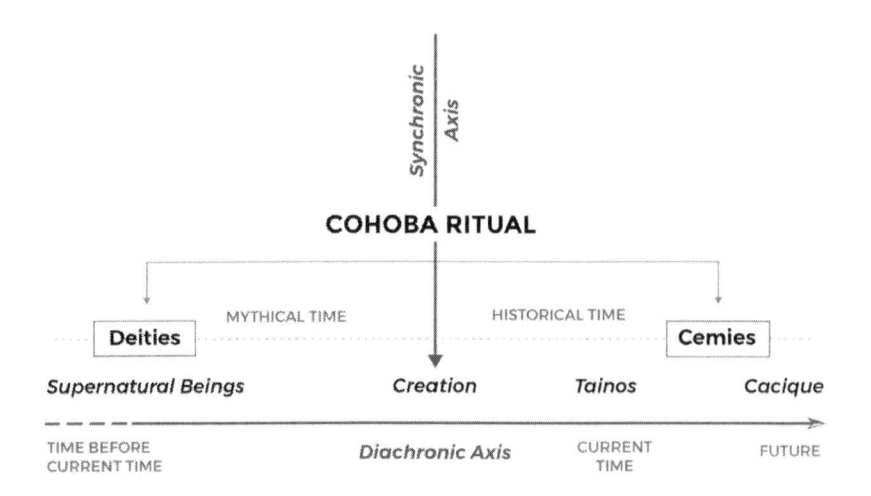

```
                    Synchronic
                       Axis
                        │
                        │
              COHOBA RITUAL
         ┌──────────────┼──────────────┐
         │  MYTHICAL TIME │ HISTORICAL TIME │
         ▼              │              ▼
     ┌────────┐          │          ┌────────┐
     │Deities │          │          │ Cemies │
     └────────┘          ▼          └────────┘
  Supernatural Beings  Creation    Tainos     Cacique
  ─ ─ ─ ─ ─────────────────────────────────────────────▶
   TIME BEFORE      Diachronic Axis   CURRENT        FUTURE
   CURRENT TIME                        TIME
```

In addition to the *cohoba*, it is very likely that the **Tainos** used other Antillean plants with hallucinogenic effects. As we saw, the *digo* was one of them. From the same family we could suggest that the "aguinaldo" or "bejuco de Pascua" (*Turbina corymbosa* or *Rivea corymbosa*), whose seeds have a strong narcotic effect, may also have been used. There is also *Datura stramonium*, called in Spanish "chamisco" or "belladona de pobre," whose fruit is covered with thorns and contains the belladonna alkaloids that have hallucinogenic properties. Certain fungi, such as those of the extended genus *Psilocybe*, also produce hallucinogenic effects.

It is necessary to point out that the investigation of the rituals carried out in South America with hallucinogenic, entheogenic or psychotropic substances equal or similar to the *cohoba*, shows that there is a repetitive pattern in the visions, according to authors such as Peter Furst, Michel Harner and Jeremy Narby. It is curious that among the predominant visions is that of a powerful serpent. José Alcina Franch has emphasized the parallelism between the visualized forms and certain designs in Colombian Tukano and **Taino art**.

In sum, these facts encourage us to consider that the configuration of deities and various elements of aboriginal art find their origin and inspiration in manifestations of the unconscious as projected in both dreams and in the visions experienced during altered states of consciousness. Perhaps this is how certain constant symbols that appear in geographically - and historically- separated cultures can be explained.

Magical plants - medicinal

In addition to the *cohoba*, the *digo* and the *güeyo*, Las Casas and mainly Oviedo offer us a list of Taino trees, plants and medicinal herbs. The **Tainos** believed that there was a magical principle that fought evil spirits lodged in a patient's body. Disease, thus, was believed to be caused by an imbalance of a spiritual nature.

The *behiques*, as Oviedo wrote, were "great herbalists" who "knew the properties of our trees and plants and herbs; and how they helped heal, had them in great veneration and obedience, as saints, held among these people as Christians hold priests." Of course, the empirical knowledge of the *behiques* was the result of centuries of oral tradition in the Antilles.

The available documentation on the Taino pharmacopoeia is very limited and what was known disappeared in a short time. However, the use of a large part of the native flora considered curative was inherited through Antillean folk medicine.

The main disease faced by the European was syphilis (called "buba" by the Spaniards and, apparently, *yaya* by the indigenous people of the Antilles), although today it is believed that syphilis existed in both continents before the discovery of the New World. Guahayona probably suffered syphilis and overcame it during his stay in Guanín. It is for this reason that the **Tainos** believed that the balm of the *guayacán* tree (*Guaiacum officinale*) cured this disease and was one of the secret remedies acquired by the First *Behique* during his mythical journey. This belief was so rooted among the **Tainos** that the Spaniards confided in the curative power of the *guayacán*, which they called "palo santo" (blessed tree), and they initiated exports of the tree itself to Spain in 1508.

But the broad healing power was specifically in the balm prepared from the resinous tree called *guaconax* (*Amyris* sp.), "guaconejo" o "palo de tea" in Santo Domingo; "cuabilla" in Puerto Rico. According to Oviedo, in Santo Domingo the pharmacist Antonio Villasante obtained "from his wife who is Indian and natural of this island" the secret of its manufacture. In 1526, Villasante sold the secret formula to none other than Diego Colón, the son of the Admiral who had been Governor of the Indies. The drug was believed to be ideal to treat "fresh slash or spear wounds, or any other recent wound, because immediately the blood stagnates, and none have seen nor known of any other medicinal remedy that so quickly welds and closes the wound." In addition, they said that "it takes care of other serious illnesses, which tend to be incurable."

The tobacco (*tabaco, Nicotiana tabacum*) smoked by the indigenous people of the Antilles "caused numbness in the flesh and in the whole body, so they neither felt hunger nor fatigue," according to Las Casas. Tobacco was quickly adopted by the Spaniards and spread throughout Europe in the 17th century and used therapeutically during the Colonial era. To this day, tobacco is part of African-American rituals, as studied by Fernando Ortiz.

There was also a bush called *perebecenuc* from which **Tainos** extracted a liquor that was believed to have ample healing power. From the *tuna* or spiny prickly pear (*Opuntia* sp.), they made a medicine that healed broken bones. For sores and other ailments, they used the *curí-a*, which today is known as "carpintero" (*Justicia pectoralis*) and is an aromatic herb whose waters "are very much procured by women, because when warm it serves their passions and tighten and dry; and if you wash her loins with it, it incites veneration." The *guao* (*Metopium brownei*), on the other hand, was a shrub whose caustic sap had dual use: "it serves to eat the rotten flesh of the wounds" and to "whiten the skin of some Indian women who imitated the Spanish women." Further, from the seed of the *mamey* (*Mammea americana*), the **Tainos** obtained a powder for sores. They also adjudicated extensive curative properties to the *yagrumo* or trumpet tree (*Cecropia peltata*). The **Tainos** boiled the bark and skin of the *jobo* (*Spondias mombin*) to wash the legs and relieve fatigue. A similar use was given to the juice or water of the *jagua* (*Genipa americana*), by virtue of its ability to "tighten the flesh and remove the fatigue of the legs."

The leaf of the *caimito* or star-apple (*Chrysophyllum cainito*) was used to clean teeth. Las Casas mentions the broad virtues of the popular "tua-tua" (*Jatropha gossypiifolia*), a tree that they planted near dwellings and is still in use today. The poisonous tree *par excellence* in the Antilles was the *guchón*, later called "manzanillo", or manchineel (*Hippomane mancinella*), whose toxicity is transmitted simply by touching it or sheltering in its shade. The French chroniclers refer to this tree as being used by the Caribs to extract venom for their arrows.

Lastly, the Tainos possessed the secret of two powerful poisons, as pointed out by the chroniclers. They used these venoms as a last resort in their desperation to rid themselves of the abusive and cruel slavery to which they were subjected. One was the *hyen*, the juice of the bitter manioc, with which they committed suicide collectively; the other was the juice of a strange grass that mothers took "to give birth prematurely, on the grounds that the fruit of their entrails would end up as a slave to the Christians."

"Manzanillo", manchineel (*Hippomane mancinella*),
Little, Wadsworth, and Marrero (1977).

CHAPTER 10

The mythical origin of art

As we have reviewed earlier in this book, Guahayona was probably among the bat-beings transformed by the Sun into an original Taino upon exiting the mythical cave. In Taino mythology, Guahayona was the First Navigator and the First *Behique.*

Various objects in Taino art represent the magical transmutation of animals into human beings. It is plausible that the images that depict a bat-being with the body of a human and features of a chiropteran, are a visual snapshot of the moment of physical transformation experienced by those avatars. Indeed, the bat motif, like that of the frog (both perhaps totemic symbols), can be found in all stages of development and illustrates the complete evolution of aboriginal art in the Antilles, from the Saladoid to the Ostionoid and, from there, to the Taino. Taino art, in fact, registers features of the bat element in a great variety of objects made across a broad range of materials (pottery, wood, rock, shell, bone, amber) and are related to

Representations of bats in pottery from the Dominican Republic

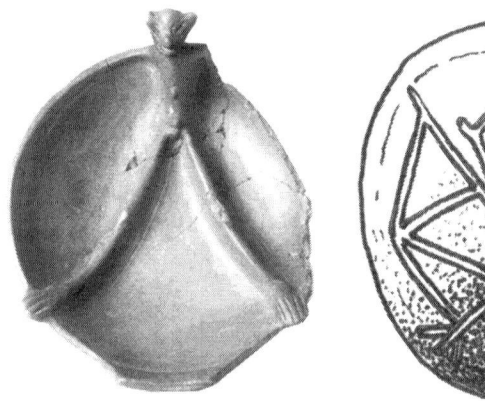

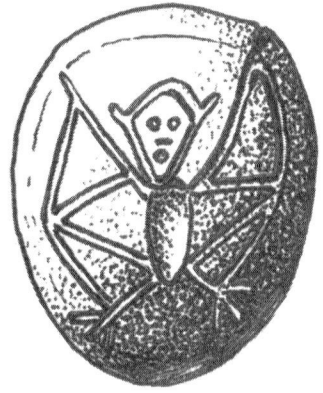

Bat motifs. Left: Ceramic dish, Tecla, Guayanilla, P. R.
Right: "Higüero" from Santiago de Cuba.

shamanism and the afterworld, as shown by Henry Petitjean Roget as well as by two Dominicans: Manuel García Arévalo, whose foundation contains one of the best collections of Taino art, and Fernando Morbán Laucer, who served for many years as the director of the Museo del Hombre Dominicano in the Dominican Republic.

Interestingly, the *cibas* and *guanines* obtained by Guahayona during his trip to the island of Guanín are the first art objects known in Taino mythology. In other words, the origin of art is linked in Taino mythology directly with the origin of the times. And the canoe is the means of dissemination of such art and knowledge between islands.

The *cibas* were "stones that very much resemble marble and are worn tied to the arms and neck" by Taino people. *Cibas* appear to be made either from the *cobo* (*Strombus gigas*), the same conch that makes an appearance in myth, or from the semiprecious reddish stone that is occasionally found in the interior of this conch, which the Taino esteemed and called *cohibici*, according to Anglería. Further, it cannot be ruled out that quartz may have been used as well, given quartz was a stone of magical virtues used for healing purposes by the *behique* and widely employed to make necklaces.

The *guanín* were decorations worn in the ears in the shape of a half moon or a disc and made using an alloy of gold and copper.

Guanín came from the South American coast, where it was called "tumbaga" by the Tairona indigenous people in Colombia. Due to its rarity and brilliance, the *guanín* became a jewel of solar connotation and a symbol of *cacique* power for the Tainos. This is why, when Columbus asked for gold during his first voyage, the Tainos thought that he was referring to the *guanín* and pointed east towards the legendary Guanín, the ancestral route to the continent through the Antillean arch. The Admiral, who travelled in those strange vessels with great wings moved by the wind, was a god "from the sky," perhaps the nautical hero returning home in search of the *cibas* and the *guanines*.

Taino navigation

Navigation can be considered an art that is learned in youth, experienced and perfected over the years with the intuition of maturity. Nautical men like "Diego Méndez," the godson, guide and interpreter of Columbus, belonged to a type of clan in which the knowledge and traditions regarding canoe construction and navigation were acquired orally.

As for the Taino canoe, first and foremost, as Columbus observed and Oviedo later explained, the canoe was made from the trunk of a tree that was "emptied by blows of stone axes… with them they cut or grind the wood with blows… and they go burning what is beaten, little by little…" This technique was identical to that used by the Caribs and other indigenous peoples in South America. While they hollowed the trunk, they placed planks transversely to serve as tables or benches for the rowers. The Taino paddle (*nahe*) was about 1.5 meters (5 feet) in length and analogous to a stylized paddle with a T-shaped top and a spear-shaped submersible blade.

The entire process of canoe construction, from the selection of the tree to its launching into the water, must have been accompanied by an elaborate ritual that has been, sadly, lost.

There were canoes of all sizes, for different uses. Among the largest reported by Columbus was the "beautiful" canoe measured in Baracoa, Cuba, which would have been about 20 meters (65 feet) in length, with an estimated capacity of 150 persons. There was also the canoe that the Jamaican *cacique* used to travel to Columbus' caravel to request to leave with the Admiral, estimated at about 30 meters (97 feet) in length and 2.5 meters (8 feet) wide. On another occasion, Columbus observed a large canoe with 70 or 80 men, in which half of the men rowed and the other half rested at the bottom of the boat.

Due to the average size of the trees used regularly for canoe construction, for example *ceiba* (*Ceiba pentandra*), cedar (*Cedrela odorata*), *tabonuco* (*Dacryodes excelsa*), the prototype Taino canoe was between 10 and 12 meters (32 to 40 feet) in length, with a capacity of 40 to 50 persons. This is the ideal dimension for navigation on the high seas because, according to the studies and experiments carried out by the famous navigator Thor Heyerdahl, "[...] primitive boats of about 10 meters (32 feet) have greater chance of surpassing a raging sea than similar, larger boats."

Canoe construction with controlled fire; engraving of an indigenous canoe (Benzoni, 1565); instruments used in the process.

According to Las Casas, canoes "traveled 7 to 8 leagues a day," which is equivalent to about 40 modern nautical miles (about 70 kilometers). In contrast, caravels sailed "in a natural day, fifty leagues," according to Bernáldez. Of course, these values varied according to the winds and the sea currents. The speed of the canoe depended on the number of rowers, but the average that we have calculated is 3 kilometers per hour or 1.7 nautical miles, similar to the one reported by Johannes Wilbert for the Warao indigenous people of South America.

Regarding canoes, Columbus affirmed, "they go in a matter you would not believe, and [...] they sail all the islands, which are innumerable, and bring their merchandise." Las Casas reported - perhaps exaggerating - that there was a daily exchange between the coasts of Hispaniola and Puerto Rico. Due to this close cultural relationship between both islands that archeology confirms, the *cacique* Andrés del Higüey of Hispaniola was considered a relative of the *cacique* Agueybaná of Puerto Rico.

Thus, the canoe, aided by the hydrology of northern South America and the Antilles, played a leading role in facilitating the migratory movements that occurred over time in the Caribbean. The importance of marine currents in these migrations was studied in a pioneering manner by Adolfo de Hostos (1922) and more recently by Richard T. Calaghan using computer models. It was precisely the strong currents between the Yucatan peninsula and Cuba that prevented an interaction between these areas, despite their relative geographical proximity. This natural barrier has been ignored by some authors who have sought to establish a direct influence of the Mayans on the Antilles.

The canoe has been a valuable means of production in all historic stages of the Antilles. Tainos used canoes to fish. Using hooks made of bone, they caught shad, sea bass, and eels, which are fish that swim upstream of rivers to spawn during the evening presence of the Orion constellation (an idealization of Yayael, from whose bones emerged the sea and the fish). Tainos also collected conch and caught fish from canoes with traps, nets, harpoons or using remora fish (*guaicano*) as bait. Remora fish, when tied to a rope, swim to stick firmly to the prey. In addition, Taino men fished in rivers with the use of the narcotic plant *baiguá*, with the bow and the arrow, or with traps. An example of Taino inventiveness was the practice of fish farming: in water pens made by driving "rods onto the river bottom," they kept fish and turtles alive for daily consumption.

It is worth adding that the often-mentioned canoe trip by Guahayona to distant islands and, similarly, that of Acáyouman, father of the lineage of the Island-Carib, as we will see later in this book, is the Antillean version of the water journey made by the cultural hero of the Guianas. Thus, there is no doubt that this mythical component - unnoticed by the chroniclers - was present among the indigenous peoples of the Antilles. The large canoes were "carved [...] in bow and stern with decorations and paints, of marvelous beauty," as reported in Jamaica, and the "very painted" canoes reported among the indigenous people in the chiefdom of Xaragua in Hispaniola, were emblematic vessels that symbolized the continuation of the cosmic-social order and the divine power held by the *cacique*.

As a matter of fact, in lieu of attributing the migrations from the South American coast to pressure from groups and the search for new natural resources, as has been the case traditionally to date, we can speculate that there was a motivation that transcended those factors and went to the mythical cause or incentive among the Tainos of recreating the journey of the cultural hero. As such, navigation rose to become a spiritual requirement, a necessity reaffirmed by the value and power of myth.

Regarding Taino artists and their work

In general terms, the visual arts of the chiefdoms analyzed throughout this fifth part, with the exception of slight regional variations, are consistent in form and symbolic element, allowing us to establish a definition of style that corresponds with the Chicoid style, also known as Boca Chica, the area in Hispaniola where it originated around the year 1,000 AC and from where it spread to the rest of the Antilles.

Given that art reflects the myths, beliefs and traditions of a culture, the distinctive features of the Chicoid style reaffirm that under the Antillean chiefdoms there existed a predominant religious world. Taino visual artists mastered artistic techniques and had a precise idea of the image they wanted to capture. What remains for us to elucidate is how their knowledge originated and was transmitted to others.

Style is anonymous but its origin responds to a gifted and experienced artist who, with her skills, managed to create unique and innovative elements at a given moment in time. Someone must have conceived and carved for the first time, perhaps using the already established form of the three-pointed stone, the unique characteristics that became associated with the *cemí* that represents Yúcahu. But this would not have been sufficient for her artistic proposal to be accepted. To be endorsed, the visual arts language used by the artist must have corresponded with the Taino worldview and the oral literature (myths, beliefs) that contain elements that guaranteed the traditional precepts of beauty, using symbols that managed to convey the esoteric message of the work.

If a skilled artist belonged to the political-religious power group (as seems to have been the case in aboriginal society), her work - inspired probably under the effects of hallucinogenic substances, that is, in an altered state of consciousness or as a result of a dream - would have been interpreted as being of divine origin and would have acquired social legitimacy. With the passage of time, the peculiarities of her work would begin to be reproduced slowly by other artists, giving way to the progressive establishment of the representative style of a cultural period. If, indeed, styles are formed in this manner, then it is tempting to think that in Taino society there existed organized groups in which a novice endowed with artistic skills would receive the traditional canons of chiefdom art from experienced teachers. And that even artistic patterns were passed from island to island.

However, as American anthropologist Franz Boas pointed out, different styles can exist in parallel in the art of a culture. Realistic, figurative, abstract and geometric motifs can coexist. The dissimilarities are mainly noticeable when comparing the different means of artistic expression and their respective uses. In the case of the Tainos, in spite of a common general iconography, the forms and styles used in pottery, sculpture or rock art differ to a greater or lesser degree. That is, each field of artistic expression has objects of specific materials with distinctive properties. Similarly, each object has its own symbolic elements that give it a precise use in society. For example, the vomiting spatula that was regularly carved on bone, with its elongated and curved shape, is linked exclusively to the *cohoba* ceremony, just as the stone *cemí* with its tricuspid form is associated with agriculture.

We may find explanations to the origin of these peculiarities in the social division of labor and in the creativity of the artists of each genre, among other reasons. We know that Taino pottery was made by women. On the other hand, sculpture and rock art (and perhaps some types of ceremonial pottery, as suggested by Veloz Maggiolo and Moscoso) were the occupation of men presumably, probably of the *behique*. Hence, even within the same ideological context, there are gradual differences between the artistic styles in each field.

When an archaeologist studies pottery styles over time, he is fundamentally analyzing the feminine perspective, the conceptual patterns of the pottery makers, not necessarily the patterns of the society. This situation, as we shall see, is of significant importance among the Caribs of the Antilles.

On the other hand, Antillean rock art (petroglyphs and pictographs) seems to have been created from the Archaic to the Taino periods, emcompassing both figurative and abstract motifs. Rock art is a relatively well-documented manifestation but it lacks more definitive studies in terms of its origins, comparative analyses, regional developments, classificatory proposals or possible interpretations. In this last sense, there is no doubt that rock art was a projection of the mythology and the cosmology of the aboriginal. Among other scholars, it is worth mentioning the works of Antonio Núñez Jiménez in Cuba, Dato Pagán Perdomo and Fernando Morbán Laucer in the Dominican Republic, Carlos Pérez Merced in Puerto Rico, and Cornelis N. Dubelaar in the Antilles, in general.

Artistic manifestations

Beyond pottery, Taino visual artists worked predominantly on stone, wood, bone and shell material. Gold nuggets were produced by means of blows or were pressed between stones, becoming either thin plates embedded in the cavities of the idols or the beads of necklaces or plates of masks. To cut and decorate pieces of hard materials, artists patiently used the bone chisel, natural abrasives, as well as flint and fiber threads with water and sand.

If we had to identify representative objects of Taino art for each one of the materials mentioned, we would choose the effigy vessels and carafes for pottery; in stone, the three-pointed *cemíes* and the stone collars; in wood, the *duhos* and the *cohoba* idols; in bone, the inhalers and the vomiting spatulas for the *cohoba*; in shell, the amulets.

The effigy vessels are modeled to represent a regular human figure by means of a realistic style. Some seem to represent a thick female figure (Itiba Cahubaba), a possible *behique* with protruding ribs and thick legs (Guahayona) or the twin Deminán Caracaracol with the turtle on its back. More than deities, it seems that the effigy pots were images of mythical characters.

The carafes or large containers for liquids (*potizas*) show definite sexual forms. The heart-shaped containers in the form of mammals resemble two immense breasts separated in the central part by a neck of phallic form.

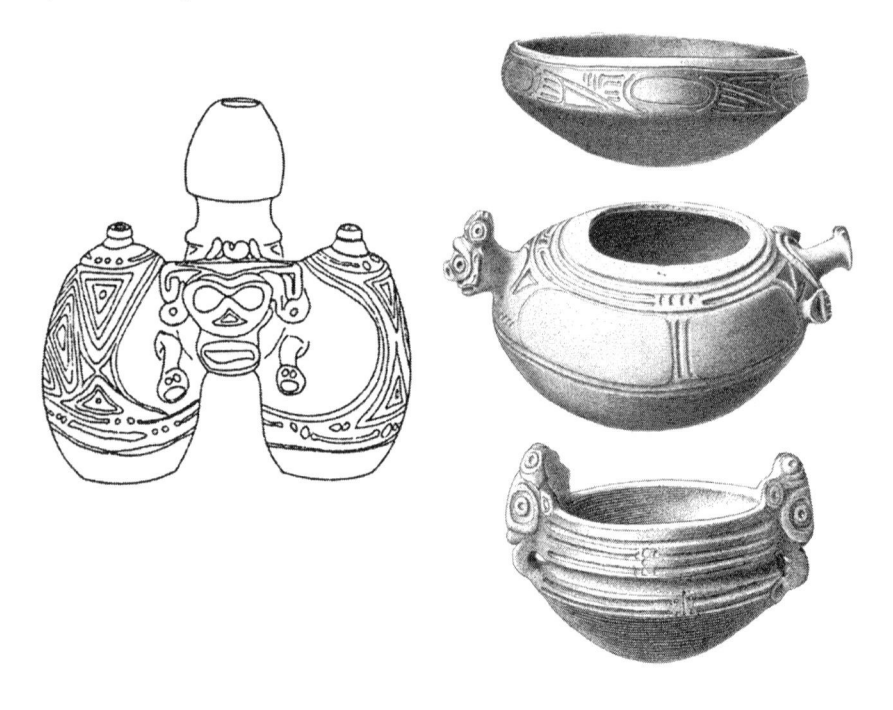

Left, then top to bottom: *potiza* in ceramic with defined sexual forms, Fundación García Arévalo, D.R.; Taino ceramic bowls from P. R. and the D. R., according to Fewkes (1922).

Different views of a three-pointed stone or *cemí* (Fewkes, 1907).

Ceremonial seat (*duho*) used by the Taino hierarchy.
The back of the seat shows an elaborated carving of circles with a central point, a recurrent motif in Taino art that probably had great symbolic importance. Museo del Hombre Dominicano, D.R.

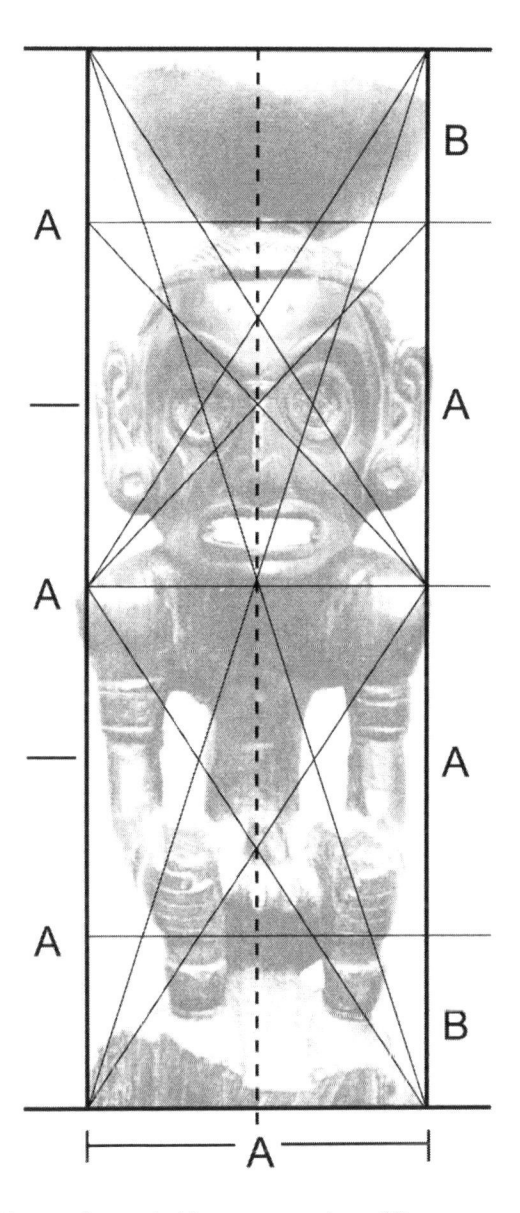

Cohoba idol in wood, a probable representation of Bayamanaco, God of Fire, from Jamaica. Metropolitan Museum of New York.
Canon of Taino art, according to the author.
Dimension A is repeated in the head, torso and width of the figure.
Dimension B occurs in the upper and lower ends. In effect, A = 2B.
In Taino art, the head occupies a relevant position.

In stone, the three-pointed *cemíes* and the stone collars are prototypical objects of the classical Taino period. These ritual objects are only reported in Puerto Rico and in the southeast region of the Dominican Republic. It is in this latter region where the faces or heads of *macorix*, carvings of great realism, are found. The stone collars, which together with the elbows and stone masks are associated with the ball game, exist in both regions but achieve their greatest abundance and artistic quality in Puerto Rico.

The *duhos*, the four-legged ceremonial seats with back support reserved for members of the high hierarchy, demonstrate the skill of the Taino wood sculptor. Typically, the head of an idol is placed between the front legs or on the high backrest. Symmetrical geometric incisions decorate the art pieces, which are most commonly carved in wood.

In contrast, the idols of the *cohoba*, also carved in wood, commonly show a male figure in a sitting position with a large head, dramatic expression, and usually with the penis erect and with the arms on the legs. Its main characteristic, nevertheless, is the circular plate on the head, which served to place the powder of the *cohoba*. These carvings probably represent the image of Bayamanaco, the God of Fire and mythical holder of the sacred hallucinogenic substance.

In bone, the decorated inhalers and the vomiting spatulas (made in wood or from the ribs of the manatee) stand out as visual art objects used for the ceremony of the *cohoba*. In shell, the amulets call the most attention due not to their size, but to their careful execution. The amulets usually represent a symmetrical humanoid figure, in a sitting position with hands on the chest or knees and head facing forward. According to Dominican art critic Darío Suro, who wrote a pioneering study on this subject, the "squatting or curled up" position is associated with the posture assumed by the Tainos during the *cohoba* ceremony or the fetal position in Taino burials. These amulets, according to the archaeologist García Arévalo, were "personified protective spirits" that hung around their necks or hugged their foreheads hanging from cotton strings. Other times, the carvings contain figures with zoomorphic features.

In general, Taino art is symmetrical and contains a series of geometric decorations - present mainly in pottery and sculpture - that alone or mixed together give rise to complex designs in "labyrinth style."

Amulet carved in shell, from D.R. Private Collection, United States.

The circle with a center point stands out among these symbols as it is used repetitively in various objects that undoubtedly must have had great religious significance. Perhaps it was a representation of the Center, associated with the Divinity, as interpreted by René Guénon in other cultures.

Other decorative motifs are group of parallel lines or a line with a point at both its ends, in a horizontal, vertical or inclined position; the spiral and the "S" inclined or intertwined; the semicircle, the circle or concentric circles; the triangle or the "V" inverted with or without a center point; the rectangle with rounded corners and a horizontal central line. In the pottery bowls, the sequence of these geometric symbols constitutes a true visual rhythm.

In Taino art, both figurative and geometric elements are part of the visual language, a symbolic code that is associated with the religious worldview of the chiefdoms. Like all art, the Taino visual arts had a canon, some rules and proportions that give it its characteristics. But, as José Juan Arrom wrote, "what we have lost is the key to their message."

Taino art symbols, according to Michael Sellon (1970).

From top: petroglyph in the Cavern of Patana, Cuba
(Fernández and González, 2001) and ensemble of petroglyphs,
Caguas, P. R. (Pérez Merced). Geometric engravings in the
Guácara de Comedero, D.R. (Morbán Laucer, 1994).
Below, pictography of the *cohoba* ritual, Cave of Borbón, D.R.

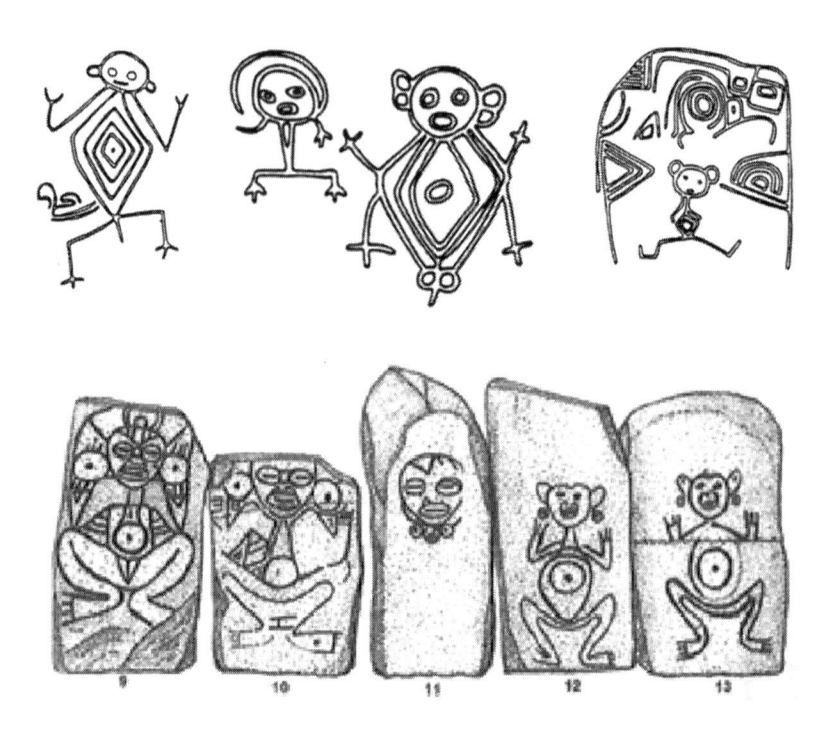

Petroglyphs from Chacuey, D.R. (Weeks and Ferbel, 1994).
and from Caguana, P.R. (Siegel, ed., 2005).

In spite of the limitations, we can summarize Taino artistic manifestations in the categories detailed below:

Body decoration. Cranial frontal deformation, designs on the body with vegetable dyes (*bija* or achiote, *jagua*), with clay seals; hierarchically: use of masks, feathers and crowns of feathers, *guaízas* (masks mainly made of shell, used in the head or in belts), necklaces (*cibas*, shells, quartz, semi-precious stones), nose rings, ear flaps, *naguas* (short skirts worn by women), *guanines* (in the form of a half moon or disk).

Music, dance and singing. *Areíto* ritual, celebrated communally with *mayohabao* (drum made of hollow trunk), *baiohabao*, maracas (made of wood or *higüero*), flutes (made of bone or reeds), whistles (made of bone), small flutes (made of clay), wind instruments (made of shell); other rituals.

Constructions. *Bohíos*, *caneyes*, *bajareques*, *yucayeques*, *bateyes* or ceremonial plazas, embankments, roads, irrigation canals, canoes.

Pottery.
Carafes or jugs of large size (heart-shaped, globular), idols, effigy vessels (representing figures of humans, humans-animals, or animals), bowls, dishes, plates, *burenes* to cook the cassava.

Fabrics. Cotton idols, *naguas*, cloth, hammocks, elastic bands for arms and legs, belts with rhinestones, several types of pennants, fishing nets, pita cord, agave fiber, agave, *bihao*.

Goldsmithing. Gold plates (*caona*), idols, masks, nose rings, ear flaps.

Basketry. Fish nets and traps for fishing, *cibucán* to squeeze manioc, baskets of *bihao*, *maguey*.

Drawing. Petroglyphs and pictographs in caves, rocks, at the margins of the rivers; recorded in various media.

Culinary. Various dishes made for the *caciques* or principals, such as the cassava *xauxau* and iguana meat.

Sculpture or carving. In wood (idols, *duhos*, inhalers and vomiting spatulas for the *cohoba*, maracas, amulets, ear flaps, urns, rafts, *coas*, bowls, bows, arrows, dart-throwers, clubs, types of trumpets, drums). In stone (three-pointed stones, rings, elbows, idols, amulets, heads, mashers, mortars, graters, axes, effigy axes). In shell, bone or nacar (*guaízas*, idols, necklaces, amulets, wind instruments, spoons, inhalers and spatulas for the *cohoba*, flutes, arrowheads).

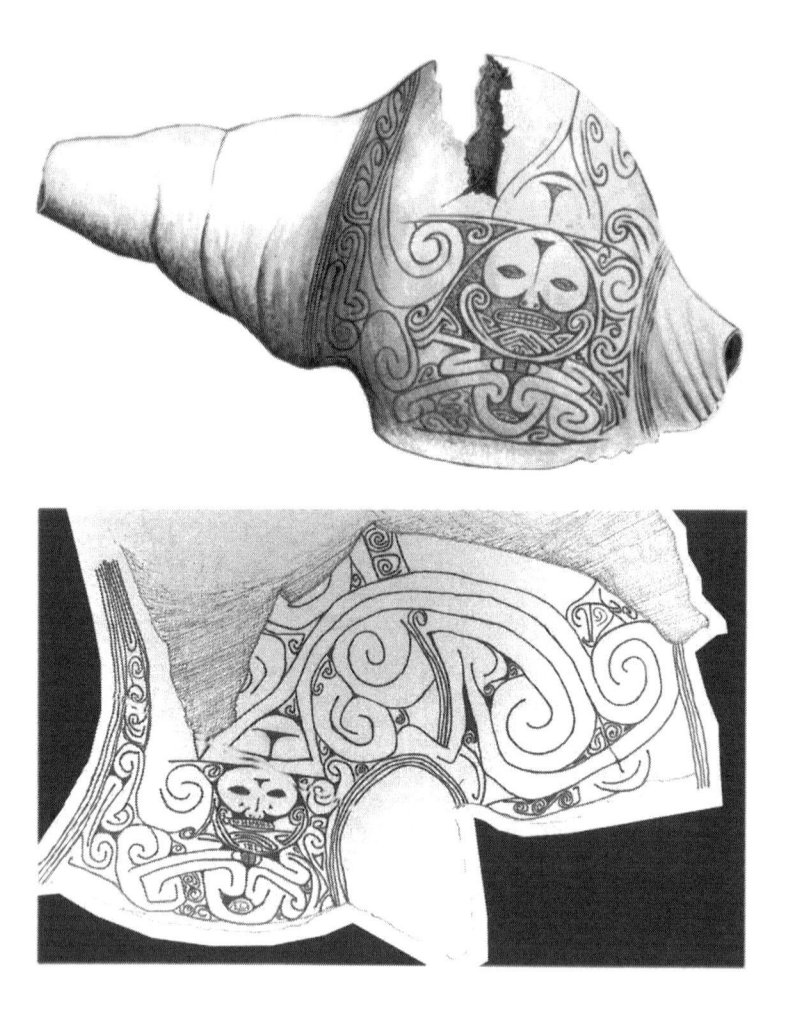

Carved shell (*Charonia variegata*) used as trumpet or "fotuto"; planimetric version. Museo del Hombre Dominicano, D.R.

Beyond Coaybay

To sum up and conclude what has been presented in the last chapters, the Taino worldview encompassed a dualistic perception of the forces that rule the universe. It is the concept of *coincidentia oppositorum* or the coincidence of opposites, as suggested by Stevens-Arroyo.

This unconscious system is characterized by two opposite terms, contradictory, but at the same time analogous, complementary and interdependent: Sun-Moon, inside-outside, up-down, man-woman, day-night, rain-drought. This system of compensatory forces (thesis and antithesis, a kind of "dynamic monism") is evidenced in different planes: in the Yúcahu and Atabey operating deities, the archetypes of the masculine-feminine; in the *cemíes* Iguanaboína and Guabancex, rulers of the triad of *cemís* that dictated the constructive-destructive water cycle; in the mythical *caciques* Mautiatihuel and Maquetaurie Guayaba, lords of the dawn and the dead and of the east-west regions. The Taino belief system seems to have been based on this principle of duality-opposition that, at the same time, manifests a unity in itself.

The stars are part of that dialectic logic and become an analogy of the terrestrial world. By day, the solar star dominates. The sun is the transformer, the creator that is associated with nature, the *guanín* and the *cacique*. At night, the beings from the origins arise from the underworld and become stars or constellations that move through the celestial vault. Night is the kingdom of the owl and the bat, of animals that live in caves, where the Tainos believed creation originated. The Moon, linked to the serpent and the *behique* by its cycle of life-death-resurrection, is a symbol of cyclic renewal and an intermediary between night and day, just like the bright Venus that is always seen in the direction of the Sun before sunrise or sunset.

The sky-earth-underworld balance, the cosmic proportion created in the beginning by the gods, is maintained because of the continuous rotation of the stars around the central axis of creation. This orderly movement of the stars, of the mythical figures in space, forges, according to what has been said, the concept of time, circular time and cycles. And that cosmic rhythm is aligned with society, giving way to the division and measurement of time. The ceremonial plazas are a projection of the divine order in a human space; an integration of the space-time duality.

The rotating dynamic of the stars constitute for the Tainos the energy of the universe. Such energy could be creative if, for example, the balance in the unity of the Sun-Moon opposites is maintained, or it could be destructive if, as in the case of an eclipse, stars come together and cause an imbalance of the established order. Moreover, this energy manifests itself in the astral personalities that were projected in nature.

For these reasons, it was important for the Tainos to stay on friendly terms with these superhuman beings by means of rituals in order to maintain, or even try to control on some occasions, the cosmic balance. By communicating through the *cohoba* ritual with these superior entities personified in the *cemí*, the *cacique* served as the mediator, the intermediary between the divine and the human forces. Hence, the *cacique* became the center of religious and social power.

The island, the society, the village, the *bohío*, the Taino's own body, was a replica of that dualistic worldview. As such, the known world was only an opposing side of true paradise. *Coaybay* was the house and room of the dead, located for the Tainos in the Hispaniola in Soraya, a place on the island ruled by Maquetaurie Guayaba. For the Tainos, the afterworld was an idyllic world in the same mythic geography.

Therefore, there was no reason to fear death; death was simply the transition to the other world. This explains the cult of the ancestors; in a certain sense, this is how collective suicides are justified in the face of the slavery condition put in place by the conqueror or the reason why they abandoned or hanged a loved one who was about to die. Among the funerary rituals, the burial of the squatting body, in a fetal position, was accompanied by their intentionally broken (that is, dead) belongings, offerings and food for the journey to the afterlife. This is why some *caciques*, not wanting to separate themselves from their favorite wife, arranged that at his death she would be buried alive next to him.

With death, *goeíza*, the spirit of a person in this world became *opía*, the spirit of that transfigured body that inhabited *Coaybay*. They were confined to this paradisiacal place during the day, but at night they went out for walks, to eat guava, to live side by side or to celebrate together with those of their former world. People living in the former world recognized them and called them *operito*, because when they touched their stomachs they could not find their navel. For these reasons, night was feared and respected, because it was the occasion of fortuitous and untimely encounters with that other world.

This was thus the manner in which the Tainos lived before the arrival of the bearded men with swords and a cross: integrated into an ideal, mythical, sacred reality.

Rare wooden funeral urn,
Musée Bar-le-Duc, France.

Idol in cotton with a human skull on its head, from the D.R.
Anthropology and Ethnography Museum of Turin, Italy.

SIXTH PART
CARIBS:
HISTORY AND SOCIETY

CHAPTER 11

Fable and reality

While Taino chiefdoms consolidated in the Greater Antilles, groups of Kalinago or *callínago* warriors arrived on the eastern Antilles from the coasts of South America. To the Europeans, these people became known as the Caribs.

Carib invaders began a transculturation process on the islands in the Lesser Antilles as they killed the men, whom they called *igneris,* and took the Arawak women for themselves. The outcome was a society called Island-Carib by anthropologists, where men were warriors and women ended up 'conquering the conqueror' by making the Awarak language predominant among all, although men kept part of their old vocabulary when talking among themselves. In this manner, the invaders became the immigrants. Something similar occurred with their pottery. Since the pottery was made by women, the identification of caribe pottery has been an archaeological problem. Veloz Maggiolo has written that, were it not for the French chronicles, "we would have never known of the Carib presence in the Antilles by way of archeology."

For these reasons, there is no categorical archeological evidence to demonstrate the Carib intrusion in the eastern part of the Antilles. Instead, it is necessary to turn to ethnohistory, to the old documents of the French chroniclers. Due to this peculiar situation, some have thought that the Caribs were no different from the Tainos and that their attacks and their cannibalism was an invention of Spanish imperialism to justify slavery. This thesis was originally supported by Cuban Juan Ignacio de Armas in his book *La fábula de los caribes* (1884) and restated almost one hundred years later by Puerto Rican Jalil Sued Badillo in *Los caribes: realidad o fábula* (1978).

Although there is no doubt that the Europeans exaggerated Carib cannibalism, this does not rule out the existence of the Caribs or their anthropophagic practice, despite their being no categorical archeological evidence of it. The ritual of cannibalism, practiced also by other American aboriginal cultures, must be interpreted anthropologically. Nor should we deny that there were parallels between Carib and Taino cultural manifestations. Despite they being at different levels of development, both societies traced their roots to the area of South America where Carib and Arawak ethnic groups influenced one other. Moreover, some similarities can be explained by the recognition that Arawak women were a common denominator between these two cultures.

In the next chapters, we will examine the Carib culture of the Lesser Antilles in an attempt to distance it from the crude stereotype to which it has been subjected and place it in its proper historical perspective. In this way, we will complete the Antillean pre-Columbian cultural panorama and better understand the Caribs, the aboriginal people who managed to survive the impact of the European conquest and who, serving as a common factor to various ethnicities of African slaves, gave way to an interesting Antillean acculturation: the blacks-Caribs.

The origin of the dichotomy

In the first part of this book we saw that, throughout his first voyage, Christopher Columbus learned of the fear experienced by the inhabitants of the Lucayas (Bahamas), as well as those in the north coast of Cuba and Hispaniola, due to the attacks of those who they originally thought were the "people of the Gran Can."

In Cuba, the Admiral notes that these aggressors were called "caniba" or "canima;" then, in Hispaniola, he writes for the first time "caribe." Columbus even believed that the armed, long-haired indigenous people he encountered in the northeast of Hispanola could be Caribs. At the beginning of his return voyage, Columbus added another feature to the ferocity of the Caribs: these people were "human flesh eaters," and, as he understood, they inhabited the Carib Island, to the east of Hispaniola. Thus, in his famous letter to the King and Queen about the discovery of the New World, which would achieve widespread dissemination throughout Europe, the terms Carib and cannibal became synonymous. Famous authors such as Cervantes and López de Vega used these terms, responding to the custom established in the old continent.

During the second voyage, in their travels through the Lesser Antilles, both Columbus and the chroniclers Chanca and Cuneo were

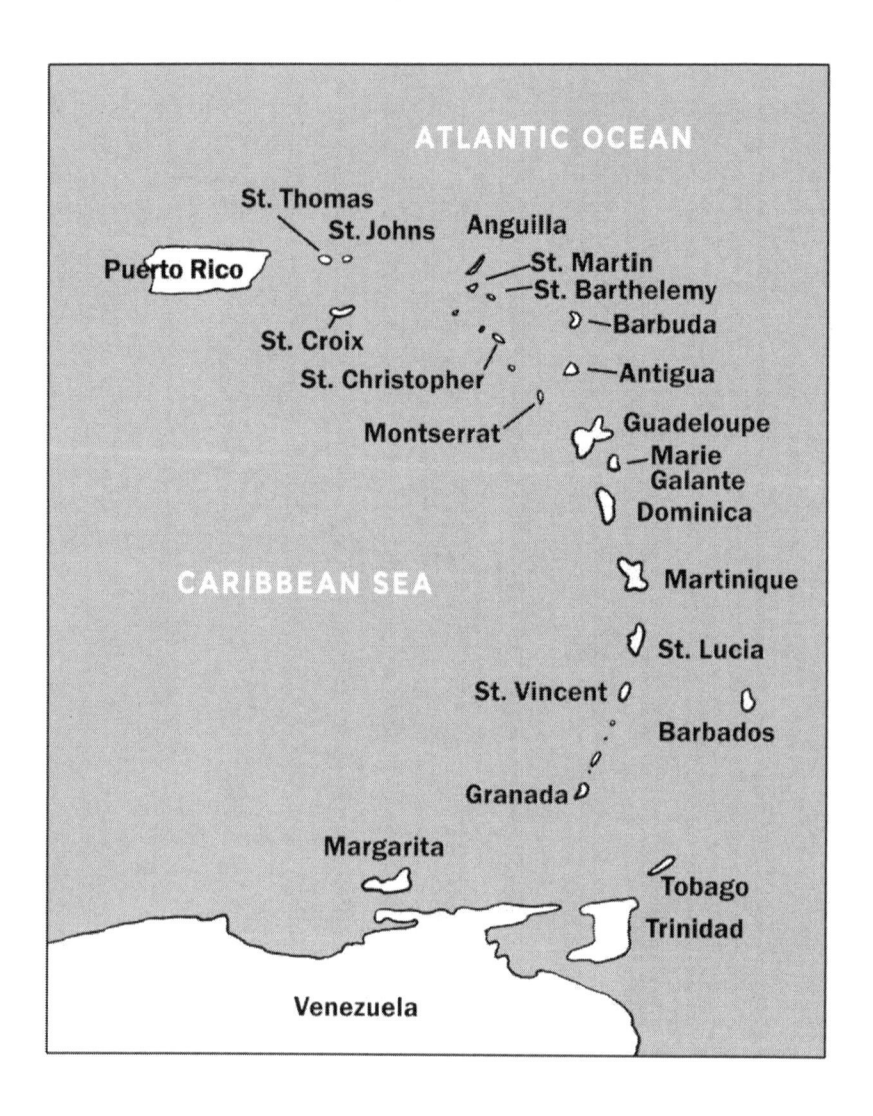

```
                ATLANTIC OCEAN
    St. Thomas
         St. Johns   Anguilla
Puerto Rico     ○ ○      ⸺St. Martin
                        ⸺St. Barthelemy
          St. Croix        ⸺Barbuda
          St. Christopher    ⸺Antigua
              Montserrat    Guadeloupe
                            ⸺Marie
                              Galante
                            Dominica
     CARIBBEAN SEA          Martinique
                            St. Lucia
              St. Vincent
                            Barbados
              Granada
         Margarita
                            Tobago
                            Trinidad
              Venezuela
```

convinced that the inhabitants of these islands were the fearsome "Carib-cannibals." And it would be on the island of Guadeloupe, where they stopped to rescue a group of Carib captives who called themselves "tayno, tayno, which means good," where the prevailing Antillean aboriginal colonial dichotomy would be established: Taino-good vs. Carib-bad.

This belief became stronger during the first years of the Spanish colonization. In October of 1503, responding to the legal mandate at the time that justified controlling barbarism, Queen Isabella the Catholic declared that rebellious and cannibal indigenous people could be imprisoned and enslaved. (Anticipating this royal disposition, Columbus captured some 300 Caribs in Martinique, upon initiating the return from his second voyage.) Later, in 1508, when Juan Ponce de León began the conquest of Puerto Rico, he learned that the Caribs had been "doing badly on the island of San Juan, as the *caciques* and Indians complained."

In the following years, several expeditions to St. Croix and nearby islands took place. These were aimed at enslaving alleged Caribs. In January of 1511, as a consequence of the rebellion of the Puerto Rican Taino people, the King himself - despite reports to the contrary - made the Caribs responsible for what happened to the Tainos, declared war on the Caribs, and reiterated that every captured Carib would be considered a slave.

As a result, any and all indigenous person that the Spanish people wished to enslave was in a short time labeled Carib; that is, cannibal. This unjustified model of conquest and colonization extended from the Antilles to South America, whose coasts frame the portion of the sea that, for this reason, became known as the Sea of the Caribs or the Caribbean Sea.

A long century of confrontations

Throughout the 16th century, Carib attacks were reported in several Spanish colonies. In Puerto Rico they occurred until 1606. Carib presence in Puerto Rico can be documented as of June 1512. This is about 18 months after the Taino uprising and the year when the destruction of several canoes allegedly belonging to Caribs is documented.

In mid-1513, some 350 Caribs landed on the eastern coast of Puerto Rico, attacked and burned Caparra, destroying the library of Bishop Alonso Manso that was considered the first in America. The attack, which some people conjecture was assisted by rebellious Tainos, resulted in the death of 16 settlers. That same year, an attack was reported in the area of the Cayrabón River (Loíza, Puerto Rico) and another in the ranch of Sancho de Arango, who was saved by his dog Becerrillo, famous for his ferocity against the indigenous people, but who was finally killed by a poisoned arrow. In the middle of September of 1520, an expedition disembarked in the Humacao River in Puerto Rico with 150 Caribs in five boats. The attack extended for

15 to 20 days, burning the structures in the area. "In total - wrote the governor two months later – thirteen Spanish were killed, a similar set of Indian women, and they took 15 native Indians captive."

The following year another attack that is poorly documented took place. Undoubtedly, one of the boldest Carib attacked occurred on October 18, 1529, when eight canoes entered San Juan Bay at dawn. As they came near the beach of Bayamón River, the Caribs attacked a boat and the structures in the area. Three blacks were killed and two were taken captive by the Caribs, who retired at dawn. A year later, on October 23, "eleven Carib canoes came to this island that could take five hundred people." They attacked the surroundings of the Daguao River, burned plantations and houses and killed the plantation owner, Cristóbal de Guzmán, and other Spaniards. Historical records document that the Caribs took with them 25 indigenous people and black slaves who worked on the farm.

Carib expeditions to Puerto Rico - as well as to other Spanish colonies - continued to be reported throughout the century. In 1534, governor Franco Manuel de Landa conveyed that the attacks took place every year. In 1546 and 1550, there are vague news of Carib incursions. In October 1564, another attack was reported. On November 23, 1567, before dawn, nine Carib canoes landed in the

Guadianilla (Guayanilla) area. Dividing forces, they attacked the structures in the area and the New Villa of San Germán.

In October of 1572, another Carib attack consisting of nine canoes with some 500 Caribs who took captive 30 blacks and many other indigenous people is known to have taken place. In 1576, the capture of the black Puerto Rican Luisa de Nabarrete took place in the Humacao region. After becoming the wife of a Carib chief in Dominica, de Nabarrete managed to escape in 1580 during a Carib attack into the Salinas area of Puerto Rico. In 1578, several incursions are reported: in July, 10 canoes attacked a sugar mill; in November, an attack resulted in 26 kidnapped black slaves.

The last Carib attacks took place at the beginning of the new century. One of these happened in 1602 in the Loíza River region, which Governor Ochoa de Castro highlights in his letter to the King with the following relevant detail: the canoes had sails, something never observed before. Another attack occurred in 1606, consisting of 20 canoes and 150 Caribs.

It is worth observing the time of year in which these attacks took place. In a letter from the Bishop of Puerto Rico dated August 11, 1531, it is established that the attacks often occurred in the months of September and October. Thus, governor Francisco de Solís, in a letter dated May 3, 1570, reaffirms that the attacks typically occurred in September and October, but that during his time in office they took place in other months. The change of pattern was perhaps the result of reactions and transformations that the Carib society experienced due to the arrival of the European. For example, the Carib attacks on Puerto Rico diminished as the presence of the French and English in the Lesser Antilles increased, eventually ceasing, as has been said, towards 1606.

During this same period, throughout the 16th century and until 1633, repeated attempts were made by the Spaniards to destroy or enslave the Caribs, and colonize the Lesser Antilles. In San Juan, it should be added, there were Carib slaves; Alegría documents the case of an important chief from Dominica, known as Pedro. For more than fifteen years his masters were so afraid that he would escape and direct an attack on the city; they sent him to the King "with his bow and arrows" so that he would decide how to handle the situation.

Some researchers have hypothesized that the Carib attacks on Puerto Rico occurred because of the Spanish presence or, moreover, as a result of an alliance with rebellious Tainos. Two facts preclude us from fully accepting either of these propositions. First, there is evidence that the Carib attacks happened before the arrival of the Spanish; second, during the colonization, the Carib attacks entailed the abduction of Tainos, to whom they would later add European and black slaves.

Some Spanish manuscripts provide valuable information in this regard. There is a letter to the King dated 1587 and written by Diego de Salamanca, Bishop of Puerto Rico, based on the information given years earlier by the aforementioned Luisa de Nabarrete. In it, he establishes - perhaps unknowingly - the fundamental reason for the Carib attacks: on the island of Dominica, the Caribs had "more than thirty people, men and women, and more than forty black slaves who they had taken from Puerto Rico" engaged in agricultural work, but they did not eat them because "they went to Trinidad to capture the Indians to eat."

And that is because the Caribs kidnapped women, then Europeans and Africans, in order to increase their production force. It was not for their cannibalistic practices, as this was a transcendental ritual that required certain characteristics be met by the men to be sacrificed.

The French chroniclers

The first information we have about the Caribs pre-date the French chroniclers and come to us from Luisa de Nabarrete, who in 1580 revealed to the authorities in San Juan her unusual experience as a Carib slave for four years in the island of Dominica. Basing himself on documents from the General Archive of the Indies, Alegría wrote a monograph on Luisa, a black Puerto Rican, in the disappeared *Revista* del Museo de Antropología, Historia y Arte de la Universidad de Puerto Rico (1980).

Almost forty years after Luisa's statements, a French commercial expedition to the Lesser Antilles led by Captain Charles Fleury suffered major hardships in Brazil and arrived in Martinique on April 21, 1619. While Fleury and his five-vessel crew did not achieve their intended economic objective, the expedition left us with a valuable enthnohistorical document.

Among the members of the crew of 350 men there was an anonymous and educated French soldier who devoted himself to learn about the flora, the fauna, and the customs of the Caribs in Martinique and Dominica for eleven months, to later write the oldest chronicle known about this island culture. This clever author has been called Anonymous of Carpentras by Jean-Pierre Moreau, who discovered, transcribed, annotated and published the unique manuscript. In contrast to later chronicles, this document was not written from the perspective of a colonialist; that is, with political, economic or religious concerns. Rather, it contains countless details of ethnohistorical significance, such as the description of an anthropophagic ceremony, and 70 new Carib words. Further, and no less important: when one compares this document with the works of the subsequent chroniclers, one can appreciate the position of the Caribs in the face of colonization.

The official French colonization of the Lesser Antilles began six years after the Anonymous of Carpentras' manuscript was written. This occurred 132 years after the founding of La Isabela in Hispaniola and 117 years after the beginning of Spanish colonization in Puerto Rico. That is to say, while the Caribs were beginning to be colonized, the Tainos had practically disintegrated.

Guillaume Coppier, who arrived in San Cristóbal in 1627, was the first and only non-religious chronicler of the century. Coppier's *Histoire et Voyage des Indes Occidentales* was published in 1645, five years after the *Relation* written by Jesuit Father Jacques Bouton based on the establishment of the French in Martinique, where he was located in 1640. In 1635, 16 years after the journey of the Anonymous of Carpentras, Dominican Father Raymond Breton arrived in Guadeloupe accompanied by three other religious men. Breton lived in Dominica from the beginning of 1641 until the end of 1653. In that span of time, he gained the respect of the indigenous population, studied their culture and learned their language better than any other missionary man. Breton then wrote ten chapters on the Caribs; the manuscript is still lost, but several other French chroniclers rely on it, for example, de la Paix. Breton managed also to publish four important works: a catechism in the Carib language (1664), *Dictionnaire Caraïbe-Français* (1665), *Dictionnaire Français-Caraïbe* (1666), and a work on Carib language grammar (1667).

Frontispiece to Rochefort's book (1658)

Before the works of Breton came to light, other chroniclers published several books: in 1646, Father Pacific of Provins; in 1647, Father Armand de la Paix, superior of the mission in Guadeloupe, probably with the help of Father Breton; in 1652, Brother Mathias du Puis and the Carmelite Maurile de St. Michel; in 1655, Jesuit Father Pierre de Pelleprat; from 1658 to 1659, the missionary André Chevillard. In 1658, Protestant César de Rochefort, doctor of law, published *Histoire Naturelle et Morale des Iles Antilles de L'Amérique*. Rochefort stresses that his book described the Caribs of St. Vincent, who "are more accurate of their ancient customs," because those of Martinique and Dominica began to alter their language and traditions after years of contact with the Europeans. This warning explains some of the contradictions between certain chroniclers.

In 1667, the Dominican Father Jean-Baptiste Du Tertre (Dutertre) published his fundamental work, *Histoire Générale des Antilles habitées par les François*. Then, in 1674, La Borde reveals his short but interesting *Relation de l'Origine, Moeurs, Coustumes, Religion, Guerres et des Caraïbes Voyages*. The extensive work of Father Jean Baptiste Labat, *Voyage aux isles de l'Amérique (1722) and Nouveau Voyage aux Isles de l'Amérique* (1724), reflect the disintegration of the Caribs by the European and the African slave.

With the help of the aforementioned works - which, with the exception of those by Anonymous of Carpentras and Breton, have been partially translated into Spanish by Manuel Cárdenas Ruíz - in the next chapter we will learn about the peculiarities of the Carib culture in the Lesser Antilles.

In the footsteps of the Caribs

The first mention of aboriginal vestiges in Guadeloupe and possibly in the Lesser Antilles comes from Raymond Breton and Armand de la Paix when in 1640 they described several engraved stones that they adjudicated to the Spaniards.

The first archaeological evidence in Guadeloupe is reported in 1805 with two skeletons found by Mathieu Guesde and Dr. Lherminier. Curiously, Guesde lived later in Humacao, Puerto Rico, where he began his collection of indigenous objects and where in 1844 his son Louis was born. Returning to Guadeloupe in 1846, he continued to enrich his collection, which he showed at the universal exhibition in Paris in 1867 along with the molded petroglyphs found in Trois Rivieres. Some of these petroglyphs were included in the paper on the Caribs presented by the *créole* historian Jules Ballet at the *First International Congress of Americanists* (1875).

From 1867 to 1884, Louis Guesde, following in the footsteps of his father, conducted research in Guadeloupe and made two albums of the objects in his collection in watercolor. One was donated to the Musée de l'Homme in Paris and another to the Smithsonian Institution of Washington D.C. Otis T. Mason later wrote a richly illustrated article on the Guesde collection in the annual report of the Smithsonian Institution published in 1885.

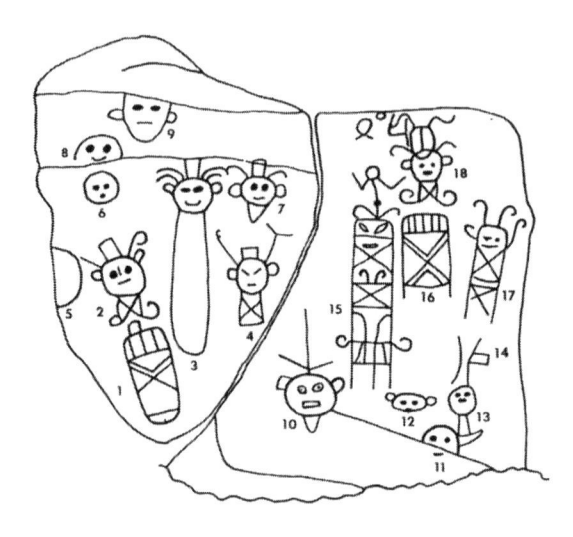

Petroglyphs in Parc Archéologique, Guadeloupe. Dubelaar (1995).

By 1880 the American ornithologist Fred Ober published *Camps of the Caribbees*, a book that narrates curious details of his visit to the Carib descendants of Dominica. This work became part of a series of articles and books about the Antilles edited by Ober.

In 1903, E.T. Hamy published a study on the petroglyphs of Guadeloupe in the *Journal de la Société des Américanistes*. And, the following year, prominent archaeologist Jesse W. Fewkes published the results of his preliminary excavations in the Lesser Antilles that continued in 1912 on behalf of the Smithsonian Institution.

From 1915 to 1929, Walter E. Roth edited his well-known research on the indigenous people of the Guianas without ceasing to refer to them as Island-Caribs. Then, between 1919 and 1922, Emile Merwart and Henri Froidevaux published several studies on the Trois Rivieres petroglyphs in Guadeloupe. In 1929, Father Joseph Rennard published in Paris *Les Caraïbes, La Guadeloupe: 1635-1656*, based on Father Breton's chronicles.

Beginning in 1931, Douglas MacRae Taylor, a British ethnologist, began to publish his field research on the Carib descendants in Dominica. Taylor's abundant work (which we will cite repeatedly) is of extraordinary value: he made note of and studied the myths, the legends and rituals, the kinship systems and social customs, the complex pharmacopoeia and knowledge of astronomy, the technique of building canoes, the games, the crafts, the practice of agriculture and fishing. From 1947 to 1948, Taylor investigated the

Black-Caribs expelled to Central America, making his findings known in *The Black Carib of British Honduras* (1951). At the same time, he contributed numerous key studies on the linguistics of the Lesser Antilles, establishing in 1961 that "the grammar and structure of the language of the islands was still fundamentally Arawak, conserving only a few Carib traits in the speech of men." His masterpiece was *Languages of the West Indies* (1977).

In 1938, Father Jean-Baptiste Delawarde published his observations on the life of the Carib descendants of Dominica in the *Journal de la Société des Américanistes*. A year later, C.H. de Goeje made public his decisive work "Nouvel examen des langues des Antilles" in the same magazine. It was Emile Revert, sent by the Musée de l'Homme in 1949, the first to excavate systematically at the Morel site (Guadeloupe). During that time, Father Robert Pinchon began his research in archeology, discovering in 1951 the Petite Riviere site (Désirade). Father Pinchon became the president of the First International Congress for the study of the cultures of the Lesser Antilles, held in Fort-de-France, in July 1961. There he presented his hypothesis that the two ancient cultures (Arawak and Carib) of Martinique were characterized by having different pottery-making techniques: with panels or with clay cylinders.

In 1951, Walter Hodge, botanist, and the aforementioned Douglas M. Taylor, published an extraordinary study on the ethnobotany of Dominica. By then, Edgar Clerc had already begun his excavations in Morel and other places in Guadeloupe, initiating in 1961 the publication of his tireless and meritorious investigations. His large collection constitutes a large part of the museum that bears his name, inaugurated in 1987, in Basse-Terre, Guadeloupe.

Since then, archaeological research in the Lesser Antilles has made decisive progress. The proceedings of the congresses of the International Association of Archeology of the Caribbean are proof of this.

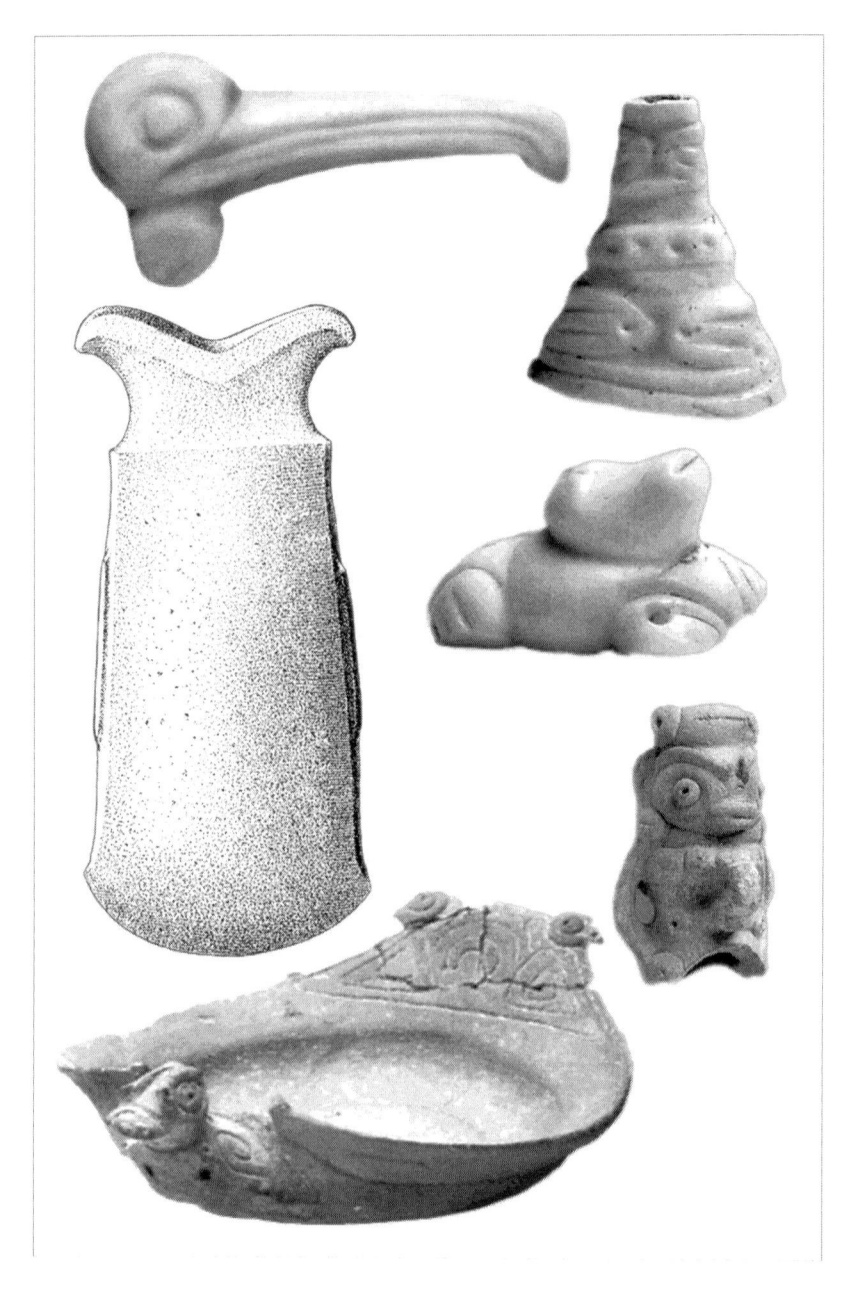

Tainos and Caribs. The Aboriginal Cultures of the Antilles

Archaeological objects of the Lesser Antilles.
Carvings in shell and pieces in ceramic Saladoid style, Musée Edgar Clerc,
Guadeloupe; typical axe with ears carved in stone, according to Fewkes (1922).

The unknown Igneri

The first archaeologists of the Lesser Antilles believed that their findings corresponded to remains of the Caribs. Today, we know that this is not necessarily true.

In chapter four we pointed out that the first settlers of the Lesser Antilles were Archaics called Banwaroides because they came from Banwari-Trace, on the island of Trinidad, and their oldest date is about 5,500 years BC. Likewise, we know that towards the year 500 BC, Agro-Ceramic groups began their entry to the Antilles from South America.

According to Henry Petitjean Roget and other researchers, the Huecoids appear in several sites in Guadeloupe before the Saladoids, and the oldest recorded deposit (450 BC) of the Lesser Antille is in Hope Estate (St. Martin). In general, the existence in the Lesser Antilles of three "Saladoid layers" is well established: island (0 to 350 AD), modified (400 to 600 AD) and terminal (600 to 800 AD). In the modified Saladoid, the pottery emphasizes the decoration with white and red, and curvilinear incisions. In this period, archeologists report "pierres à trois pointes" or small three-pointed stones. The diet changes towards an increase in the consumption of marine conchs. In the terminal Saladoid, the pottery becomes coarse, painted only in red and black. Some archaeologists postulate that the end of the Saladoid is due to the arrival from the south of a new style called Caliviny (name of an islet south of Granada), that finally gives way to the period called Suazey.

According to Irving Rouse, the old Saladoid series becomes the Troumassoide series around 500 to 600 AD (equivalent to the beginning of the modified Saladoid) in much of the Lesser Antilles. This coincides with the time period in which the Saladoids in Puerto Rico began their transition to Ostionid. Rouse argues that the Troumassoide around 1000 AD gives way to the Suazoid series, named by the Suazey site in St. Vincent and the Savanne Suazey site in Granada. This new series showcases for the most part course pottery, although a small amount of the pottery is of fine design. There is also a variety of artifacts and ritual objects of Ostinoid-Chicoid influence.

For his part, Louis Allaire has shown that, in a certain part of Martinique, the Suazoid pottery abruptly disappeared around the year

1450. This archaeological question finds a probable explanation if we turn to ethnohistory. It is feasible that the Suazoids of the Lesser Antilles - who served as intermediaries between the Tainos in the center of the Antilles and South America - were the Igneris, those ancient island inhabitants whose men the Caribs claimed to have annihilated, according to the French chroniclers. The Igneris women, abducted by the Caribs, continued to manufacture pottery in the new villages probably influenced by the South American Cayo Complex, such as Arie Boomert has suggested.

The unique juncture of cultures in the Lesser Antilles teaches us that a cultural manifestation such as pottery does not necessarily respond to the dominant ethnic group and that, therefore, ethnohistory is decisive in helping us solve the unknowns posed by archeology. Hence, the great merit of interdisciplinary studies.

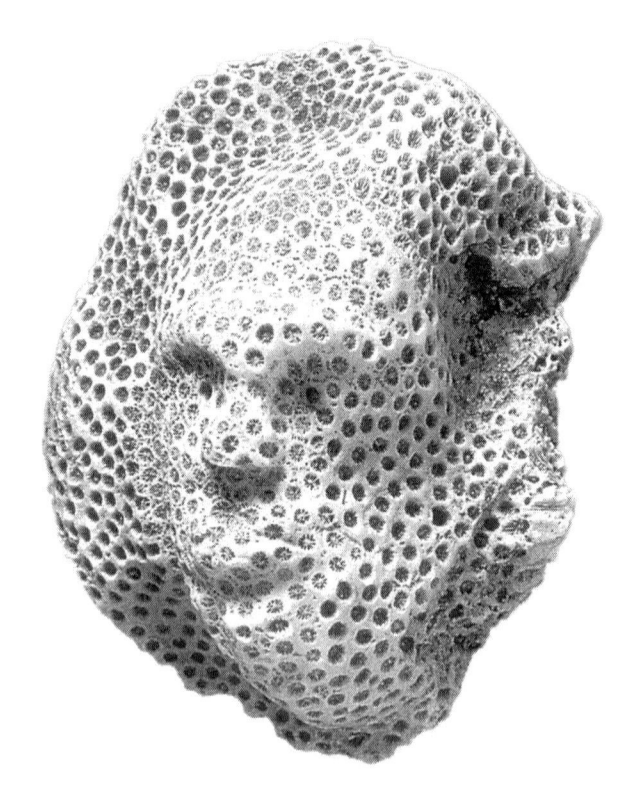

Human head carved in coral. Anse à la Gourde, Guadeloupe
(Delpuech, 2001).

CHAPTER 12

Two societies in one

In spite of what we have said above, it is difficult to establish when the continental Caribs arrived in the eastern part of the Antilles. It is very probable that a gradual, island by island, immigration occurred. In any case, by the time the European made contact it seems that Tobago, Grenada, St. Vincent, St. Lucia, Martinique, Dominica, Marigalante and Guadeloupe were under Carib control, while Monserrat, St. Kitts and St. Croix were beginning to be raided. Estimates indicate that at the beginning of the 17th century there were at least 10,000 inhabitants in the Lesser Antilles, including approximately 3,000 in Dominica, the most populated island.

The fact that the first French chroniclers heard the story of the Carib's origin and arrival from the Caribs themselves is an indication that the oral tradition had neither disappeared nor become myth, as was the case with the Tainos. "The only thing that can be inferred is that they are descendants of the peoples closest to the islands, which are those in the mainland, which is totally true," wrote de la Paix, consistent with later chroniclers. And he added: "They are called, namely, Kalinago, according to the language of men, and Kaliponam according to the language of women."

Du Puis and Dutertre also wrote *kalinago*. Breton, meanwhile, wrote *callínago* ("c'est le veritable nom de nos Caraïbes insulaires; sont ces cannibales et anthropophages"…"les femmes les appellent *callíponan*"), noting that the plural was *calinagoium*, the "old name they gave themselves." Later, Rochefort employed the terms *calinago* and *callíponam*. This is why the South American Caribs are called *kaliñas* or *karinyas*. As Columbus noted during his first voyage, *canibe* (later converted into a cannibal) and *caribe* were the names given to the man-eating indigenous people by the Tainos of the northern coast of Cuba and Hispaniola. It is curious that the *caraïbes* were shamans endowed with exceptional messianic power and therefore considered semi-gods by the Tupinamba people of Brazil, according to the old French chronicles written by André Thevet and Jean de Léry.

There is no doubt about how the Caribs settled on the islands: in the beginning of the French colonization, among the old inhabitants of St. Kitts, "it was known publicly [...] that the natives had been captured or killed by the *galibis*," [the Caribs of Guiana, known in this manner by the French], wrote Du Puis. Pellerat, similar to other chroniclers, wrote: the Caribs "made war, several centuries ago, to the *iñeri* [also written *inibis, igniris, iñiris, igneris*], former inhabitants of the islands, and [...] killed all men and all children, preserving women and girls, according to the custom of the savages of these regions." It was even mentioned that some *Igneri* survivors had taken refuge in the mountains of the islands. La Borde affirmed: "The old savages have told me that they come from the *galibis* of the mainland, neighbors of the *aluages* [Arawak], their enemies [...] and that they had completely destroyed a nation in these islands, with the exception of women, who they had taken for themselves, and that is the reason why the language of men does not resemble that of women in several ways."

Therefore, the social structure in the Lesser Antilles consisted of two societies in one. That is, a society composed of two ethnic groups of different origins: that of continental Carib men and those of *Igneris* or Island-Arawak women. Black and European slaves were incorporated later.

The woman: force of production and reproduction

Jesuit Jacques Bouton was the first to emphasize that the women of the Caribs "are unhappy and treated as slaves" because they had to "do the work of the gardens, the housework and everything, except war, fishing and hunting."

This observation was reaffirmed by later chroniclers. The women, as soon as they woke up and bathed, began to grate the manioc and prepare it for the men; then they combed the men's long hair with oil and annointed their bodies with *surúkuli*, a red paint made of *roucou* (*Bixa orellana*), that protected them from the sun and insects. This body paint was also used by women.

Later in the day, some women went to work in the gardens (originally called *moanna* or *maynabou*) while others stayed in the village making pottery, hammocks or spinning cotton, among various other domestic activities. Women were also in charge of raising the children

Carib woman, watercolor by C. Plumier (1688)

until they were initiated as warriors or became fertile women. When a young girl became a woman, she retired to a small hut with her hammock, where she fasted on dry cassava and water for ten days.

As the chroniclers noted, a large part of the females came from the Carib way of capturing women during their attacks against their eternal enemies, the continental or island *aruagues* (Arawak). The captives, called *oubéerou*, according to Breton, integrated themselves to the functions being performed by other women, but, contrary to these, were distinguished by not wearing "a type of knitted cotton boot on the leg itself ... from above the ankle up to the calves." This ligature that was tied to the legs was one of the distinctive features of Carib women, as Chanca also noted in 1493.

Captive women could become wife of a Carib man. And although she remained a slave, her children were considered free and Caribs. A black captive could also become a wife. The children begotten in these relationships were called *chibárali*. We have already referred to the case of Luisa de Nabarrete, a 19-year-old freed slave of Puerto Rico who was kidnapped in a Carib attack in 1576 and who became the wife of a Carib chief in Dominica. In contrast, many Carib women would later procreate with African refugees in St. Vincent, giving rise to the black-Carib culture.

Following matrilineal kinship relationships, the women married their crossed first cousins-brothers (*yapataganim*), that is, the children of the maternal uncle (*akátobu*). The fact that the cousins considered themselves brothers made some chroniclers think that the Caribs were married between brothers. This kindship wife (*yenérery*) became the preferred one, even if the man later had other women, as it happened among the principals. Yet, any man could ask a father (*bába*) and mother (*bíbi*) for a woman's hand in marriage. In such cases, the suitor had to prove that he was capable of building a house, fishing and hunting. Likewise, the parents offered their daughters (*niananti* or *nirahei*) as a reward to the warriors who had shown their bravery and cunning in the war excursions. Having several women was considered a great social prestige. Usually, the marriage (*yuelleteli*) consisted of the presentation by the parents of the daughter to the young suitor at a dinner between the couple with the food supplied, as all food always was, by the woman.

When she married, the woman did not leave her parents' house; it was the man who moved to the family nucleus of his mother-in-law (*imenuti*). This matrilocal practice, however, changed to patrilocal when the woman married a Carib chief or her son, because then she was taken to the husband's house by her father and mother. Even then, the husband only spoke with his wife's father, mother or brothers in extraordinary occasions. In the case of the death of her husband (*nireti*) - as Chevillard wrote - the woman became the wife of her brother-in-law and cousin on the mother's side (*nikeliri*), a practice that anthropologists have called "sororato."

Except for occasions in which she participated in communal ceremonies or cohabited with the husband, the woman led a life completely independent of the man. She ate with her children (*nirahei*) and the other women, while the men ate in the communal house (*tabui*), called *carbet* by the French. However, some women accompanied their husbands on expeditions to prepare food. To all this, when the husband had suspicion of infidelity, he could kill his wife without her father being angry. Quite the contrary, if he had another marriageable daughter, he promised her immediately.

Apparently, women, who were "more slaves than partners" as Rochefort wrote, had clearly defined production and reproduction functions in Carib society.

The raison d'être of men

As a result of the enslaving position of women, Carib men were branded as "wonderfully lazy" or "extremely lazy" by the French. However, in this tribal society, men had a series of occupations in daily life, perhaps considered less arduous than those of women.

When they were not on war missions, the men, after getting up at dawn and bathing in the river, met in the *carbet* to talk or play the flute (made of the bones of their enemies or wood), while the women prepared breakfast. After the women combed their hair and painted their bodies, some men went fishing in the sea or in rivers; others cut and burned trees to prepare the planting area, built or repaired houses, manufactured certain types of woven baskets *(paniers* and *catolis)*, wooden seats, small tables made of fiber *(matutus)*, and sieves for manioc flour *(ibichets)*. Some men made cotton belts, feather crowns, and various types of ropes. Special attention was given to the manufacture of their weapons: bows *(chimala)*, six different types of arrows *(chiribali* was poisonous) and *boutou* or *butu (amoulitanum*, in Carib), the large flat macana polished in hard wood and curiously adorned in its handle. "The most diligent men - Dutertre writes - are engaged in making canoes."

Above all, the raison d'être of the Carib man was to become a brave warrior and a fearless navigator. This was the only means of gaining prestige, recognition and power in society. According to the Anonymous of Carpentras, there were three "degrees of honor" to be "capitaine," that is, *ouboutou* or *ubutu*, as written by Breton and Rochefort.

The first grade - only reported by Anonymous - was achieved at 9 or 10 years old in a *courana ouiycou* (called *caouynage* by the chronicler), which was a feast or communal assembly held in the *carbet*. This ceremony was called "vins" by the French given how much *uicú*, the intoxicating drink regularly made from manioc and sweet potato fermented in water, was served. In this feast the parents presented the son, who stood in the middle of four arrows nailed to the ground. Then, an old warrior pronounced a *harenga* inciting him to have courage and never to forgive any enemy; then, he received a bow with arrows and a necklace of small gourd filled with the bones of enemies. The future warrior began then to eat with men and become a skilled archer.

The second "degree of honor" occurred when the young man was around 15 or 16 years old. If the young man passed this initiation, in which some died, he became a Carib warrior. The ceremony is discussed by chroniclers such as de la Paix, Chevillard, Rochefort and Dutertre, although certain details vary with respect to the older description offered by the Anonymous of Carpentras, perhaps due to alterations in the ritual suffered over the years.

Prior to the ceremony, the neophyte had to previously capture and feed a bird of prey called *anana* by the Anonymous, or *mansfenis*, *manfenit* or *mancephenil* by others, and *uachi* by La Borde. This bird was a species of local *guaraguao* (*Buteo platypterus*) and was the Antillean substitution to the giant harpy eagle (*Harpia harpyja*) of the Guianas, a celestial bird of masculine-solar symbolism.

Then, the parents called a great feast. On that day, the young man sat in the middle of the assembly. After telling him what his warrior duties were, making him promise that he would not do anything against the glory of his predecessors and that he would avenge himself with all his strength from the enemies, the father or an old warrior would beat the bird with blows on top of the young man's head. Then, his entire body was teared apart with an *acoulari*, an instrument composed of a sharp tooth of the rodent called *agouti* (*Dasyprocta* sp.) attached to a wooden handle.

The sacrificed bird was then submerged in an infusion of chili pepper grains and passed over the wounds of the young man without him showing any signs of pain. Next, he was made to eat the heart of the bird so that he would gain more courage. Finally, he would lie down in a hammock on a small cabin far from the village, where he fasted typically for the length of a moon. The physical separation of the candidate is common in all rites of initiation.

Carib warrior with *butu* or *boutou,* watercolor by C. Plumier (1688). *Mansfenis,* celestial bird sacrificed in the warrior initiation ceremony.

During this period of marginalization, the candidate departs from his normal existence by accepting a series of prohibitions regarding food and movement. While this stage takes place, the candidate is marginalized, outside of society and out of time. These tests represent the death of the previous status. Only after these tests are overcome is the candidate reborn socially as a Carib warrior.

The third "degree of honor" mentioned by the Anonymous of Carpentras was achieved before conferring the Carib warrior title to the son of an *ubutu* ("capitaine") or an experienced warrior. In short, the candidate had to submit himself again to a rite of marginalization ("*rites de margé*") in a secluded hut, fast for two months, receive certain blows from other future classmates, sleep on a pile of stones, to receive in the end from the oldest of the principals among the Caribs, in a great festive assembly, the following symbols of his rank: a garland of parrot feathers, a flute made from the bone of an enemy's leg, and other objects. Other than Anonymous, no other chronicler mentions this ceremony, indicating only that the title was obtained by inheritance or by the recognition of warrior prestige.

In sum, ascent in the Carib social structure - reserved exclusively for men - was obtained, rather than by inheritance, through specific sacrifices in initiatory rituals characterized by extensive fasting, corporal punishments and demonstrations of value in war-like confrontations. The war erased, after all, any privilege of birth. The chronicles also indicate that the title of *ubutu* was conferred only to men of age, never to young people, so there was a kind of gerontocracy. However, the authority of the *ubutu*, as we shall see, was restricted.

The dynamics of Carib society can be compared to a circular process. The man had to become a warrior because the moral essence that sustained the society was to revenge against his ancient Arawak enemies. This was only achieved by means of military expeditions in canoes that allowed them to capture, in nearby islands and far away lands, women (and then Europeans and Africans) to reinforce production and reproduction, and enemy warriors that allowed them to carry out the main communal ceremony in which they revalidated and reaffirmed their social values.

Time of peace or how to prepare for war

The activities of the Caribs were grouped around two seasons: when the men resided in the islands (January-July) and when they were on war excursions (August-December). We will see that this annual cycle was governed by a complex calendar, consisting of constellations closely linked to their mythology.

For now, it is worth highlighting some Carib customs observed by French historians during peace time, when men inhabited the islands and performed the aforementioned tasks. Caribs practiced a well-defined, gender-based, and unbreakable division of labor, which is a characteristic of tribal societies, about which La Borde went as far as to write that men "would die of hunger rather than prepare cassava."

A curious tradition involved abstinence carried out by men as a result of the birth of a child. This practice is called *couvade* (from the French "couver," "incubar" in Spanish), because when the woman gave birth, it was the husband who complained of pain, rested and submitted to a strict diet. It seems that this custom did not exist among the Tainos.

If the newborn was the firstborn male, the ritual was more extensive. The husband retired to a small hut where, lying in a hammock, he fasted for up to three moons. In the first days he ate only dried cassava and water; then he could drink a little *uicú*, the fermented manioc drink. However, only the center of the cassava cake was eaten. The edges were kept and hung for the feast that was celebrated at the end of the fasting period. On the day of the feast, the subject was taken to the village plaza where he was placed in front of two large white cassava. Then, despite his weakness, his whole body was torn with *agoutí* teeth and rubbed with chili water, and he could not express a moan. With the spilled blood, he rubbed the newborn's face to stimulate his courage. Next, the elders distributed among the participants the pieces of cassava that the faster had kept, while he was fed and given something to drink. For other children, the fast lasted no more than four or five days.

But there was still more: for the next six moons after the delivery of any male child or while he was tender and weak, the father refrained from feeding on certain animals because he believed that the son would reflect the characteristics of the animals he ate. Breton was informed that if turtle was eaten, then the son would be slow and heavy; if eels were eaten, then he would have a long snout, if parrots and manatees were consumed, then he would grow to have small eyes. The Caribs believed that all the fasting and abstinence magically completed shaping the body and character of the newborn son.

In contrast, the woman returned to her daily work the day after giving birth. Away from her husband during pregnancy, she would not have sexual intercourse until about six months later. From the day of a child's birth, the mother began to press the forehead of the creature little by little with her hand, creating the typical craneal deformation of the Caribs. Fifteen days later, the child was given a name and the nose and lower lip were pierced. In the case of a male child, this name could be changed later when he was initiated as a warrior, or it could be added to upon the exchange of names with a friend, or he could adopt a new name upon the sacrifice of an enemy warrior. After one year, the father held a party called *eletoaz* in which he would cut his son's hair entirely.

Adult men and women in Carib society went about completely naked and wore their hair long. This was not the case with the captives. For this reason, long hair was another characteristic feature of the Caribs, contrary to the Tainos who, according to Spanish chroniclers, wore their hair short. Sometimes Caribs held their hair in braids; men could use feathers. They were adorned with different necklaces: some made of shell beads, others made of green stone beads obtained in South America. Bird wings, *agoutí* teeth or a whistle made of human bone were hung as decorations. The most esteemed jewel, however, was the *caracoli*, the *guanín* of the Tainos, with a half-moon shape and placed on a piece of precious wood. They hung it from the ears, the nose or the neck. They said that they got them from the *aluagues* or *araguacos* (Arawaks), their continental enemies, or from further away even, perhaps through the exchange of slave women, as historian Adam Szaszdi Nagy has suggested.

Due to the island ecosystem, Caribs fed primarily on crabs, turtles and their eggs, certain marine conchs such as the *burgao* (*Cittarium pica*) and the *ottabou* (*Strombus gigas*), as well as fish and birds. They ate nothing boiled, but roasted or smoked. They did not use salt either, but a sauce (*tomali*) made of chili with manioc juice. Agriculture was based on the slash and burn system and the work that men performed during their stay in the islands. It does not seem that sowing on mounds of earth was used as an agricultural technique, as in the case of the Tainos.

Among the crops tended to by women, the main one was the manioc (*kiere*) for making the daily cassava. Sweet potato (*mábi*), tannia (*chou*), corn (*anási*), and pineapple (*kuráua, ananas*) were also cultivated. Various wild fruits were consumed, such as guava (*oriapa, ualíapa*), papaya (*abábai*), carob (*caouhari*), jobo (*oúbou, monben*), and ausubo (*bálata*). Among the infinity of plants and trees that had utilitarian purposes were the gourd (*camoury*) used for utensils, a poisonous herb (*conami*) used for fishing; *allougati* used to make strings; the candlewood or tabonuco (*chíbou*), the cedar (*chimalouba*), and the ceiba (*comaca*) used for the construction of boats.

As for medicinal plants, Breton cited at least 19 aboriginal names. The magical-medicinal plant *par excellence* was *toúlála* (arrowroot, *Maranta arundinacea*), later called in French "l'envers tête chien" because of the belief that it had been obtained from the Great Serpent. From the arrowroot, Caribs prepared a nutritional flour (*sagú*), an antidote for poisonous arrows, and a talisman against Maboya, the evil spirit. Rochefort reported that they ate sea turtle or manatee to protect against syphilis; for skin rashes, they used the bark of a tree called *chipiu* that they diluted in water inside the large *ottabou* shell. For cutaneous infections, they composed remedies with the ashes of certain burned shrubs "that they dilute in water collected in some leaves of the stem of the bamboo." The juice of *quenepa* (*Melicoccus bijugatus*) was likewise used. Baths were quite common and they were prepared with a diverse set of plants. Women - reported Dutertre - used a kind of fungus to get pregnant, while a kind of reed with aromatic smell was used to give birth.

To eat, they commonly used grouds of "higüero" that they called *cuys*. These were carved, polished and painted by men "as delicately as possible." The Anonymous of Carpentras distinguished them by their size and use: *lita*, where they placed meat or sauce; *rita*, the largest, used to store water; *taba*, the smallest, used as a glass. Perhaps the *dita* of the Puerto Rican peasant comes from these words.

The need to cook the cassava, prepare and store the ingredients of the chili sauce or the fermented drink, involved the use of ceramic utensils. As has been emphasized above, pottery was made by women. Breton and La Borde confirmed this. In fact, research conducted on the French chronicles has allowed us to establish about 15 terms related to Carib pottery alone. As the words are probably of female Arawak origin, they provide a glimpse of a possible Taino pottery vocabulary that was not recorded by the Spanish chroniclers.

Lastly, the clay was called *teútéli*, like the pots in general. Hence, the pottery-maker was called *Ategoútimun*, "maker of pottery," according to Breton. *Bourrélet* was the thick round dish used to cook cassava; this word seems to be the origin of the Taino term *burén*, still in use today. *Canali* or *canari* was the great urn of four or five feet in diameter, with a pointed bottom, where the *uicú* (also written *ouirou* or *ouecou*) was prepared. The *iucú* is the manioc drink that was served in the bowl called *chamácou* or *taólöüa*. In another bowl named *iáligali* the fish was roasted, while *loura* was a pot used to prepare some kind of drink. Sweet potatoes were cooked in the *roüra*. The *toumalacai* (Anonymous), *tómayhiem* (Breton), and *tomali-akae* (Rochefort) corresponds to the bowl where women made the typical chili pepper sauce (*tomali*) that accompanied all food. Apparently, each container had a specific use - perhaps magical - in the preparation of food.

In short, it can be said that the Caribs used ceramics to produce food, and materials made with "higüero" to distribute and consume food. And it would be in the *caouynage*, the great communal festive assembly, where the Carib tableware would be put to use and where the next attack against their enemies would be decided.

Matoutou, canari or *canali* (La Borde, 1674).

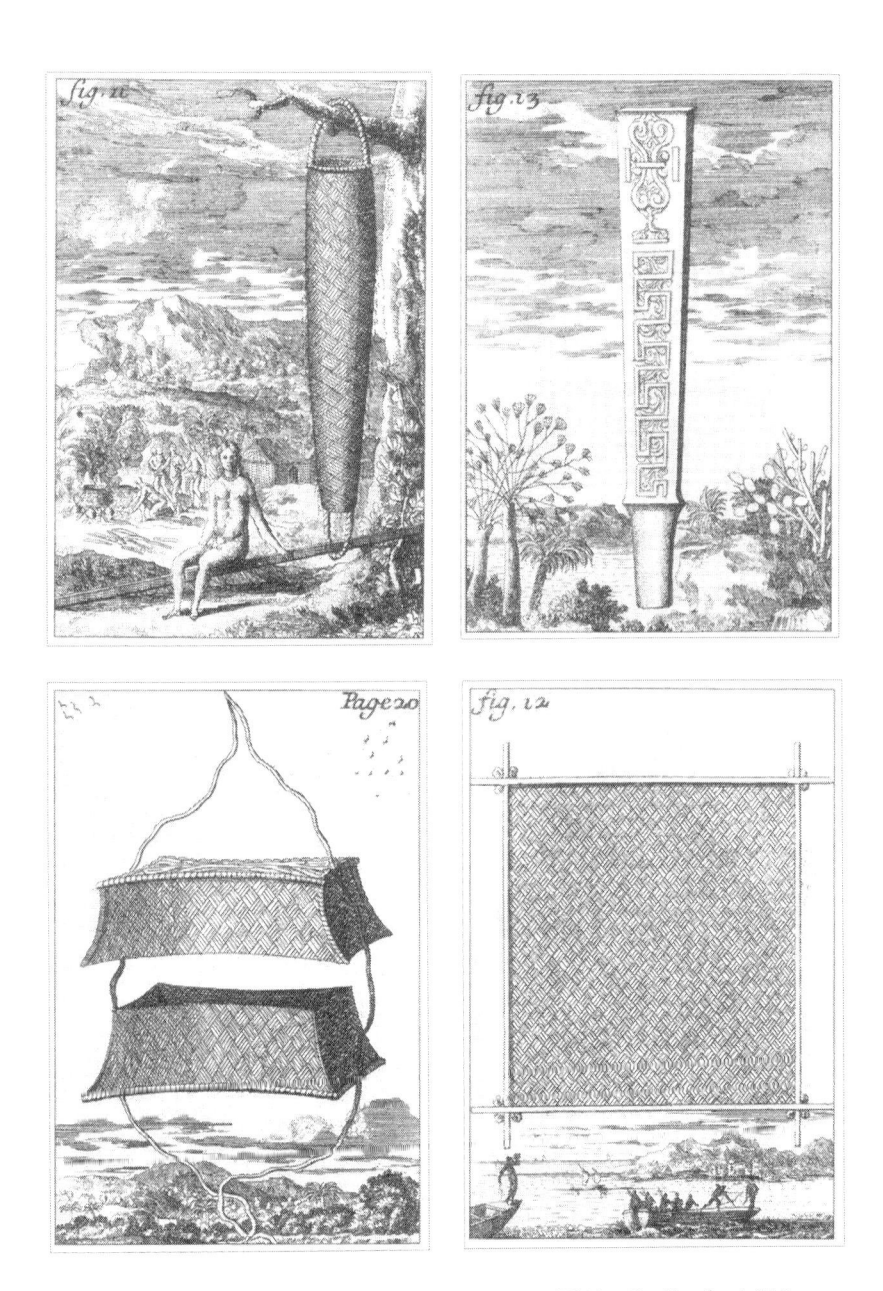

Top to botton: *mátabi, boutou* or *butu, panier, hibichet* (La Borde, 1674).

Island-Carib camp for interchanging goods with the French.
Engraved by Sébastien Leclerc (Dutertre, 1667).

SEVENTH PART

CARIBS: FROM SLAVERY TO ANTHROPOPHAGY

CHAPTER 13

A slave society

In the previous chapter, we proposed that the Caribs were a dual society in regards to both their ethnic origin and how they divided labor between the genders. Men, whose goal was to become great warriors, controlled the power structure subjecting women to a type of slavery.

The arrival of Europeans and Africans brought a new dimension to Carib society. The Caribs began to take captive people who stopped over their islands as part of their journeys and whose vessels shipwrecked on their coasts. And, as we have seen, they were quick to kidnap colonizers and black slaves in their attacks on the Spanish colonies. Contrary to what many people believe, these captives were not sacrificed in a cannibalistic ritual. Rather, they were used to supplement the production force provided by women traditionally. In this manner, the Caribs created a heterogeneous slave society. This practice developed to the point that the Caribs had, in the early years of the 17th century, approximately two thousand European and African slaves in the Lesser Antilles, or 20 percent of their population, according to historian Jean-Pierre Moreau.

Luisa de Nabarrete, the black Puerto Rican woman who in 1580 and at the age of 23 declared to the authorities of Puerto Rico that she had managed to escape the Caribs, was a witness to the Carib slavery system. She reported that the Caribs kidnapped "a lot of blacks" who they would then distribute among the Carib-dominated islands. In Dominica, where Luisa was the wife of a Carib chief, she had seen "more than forty black slaves." She had several acquaintances among the Spanish captives in Dominica, which totaled "more than thirty people, men and women." She told authorities that there was "a white young man, son of Domingo Pizarro;" and that, from a group of "six women and ten to twelve men" taken from a Spanish ship, there was a woman named Juana Díaz.

According to Luisa, some of the captives "were as Carib as the Caribs themselves" given the many years they had been enslaved, and that they "do not remember God anymore... and eat human flesh and do as they are told, without argument." She also spoke about a practice that was confirmed later by the French chroniclers: when a Carib slave master died, some of the slaves were killed "so that they could serve him" in the afterlife.

García Troche, the son of Juan Ponce de León II (also known as Juan Troche Ponce de León) and great-grandson to the conqueror of Puerto Rico, was the best-known Carib captive identified by Luisa de Nabarrete. In 1569, he was presumed dead during his father's attempt to colonize Trinidad. Luisa's revelations motivated Ponce de León II, together with the governor and the bishop, to ask the king of Spain to organize an expedition to rescue the Spaniards and bring back an alleged treasure in gold. The expedition, however, did not take place. The final fate of Ponce de León's great-grandson and his companions was never known.

Etiquette and protocol

Any internal discord and tautness among the Caribs balanced itself out during the *caouynage*, the festive assembly in which men, women and children participated. Given the variety of reasons why it was celebrated, this communal activity occurred quite frequently. In some ways, the Carib *caouynage* was equivalent to the *areíto* of the Tainos.

The *caouynage* was summoned by the *ubutu* (chief) of the village. The women organized the tableware, prepared a lot of cassava and a large quantity of *uicú*, the intoxicating drink, while the men brought fish and iguanas to eat. On the appointed day, men and women painted their entire bodies in different colors and designs. The men adorned themselves with crowns of feathers, *caraçolis* and necklaces. Others smeared sticky liquids on their bodies to then blow loose feathers over themselves.

About 200 or 300 people gathered in the *carbet*. There they celebrated the birth of a male firstborn, the son's haircut or his initiation as a warrior. They also celebrated the preparation of an orchard, the capture of a turtle, the construction or launching to the sea of a canoe. The event, which in some cases could last eight days, served also to commemorate the appointment of a captain, the formation of a council to go to war, or the celebration of the return from war. Participants sung and played the flute of bone or wood (*couloura*), accompanied by maracas and certain drums made from a hollow tree.

The *carbet* was also where the Caribs tended to their European friends (mainly French), relatives or representatives from other villages. The protocol manager was called *niuaketi*. When foreigners visited, the *niuaketi* welcomed them to the village and directed them to the *carbet*, where they were received kindly by the *ubutu* and the rest of the community. The first sign of affection was the exchange of names with a guest, who was called *banari* (a pal, buddy, or mate); then they made the visitor rest in a hammock, women combed his hair, and then each visitor was served food and *uicú*. Afterwards, the Caribs showed the visitor their homes, weapons, curiosities and, finally, they said goodbye with signs of sadness.

If they were visited by an *ubutu* or a relative, they would also hang a hammock and serve him food and drink. The women stood at his feet and the men showed him the food while standing next to him. The placement of the cassava was dictated by the hierarchy of the visitor: if the visitor was important the cassava was displayed, meaning that he could eat it and take the remainder home to eat; for others, cassava was folded, meaning that he could eat it and leave the remainder. Once the guest finished eating, he received a welcome from each warrior.

The courtesy and kindness with which the Caribs treated their friends impressed some chroniclers even more than the cruelty they employed against their enemies.

A chiefdom in gestation

Carib villages - separated from one another by about half a league - had a *carbet* or communal house about thirty per one hundred feet long, its only entrance was facing east, and the straw roof fell almost to the ground. Around the *carbet* they built "up to 50 oval houses in straw" (*muena*) for married couples and relatives of the "captain" of the family and they called them *tiubutuli hothe*, according to Rochefort. Unlike the Taino *cacique*, the Carib chief did not occupy special housing and his authority, based on kinship relations, was limited to his village.

The Carib who directed the construction of a canoe and who was typically elected to lead it when they went to war, was called *tiubutli canaoa* (*noubacáboüenoucou*, according to Breton). Rochefort added that they also chose an "admiral," called *nhalene*, who commanded the expeditionary fleet. They also elected a "great captain," called *ubutu* (*ubutunum* in the plural), an adult of great prestige as a warrior. Rochefort gave the name *cacique* to the *ubutu*, an error that Dutertre criticized because "neither the savages nor most of the French" had "heard mention of this name." The main function of the *ubutu* was to summon the assemblies in the *carbet* for the village to decide on the war missions; he was always accompanied and when he spoke, everyone listened attentively. He had an assistant, called *ubutu maliarici*, the "captain's trail."

Importantly, the chroniclers emphasized that among the Caribs there was no established authority, that "captains" had authority only at war, and that their power ceased as soon as they returned. From an anthropological perspective, these characteristics are typical of a tribal society or an "undivided society," according to anthropologist Pierre Clastres. That is to say, a society that maintains the power among all of its members.

Given the incessant state of war against the Arawaks and the increasing presence of the European, alliances formed between Carib villages on the same island and between islands. Some of the *ubutus* distinguished themselves and acquired prestige due to military successes, thereby extending their influence, through polygamy, to other towns and nearby islands. Over time, these bonds allowed for decisions to be delegated and authority to be centralized on certain leaders. Undoubtedly, war forged hierarchy. Hence, some "captains" that were known to the French, such as Piloto in Martinique, Ukalé and Kalamiena in Dominica, became the ideal candidates for the emerging Carib chiefdown system.

Despite all this, these Carib leaders lacked something that their Taino counterparts had. The Caribs were outstanding warriors and navigators, but they did not have the divine connection that the Taino *caciques* possessed. That divine connection gave the *caciques* the authority in political and economic matters, and allowed them to control the ideology of their subordinates.

The spirit world

If in Taino chiefdoms the social hierarchy was legitimized because it was considered to be a reflection of a divine hierarchy, the opposite occurred in Carib tribal society: the absence of a defined social hierarchy did not demand the existence of a model divine pantheon. In other words, as there was no ruling class, there were no commonly accepted deities. To this we add the different ethnic backgrounds of the men and women who lived among the Caribs. The result was an animistic and individualistic conception of the world in which each person had a personal protective spirit. This is why Rochefort wrote that "when each person speaks of their personal god, they say *Ichetriku*, which is the word of men, and *Nechemeraku*, which is that of women."

In general, men called the soul *akambue* and women called it *opoyem*. *Opoyem* seems to be related to the Taino *opia*, the soul of a person after death. More specifically, men called the spirit that performed good deeds *Icheíri*, which is why Breton interpreted that *Icheíri Iouloúca* was equivalent to God; for women, the spirit that performed good deeds was *Chemyn* or *Chemijn*, words that by their Arawak origin correspond, without a doubt, to the *cemí* in Taino.

On the contrary, the spirit that caused upsets or disruptions was common for men and women; it was called *Mabouya*, *Mapoya* or *Maboya*. To be sure and despite the arbitrary dichotomy created by Christian chroniclers between "good" and "evil" spirits, *Maboya* did not necessarily equate to the Christian devil. For the Carib, a spirit could be good or bad depending on its behavior.

As Rochefort and Dutertre noted, *Maboya* was a spirit that originated from one of the three "souls" present in the human body. After death, the main spirit (*Yuanni* or *Lanichi*) that resided in the heart, moved to the other world, a place that chronicler St. Michel said was in a distant region to the west. Rochefort wrote that, if the deceased had been a courageous warrior, his main spirit went to idyllic islands where there was abundant food and all time was spent in dances, games and parties with Arawak slaves. In contrast, if the deceased had been a timid warrior, his main spirit would go to a desert region where Arawak enemies reigned.

The second spirit, called *Uméku*, was located in the head and went after death to the edge of the sea to wreck boats. The third,

Maboya, resided in the arms and moved after death to the woods becoming the Spirit of the Forest. There - according to Taylor, who managed to collect this information among the Carib descendants of Dominica - *Maboya* dwelt in the *guano* or balsa tree (*Ochroma pyramidale*). Taken in sum, the Caribs believed that one of the three spirits transformed into *Maboyas*, the "evil spirits to which they attributed everything sinister and ill-fated."

The shaman was in charge of the spirit world and was called *bóyez*, *boyez* or *boye*. The shaman was a well-known person who was respected and distinguished by all, and had decided to dedicate to this practice since youth. The consecration of a new *boyez* occurred also in the *carbet*, where a small opening (*tourar*) allowed the nocturnal entrance of the *coribib chemin*, the messanger bird of the afterlife and of the ancestral spirits, identified with a species of owl (*Spéoyto cunincularia*) whose song was a sign of bad omen or death itself. Bats occupied the opposite position, "those that they call *bulliri*, who fly around their houses at night, are *cemíes* because they protect them, and will sick anybody who does them harm," according to La Borde.

In the *carbet*, Caribs placed an offering of fresh cassava and *uicú* in new bowls over a small table (*matutu*) for the veneration of the family spirit. The elder *boyez* conducted a ceremony in the dark, sang mournful songs, blew tobacco smoke, and entered into a trance in the middle of the *carbet*. Lying on a hammock, he presented the offering while he began to ask for "a god for whom he wishes and who is very purified because of the rigorous fasting." This god manifested itself as a man "and if it is a woman, he gave a female god that manifested herself as a woman." Rochefort added an important detail to his account of the shaman: "each *boyez* has a particular god [...] who he invokes while singing words accompanied with the tobacco smoke." De Puis mentioned a *boyez* who had inherited one of two "gods" from his father.

As a tribal shaman, the *boyez* was the controller of the spirits, more so than of the gods. His interventions were requested in four circumstances: to cure an illness, to avenge a wrong received from someone, to decide the appropriateness of a war or to succeed in expelling an evil spirit. When a relative became ill, they did not visit him because they believed that this could afflict him even more. As for the healing ceremony performed by the *boyez*, it was very similar to that of the *behique* among the Tainos: they rubbed, blew and sucked the sick part of the patient to extract the spirit that caused the disease.

Coribib chemin, the messenger bird of the afterlife for the Island-Carib. Illustration of a ceremony carried out by the *boyez* (Lafitau, 1724).

Unlike the *behique* who used the *cohoba* and *güeyo*, the *boyez* smoked tobacco and, "squeezing it in his hands, he blows it up like raising it with both hands" or "takes it in his mouth, and throws it into the air in puffs" to invoke the presence of his protective spirit.

It is curious that with the exception of tobacco, no French chronicler mentions the use of hallucinogenic substances among the Caribs. The descriptions of the use of tobacco do not establish with certainty that it produced effects similar to those experienced by the Tainos with the *cohoba*. Perhaps this is because in Carib society religious ceremonialism never reached the level of sophistication that it did among the Tainos. Moreover, there is no reported elaborate religious activity among the Caribs, nor the existence of temples or sacred figures. The only offering of a religious nature noted by the chroniclers is the offering of cassava (*anacri*) and the first fruit harvest that each villager could perform in their home.

The single communal ceremony that united the main ideological values of Carib society was the sacrifice of an enemy warrior.

The nautical warriors

Beyond being warriors, the Caribs were men of the sea. The sea played a large role as a food source and was the only means to fulfill their war mission. The Caribs were, therefore, nautical warriors.

The Caribs had two types of boats adapted to the island environment. The smallest boat (*cohala, culiala*) was for coastal use and did not exceed more than six meters (20 feet) in length and one meter (three to four feet) in width. The largest boat (*canobes, cannüa*), the one the French called *piraguа* or canoe, was about 15 meters (50 feet) in length and about two meters (five to eight feet) in width, and could carry 50 to 60 persons. The large canoes were used to travel between the islands and on distant journeys. Due to their common South American origin, the canoe construction method was the same as that described for the Tainos: they patiently hollowed out a trunk with stone axes (they later used iron) and controlled the fire.

Boats were built from three possible straight trees. One was called *chibou*, "gommier blanc" in French or *tabonuco* (*Dacryodes excelsa*), from which they also extracted a fragrant resin. Another was the *chimalouba*, "acajou blanc" or cedar (*Cedrela odorata*), from which they made the side boards to "increase the height of the edge of the canoe and thus be able to withstand the great waves of the high seas," as Breton wrote, a characteristic exclusive to Carib canoes. Lastly, from the *comaca*, "fromage d'hollande" or *ceiba* (*Ceiba pentandra*). The Caribs believed that the Great Spirit of the Trees lived in the gigantic *comaca*, which was why it could be knocked down only when the spirit was absent. This happened at the beginning of the year when the tree lost all its leaves to give them the signal. Breton noted that the oars were called *nenene* and that they were lined with the rough skin of the shark (*ouaibayaona*).

Before, during and after the construction of a canoe - an activity for men exclusively - a series of ceremonies was held: a *caouynage* to summon its construction, a ritual to choose and knock down the tree, and another for its launching to the sea. The women had to stay away during the entire construction process; they believed that the canoe would crack if touched by women at any time.

The French chroniclers regularly mentioned the use of cotton-woven sails or leaves of a certain palm, which has made it possible to postulate that this technique was known by the Caribs before the arrival of the European. However, Anonymous of Carpentras shed light on this problem as he pointed out that the use of sails was learned from the Europeans. You will recall that the governor of Puerto Rico reported in 1602 the presence of Carib canoes with sails for the first time. Another source reported that three years later, Father Blasius, a Franciscan, obtained his freedom from the Caribs by teaching them the use of the sail.

The Europeans were impressed, for good reason, by the nautical skills of the Caribs. They were surprised that Caribs sailed from 200 to 300 leagues to attack their enemies. To accomplish this, the Caribs used their ample empirical knowledge - together with their animistic beliefs - to predict the weather conditions by observing the shape and movement of the clouds, the color of the sky, the direction of the wind and the waves, and the behavior of the birds, as compiled curiously by Dutertre.

Anonymous of Carpentras was the first to note that the Caribs "are guided according to the sun and the stars and their trajectory, and they show us a large and varied quantity of stars, that is almost unbelievable." Bouton later wrote: "they go from island to island and foresee with sufficient certainty the bad weather and the storms based on their inspection of the sky and the stars, of which they have wonderful knowledge." And Coppier added: "even when they have no compass [...], they do not cease to navigate, taking their route by looking at the trajectory of some stars, of which I have not been able to have knowledge despite having studied it." Years later, Breton recorded the names of eight stars or constellations and La Borde highlighted the position of the stars in the Carib worldview.

Later, we will see that certain stars or constellations marked the time for Caribs to start navigation, to attack their enemies, and to celebrate the anthropophagic ritual.

Round trip to dry land

After residing in the islands for about seven months, Carib men returned for about five months to the warring activities that allowed them to exercise their raison d'être: to attack their enemies on other islands and distant lands. As we have seen, the endemic state of war had an ideological and an economic function: to feed the cannibalistic ritual with victims and to reinforce the production force with slaves, particularly women.

Before embarking, a festive assembly was held to decide on the war expedition. The elder women first addressed those present remembering the affronts and damages that their former enemies had caused them; they recounted how the enemies had killed or taken prisoner their relatives and, in the midst of the excitement produced by drinking, demanded revenge. Then, the *ubutu* pronounced another compelling and emotional pep talk (*caramento*), extolling his military prowess, to obtain the support of the warriors.

Once the expedition was approved, the elder men talked to one another in some gibberish that only they understood to agree on the secrets of the mission. In order to establish the time of departure, they usually distributed bowls with a number of seeds equal to the days remaining; thus, each morning they discarded a seed. This period probably did not exceed 20 days, because this was the highest number used by the Caribs and counting was achieved by using the fingers and toes. We also know that they kept track of the days by looking at the moon.

During the waiting period, the men prepared their bows and arrows - which, as is known, were poisoned with the sap of the *paraboucoul* (manchineel, *Hippomane mancinella*), the *guao* or *guchón* of the

Tainos - and the *butus* or hardwood macanas that were two to three feet long and three fingers wide, with elaborate engravings filled with white paint. The women prepared the provisions, including manioc flour. Messengers were also sent to neighboring villages to invite them to join the war. However, no one was forced to participate.

On the agreed day of departure, the warriors and the chosen women left on the canoes. A typical expeditionary fleet consisted of 8 to 10 canoes, with an average of 500 warriors accompanied by the women they needed to cook and serve them. They fed themselves in the islands they passed and more canoes could join them then. Luisa de Nabarrete, who said she participated in several expeditions, said that on one occasion there was an "armada of fifteen canoes, five from Dominica, five from Marigalante and five from Grenada, that went to Trinidad Island to take indians to eat."

Carib seamen held fast a number of beliefs during their journey: they did not eat crabs or iguanas, because they thought that the animals that lived in holes prevented them from reaching the other shore; drinking water could not be dumped in the canoe or at sea, since it would produce bad weather; when passing through certain places, they threw food to sea because some Caribs had perished there and needed food to live; if they saw a cloud of bad weather, everyone blew to drive it away; to calm a storm, they chewed cassava and spit it skyward to please the angry spirit.

When arriving on land, generally in the area of the Guianas, the strategy was to send spies (*nábara*) to learn the enemy's situation. The attack had to occur at a precise cosmic moment: "they wait (I do not know why) for the moon to be in the perpendicular, that is to be in its fullness," observed Dutertre. Father de la Paix wrote that they always attacked at dawn and that they fought "more agreeably under the full moon" and Chevillard pointed out that they never fought in the open field, but by surprise "shortly before dawn, or else in the moonlight."

In fact, the best documented Carib attack in terms of its date, time and location, occurred on October 18, 1529 around midnight in San Juan Bay. The full moon was at its zenith, as we have confirmed using a computerized astronomy program.

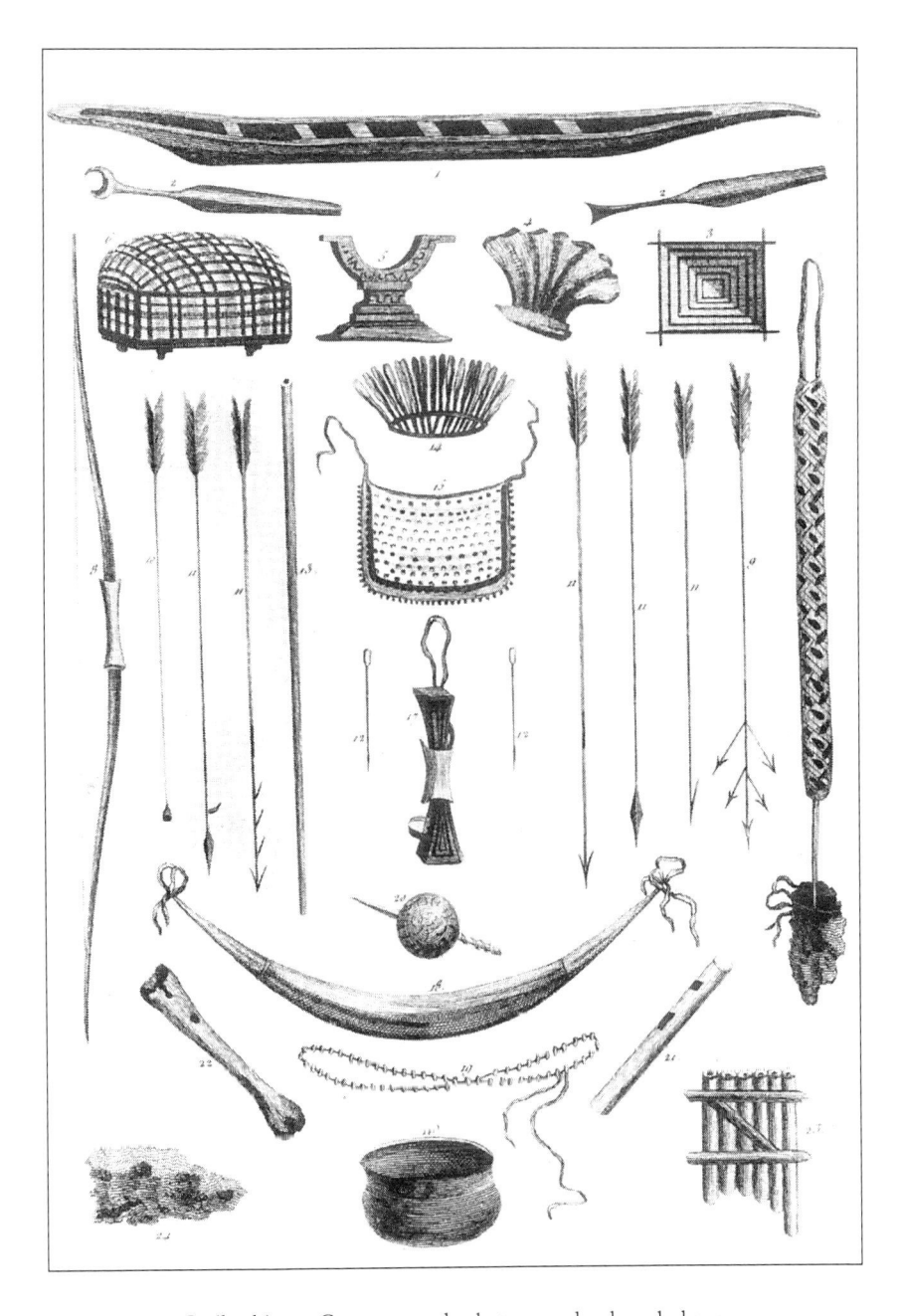

Carib objects. Canoe, oars, baskets, wooden bench, bow, arrows, ornaments, cassava squeezer, hammock, musical instruments. *Narrative of a Five Years Expedition…*, John G. Stedman (1796).

If all elements favored them, Caribs attacked a village by surprise with their bodies painted black with dye of *jagua* (*Genipa americana*), giving horrible and frightful cries to create fear. But, if they were discovered before an attack, they surrounded the village and threw arrows with burning cottons to burn the houses and force the enemy to leave. Then, they attacked with arrows and clubs. Several chroniclers claim that the enemies killed in the confrontation were roasted and eaten at the site. To prevent this from happening to their dead comrades, they never left the body of a Carib at the mercy of the enemy.

It is worth mentioning Dutertre when he synthesized the purpose of any Carib attack: "They never seize their enemy's land; all wars have no other purpose but to exterminate them, in revenge for the insults they believe they have received. They take the women as prisoners and destine men to death without remission and women to slavery."

Having captured women and enemy warriors, the Carib fleet returned triumphantly to their islands. This ended a cycle of eternal revenge, until another one began.

Island-Carib couple next to a *papaya* tree, resembling Adam and Eve.
Engraved by Sébastien Leclerc (Dutertre, 1667).

CHAPTER 14

The cannibalistic ritual

Although the main French chroniclers of the 17th century mention the cannibalistic ritual of the Caribs, it was not known in detail until Anonymous of Carpentras' manuscript was published in 1990. Let us synthesize the ritual itself.

The captive warrior (*tamon*) had his hair cut off, since long hair was a distinction of the Caribs. If the captive was very young, he was assimilated into the daily life of the village until he was between 18 and 20 years old. For about five or six months before the sacrifice, the captive was fed and he drank everything he wanted while resting in a hammock. (Later chroniclers, in contrary, point out that the captive underwent an intense fast, possibly some time before sacrifice.) To all of this, the captive showed no sign of fear or sadness.

On the selected day of the sacrifice, the warrior who had captured the victim celebrated a great night feast with all villagers. The attendees adorned themselves as usual: everyone painted their bodies with *rocou* or *rucú*; the "captains" wore crowns of feathers on the head and ornaments on the arms and waist; on the legs, they wore garlands made of shells. In their hands, some "captains" wore a *boutou* and others a long staff adorned with parrot feathers. Everyone, including the captive, drank the intoxicating *uicú*.

Once drunk, they paraded with the captive around the village. They had the captive sit in a small chair and offered him drinks continuously. The women surrounded the captive dancing and singing repetitively: *"Tamon Tamon éhé éhé, Tamon Tamon éhe éhe."* The children followed the women; that is, the children joined the women in the ceremony and later left the ceremony with them. Then, the men approached the captive and, hitting the ground with the stick, formed a semicircle and sang the same refrain for a long time. Meanwhile, they drank and gave the enemy to drink, while insulting him. Those who had the *butus* threatened to hit him repeatedly; until one of them - probably the captive's master - surprised him with a fatal blow to the head.

Next, the oldest "captain" butchered the body and gave the young people the parts to be roasted on the *boucan*, barbecue or wooden grill. At dawn, everyone eagerly ate the slaughtered man. They reserved nothing but his private parts (which were thrown into the sea), his skull (which was thrown into the ashes and then kept as a trophy of great merit), and the bones of the legs that were used to make flutes.

Rochefort and Dutertre added other important details to the valuable description by Anonymous of Carpentras. Rochefort wrote that the fat of the sacrificed man was distributed among the principals, "who receive it and carefully preserve it in small gourd so that they may pour some drops into sauces on solemn feasts, and thus perpetuate as much as possible the food of his revenge." Dutertre emphasized that the victim showed courage by remaining calm during the ceremony and that he even provoked his victimizers by showing pride in having eaten other Caribs in the past, assuring them that his parents and friends would avenge his death.

Dutertre added other details: the bravest ate the heart, women the legs and thighs. Each participant took a roasted portion to their house and kept it there to be eaten in another occasion. In Martinique, Dutertre saw a roasted leg "as dry and hard as wood" and Caribs believed eating it "would make them very brave." He concluded with a very important observation: "They eat this meat more out of rage than appetite, to get revenge and not to feed themselves, for they do not find pleasure in its taste, since most of them get sick from this abominable food."

Despite the ethnohistorical documentation, no categorical human remains have been found in archeological digs to document the Carib anthropophagic practice. If it were not for the French chroniclers, neither would we know of the presence of the Caribs in the Lesser Antilles.

Why anthropophagy?

Misunderstood, badly exaggerated and maliciously manipulated by the European conquerors and colonizers, Carib cannibalism needs to be analyzed in its proper context. Above all, Carib cannibalism was not intended as a practice to consume human flesh. The French chroniclers themselves realized and confirmed that it had another meaning.

The sacrifice of an enemy warrior was the central ritual around which and for which Carib society revolved. It was the apex of the annual cycle of festive rituals, the feast of feasts. All social activities were oriented towards that moment, a communal climax. It is only through this lens that we can explain the extraordinary effort deployed by Caribs through time and space to capture enemy warriors in order to sacrifice them ritually.

While strict and demanding rules existed for the rituals that took place when Caribs were home, no such limits existed when they were at war. The type of cannibalism practiced when an Arawak village was attacked and a dead enemy was eaten in battle, was without ritual. Yet, the objective of the Carib attack was not cannibalism, much less territorial conquest. An entire social context was at play during war raids. For the Caribs, the feat of greatest merit and honor was to capture an enemy warrior alive and bring him back to the village. The Carib man was communally recognized among his people for the capture, but he had to donate the enemy to the community for a sacrifice from which everyone would benefit.

Further, the captive had to meet certain requirements and undergo an initiation process. He could not be less than 18 or 20 years old. This was perhaps a guarantee that he was a warrior or had the age to be one. There was also a period of time during which the captive lived in community with the Caribs. They believed this was the time when the prisoner attracted to himself the tensions, hatreds and grudges accumulated by Carib society. At all times - even at the moment of sacrifice - the captive had to behave like a proud enemy; otherwise, he would be considered unworthy of the death that awaited him. The captive had to see in his sacrifice crowning proof of the courage that a warrior of his ethnicity had to face with dignity. He accepted his destiny because he was convinced that his death guaranteed him a place in the afterworld and that he would soon be avenged by his own people.

Ritual cannibalism is the response to a complex ideology that we intend only to sketch here. Due to the parallelisms between the cannibalism of the Caribs and that of the Tupinambá of Brazil, it is worth mentioning the analysis of the latter done by the French anthropologist René Girard.

Stages of the anthropophagic rite, based on the Tupinambá of Brazil
(Theodor de Bry, 1557).

For Girard, "a victim is not sacrificed in the cannibalistic ritual to be eaten, but eaten because he sacrificed himself." That is, sacrifice - as in the case of the Caribs - does not have a material, but a symbolic, end. Girard interpreted the adoption of the enemy warrior in the community as a representation of the myth of origins, since "in the eyes of those who practice it, the ritual of cannibalism is a repetition of a vital event." It is tribal warfare with members of other ethnic groups (exogamic). It allows "a displacement of internal violence towards the outside" and, thereby, "prevents violence from being unleashed where it does not have to."

That is why the prisoner must go through a process of social assimilation: the victim comes from the outside, "from the undifferentiated sacred. He is too foreign to the community to be immediately sacrificed. You have to give him what he lacks, a certain belonging to the group. You have to turn him into a creature of the 'inside' without snatching, however, his quality as an 'outside' creature." The captive must, therefore, show "through his courage, that he is really the embodiment of violence." In this manner, when the victim's flesh is consumed after the sacrifice, "once the evil violence metamorphosizes into a beneficial substance," it becomes "a source of peace as well as good vitality and fertility."

More recently, Isabelle Combes conducted a complex analysis with ethnohistorical documentation on the cannibalism of the Tupi-Guarani in South America. Christian Duverger, in his study of Aztec anthropophagy, conveyed that, to understand the human sacrifice, "the sacrifice *par excellence*," we must recognize that the body hides a potential source of energy that can be released. Inevitably, this "vital energy" is released with death. Therefore, ritual anthropophagy is the liberation of that energy in order to acquire it through the ingestion of the sacrificed body. Duverger sustained that human sacrifice is an artificial rupture of the natural process and that, however abhorrent it may seem, is not an act of pure cruelty because it is entirely sacralized ritually.

Similarly, Peggy R. Sanday, after studying anthropophagy worldwide as well as various anthropological, psychological and sociological hypotheses that try to explain it, concluded that the cannibalistic ritual entails "messages that have to do with the maintenance, the regeneration and, in some cases, the bases of the cultural order."

In conclusion, cannibalism could only be performed if the sacrificed person was an enemy warrior. The practice constituted a very important ritual of religious character and social function. Communally, it allowed Carib people to remember the myths of origins, to pay homage to their ancestors, to avenge enemy insults, to redeem the lives of Caribs killed in battle; in sum, to maintain and reaffirm traditional values and social cohesion.

At the individual level, the anthropophagic ritual was the ideal means for the Carib man, the controller of the society, to acquire the warrior spirit of the sacrificed enemy. It was because of this belief in the animistic principle that allowed Caribs to magically absorb the essence and spirit of animated bodies, that Caribs never practiced cannibalism with women or consumed animals whose characteristics they rejected. Carib cannibalism answers to male dominance and the warrior purpose of society.

Acáyouman: the father of the lineage

We now explore the extent to which Carib cannibalism had a cosmological component related to *Acáyouman*, an important mythical character.

According to the legend documented by Breton, the first "captain" who led the Caribs from the mainland to the islands was "small in body, but great in courage," exterminated all the natives except for the women, and ordered others to save the skull of their sacrificed enemies to preserve the memory of their conquest for later generations. Breton, however, was unable to record the name of this first "captain." It is other chroniclers who offer such detail. Father de la Paix added that this historical character established himself in Dominica: "There, he had many descendants and the children of his children lived, it was them who by extreme cruelty poisoned him." He became a "monstrous fish" that they called *Akeuman*, he "who still lives in a river full of life." Du Puis and Dutertre essentially repeat the same narrative, although they call the "large fish" *Akayoman* or *Atroiman*.

Akeuman, *Akayoman*, *Atroiman* correspond to the word *acáyouma* that meant "cayman," as Breton registered. Curiously, the cayman did not exist in the Lesser Antilles. This ambiguity explains why the other chroniclers interpreted that *Acáyouman* was a "horrible looking fish" that lived in their river. Having said that, there is no doubt that such name, and its association with fluvial matters, originated in the South American continent. *Acáyouman* seems to be related to *Okoyumo*, the aquatic spirit owner of fish for the continental Caribs. Further, one of the myths of origins among the continental Caribs narrates that Sun was the owner of the fish and Cayman was entrusted to their care. But Cayman eats the fish and, as punishment, Sun injures Cayman with cuts along his back, forming scales. In exchange for his life, Cayman promises Sun his daughter, who he carves out of the trunk of a *jobo* tree. She gives birth to twins, where Caribs come from. Since then, Cayman hides in the water.

As can be glimpsed immediately, there is a South American myth that explains the Carib legend about the origin of their system of kindship. We think that *Acáyouman* is the island equivalent to the continental mythical Cayman, who at the same time was associated with "the World Tree (*ceiba*) and the Milky Way", according to Peter

Roe. As such, it carries with it an astronomical connotation that none of the French chroniclers documented.

When we consult the Carib vocabulary compiled by C. H. de Goeje, we can divide *Acáyouman* into the prefix "*aká*", "*ká*" that means "luminary, sky" and the suffix "*-yumu, -yuman*" that means "old, father, spirit, constellation." Therefore, *Acáyouman* can be translated as "the spirit of the old father in the sky," "the spirit-constellation of the father" or, more to our point, "the constellation of the father of the lineage." Now, the assertion that *Acáyouman* "still lives in a river full of life" gives us the key to decipher this enigma. In many myths documented in the Guianas - and in the Carib islands, as it turns out - the Milky Way was conceptualized as a Celestial River that communicated the sky and the earth. It can then be understood that *Acáyouman*, as father of the island-Carib lineage, was visualized in the celestial vault in the form of a "monstrous fish." That is, in the mythical Grand Cayman known in South America. The Celestial Cayman was then where "the spirit of the old father" lived in the middle of "his river full of life," the Milky Way. And, nearby, as we will analyze in the next chapter, we can find in the sky the constellations that represented the Carib system of kindship.

In sum, *Acáyouman* was the Celestial Cayman (the Milky Way) that was observed in the sky principally during the months of September-October. When we examine the morning configuration of the stars in the Milky Way, we notice that they look like the body of a cayman: its head is located in front of the Hyades, its torso begins to form in front of Orion and extends to the Canis Major, and its tail ends at the lower end of the Milky Way. In fact, the months of September-October correspond with the "month" that Caribs called *mubé*, the name the aboriginals gave to the West Indian *jobo* tree that bears fruit during this season. The *jobo* tree has a mythical connotation for the Caribs because it was used by Cayman to sculpt his daughter. Also, remember that in Taino mythology, asexual beings descended from the *jobo* tree before being carved as women by the woodpecker.

If Carib attacks occurred during the months of September-November (Robiou, 2009), it is reasonable to assume that there was a link between the presence in the sky of *Acáyouman*, the father of the lineage that established anthropophagy, and the beginning of warrior expeditions in canoes (mades of *ceiba*, where the Great Spirit of the Trees lived) and whose purpose was to capture enemies to carry out the ritual. In other words, the presence of *Acáyouman* in the sky was the cosmic signal to remember the original achievement.

In the next part, we will examine Carib mythical astronomy to understand how the cyclic movement of the stars and constellations formed the basis of a calendar that governed the activities in Carib society.

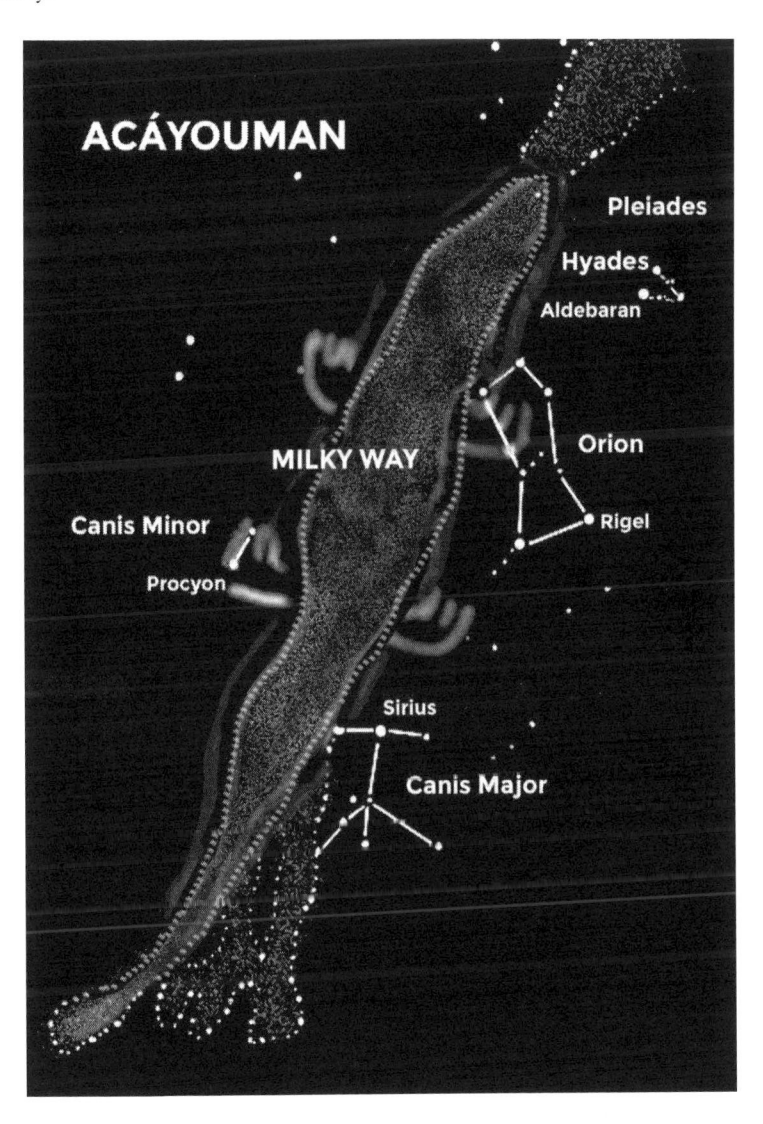

Acáyouman, the Celestial Cayman, the father of the Islad-Carib lineage, visualized in the Milky Way, according to the author.

Comaca, ceiba *(Ceiba pentandra)*,
residence of the Great Spirit of the Trees.

Sebastián Robiou Lamarche

EIGTH PART

CARIBS:
MYTHOLOGY AND COSMOLOGY

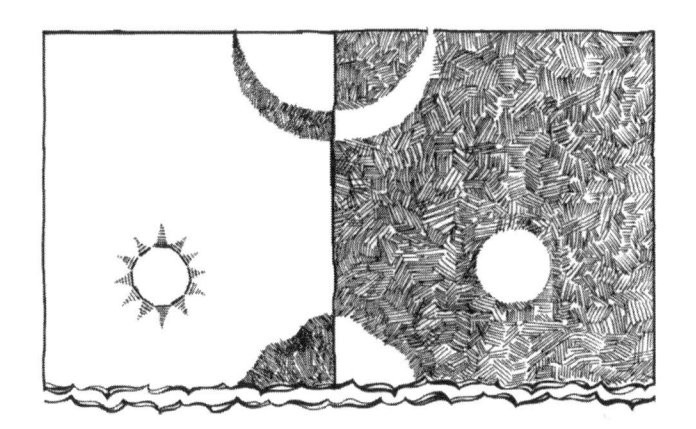

CHAPTER 15

Carib Myth-Astronomy

The chronical writings of Breton and La Borde together with the ethnological investigations conducted by Douglas M. Taylor in Dominica in the middle of the 20th century, allow us to identify fifteen Carib constellations. Some of these constellations were configured totally or partially by the light and dark areas of the Milky Way. For this reason, they are called "negative constellations."

Generally, Antillean myths associated with constellations are of South American origin. However, they underwent substitutions and transformations as they were adapted over time to the island ecosystem. Since this process did not occur overnight in the short period of time that Carib warriors inhabited the islands, it is likely that the astronomical idealizations of the people of the Lesser Antilles came from the beliefs of ancient Arawak women.

This is true despite the fact that some constellations are common to both Arawaks and Caribs in the continent. In fact, the names given to the stars by Carib Arawak women were identical or similar to the names used by the Tainos. Nevertheless, Breton regularly cited to the names given to stars and constellations by both women and men.

For the Caribs, the same celestial body could have several idealizations and meanings. We also know that, in general, Caribs observed preferably the morning stars, called *wálukuma*. They also believed that the celestial spirit of terrestrial things and the mythical heroes resided in the stars and the constellations, thus representing nature and society.

Importantly, the myth-astronomical beliefs of the Caribs reflect male dominance. As such, the constellations answer primarily to the ideology, the activities and the needs of men, as was the case for the continental Caribs, according to Edmundo Magaña. There were no large constellations related to agriculture - a women's occupation - but to the beliefs and activities of men exclusively: their mythical origin, the jobs of fishing and gathering, navigation, and the cannibalistic ritual.

The creation of the world and the stars

The short book *Relation* written by La Borde (1674) contains a valuable chapter on the beliefs of the Caribs in relation to the creation of the universe. The author himself emphasized that what he wrote "I can attest to, because of the great deal of contact that I have had with them, and for having been very curious and having taken care to inform myself."

We summarize the paragraphs that are of most interest to us, using the Spanish translation prepared by Cárdenas Ruiz (1981):

Luquo was the first man and the first Carib; he was not made from anyone, but came down here from Heaven, where he lived for a long time. He had a large navel from which he let the first men out, as well as from his leg after making an incision. He made the fish from scrapings and small pieces of cassava that he threw to sea.

They believe that Heaven, not the earth and the sea, has always existed. Being its engine and first representative, Luquo first made the land soft, smooth, without mountains. The Moon came next and she thought herself very beautiful, but after she had seen the Sun, she went to hide from her shame, and since then has only appeared at night.

All the stars are Caribs; they make the Moon male and call it Nonun, and call the Sun Huoiu; they attribute the eclipses to Mapoia, the Devil, who tries to make them die. They are fonder of the Moon than of the Sun, and in every new moon, they all leave their huts to see it from the moment she begins to appear, shouting: "There it is, the Moon." They count the days by the moons, and not by the Sun; instead of saying a month, they say a moon.

Racumon was one of the first Caribs made by Luquo. He became a great serpent and had the head of a man; he was always on top of the cabata, which is a big tree, very hard, tall and erect; he lived off the tree's fruit, which is a thick plum, and gave them to people who would pass by; now he has become a star. Savacu was also Carib; he became a crabier, which is a great bird; he is the captain of hurricanes, of lightning, and of thunder; he is the one who produces the great rains; he is also a star.

Achinaon Caribe, currently a star, produces small rain and great wind. Curumon Caribe, also a star, is who makes the great waves of the sea and overturns the canoes. He is also who, given his winds, produces the ebb and flow of the sea.

They use the Pleiades constellation to count and observe the years. They call the Sun governor of the stars and they well say that he prevents stars from appearing during the day due to his great light. They believe, however, that the stars leave and that they descend at night. Savacu makes lightning when he blows fire through a small tube. Thunder and lightning occur when the Master or captain of the cemíes shooes away the small cemíes that are not clever, and this is when they flee and fall in fear, and that is the great noise one hears; they are also the ones who make the earth tremble.

Cualina is the captain of the cemíes; Limacani is the comet sent by the captain of the cemíes to do wrong when he is angry. Juluca, the rainbow, is a cemí that feeds on fish, lizards, pigeons and hummingbirds; it is covered with beautiful feathers of all colors, particularly the head; his head is half round and only the limit is what is seen; the clouds prevent the rest of his body from being seen. He makes the Caribs sick when he finds nothing to eat there on high; if the rainbow appears when they are at sea, they welcome it and say that it comes to accompany them and secure a good voyague; but if it appears on land, they hide inside their houses and think that this is a strange cemí that has no Master, that is, Piayé [shaman].

The stellar kinship system

In the previous chapter we mentioned *Acáyouman*, the Celestial Cayman idealized by the father of Island-Carib lineage. We discussed that he appeared in the sky next to the constellations that represented the Carib system of kinship. In South America, these constellations are regularly Hyades, Pleiades, and Orion. This important mythical-astronomical structure was compiled centuries later by Taylor among the Carib descendants of Dominica. Here is his version:

Three Kings, the younger brother to Pleiades, was in love with the daughter of Bíhi, an old woman. The old woman hated the boy so much that when he laid down on his hammock, she sat on him and farted. As a result, Three Kings became ill. He then consults a shaman, who tells him what to do. One day he pretends to sleep and when the old woman approaches him, he hurts her with a knife. He runs away with his beloved, but the old woman follows him. When they take the road to the sky (Milky Way), the old woman cuts his leg. They can now be seen in the sky: the girl is the star Aldebaran of Hyades, her suitor Three Kings is Orion's belt, and the star Rigel is the mutilated leg; the mother-in-law is the star, Sirius, who still chases them with knife on hand.

Let us analyze the myth in parts. As noted by Breton, the Orion constellation was called *Ebétiouman* by men and *Mambouicayen* by women, corresponding to "Orion's belt" and the "Orion constellation, what they call the man without a leg." The name used by men is a derivation of *Epietembo*, the constellation of the mutilated or one-legged hero in the Guianas. As we saw earlier, among the Tainos, Yayael was the mutilated character; he was murdered and dismembered. As such, Yayael was most likely visualized in Orion.

In this myth, Pleiades was Orion's older brother. The Pleiades, a set of small but very important mythical stars, were called *Iromobouléme* by men and *Chiric* or *Siric* by women, according to Breton. In addition to being part of the star kinship system, the Pleiades possessed multiple meanings. They signaled the beginning of the year with their morning rise in early June ("They count their years using the trajectory of the Pleiades constellation, which they call Siric"); the term that the Caribs used to signify 'year' included the name of these stars (*chiriqui* or *chiric assoura*, according to Anonymous of Carpentras); the morning rise of the Pleiades coincided with the rainy season, the time of year when the land crab (*Cardisoma guanhumi*, the Puerto Rican *juey*, also called *Sirik* and an important crustacean in the Carib diet) was plentiful.

We should be reminded that Tainos associated the Pleiades with the frog, a symbol of rain in an agriculturally-developed society. Due to the Arawak origin of the word *Chiric* or *Siric*, it is probable that was also the name the Tainos gave to this important cluster of stars.

In the aforementioned Carib myth, *Bíhi* is the windy old woman who farts Orion, her daughter's suitor. *Bíhi* is who provokes the family conflict that results in she being transformed into Sirius. Sirius is a bright star in the Canis Major constellation that is identified with the eye of the old mother-in-law in South American mythology. Among the Island-Caribs, this constellation was called *Maliroúbana*. As *Mali* was the name given to Sirius by the continental Arawaks, we speculate that *Maliroúbana* was an Island-Arawak word.

Breton defines *Maliroúbana* as "the star of the great dog," that is, the constellation Canis Major, and stated that Canis Major, together with Canis Minor (*Maliroúbana-oporcou*, "the little dog"), were the stars that "cause hurricanes in the islands." According to Breton, Caribs were "very careful to not go out to sea when they see [these stars] rise" because they are wind stars; they also believed that the appearance of these stars was unhealthy, unsanitary. In fact, the rise before dawn of Sirius and Procyon, the main stars of Canis Major and Canis Minor, occurs in the middle and the end of July in the Lesser Antilles, so their ascension on the eastern horizon predicts the hurricane season.

Bíhi was also the name of a small land crab and a species of wild yam (*Rajania cordata*, "guáyaro", "bejuco de guaraguao" or "ñame gulembo" in Spanish) that was commonly consumed but not cultivated by the Caribs, because they believed that the family of the person who sowed it would end up broken. A fate that is turns out to be similar to that of the old farting woman's family.

In the above myth, the bride became *Aldebarán*, the main star of the Hyades constellation. There exists no historical documentation of the Carib name of this star or constellation. We could conjecture that the name *Aldebarán* was linked to *mubé*, the *jobo* tree (*Spondias mombin*). If true, *mubé* would also correspond to the name of the Carib 'month' in which *Acáyouman* was observed in the sky. In any case, *Aldebarán*, the star that became Orion's girlfriend, may have been called *Mubéyuman*, the star of the *jobo* or Celestial *Jobo*.

It would seem, in sum, that a great part of the celestial vault during the months of September and October was a canvas that painted the complex Carib kinship system. In the sky, the constellations of consanguinity (Orion and Pleiades), affinity (Canis Major*)* and ancestry (Hyades) make their appearance contiguous to the father of the lineage (Milky Way). In other words, the Celestial Cayman, the father of the Caribs in the islands, transports on his back the constellations of his ancestors, just as in life the first canoes transported the first Carib men from the continent to the islands. And it was by means of the canoe that their descendants maintained the anthropophagic tradition he established.

The Big Dipper: the heron's canoe

The canoe, one of the Caribs' most precious cultural objects, was idealized in the Big Dipper (Ursa Major), called *Lukúni-yábura* or the "heron's canoe," according to Breton.

The myth of origin of the Celestial Canoe remains unknown, although it apparently had to do with a wife who turned into a heron. The heron was called *iáboura* or *yábura* by the women. Therefore, it is likely that *Lukúni-yábura* was a constellation of island origin. *Yábura* was also another "constellation composed of small stars in the shape of a triangle, located next to the Big Dipper," according to Breton.

If we rely on a drawing given to Taylor by a Carib descendant in Dominica, the stars of this constellation are the beak or the plume of feathers of the heron, with the heron being the canoe. The *yábura*, a nocturnal hunter of crabs with several long feathers on its head as described by Breton, we have identified it with the *cabrier* or *gaulin* (*Nyctanassa violacea bancrofti*) of the Lesser Antilles, a bird known as *guanabá* in Cuba and *yaboa* in the Dominican Republic, with the latter name most likely deriving from the original Carib *yábura*.

This heron's food was represented in another small constellation located also near the Big Dipper. It was called *Túlulu*, which is the name of a small reddish crab (*Gecarcinus lateralis*) that Anonymous of Carpentras documented as *Itouloulou*.

La Borde wrote that *Savacu* was a "crabbier" (a crab-eating heron) and the "captain of hurricanes, of lightning, and of thunder." Evidently, *Savacu* was the name given by the Island-Caribs to the aforementioned crab-eating heron, as Breton recorded it as *Sawaku*.

Lukúni-Yábura, the Heron's Canoe, the constellation of the Big Dipper.

You will recall that the Tainos associated the Big Dipper with the mythical *cacique* Anacacuya, Central Spirit (Polaris, Center of the Universe), a name that appears to be related to *Anulakuya*, the "spirit of the heron in his canoe," visualized also in the Big Dipper by some continental Caribs. We have discussed that the morning rise of the Big Dipper in August could have announced the busiest hurricane season in the Antilles. This hypothesis is verified in the case of the Caribs: Breton himself reported that the entry and exit cycle of the Big Dipper in relation to the sea was considered to be the "leap of the celestial heron," which the Carib believed produced the storms and the strong rains.

Perhaps this is why the heron - with or without a crab in its beak - is a recurrent figure in Antillean rock art. The representation of the heron does not necessarily mean that the intention was to objectively draw or record a bird, but rather to capture what that bird symbolized for the aboriginal people. In this case, it is possible that the crab-eating heron - like *Savacu* – was associated with the hurricane among the Island-Caribs and the Tainos.

The Big Dipper's morning cycle around Polaris that served as a maritime-seasonal calendar for the Tainos could have had a similar purpose for the Caribs. The appearance of the Big Dipper on the horizon starting in August coincides, should a hurricane (*ioüállou*) not occur, with the most propitious time to navigate in the eastern Antilles. Therefore, the presence in the sky of the Celestial Canoe was the cosmic signal that marked the beginning of war expeditions and the time period (August-December) for Carib men to be gone from their islands. Historically, we know that Carib attacks occurred mainly in the months from September to November, a time period when, as we have seen, *Acáyouman* dominated the morning sky. When the Big Dipper reached the top position in its cycle in November, it was time for Carib men to return home. It is documented that by December "the Caribs were in their homes."

Isúla, the celestial barbecue

Carib men returned home having captured slave women and warriors and stayed in the islands from January to July. It was during this period of rest when the important anthropophagic ritual took place.

Anonymous of Carpentras provided the only known evidence that allows us to assign a timeframe to the cannibalistic ritual. In his work he wrote that when they arrived in Martinique, there was a captive in the house of Captain Louise, the principal captain of the island, who was eaten about two months later. "When we approached him, the captive showed us with his fingers how many moons he still had of life." Their arrival to the island took place on April 21, 1619, according to Anonymous, so the sacrifice of the prisoner must have taken place towards the end of June. In other words, the anthropophagic ceremony coincided with the great Celestial Barbecue (Pegasus constellation) in the top position of its cycle and with its maximum display in the celestial vault before sunrise.

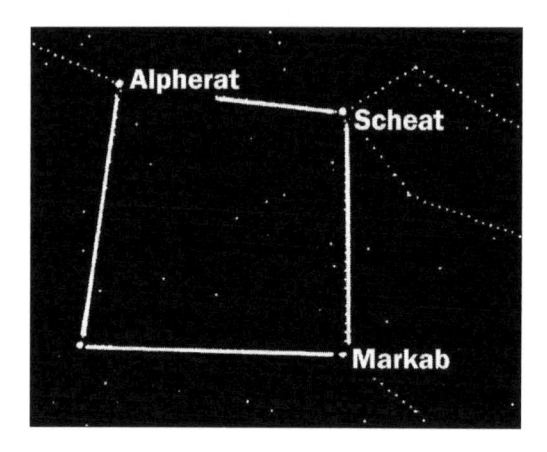

Isúla, the Celestial Barbecue, the constellation of Pegasus.

The stars Sheat and Markab can be seen in the Lesser Antilles starting in early March. These stars are the corners to the constellation Great Square of Pegasus that rises above the horizon before dawn. By mid-March, the entire constellation is over the horizon. Breton documented that this constellation was called *Isúla* or *Iúla*, a word that means *boucan* or barbecue, the square structure with vertical sticks on its vertices and in the upper part of which a kind of grill was built in to roast meat. It was at the barbecue where the torn body of the enemy warrior, ritually sacrificed, was roasted.

We propose that the presence in the sky of *Isúla*, the Celestial Barbecue, could have signaled to the Carib men the time to celebrate the anthropophagic ritual. Indeed, *Lukúni-yábura* (Big Dipper) and *Isúla* (Pegasus), although opposed in the celestial vault in time, idealized the two main cultural objects of this society of nautical warriors: the canoe and the barbecue.

Coulúmon, the celestial lobster

Anonymous of Carpentras wrote that *ychourou* was the name of a tasty river lobster whose "right clamp was as long and thick as its body." Breton documented this crustacean as "a kind of river lobster with a big yellow lever" and wrote that women called it *kulúano* and the Carib descendants *kulúmo*. We believe it corresponds to "écrevisse" in French and "crayfish" in English, which is a large, fluvial crustacean of nocturnal habits (*Macrobrachium* sp.). In Puerto

Rico, the species has several popular names in Spanish: "boquiguayo," "palancú," "rabicaña," "chiflú," "popeye."

Coulúmon was also the name given by women to a constellation, not identified by name by Breton, that was positioned a little high in the morning sky when "the sea is choppy on the coast and calm on the high seas." He added that the men called it *Oulíao*, which seems to correspond with *Uráu*, one of the Pleiades and Orion brothers among the Carib descendants. For his part, La Borde registered this constellation as *Curumon*, the star that "makes the great waves of the sea and overturns the canoes."

In 1944, an informant from Dominica pointed out this constellation to Douglas Taylor. However, the drawing Taylor made showed that he did not really see the shape of this fluvial crustacean in the sky, as described by the Carib descendant. Taylor indicated that the constellation was visible during April and that it corresponded in part to Cetus and Aquarius.

To our knowledge, the reason why Taylor did not "see" *Coulúmon* was that it was conceptualized in the Milky Way, the Celestial River, as a constellation formed by its light and dark spots. *Coulúmon* was, then, a negative constellation that could be observed before dawn from February to April: its tail corresponded to the constellation Cygnus; its body was delianeated by the long dark strip, the Great Rift of the Milky Way, extending with its great pincers, thus configured, to the Scorpio constellation. In *Coulúmon*, thus, was the Lobster of the Celestial River.

In fact, the presence in the sky of this great "negative constellation" in the months of February to April coincides with the dry season in the islands - called *isura* - the most propitious season to capture the crustacean under the rocks of rivers as there is less flow and depth. Next to *Coulúmon*, there was another constellation of stars called *Achínnao*. It corresponded to "a fish called bourse" by the French, wrote Breton. It is called "peje puerco" or "varraco" in Spanish, or old wife (*Balistes vetula*), and it is a very attractive fish that is common in reefs. La Borde used the term *Achínao Caribe* to identify a star that "produces the small rain and the great wind."

Taylor, for his part, believed that this constellation was composed of the star Altair of the constellation Aquila, noting that when it came out on the eastern horizon, it was the time of fresh winds, light rain and this fish's abundance. Thus, *Achinnao* is the Celestial Fish.

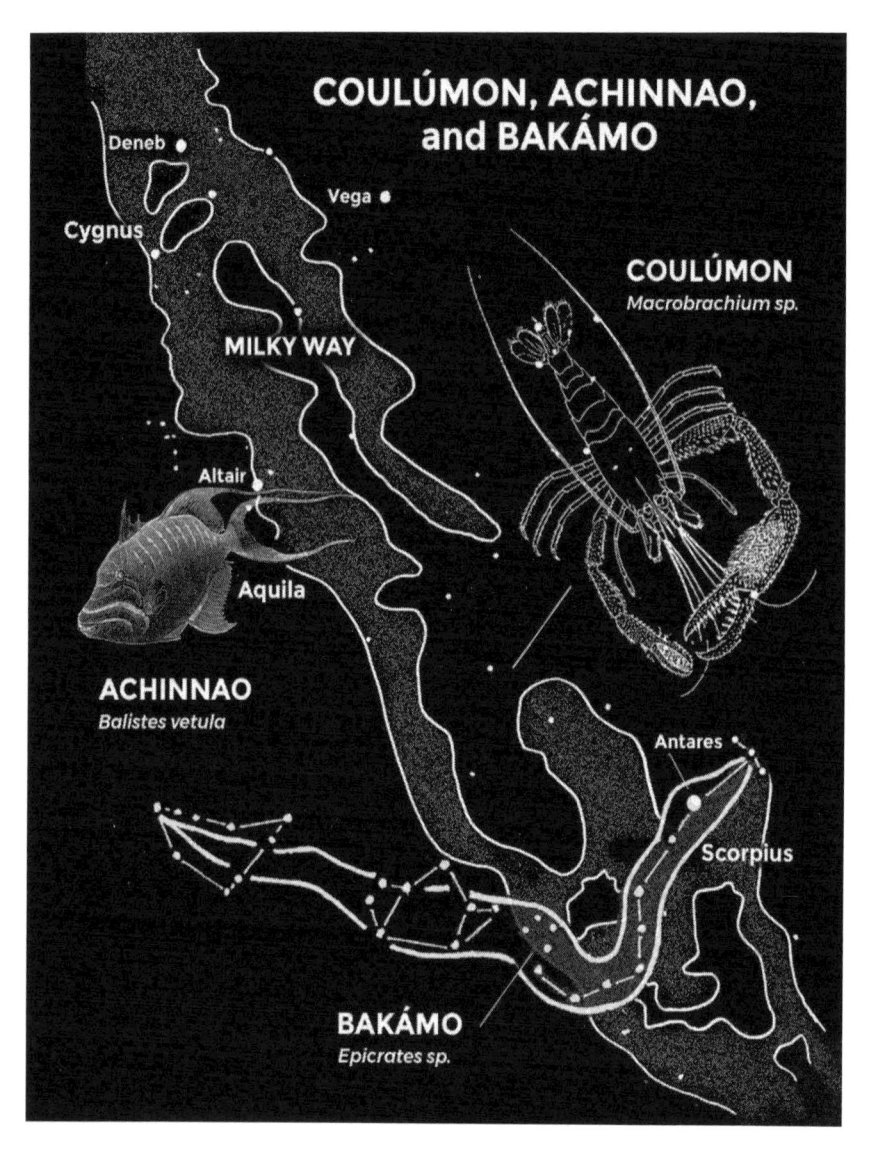

Coulúmon, Achinnao, and *Bakámo*, displayed in the Milky Way.

In this manner, *Siric* (Pleiades) and *Coulúmon* (Great Rift of the Milky Way) were two constellations seasonally opposed but symbolically united by a food collection code composed of two crustaceans occupying different habitats: one was land-based, the other river-based.

Bakámo, the Great Serpent

According to aforementioned La Borde, *Racumon* was "a great serpent" with the head of a man who was always on a *cabata* tree and ended up becoming a great star.

Unknowingly, the French chronicler was transcribing a fragment of a complex continental myth about the origin of the Caribs. Briefly, these myths narrate that a young woman has intimate relations with the great aquatic serpent, the Anaconda (*Eunectes murinus*) or *Camudi* (commonly represented by the Scorpio constellation) that was transformed into a human being. The young woman procreates a son. The serpent lived in or was related to the *balata* tree, whose fruit it offered to the lover. Her brother or brothers find out and kill the serpent, cutting it into small pieces that they throw to the river. Caribs are born from these small serpent pieces.

These beliefs, transformed and adapted to the island environment, were compiled by Taylor in Dominica centuries later:

> *A young woman met a man in the mountains who became a serpent. As a consequence, the young woman conceived and gave birth to a serpent with a human head that always wanted to return to the womb. When she consulted a boyez, he showed her how to solve the problem: she should find a balata tree where the serpent would look for the sweet fruit and, when the serpent descends the tree, she should put its head inside a burgao, spit around the tree, and run away. If the serpent chased after her, then she had to urinate on a mound of sand to confuse the serpent. The young mother did everything that was recommended and, when the serpent chased her, the urine became a great river that dragged the serpent towards the sea, transforming it into the Bakámo constellation.*

Let us analyze certain details of the myth. The *cabata*, *balata* tree or "ausubo" in Spanish (*Manilkara bidentata*), whose fruit was food for the Caribs, symbolizes the "food tree" in other South American myths. The *burgao* (*Cittarium pica*), the peculiar food source of the Saladoid, as we saw previously, is a conch with nocturnal habits that is common in the islands and is of a grayish-white color with black zigzag spots.

Contrary to the continental myth, however, the Island-Caribs did not believe that they originated from a serpent. Rather, they believed to be descendants of *Luquo*, the first man and the first Carib that created *Racumon* and the other ancestors, as La Borde documented. And, they believed that fish, not Carib men, were made of pieces of manioc, not serpent.

In addition, note the fluvial to terrestrial transformation experienced by the mythical serpent as the myth migrates from the continent to the islands. The mythical substitution is obvious: in the island myth there is no *anaconda*, the central motif of significant myths in the South American worldview. Similar to the Taino myth with *Iguanoboína*, the Great Serpent, the Island-Carib myth had to be inspired by the largest ophidian in the Antilles, called *Tête Chien* (Dog's Head) in the Lesser Antilles. Other names given to this serpent are boa or "culebrón" in Puerto Rico, "culebra jabada" in the Dominican Republic, and "majá" in Cuba (*Epicrates* sp.). This is a nocturnal, terrestrial serpent that lives in caves and measures about seven or eight feet in length.

For Breton, *Baccámon* was the name that the Caribs gave to the "constellation that we call Scorpio, which follows the dog [Canis Major]," although in another part he mentioned that *Ouanáche* was "a great serpent," that "becomes the constellation that we call *bacamon* or Scorpio when it rises in the morning." Thus, *Baccámon*, *Racumon* or *Bakámo* were all equivalent to the great Celestial Serpent.

In Dominica, Taylor wrote that his informant pointed to the star Antares as the eye of *Bakámo* and conveyed to him that Scorpius, Sagittarius and Capricornus constituted the head, body and tail of the great serpent, respectively. Taylor, however, confessed that he could not observe the *burgao* inside which the head of the serpent was found, as indicated by the Carib descendant. Further, he added that the island colloquial expression "*Bakámo* brings great winds" came from the observation that "the rising at dawn of Scorpio at the end of November coincided with the renewal of the trade winds and a decrease in rainfall."

Indeed, the magnificent presence of *Bakámo* in the celestial vault before dawn from January to April made it the quintessential symbol of the drought season (*isura*) and places it opposite to *Siric* (Pleiades), the stars of the rain, seasonally. Therefore, when *Bakámo* emerges on the eastern horizon, *Siric* hides behind the west horizon, and vice versa.

The reason why Taylor could not contemplate the Celestial Conch (*burgao*) was probably because it was configured not by stars, but by the Milky Way. The "great river that dragged the serpent to the sea" is, we repeat, a clear allusion to the conceptualization of the Milky Way as the Celestial River. The conch's white-grayish color with black blotches resembles the portion of the Milky Way around the Antares star of Scorpio, the eye of the great Celestial Serpent whose head was inside the Celestial Conch. In sum, *Bakámo* was the largest of the Carib constellations. And so was its mythical importance.

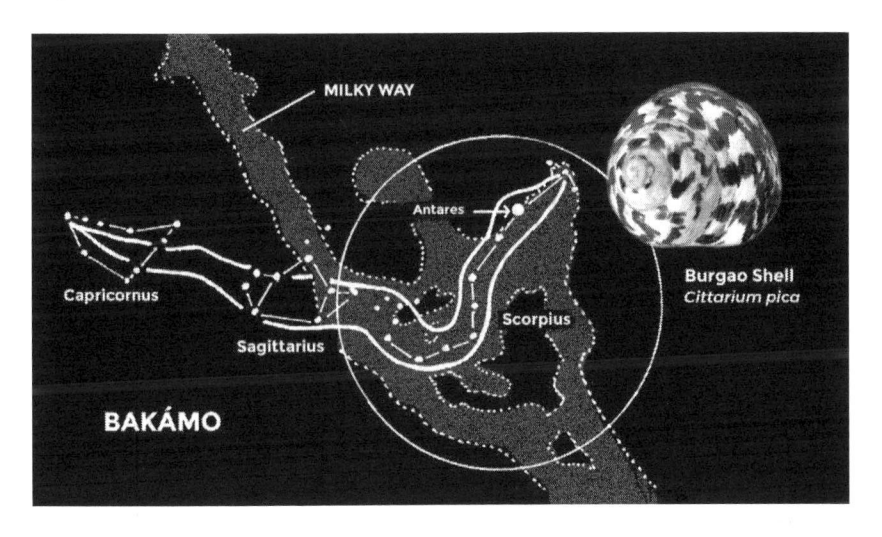

Bakámo, the Great Serpent.
The head was inside the Celestial Conch, part of the Milky Way.

As it is, the Great Serpent as a mythical entity occupied an important place in Carib cosmovision and among black-Carib descendants. There is no doubt of the influence of former black slaves on the black-Carib people given that the serpent also had cult status in African religions. In Dominica, the Great Serpent was believed to live in a "dreadful cavern." Bouton wrote that the serpent "grows large or small," had on "half of its forehead a garnet or very bright stone, which he takes out when he wants to drink," and that nobody dared go visit it if they had not fasted for three days and abstained from his wife, because the serpent "would not see him and [the visitor] would be in danger of being killed." In his version, de la Paix documented its name as *Oloubera*.

As late as in the 20th century, Taylor reaffirmed that the legend still existed among Carib descendants and that offerings consisting of pulverized tobacco leaves were made to the spirit of the Great Serpent. Taylor reported that it was because of those offerings that two brothers - perhaps twins - managed to make the serpent vomit the *túlala* ("l'envers tête chien" or arrowroot, *Maranta arundinacea*), the magical plant *par excellence* of Dominica from which they extracted an antidote against poisonous arrows, food flour, and an amulet used against *Maboya*, the spirit that tormented them.

It would appear that, in spite of the differences between the Carib tribal community and the Taino chiefdom society, the Great Serpent was an essential part of the mythical substratum common to both Antillean cultures. Hence, a parallelism can be established between the cave of *Iguanaboína* in Hispaniola and the cave where *Oloubera* lived in Dominica; between *Boinayel*, the son of the Great Taino Serpent, and *Racumon*, the son of the Carib serpent transmuted in the great *Bakámo* constellation.

The Milky Way: the path of the turtle

Carib descendants in Dominica told Taylor that they knew when turtles came to the beaches to spawn by looking at the Milky Way. In Dominica, the Milky Way was called, in French, "chemin la tortue" (the path of the turtle). Some descendants told Taylor that they could read the sky by "observing the position of the marks at the beginning and at the end" of the Milky Way; others told him that they would notice the direction of two lines of stars on the head of the celestial turtle vis-a-vis the "path" in the sky.

We thus face yet another meaning to the Milky Way. We saw the concept of the Celestial River where *Acáyouman*, the Celestial Cayman lived; we learned about *Coulúmon*, the Celestial Lobster, and about the Celestial Conch that contained the head of *Bakámo*, the Great Serpent. Now, it turns out that the Milky Way was considered "the path of the turtle." This tapestry demands analysis.

In American continent, the Milky Way was idealized in a variety of ways. In the Guianas, in particular, it was believed that the orientation of the large river in the sky established the two primary seasons of the year, as Edmundo Magaña found in his studies. Further, one of the most widespread meanings of the Milky Way in Guiana is that of the "path of the tapir" due to the footprints left on the riverbank by this important South American animal. Since the tapir (*Tapirus terrestris*) does not exist in the Antilles, we believe that the sea turtle replaced the tapir in the mythological system.

In the Antilles, the spawning season of sea turtles varies slightly. The turtle in greatest demand for its meat and eggs, the green turtle (*Chelonia mydas*), nests mainly at night from June to August. According to Taylor, the head of the turtle in the sky was formed by two lines of stars. Now, the morning rise of Capella, the most brilliant star of the Auriga constellation, takes place at the beginning of June in Dominica. If we look at the Auriga constellation, we will notice that its shape resembles a turtle. The head is the intersection of the lines formed by the star Beta with Theta, and the brilliant Capella. It is plausible, then, that the rise of Capella and, later, of the entire constellation, was the signal expected by the Carib to mark the beginning of the sea turtle's spawning season.

But there is more. The Auriga constellation is observed higher each day above the horizon before dawn in June and until its disappearance in September. The movement of the constellation simulates a march over the Milky Way that coincides with the months of the turtle's spawning season. In short, it is as if Auriga's trajectory forms the "path of the turtle" in the Milky Way, whose elongated shape is similar to the marks left behind by turtles as they move slowly over the sand to spawn.

All we have seen buttresses the theory that the Auriga constellation was the Celestial Turtle for the Caribs and that the trail left in the sand by the turtles was conceptualized, from June to September, in the Path of the Turtle or the Milky Way. Further, although the name the Caribs gave to both celestial bodies is unknown, we conjecture that the Celestial Turtle could have been called *Catállou-yuman* (from *catállou* = marine turtle, *yuman* = spirit, constellation), or perhaps *Catáluyuman*. In the same manner, the Path of the Turtle could be *Catállou-éma*, because *éma* was equivalent to "chemin" (path in French), as noted by Breton in his *Dictionaire Français-Caraibe* (1666).

In sum, the Milky Way embodied a large part of the Antillean ecosystem: in the shore, the footprints left in the sand by the turtles when they spawn; in the river, a mythical cayman, a conch whose insides were inhabited by the human head of a mythical serpent, and a tasty river lobster. Similarly, all the animals represented in the Milky Way's "negative constellations" or in the other constellations analyzed, appear at night or relate to the night: the cayman, the land crab, the crab-eating heron, the river lobster, the marine fish, the terrestrial serpent, the conch, the sea turtle. Also, the animals represented in the celestial fauna have an economic value and correspond to activities carried out by men in Island-Carib society. Likewise, the cultural objects represented in the constellations, the canoe and the barbecue, answer to the superiority of men in the society.

Catáluyuman, the Celestial Turtle, idealized in the constellation of Auriga. The marks left behind by the turtles in the sand resemble the Auriga's trajectory in the Milky Way.

CHAPTER 16

Lost wisdom

The astronomical idealizations of the Caribs that we discussed in the previous chapter are undoubtedly the result of an adaptation process that occurred in the eastern Antilles over time. The main stars and the Milky Way had various meanings: they were associated simultaneously with a kinship system, a food code, a seasonal cycle or a social activity. In this chapter, we will propose that the movement of the Milky Way and the constellations constituted a Carib stellar calendar.

Broadly speaking, the constellations can be grouped in two opposing, seasonal symbolic sets. The group of constellations that appear in the rainy season (*Siric, Catáluyuman, Ebétiouman*) move in the northern hemisphere of the celestial vault, opposed symbolically to the set of constellations of the dry season (*Bakámo, Achinnao, Coulúmon*) that move in the southern hemisphere. In short, the Milky Way is divided into two seasonally opposite segments: one corresponding to the "wet" and the other to the "dry" constellations.

The documented evidence about Carib cosmology and the corollaries that can be inferred from it are a mere speck of a vast oral tradition regrettably and irremediably lost. "Many of my informants," wrote Taylor in the midst of the 20th century in Dominica, "say that the ancient *boyez* had much more extensive knowledge of the stars, but they always refused to communicate what they knew to the new generations."

Moon, Sun, comets and planets

In addition to the stars, the Caribs observed the phases of the Moon and the apparent movement of the Sun. Also, to a greater or lesser degree, they feared eclipses, rainbows and comets.

The Moon, considered being more important than the Sun, according to La Borde, was called *Cáti* by women and *Nónum* by men, according to Breton. La Borde captured the same word (*Nónum*) for males, while Rochefort documented *Káti* and *Nonim*, respectively.

Moon was a mythical male character, whose existence among the Carib descendants we know thanks to Taylor:

Moon originated from a young man who, sheltered in darkness, coinhabited with the daughter of an old woman. One of the women dirties the man's face with the juice of genipa [Melicoccus bijugatus] to discover his true identity. The next day, they find out that he was the girl's brother who, upon being identified, becomes ashamed and ascends to heaven becoming Luna. His stained face can be seen from afar. The son of this incestuous relationship was Híali, 'the one who became bright,' the founder of the Carib nation. The yeretté took Híali to Moon, his father. In return, the bird received the beautiful colors of its plumage.

Yeretté, the Crested Hummingbird (*Orthorhyncus cristatus*), a bird of mythical importance to the Island-Carib.

This myth is widespread throughout the American continent and was called the "American vulgate" by Lévi-Strauss. In other variants that do not reflect the Antillean myth, Moon is linked to the Great Serpent and the origin of clay, or is who teaches women the art of pottery. That is why pottery is intimately associated with the Moon and is usually a female function. Additionally, the name *Híali* reminds us of Taino mythology, because the son of the hero *Guahayona* was called *Hiaguaili Guanín*. Consequently, it is likely that the original myth entered the Antilles with the first migrations of Agro-Ceramic people when, perhaps, it had - in analogy with the South American myths - a link with the origin of pottery, a subject that disappears completely in Antillean mythology as we know it today.

Phrases related to the Moon abound in Breton's dictionary. For example, *atupikali-nónum* was the coming out of the Moon, while *chiríali nónum* was a full moon and *chiléali nónum* was a new moon. The first night that the Moon reappeared was called *tihuenébouli nónum*, an occasion that prompted everyone to come out of their dwellings to see it, according to La Borde. In Guianas, clay for pottery making was collected precisely on this night. If it was not collected, it was believed that the pottery would break or the food deposited in the pots could cause diseases. Similar to the Taino belief, the new moon had a magical connotation for the Carib people: the fifth day of the new moon was the most appropriate for planting corn (*anási*, *Zea mays*) or fishing in the high seas. During the new moon, it was necessary to cut down the *chíbou* or *tabonuco* (*Dacryodes excelsa*) for the construction of the canoe. Of course, we already saw that Carib attacks were carried out under a full moon.

The main French chroniclers clearly point out that the Moon served to count the months. The Caribs counted nine moons to harvest manioc, just as the ancestor who first cultivated it. To be sure, Coppier claims that the Carib year consisted of 12 moons.

The Sun - whose myth of origin is unknown - was called *Cáchi* by women and *Huéyou* by men, according to Breton. Rochefort registers *Káohi* for women and *Hiieiu* for men. The position of the Sun in the sky marked the principal times of the day, each with its own name. As we saw earlier, the trajectory of the Sun was used in navigation.

Importantly, the Caribs observed the passage of the Sun through the zenith. During two days of its apparent annual movement (when the latitude of the location is equal to the declination of the Sun), the solar star will pass through the zenith of a locality and, consequently, the solar rays will strike on the ground perpendicularly. For Dominica, this occurs on May 1 and August 12. Breton reported that the Caribs called this phenomenon *Leouallágonirocou chéenli huéyou*, which meant that "the Sun is in its middle, in its equality" because "they know well that the Sun goes over the zenith again and again, they say over the head, and this is what this expression means."

None of the terms documented by the chroniclers refers to the equinoxes or the solstices. It is difficult to establish if these significant days were observed by the Caribs. In the case of the Tainos, despite the absence of ethnohistorical evidence, the astronomical orientations of ceremonial plazas such as that in Chacuey (analyzed in chapter eight) allow us to postulate that it was a kind of astronomical observatory where the solar cycle was correlated with that of several important constellations, serving as the basis for a probable Taino calendar.

What is more, unusual astronomical phenomena inspired fear among the Caribs. Breton wrote: "When they saw a comet (*boukébonun*), they said it was a warning, a signal." La Borde gave the name of *Limacani* to "the comet that *Cualina*, the captain of the *cemíes*, sent to do evil when he was angry." However, Breton identified *Limagani* ("his principal son") with Venus, a planet that was also called *Toubayoula* (from the twilight side). Among Carib descendants, *Wálibuka* corresponded to the planet Mars. The Moon and Sun eclipses were the Carib's most feared phenomena.

Eclipses and cosmic chaos

Christopher Columbus was the first to learn the effects of an eclipse among the aboriginals of the Antilles. In February of 1504, the caravels stranded in a bay in Jamaica and Columbus was unable to obtain food from the natives. He used astronomical tables he carried with him to learn of the proximity of a lunar eclipse. Being no fool, he summoned the rebellious Jamaican *caciques* and told them that the wrath of his God would be manifested in the paleness of the Moon. The plan worked: the next day, as soon as the eclipse occurred, the Tainos panicked and, all doubts of his divine connection vanished, offered him all the food he desired.

In the case of the Caribs, Anonymous of Carpentras was the first to learn of the ritual that was performed as a result of an eclipse given that, during his stay in the islands, two lunar eclipses occurred. Both he and later chroniclers pointed out that the Caribs believed that it was *Maboya*, the "evil spirit," who ate the star being eclipsed. That is why the Caribs called the eclipses *Laikua-noquian*, the consumption of the Moon, or *Laikua-vicu*, the consumption of the Sun. For the Caribs, the eclipse was an act of cosmic anthropophagy.

The ritual that was celebrated to help revive the eclipsed star began when the men burned the tips of their arrows and shot them into the sky to scare off *Maboya*. Meanwhile, in the *carbet*, the three eldest women dyed in black and a young woman who made sounds by shaking a gourd with small pebbles inside, sang a lugubrious, rhythmic song. This music caused the women to initiate a dance that lasted four to five hours; at that time, the men joined the dance for the rest of the night. They did not hold hands. Rather, separated from each other, they put their feet together and leaped forward while hunched, putting one hand on their head and the other on their sex, constantly changing their position.

The Island-Carib believed that the eclipse was an act of cosmic cannibalism caused by *Maboya*.

Perhaps the intent of the music was to return the cosmos to its harmonious rhythm while the dance imitated the sinuous movement of the Milky Way in the celestial vault, as occurs in certain aboriginal dances in South America. Another possibility is that the music reminded the Carib people of the venerated Great Serpent, who gave to humans the magical plant from which they made the amulet used against *Maboya*. The celebration of this ceremony from night to dawn was perhaps a way to re-establish the balance between night and day, the Moon and the Sun.

Carib dance.
"Manière dont les prêtres Caraïbes soufflent le courage" (Picard, 1723).

In any case, the impact of the eclipses among the indigenous Antillean people can be better understood if we accept that eclipses were considered a rupture of the cosmic order established in the time of the origins. The same was believed to be true in South America. If, due to an eclipse, the Moon or the Sun died, the world would return to the original chaos, to the imbalance prior to creation, to social disorder. That is why the ritual dance, as in the case of the Caribs, entailed the joint, yet separate, rhythmic participation of women and men to encourage the stars to return to normalcy, to their cyclic periodicity, to the cosmic equilibrium that ensured the continuity of creation and culture.

The Carib stellar calendar

Douglas Taylor established that Carib descendants used a calendar of nine "months" where each month bore the name of the predominant constellation in the sky for that period. Using the morning rise of the stars, the "months" that constituted the ancient Carib calendar were *Sirigo, Ebedimu, Mariru-bana, Iábura, Mubé, Uráu, Bagamu, Asinau* and *Isura*. Let us examine several details of this Carib star calendar.

Sirigo. This "month" began in early June with the rise, before sunrise, of *Siric* (Pleiades), stars that marked the beginning of the year and the rainy season. To the Caribs, *Sirigo* was synonymous with "year" and represented a mythical character and a terrestrial crab abundant at this time of year. Present in the sky also during this time was *Catáluyuman*, the Celestial Turtle (Auriga), signaling the start of the turtle spawning season that lasted until September. In this time period the Milky Way became the Way of the Turtle, an analogy of the footprints left in the sand by the turtles when spawning.

Ebedimu. The rise of *Ebétiouman* (Orion), a constellation that delineated a one-foot character belonging to the kinship system, occurred during the first few days of this "month." This month aligns more or less with July. The bright star *Bíhi* comes out towards the end of this "month." You will recall that *Bíhi* was the windy mother-in-law (Sirius), a star in the *Maliroúbana* (Canis Major) constellation. Also, this month, the *Maliroúbana opourcou* (Canis Minor) constellation emerges. Both constellations signaled the storm and hurricane season.

Mariru-bana. The predominance in the morning sky of the previous constellations gives the name to this "month" that occurred towards the end of July and the beginning of August. At the end of this period, the star *Lukúni-yábura*, or Celestial Canoe (Big Dipper, Ursa Major), rose high above the sea. This was probably a sign of organize the next warrior expeditions.

Iábura. In this "month," corresponding to the majority of August, *Lukúni-yábura* (the crab-eating heron) continues its ascent above the horizon. As such, the nocturnal bird gives name to this time period. Meanwhile, *Isúla*, the Celestial Barbecue (Square of Pegasus), is hidden behind the western horizon. These two constellations, although opposed in their period of visibility, are identified with the two main objects of anthropophagic practice: the canoe and the barbecue.

Mubé. This "month" corresponds to September and October. It is the time of year when the *mombin* tree (*jobo, Spondias mombin*) gives fruit and when *Acáyouman*, the Celestial Cayman and father of the Carib lineage, appears in the center of the celestial vault accompanied by the system of stellar kinship stars composed by *Mubéyuman*, the bride (Hyades), *Ebétiouman*, the mutilated boyfriend (Orion), and *Maliroúbana*, the windy mother-in-law (Canis Major). This was the first "month" of Carib expeditions.

Uráu. This "month" aligns with November and is when *Lukúni-yábura* (Big Dipper) appears at the peak of its cycle around Polaris, marking the culmination of the war excursion season. Also, in the first days of November, the rain-related *Siric* (Pleiades) disappears on the western horizon before dawn, announcing the forthcoming appearance on the eastern horizon of *Bakámo*, the Great Serpent, identified with the drought season. *Siric* and *Bakámo* are opposed, symbolically and seasonally.

Bagamu. Towards the beginning of December, Antares (brightest star of Scorpius) rises in the morning. Antares is the eye of the Great Serpent (*Bakámo*) inside the Celestial Conch (*Burgao*) and its appearance in the sky corresponds to the renewal of trade winds and a decrease in rainfall. The morning presence of *Bakámo*, the Great Serpent that gives the name to this "month," dominates during this drought season. In the course of this period, the Milky Way disappears in the western horizon along with the constellations associated with the rainy months.

Asinau. This "month" aligns with January and is when *Achinnao*, the Celestial Fish (Altair), emerges on the eastern horizon. It is a period of cool winds, light rain and abundant fish. During this time, the Milky Way disappears from the centre of the celestial vault and can be barely observed on the horizon. Its later reappearance marks a seasonal change, since it takes place with the constellations of the drought set.

Isura. This long "month" begins in or before February and lasts until the end of April. It bears the name of drought and aligns with the drought season in the islands, the time when men were home and carried out their communal activities. This was also the "month" when *Coulúmon*, the Lobster of the Celestial River, was present. It was also the time when *Lukúni-yábura*, the Celestial Canoe (Big Dipper), began to descend towards the sea while *Isúla*, the Celestial Barbecue (Square of Pegasus), rose before dawn over the horizon, announcing the beginning of the season when the anthropophagic ritual took place. As has been said, *Lukúni-yábura* and *Isúla* represent the main objects of this practice. They are opposing constellations, astronomically and seasonally.

Finally, the gradual disappearance of the set of "dry" constellations (*Bakámo, Achinnao, Coulúmon*) that move in the southern hemisphere gave rise to the start of a new stellar year with the reappearance of the Pleiades in early June and the eventual prevalence of the "wet" constellations (*Siric, Cataluyuman, Ebétiouman*) moving in the northern hemisphere. Both sets of constellations were in the vicinity of or over the Milky Way.

The opposition between the "dry" and "wet" constellations mimics the dual and interrelated classification of the Carib worldview, based on a human and animal system.

The Carib worldview

The Carib worldview, similar to the Taino worldview, stipulated sets of opposite, yet complementary, terms. As we have said, the Carib society of the Lesser Antilles consisted of two societies in one: the first society was that of Arawak women from the islands and the second consisted of Carib men of recent arrival.

As part of the process of cultural syncretism that occurred in the eastern Antilles, the Carib immigrants adopted, to some degree, a belief in animistic conceptions. This is the belief in spirits of nature, such as the fauna and flora present in the islands at the time. For instance, the Great Serpent held an important role in the Carib belief system and was present in the constellation *Bakámo*. The Great Serpent was associated with the *boyez* and received veneration and tobacco offerings. You will call that the Caribs believed that they acquired from the Great Serpent the magic *toúlála*, a plant with a small edible tuber from which an antidote against poisonous arrows and an amulet against the malignant *Maboya* spirit was obtained.

The position of the stars in the sky governed the social life of the Caribs. Stars were considered to abode the spirit of terrestrial things. Stars were analogous to animals, plants, objects and ancestors themselves. Importantly, the celestial spirit of these objects descended to their earthly body when the corresponding star was visible in heaven. Therefore, the presence of the Celestial Turtle in the sky was what allowed the sea turtles to spawn; the departure of the Celestial Canoe marked the beginning of expeditions; the ascension, months later, of the Celestial Barbecue, was the cosmic signal that allowed the ritual sacrifice of the captive enemy warrior to occur.

In contrast, the absence of that celestial spirit in heaven authorized the Caribs to violate the sacred prohibition imposed otherwise when the object resided on earth. Thus, the giant *ceiba* tree, home to the Great Spirit of the Trees, could only be demolished to build a canoe when that spirit was absent and, consequently, when the tree lost all its leaves. This worldview allows us to comprehend how *Maboya*, a spirit of human origin sheltered in the forest, could elevate itself to produce an act of cosmic cannibalism when he "ate" a piece of the Moon or the Sun, thereby producing a cosmic imbalance: an eclipse.

This system of interdependence and contradiction is manifested throughout the Carib worldview. *Olubera*, the Great Serpent of the Dominica, was beneficial but could kill if certain terms were not followed when looking at her. The favored *cemí* was opposed to the feared *Maboya*. The rainbow, *Juluca*, was evil on land because it could cause death, but it was beneficial if seen at sea. The navigation season follow the hurricane season. The solar, diurnal birds (*guaraguao* and *yeretté* or hummingbird, both solar birds) were opposed to the nocturnal, messenger birds from the afterlife (*Coribib chemin*, a species of owl). The *toúlála* (arrowroot, *Maranta arundinacea*), the magical plant *par excellence*, had its rival in the poisonous *mancenillier* (*Hippomane mancinella*).

This universe of complementary and contradictory elements seems sometimes to unfold onto itself: the iguana, an edible diurnal reptile, had immunity to consume the *guano* leaves from the *Maboya* tree and the poisonous fruit of the *mancenillier*; while the nocturnal serpent, an inedible reptile, ingested bats, the protective nocturnal spirit of the Caribs.

If we increase the scale of space and time, a symmetry of astronomical-seasonal oppositions arises. We saw that the Milky Way contains "wet" or "dry" constellations that move in the northern or in southern hemisphere in opposing seasons. Hence, when in the eastern horizon *Siric* (Pleiades, the stars of the rain) rises, *Bakámo* (Great Serpent, the constellation of the dry season) hides in the western hemisphere, and vice versa. Similarly, the two constellations that represent objects common to anthropophagic practice - the barbecue and the canoe - are diametrically opposed in time, symbolizing the two spatially opposite seasons of the Carib man: when he was on or off the islands. Both seasons revolved around the central ritual of Carib society: the cannibal sacrifice of an enemy warrior.

The fundamental difference between the Carib tribal society and the Taino chiefdom lies in the different levels of ideological evolution that they had achieved at the time of the European discovery. The animistic conception of the Caribs did not reach the level of theocratism - the belief in gods that control nature - of the Tainos. In contrast to the Caribs, the Tainos achieved a characteristic social structure and a sophisticated religion composed of hierarchical deities embodied in a multi-faceted and defined iconography. Neither did the Caribs seem to have projected in space the concept of time visualized in the movement of the stars, notions that the Taino people managed to integrate in the construction of astronomically-oriented ceremonial plazas.

Regardless of their similarities and differences, the Taino and Carib cultures were the first to suffer the impact of the European colonization.

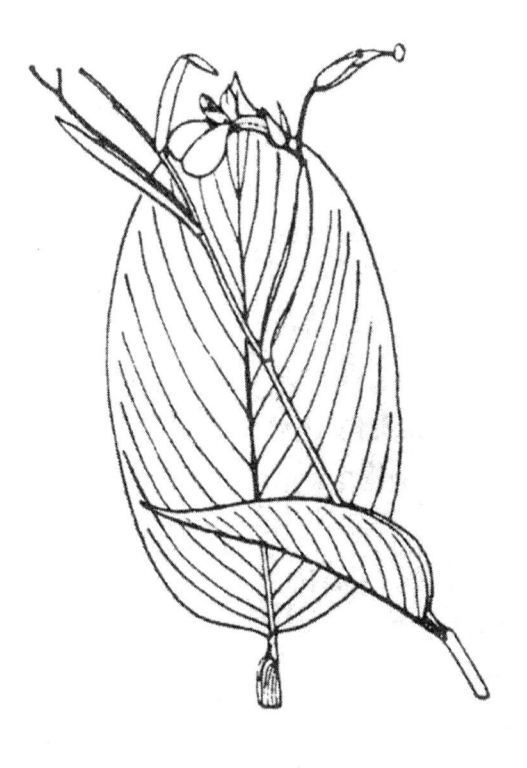

Magic *toúlála* or *túlala,*
arrowroot (*Maranta arundinacea*)

NINTH PART

DISINTEGRATION AND LEGACY

CHAPTER 17

An imminent end

The Tainos and the Caribs were the first American aboriginal societies to experience the clash that occurred with the arrival of the European.

The Spanish discovery and colonization impacted the Tainos so severely that they were physically and socially on their way to extinction in a few decades. In fact, the Tainos of Hispaniola were the first to suffer the exploitation systems successively imposed by the colonizer: the factories, the taxes and the enslaving *encomienda* system. With the exception of the first impressions of the Tainos written by Columbus himself and the fragmented indigenous beliefs recorded by Ramón Pané, the main chroniclers of the Tainos arrived when this society was already in marked decay. Las Casas arrived in 1502 and wrote only decades later; Oviedo arrived in 1514, when Taino society had been practically destroyed and its population completely decimated. Consequently, most of the details of Taino culture were lost in the first years of Spanish conquest and colonization.

The Caribs of the eastern Antilles, who were attacked initially by the Spaniards and then struggled with the French and the English for almost two centuries, managed to survive over time thanks to their individualistic character and their warrior spirit. A plethora of French chroniclers - among which Raymond Breton stands out - were able to compile considerable ethnohistorical and linguistic documentation.

From the start, the Spanish colonizer did not hesitate to mix with Taino women. That did not happen with the French and the English in relation to Carib women. The arrival of the black slave added a new racial and cultural dimension. As a result, Africans became the unifying force in the Antilles. The Tainos, the Spanish and the Africans forged the mestizo society of the Hispanic Antilles. In the smaller Antilles, those Africans who adopted a large part of the Carib culture molded the peculiar culture of the Black-Caribs;

meanwhile, Africans and French descendants gave way to the rich creole culture.

In this last part of this book, we will briefly discuss the disintegration of aboriginal Antillean societies as a result of the European colonization. And, at the same time, we will expose the legacy that Taino and Carib people left in the cultures of the Caribbean.

The apparition at Santo Cerro

As discussed in the second chapter, after founding La Isabela, the first city-factory of the New World, the Admiral decided to explore the interior of Hispaniola in search of gold.

The first confrontations between the Tainos and Spaniards occurred in the Cibao mountains of Hispaniola during an expedition commanded by Alonso de Ojeda. Doubting that the Spaniards were beings that had "come from heaven," the Tainos of Cibao drowned some of them in the Yaque River to test their mortality. (Something similar would happen years later in Puerto Rico, according to Oviedo). Ojeda reacted immediately by executing and capturing many aboriginals, an action that produced the first attempt at a Taino rebellion. Yet Ojeda's underlying purpose was to defeat Caonabo, the intrepid *cacique* who had allegedly attacked and killed all the Spaniards left there during Columbus' first voyage.

In a bold act, Ojeda visited Caonabo with alleged friendly intentions. It was then that he showed Caonabo a pair of copper handcuffs, saying that they were a gift from the kings. Believing that they were made of *guanín*, the mythical metal highly esteemed by the Tainos, Caonabo innocently allowed Ojeda to put them on him. Caonabo also accepted with pleasure Ojeda's invitation to ride with him on his horse, an animal unknown to the Tainos. Caonabo soon realized that he had been captured and that not everything that shone was *guanín*. The courageous Caonabo died, angered by the vile deception he suffered. Caonabo's fate illustrated the differences between two worlds that were beginning to come face to face with one another.

By then, Columbus had returned to La Isabela from his exploration trip through Cuba and Jamaica. In March of 1495, he led an armed contingent with the purpose of subjecting the Cibao *caciques* to pay a gold tax, "urged - as the historian Cassá wrote – to make the factory work."

As he arrived in the mountains of the valley of La Vega Real, Columbus faced *cacique* Guarionex, who directed an attack of approximately 5,000 Tainos, most likely armed with bows and arrows, clubs (in the "form of a palette until the end," with a width of "two or three fingers" and "long as a man") and dart-throwers ("they had wood throwers" with which they threw "rods as darts"). Probably they also used toxic gases produced by burning chili pepper (*Capsicum* sp.) in a container, a war technique used by both Tainos and Caribs. Not long after the battle began, the Spaniards were forced to withdraw from a hill where they had planted a cross that was made, according to tradition, from a sapodilla tree ("níspero", *Manilkara zapota*).

As recorded later by Luis Jerónimo Alcocer, Canon of the Cathedral of Santo Domingo, the Tainos occupied the hill and tried to tear down the cross with "many ropes and vines, yet despite the innumerable amount of people pulling it, the cross would not move." They could not cut it either. So, they chose to burn it. But the fire "[...] would not burn on the Cross, regardless of how much time they spent on it and how much fire they burnt, the Holy Cross remained intact." Then emerges what legend and tradition consider a miracle:

> *When they were stoking the fire, the Indians saw our Blessed Lady the Virgin Mary sitting on one arm of the Holy Cross, and it looked as if she diverted the fire and defended the cross from burning, for which the indignant Indians, thinking that she was a Spanish woman, set arms against her with their bows and arrows, throwing many of them at her and the arrows returned to them; seeing so many wonders, they gave up.*

It is necessary to make several observations about what became the first alleged apparition of the Virgin Mary in the New World.

First of all, the chaplain of the troops was a man named Juan Infante, who belonged to the Order of Mercy, a detail that could have had a great influence on the original interpretation of what happened. Being Juan a father of the Mercedarian tradition, it is not at all strange that what occurred was taken as the appearance of his patron, the Virgin of Mercy. Conversely, it would be interesting to know how the Tainos judged the supposedly divine manifestation. At any rate, the

Santo Cerro Church, La Vega, D.R. *In the Wake of Columbus* (Ober, 1893).

veneration of the Virgin of Mercy or Mercedes increased over the years in Hispaniola until she was declared the Patron of the colony in 1691.

Despite the superiority in numbers of the aboriginal population, the Spaniards had a more developed military strategy and the technology to assure victory: horses, dogs, spears, swords, armor and firearms. Plunged into a new world full of uncertainties, challenges and dangers, the Spaniards needed a divine sign to approve of their deed. Thus, the appearance of the Virgin filled a psychological need and legitimized the conquest in the name of Christianity.

The battle of Santo Cerro or La Vega Real soon progressed from legend to history. This was not the first time - nor would it be the last time - that divine favor was invoked to justify the human goals of ambition and domination.

The Moon and the Taino rebellion

The defeated Guarionex accepted to pay taxes. Likewise, so did the *caciques* who were allied with him in Cibao. But the tax demands - that any Taino older than 14 years old deliver a little cooper bell full of gold every three months or moons - ran into an obstacle of ideological nature that has hardly been evaluated. It turns out that gold was held as a divine mineral that required a certain ritual be performed before it could be obtained. Oviedo wrote the following description of the ritualistic beliefs in reference to the Tainos of Hispaniola:

> *[...] the Indians spent the first twenty days without reaching their women (or other women), and being apart from them, and they fasted, and they said that when they saw their woman, they did not find gold.*

Anglería reaffirmed this practice:

> *They believe that a deity resides in this metal and, for this reason, they never devote themselves to extracting it without having purified themselves, based on the religion of their ancestors, meaning that they abstain from intercourse and any other delight and use food and drink with great moderation for the full length of time that the operation lasts.*

Apparently, extracting gold was equivalent for the Tainos to performing a "sacred terrestrial" act that required a previous sacrifice so that Mother Earth would allow the mineral to be granted. Therefore, the intended gold tax prevented full compliance with the religious precepts. Tainos believed that, should their ritual be violated, an alteration to the established social and cosmic order would occur. Perhaps this was one of the main reasons why Guarionex proposed taxing manioc instead of gold, suggesting an immense parcel of manioc planted in heaps.

Yet, for the Admiral, manioc and gold were not synonymous, and repressions, punishments and abuses did not wait. Tainos then chose to fight the Spaniards with hunger: their plan was to destroy the existing plots and not sow the land. In the long run, however, that tactic did not work well because they suffered famine, death and revenge of all kinds from the resentful conqueror. Overwhelmed by the critical situation, Guarionex held an assembly with the allied *caciques* of the central zone of Hispaniola. They decided to start the rebellion using the next full moon as the sign. This is what Fernando Colón narrated:

> *[...] they agreed that each would be willing to kill the Christians on the first day of the full moon. The mentioned Guarionex prepared his caciques for this and one of them, the principal, eager to acquire honor,*

and believing it to be very easy business, despite not being a good astrologer to know with certainty the day of the full moon, assaulted land before the time agreed between them; poorly positioned, he had to flee and, thinking that he would find help in Guarionex, found his ruin, because he punished him with death [...]

The mistake made by this deficient Taino astronomer alerted the Spaniards and resulted in the failure of the Taino rebellion. Bartolomé Colón, in charge of the colony at the time, carried out a series of executions and repressive attacks that ended with the capture of Guarionex himself.

Xaragua, genocide in action

The failure of the Taino rebellion and its repressive sequel led to the disappearance of the useless tax system and the imposition of slavery. The conqueror began to convince himself that "indigenous labor was the true source of wealth," as the Puerto Rican historian Francisco A. Scarano wrote.

Around 1503, forced labor of the Tainos culminated in the *encomienda* system, a Spanish form of communal slavery that rewarded conquerors with the labor of particular groups of subject people. In the *encomienda*, the Crown granted a person a group of Tainos that could range from a few to two or three hundred. They had to watch over the clothing and health of natives, as well as their formation in the Christian faith and Spanish language, while working in mining or agriculture. Indigenous leaders were charged with mobilizing labor. In the Antilles, each *encomienda* group was headed by a *cacique* and several *naborías*: the Taino social structure itself was used by the colonizer to make the system work.

Nicolás de Ovando, governor of Hispaniola at the time and the person responsible for the establishment of the main administrative functions, was convinced that the enslavement of the Tainos by an elite of *encomenderos* was the only path to a productive economy. Therefore, he did not hesitate to implement an oppressive and bloodthirsty policy to finish conquering the entire island of Hispaniola and thus transfer in succession captured natives to the *encomienda* group of power being created. Conquest, slavery and production were the order of the day.

Ovando personally decided to conquer the powerful and hitherto intact chiefdom of Xaragua in Hispaniola, where years before Bartolomé Colón had been received with all honors by the *cacique* Behechío and his sister, Anacaona, when he imposed a cotton tax. Although Behechío had died, Anacaona received Ovando and his entourage with great celebrations. The *caciques* and principal leaders of the region were summoned to participate in the entertainment and celebrated a great *areíto* with hundreds of participants led by Anacaona herself. In the middle of the crowded celebration, the Governor gave the signal that initiated the criminal attack that resulted in the death of thousands of surprised Tainos. The gathered *caciques* and principals did not escape the fury: they were locked in a *caney* and burned alive. The scribe Diego Méndez, witness to the horrendous event, wrote that Ovando "burned and hung 84 Caciques, Masters of vassals." Anacaona was hung months later in Santo Domingo.

Xaragua genocide (Theodor de Bry, 1597).

The number of indigenous people who survived the genocide in Xaragua did not satisfy the demand for slaves. Each indigenous population had to be subjugated in every corner of Hispaniola. Ovando's campaigns of conquest and enslavement culminated in the eastern region of Higüey with the hanging of *cacique* Cotubanamá and the death of other *caciques* at the stake. It is not surprising that three "peacemakers" and rich *encomenderos* of Hispaniola became the future conquerors of the remaining Greater Antilles: Juan Ponce de León of Puerto Rico, Diego de Velázquez of Cuba and Juan de Esquivel of Jamaica.

Hispaniola was the land where Spain rehearsed for fifteen years the conquest and colonization of the rest of America.

Expansion to Puerto Rico, Cuba and Jamaica

Initiated in August of 1508, the conquest of the island of San Juan Bautista (a name that would be later exchanged with that of its port) would be a small-scale replica of what happened in Hispaniola.

Due to the communications between islands, there is no doubt that the Tainos in Puerto Rico knew what was occurring in Hispaniola. For this reason, Agüeybana, the supreme *cacique* in Puerto Rico, acted with extreme caution and established, without hesitation, friendly relations with Juan Ponce de León as soon as the latter arrived at his chiefdom in the southern region of the island. According to aboriginal custom, both men exchanged names ceremonially (*guaitiao*). And, in the face of Carib attacks that "the *caciques* and indians complained about," the future conqueror did not hesitate to offer protection. It was in those days that Agüeybana himself traveled to Higüey invited by Ponce de León, who later invited him to visit the city of Santo Domingo.

When the old Agüeybana died, his nephew Agüeybana II succeeded him. By then, the abuses of the *encomenderos* were felt in the indigenous population who were subject to the enslaving search for gold. The former cordial relations between the Tainos and the Spaniards began to disappear. A turning point occurred when the Tainos realized that the colonizer was mortal. The spark of the Taino rebellion in Puerto Rico was lit after the *cacique* Urayoán drowned the young Diego Salcedo in the Guaorabo River, according to Oviedo.

"The Indians wanted to prove if the Spaniards were immortal ..."
Drowning of Salcedo. *Great Travelers,* Book IV (Theodor de Bry, 1594).

In an *areíto* summoned by Agüeybana II and attended by the main *caciques*, it was decided that the Tainos would attack the Spaniards scattered around the island in towns and haciendas in the near future. However, Juan González, infiltrated among the assistants and perhaps the first spy in Puerto Rican history, managed to alert his countrymen of the plans. Despite the rebellion achieving some degree of initial success, Ponce de León faced the Tainos and, in the battle of Yagüeca, delivered the decisive blow of the conquest when, in the midst of the battle, Agüeybana II himself is said to have lost his life.

Some *caciques* retreated with their people to the mountainous area and skirmishes occurred over the years. Other Tainos, on the other hand, chose to emigrate to the neighboring eastern islands from where, according to some historians, they organized attacks against the colonizers with the help of the Caribs.

Now, it is worth wondering if the beginning of the Taino rebellion in Puerto Rico was marked by some phase of the Moon, as happened in the case of the Tainos in Hispaniola with the full moon.

Although the date of the beginning of the rebellion has not been specified, it is known that it happened "at the beginning of January of 1511." Based on ancient documents, historian Francisco Moscoso established the date of this memorable event as January 3. Using a computerized astronomy program, it can be seen that, on the evening of January 3, 1511, the Moon appears in the western sky in its new phase. It is feasible to think that the new moon of January was the cosmic signal agreed by the Tainos in Puerto Rico to start their rebellion.

Viceroy Diego Colón, a substitute to Ovando, designated Diego de Velázquez to conquer Cuba. The Tainos in the eastern part of Cuba were well aware of what awaited them before Diego de Velázquez began his expedition in the beginning of 1511. *Cacique* Hatuey, a survivor of the massacre in Xaragua in Hispaniola, arrived to warn them of the Spaniard's upcoming arrival, their evil intention, and their excessive desire for gold, "the God of Christians." Hatuey himself organized the first resistance of the Cuban Tainos. But after several months of skirmishes, he decided that the best strategy was to hide in the mountains hoping to escape the 300-strong armed men commanded by Velázquez. Woefully, the Tainos were pursued with horses and dogs and, when found, the Spaniards "killed men and women and even children with lunges and slashes," according to Las Casas. Others were tortured to disclose where Hatuey was hiding. Finally imprisoned, Hatuey was sentenced to the stake.

Las Casas wrote that, when Hatuey was going to be burned alive, a Franciscan man suggested to Hatuey that he be baptized so that he would die a Christian. The *cacique* asked "why he should be like the Christians, who were bad" and the father answered him: "Because those who die Christians go to heaven and there they see God always." To which Hatuey replied that he did not want to go to heaven if that is where Christians went.

There is no doubt that Velázquez applied and justified force to "pacify" the largest of the Great Antilles, colonize it from east to west, and establish the *encomienda* system that converted it into a prosperous colony. Meanwhile, the *encomendero* Juan de Esquivel had been put in charge of the conquest of Jamaica since 1509. Esquivel managed to "pacify" the island relatively quickly with a mere 60 soldiers and established a limited *encomienda* system based mainly on cotton production.

The death of Hatuey.
He did not want to go to Heaven if that is where Christians went.
(Theodor de Bry, 1597).

CHAPTER 18

The rebellion of the Dominicans

Important events unfolded in the Greater Antilles in 1511. The beginning of the year was witness to the Taino rebellion in Puerto Rico and the commencement of the conquest in Cuba, while in the latter part of the year, in December, Antón de Montesino pronounced in Santo Domingo his famous sermon denouncing the actions of viceroy Diego Colón and other authorities and colonial personalities. Without fear or qualms, the Dominican priest condemned the treatment given to the Tainos by the Spaniards and warned them that they lived and died in mortal sin because of the abusive treatment to which they subjected the native.

Monument to Fray Antón de Montesino. Santo Domingo, D.R.

The strong criticism made by the Dominican, repeated the following Sunday and seconded by his superiors, reached King Ferdinand, who decided to call a group of specialists to analyze the theological and legal implications of the Taino situation. As a result, the Laws of Burgos were promulgated in 1512. These set of laws governed the behavior of Spaniards in the Americas, particularly with regards to the indigenous people. The Laws of Burgos established the principle of freedom for the indigenous population and dictated the Christian duties of the Spaniards towards them. Working hours were reduced, married women were excluded from the mines, and the type of work that could be performed by children under the age of 14 was restricted.

In practice, the Laws of Burgos achieved some of the principles intended, but were generally overlooked by the dominant class of Antillean *encomenderos*. As such, the Taino population continued to decline rapidly. It was not until 1516 that, influenced by Las Casas, the government of the New World was entrusted to a council of three friars of the Order of St. Jerome that proposed the introduction of black slaves - a practice that had begun timidly years earlier, along with the import of natives from neighboring islands and South America - as the solution to avoid the disappearance of the Tainos.

Notwithstanding, the policy had adverse consequences for the Tainos. Rather than help their survival, the arrival of black slaves caused the death of a third of the already-diminished Taino population due to the smallpox epidemic of 1518 and 1519. Likewise, the arrival of predominantly male African slaves led to their union with Taino women, giving way to an increase in the miscegenation that had begun with the arrival of the Spaniards.

The demographic catastrophe

Be it because of the indiscriminate and unjustified massacres, the unequal warlike confrontations, the imposition of taxes, the forced labor in the *encomienda* system, the introduction of new diseases and epidemics, or the suicides and induced abortions that resulted from the psychological confusion and the spiritual breakdown caused by the conquest, the reality is that the Taino population was reduced dramatically in a matter of a few years and virtually disappeared. Little did subsequent uprisings, like that led by the christened *cacique* Enriquillo in Hispaniola in 1519, do to change the historical outcome for the Tainos. Neither were the New Laws promulgated by Charles V in 1542 of much use to the Tainos. These laws guaranteed freedom and protection to the indigenous population, but they arrived too late.

Let us use Hispaniola to illustrate the degree to which the conquest and colonization decimated the Tainos of the Antilles. Some authors estimate that there were between a million and three million inhabitants in Hispaniola at time of the discovery. Believing those numbers are exaggerated, others have suggested a quantity that ranges from 100,000 to 600,000. In Chapter 8, we estimated 350,000 Taino inhabitants in Hispaniola as a conservative, yet very likely, number. In 1508, the same year that the conquest began in Puerto Rico, the first census was conducted in Hispaniola. This census reported the existence of 60,000 persons. It follows that 300,000 aboriginals perished in Hispaniola in the first fifteen years of colonization. In 1514, 30,000 Tainos were counted in a census of *encomendados*. Four years later, in 1518, documents point to 11,000 Tainos. And in 1570, there were only approximately 750 survivors.

Despite the fact that the colonizers generally did not consider the mestizos to be indigenous people nor did they count people who had gone deep into the mountains, the demographic catastrophe undoubtedly suffered by the Tainos was tremendous and few examples are comparable in the history of mankind. To a certain extent, what happened in Hispaniola was repeated in Puerto Rico, Cuba and Jamaica. In Puerto Rico, approximately 5,500 Tainos were originally registered as *encomendados* and, from there, their numbers decreased over the years. The late census of 1530 yields a little more than a thousand Tainos in Puerto Rico, while in 1544 there were only sixty *encomendados*.

The New Laws (1542?) gave complete freedom to the indigenous people. As a result, some villages were created to group the few surviving Tainos and their descendants. Such was the case of Boyá and Bánica (where in 1744 "some Indians were still seen") in Hispaniola, and Guanabacoa in Cuba. In Cuba, isolated groups of Tainos persisted in the east (Guantánamo, Santiago de Cuba, Bayamo) and their descendants remain today. In Puerto Rico, Father Abbad alleged the existence of Taino people in the mountains of Añasco and San Germán in 1775.

Indigenous woman in Yateras, Cuba,
with her husband of Spanish origin and family (Harrington, 1921).

It is possible that these people were related to the inhabitants of Mona, a small island to the west and belonging to the archipelago of Puerto Rico, who moved to the main island years earlier. In Jamaica, the Taino population declined due to the conquest and apparently disappeared with the arrival of black slaves.

In sum, the evidence points to the substantial disappearance in the Greater Antilles of the Tainos and the main elements of their culture, religion and language, by the end of the 16th century. From then on, we cannot refer to the existence of Taino people. Rather, we can refer to the presence of mestizo individuals, who were the result of the union of the aboriginal woman with either a Spanish colonizer or an African slave.

In this sense, although the study by Ángel Rodríguez Olleros (1974) did not establish a correlation between blood groups, the Rh factor and "the different racial groups that make up our people," the genetic investigations conducted by Juan C. Martínez Cruzado at the University of Puerto Rico in Mayagüez show that 62% of Puerto Ricans possess the indigenous mitochondrial DNA, 30% possess the African, and 8% the Caucasian, regardless of their physical appearance. Cautiously, this does not mean that six out of every ten Puerto Ricans are either Taino, have aboriginal blood or have their traits. This means that an indigenous woman intervened at some point in the feminine ascendant lineage of these six people. This is because the female mitochondrion is transmitted intact from generation to generation, without it being combined with the masculine version. As such, these results demonstrate the considerable participation that Taino women had in miscegenation. It was through this process that the Taino heritage was transmitted to the culture of the Antilles that exists today.

Caribs: between war and peace

Lacking gold, the Lesser Antilles were not the main attraction to the Spanish colonizer. However, as we saw in chapter 11, several confrontations occurred between Spaniards and Caribs during the 16th and into the 17th century.

The Spaniard became the Carib's staunch enemy. Twelve Dominican priests who attempted to evangelize and win over the Carib people were assassinated in three distinct occasions; in 1603, 1606 and 1611. The French and English took advantage of the Carib's loathe towards the Spaniard to enter the New World through the eastern Antilles. Long before the first French and English settlements, the Caribs exchanged tobacco, cotton, wood and salt with European ships. Among those ships was the expedition that brought Anonymous of Carpentras to the New World.

When a handful of French and English settlers arrived on the small island of St. Kitts between 1622 and 1623, the Caribs welcomed the enemy of their enemies with some kindness. But, in 1625, they did not take long to plan a revolt and kill both groups of Europeans led by Pierre Belain of Esnambuc and Thomas Warner. Esnambuc and Warner, aware of the plan, hesitated even less to defend themselves and massacred in a blow the entire Carib population of the island. This was the first bloody clash between the French, the English and the Caribs in a struggle that would go on, with ups and downs, for almost two centuries. Despite their courage, the Caribs suffered the consequences of the colonial expansion of these two European rival powers. Due to the constant upheaval and mainly as a result of war, the Caribs practically disappeared from the small islands in the Antilles.

The year 1635 turned out to be very significant. A French colonizing expedition supported by the government and directed by L'Olive settled in Guadeloupe. Raymond Breton was among the four Dominicans to arrive on that trip. Separately, settlers from St. Kitts under the command of Esnambuc colonized Martinique. On both islands the French settled without confrontation with the Caribs, but with a suspicion that soon exploded. Also, that year, a shipwreck of two vessels with African slaves was reported off the coast of St. Vincent. This episode led to the settlement in the Antilles of the first group of black people who, having escaped capture in the Spanish colonies, lived in freedom with the Caribs.

In the years that followed the relationship between the Caribs and the French fluctuated between war and peace. The indigenous population was progressively stripped off the islands of Guadeloupe and Martinique, migrating to Dominica, an island that became the center of operation for the Caribs. In 1660, a Franco-Anglo-Carib treaty recognized the sovereignty of the indigenous people in Dominica and St. Vincent. It was around this time that French missionaries resided in the islands and succeeded in documenting the main features of Carib culture. They failed, however, to preach the Gospel and convert Caribs to Christianity.

It should be noted that, in contrast to the variety of exploitation methods imposed by the Spanish on the Tainos, the Caribs were not subjected to slavery. From the beginning, the economy in the French Antilles was based on tobacco and cotton produced by colonists and European workers under contract, or "engagés." These workers committed to work for thirty-six months before gaining independence. But, by 1654, the economy shifted to sugar production, giving way to the massive importation of African slaves that in a few years surpassed both the aboriginal and European populations.

Throughout the 18th century the Caribs and the French benefited from each other's alliances against English expansion. However, as a result of the Seven Years War in Europe and the Treaty of Paris of 1763, France was forced to recognize English sovereignty over Dominica and St. Vincent. By then, the black population had lived in St. Vincent for more than a century. The island was a refuge for black slaves who escaped from the plantations or "habitations" managed by the English and French in neighboring islands.

Because these free Africans came from different ethnic groups, their adoption of the Carib language and culture became the common denominator that permitted their integration.

Moreover, the fact that, as a consequence of continuous wars, women constituted the majority of the aboriginal population in St. Vincent, the progressive miscegenation forged a distinctive black-Carib culture. Notwithstanding the fact that in St. Vincent the black-Caribs were in the majority, the island continued to house nuclei of autochthonous Caribs, called "reds" by the English.

Up until 1796, in spite of the British possession, several wars took place between the Franco-Carib alliance and the English for the control of St. Vincent. Finally, in the summer of 1796, the English army prevailed and General Ralph Abercromby decided to depopulate the island of natives. In February of 1797, 5,080 black-Caribs set sail from St. Vincent. A mere two thousand people arrived at their final destination: the island of Roatan, off the coast of Honduras. Their descendants, the Garifuna people, scattered around 60 fishing villages along the Caribbean coast of Central America in what is today Honduras, Guatemala, Nicaragua and Belize. They commemorate their arrival on April 12.

In 2001, the UNESCO designated the Garifuna language as a "Masterpiece of the Oral and Intangible Heritage of Humanity." The Garifuna language belongs to the Arawakan group of languages and has survived centuries of discrimination and linguistic domination. It is rich in tales originally recited during wakes or large gatherings. The melodies bring together African and Amerindian elements, and the texts are a veritable repository of the history and traditional knowledge of the Garifuna, such as manioc-growing, fishing, and canoe-building.

The rediscovery of the Carib

In Dominica, contrary to what happened in St. Vincent, the English decided to establish a policy of coexistence with the remaining Caribs. A few hundred Caribs established the villages of Salybia and Bataka in the northeastern part of the island. Located opposite an inhospitable coast and protected by a mountainous area of dense forest, these people endured without major cultural changes for many years.

Captain George and his family in Dominica, according to Ober (1880)

In 1853, due to Methodist proselytism, Father Létrée was recruited to convert the remaining Caribs in Dominica to Catholicism. With the help of a guide, he crossed the mountains until he reached "three small villages of about 40 people each." The initial reaction of the inhabitants was to hide in the forest. When he managed to have them return, Létrée noticed that their faces were neither European nor African; "they seem more likely to descend from Asian people," he wrote to the bishop. Létrée also observed that they retained their language, but that they knew "creole" to communicate with foreigners. During his regular visits, Father Létrée managed to catechize many Caribs, built several chapels and, in the summer of 1854, he gave Communion to the first fifteen Caribs.

The rediscovery and conversion of the Caribs of Dominica by Father Létrée had other consequences. When, in 1887, the town of Salybia was visited by Frederick Ober, the American ornithologist and explorer, he noted that the assimilation process of the Caribs had accelerated. Ober reported that only some elders spoke the Carib language, despite the persistence of many ancient customs. Further, as a consequence of the progressive racial mixture of the Caribs with the creole and the black population, which he attributed to the religious men, Ober estimated that there were no more than twenty families of pure Caribs.

In 1903, due to the need for land by creole families, the British government increased the Carib Reserve from 300 to 3,700 acres and better defined its geographical limits. Frederic A. Fenger, during his companionless sailing trip from Grenada to the Virgin Islands in 1911, recorded and photographed certain aspects of the Carib people.

In 1936, Father Jean-Baptiste Delawarde published an important article about Carib villages. Years later, in 1938, Douglas Taylor began to publish important ethnographical research regarding the Carib descendants in Dominica. Despite maintaining many Carib traditions, Taylor found that, out of the 450 inhabitants residing in the reserve, only about 100 "looked like and thought of themselves as purebred Carib." As for the language, he documented that they spoke "*créole-patois*" and that the last Caribs to speak the native language had died some 20 or 25 years earlier.

Thus, the last vestige of the indigenous people of the Antilles vanished a little more than four hundred years after the European discovery and about three hundred years after the disappearance of the Tainos. What remains is a rich cultural legacy.

The aboriginal patrimony

Exchanges of various kinds occurred between the Europeans and the indigenous inhabitants of the Antilles. The first manner in which they made contact involved the barter of material goods: rattles were traded for gold and knives for tobacco. Later, the exchange was cultural in nature: for example, the Spaniard adopted important cultural elements of the aboriginal while attempting to Christianize the Tainos.

The indigenous people contributed their labor, technology and knowledge of the natural world in exchange for a European who adapted to the island environment. In a few more years, Taino women were responsible for initiating the fusion, first with Spaniard and later with African men, in the same matter that the Carib women would mix with the latter. After all, the hybrid Antillean culture that emerged denoted elements from all three groups. Many of these elements lingered for hundreds of years and survive to this day.

From the beginning, the agricultural technology of the indigenous people of the Antilles served as the foundation of the colonial diet. Slash and burn techniques were employed in the *conuco* (small plots of land) and, especially, the skill of sowing in heaps used by the Tainos, came to constitute an agrarian measure and a very important feature of the agricultural production system.

From there came the consumption of the cassava (the native processing technique that is still employed in some places), the tobacco (that was eventually exported from the Antilles to conquer the world), the *guáyiga* (the tuber that is used in the south of the Dominican Republic to extract starch and make the "chola," a kind of bread), and an infinite number of agricultural products (*maíz, yautía*, peanut, sweet potato, *lerén*, pineapple, guava, *guanábana, papaya, jagua, caimito, jobo, mamey*) as well as the use of *coa* and the barbecue (now replaced by metal instruments). Similarly, a critical legacy left behind by the indigenous people was the knowledge about medicinal plants. Such knowledge was kept by the *behique* (Taino) and *boyez* (Carib). Earlier in this book we mentioned the trees, plants and healing herbs that the colonizer used in the early years since their arrival. The aboriginal pharmacopoeia served as the basis for colonial medicine, although many original names were replaced little by little by European designations.

For example, in Puerto Rico, in the *Memoria de Melgarejo* of 1582, the poisonous *guchón* is called "manzanillo". Likewise, in Hispaniola, the educated landowner Luis Joseph Peguero recorded in 1762 about 20 native medicinal plants. He transcribed plants with the names given to them by the colonizer: palma *dey (jiguereta), babey (alpargate), busuga (sarzamora), cabima* or *curucay (azeyte), amasey* or *boaconar* (Tree of God), *dividibe (guatapaná)*. In 1775, again in Puerto Rico, Captain Miyares González made a list of native plants and fruits used by the apothecaries of the time: *pajuil, tabonuco, carob, guanábana, corozo, pitahaya, tua-tua, higüereta*. And, in Dominica, the ethnobotanical research carried out by Hodge and Taylor in the middle of the 20th century yielded a total of 134 magical-medicinal plants used by Carib descendants.

The fishing technique is also an important legacy of the aboriginal cultures of the Antilles. Fishing with poison, with nets (*tarrayas*), and in pens, is still in vogue. Also, the names of many fish (Taino: *carite, cojinúa, jurel, dajao, guábina*; Carib: *titiri, matawale, couloné, wakawa, coulirou, balaou*) are also part of history. The skill and nautical experience of the natives was taken advantage of at all times; remember "Diego Colón," the guide-interpreter to the Admiral, and the prowess of the scribe Diego Méndez when he sailed from Jamaica to Hispaniola in two canoes led by Taino men. In addition, the European would make extensive use of the canoe. In the Dominican Republic, the old canoe gave way to the "cayuco," today's primary means of fishing in the Bay of Samaná; in Martinique and Dominica, the "bacassa" mentioned by the chronicler Labat (1722) and the current "gommier" of the fishermen, emerged from the canoe. The trees with which these boats were built are the same ones that the colonizer used to repair or build his ships. For centuries, the *bohío* (Taino) and the *carbet* (Carib) were reflected in the construction of Antillean popular housing. This happened also with the fabrication of household items such as the hammock, basket weaving with cotton fibers (*cabuya* and *henequén*), and pottery made with clay or *higüero* pots. The Puerto Rican *dita*, a pot made with half an *higüera*, owes its name and its use to the native.

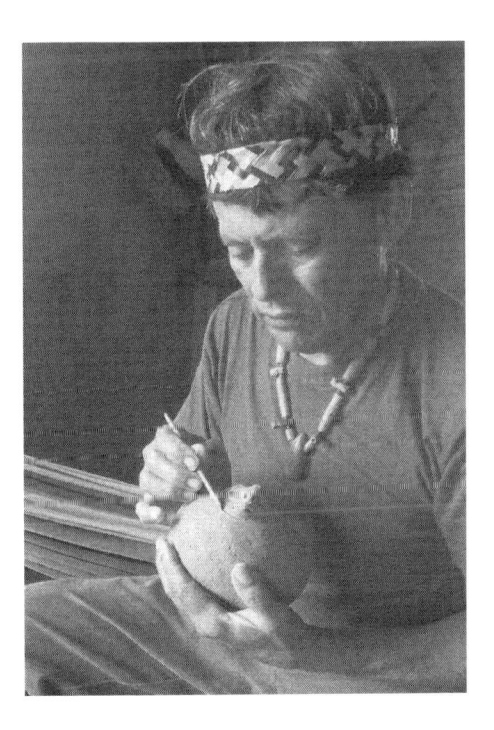

Daniel Silva Pagán,
Puerto Rican artisan who makes various types of Taino objects (2018).

It was in the language, however, that Taino and Caribe heritage would achieve its maximum recognition. Linguists estimate that there are about 700 Taino words and their derivatives in the Spanish language of the Greater Antilles. Among them, place names prevail (regions, cities, towns, neighborhoods, mountains, savannas, rivers, islands, cays, bays), anthroponyms (names of characters), names of flora (trees, shrubs, vines, herbs, vegetables, tubers, fruits), wildlife (birds, reptiles, mammals, fish, crustaceans, amphibians, insects) and endless number of words related to the spiritual life, the person, objects and tools for domestic or ceremonial use, food and drink, communal activities, etc.

Some words used by the Tainos - *canoa*, *cacique*, *huracán* - gained an international passport and belong today to the lexicon of other languages. The word *huracán*, for example: "hurricane" in English, "ouragan" in French, "orkan" in German, and "uragano" in Italian.

In the case of the Caribs, their language was Island-Arawak which was adopted presumably by the Carib invaders from the ancient island women. The Carib language went extinct in Dominica and the rest of the smaller Antilles, except for certain words that persist in *créole*. In Central America, however, the Carib language survives thanks to the Garifuna, the descendants of the Black-Caribs of St. Vincent. The Garifuna language became the unifying element of peoples of various backgrounds and cultures. According to Taylor, Garifuna people speak a dialect whose vocabulary is, fundamentally, that of the ancient Caribs but peppered with words from Spanish, French and English. In effect, Taylor managed to compile approximately 800 words of the lexical Carib legacy. Interestingly, when Taylor compared the Garifuna beliefs, customs and ceremonies to the chroniclers who wrote about the Tainos and Caribs, he concluded that in the blending that occurred, the indigenous element took precedence over the African.

In this context, it is necessary to mention the ideological contribution of the Tainos to the Afro-Antillean religions. Perhaps because they shared a similar level of socio-cultural development, the African people found a parallelism between their beliefs and those of the Antillean native. Among the similarities is the cult to ancestors and the plurality of deities. Hence, in the blending of religions that occurred between the Spanish and the African, the Catholic saints became equivalent to the *luás* of voodoo and the *orishas* of Santería. In the case of the interaction between the Tainos and the African, Carlos Esteban Deive noted that in the Dominican voodoo some *luás* have names of well-known Taino *caciques*, while Geo Ripley emphasized that Gamao, the head of the Indigenous Division, uses fragments of archaeological pieces in the altar.

Further, Cuban archaeologist Lourdes Domínguez suggested "the possible interrelation of the Yoruba and Arawak pantheons." For example, Shangó, the major *orisha* of fertility and fire, chief of thunder and war and identified with St. Barbara, could be equivalent to Bayamanaco, the Taino Fire God who possessed the secret of making the cassava and the *cohoba*.

Professing the indigenous heritage

During the 19th century, the era of liberalism and of independence movements, the indigenist theme became a symbol of national identity for writers who were followers of romanticism throughout Latin America. The Hispanic Antilles was not an exception.

In the case of the Dominican Republic, which gained its independence first from Haiti and then from Spain, the use of the Taino theme in prose and verse was a means to search for autochthonous values and to reaffirm nationalist ideals. The heroic past of the indigenous people was extolled and their physical and spiritual merits poetized. It is for this reason that the first national heroes in the Dominican Republic are the indigenous heroes: Caonabo, Guarionex, Hatuey, Enriquillo. All of these, together with Anacaona, Quisqueya, and Mencía, are names carried by many Dominicans. Today, Dominicans refer to the mestizo as "indio." Among the extensive pro-indigenous literature in the Dominican Republic, the poetic work of José Joaquín Pérez stands out. In some of his works, he builds on the fantastic *Historia de los Caciques de Haití* by Haitian author Emilio Nau, and the historical legend *Enriquillo* (1879) by Manuel de Jesús Galván, considered a "novel, poem and history" by José Martí.

In Cuba, some of the romanticism of the period expressed itself in an indigenist tendency that led to the creation of national and creole poetry. In it, authors praised the heroism of the ancient Tainos and the natural beauty of the country, conveying at once political criticisms of the Spanish government. *Siboneyismo* was a literary movement of nationalist affirmation whose maximum figure was José Fornaris, author of the popular book *Cantos del Siboney* (1855) and founder of the weekly *La piragua* with Joaquín Lorenzo Luaces.

Like Cuba, Puerto Rico was a colony of Spain until the end of the 19th century. The romantic indigenist tendency manifested itself in written works that highlighted the opposition and rebellion of the Tainos to Spanish colonization, a simile of the sustained struggle against Spanish colonialism and a reaffirmation of Puerto Rican nationality. In addition to the well-known pro-indigenous works by Alejandro Tapia and Eugenio María de Hostos, it is worth mentioning a less known work: *Los dos indios, episodio de la conquista de Borinquen* by Ramón Emeterio Betances. This short anticolonialism novel was written in French around 1855. It was later translated and published in 1998 to commemorate the centenary of the death of its author and as a valid statement against the American colonial presence.

During the 20th century, the aboriginal theme became a symbol of national identity expressed in crafts, the fine arts and music. Matilde Pérez de Silva published *Aplicaciones industriales del diseño indígena de Puerto Rico* (1939) with a companion text by Adolfo de Hostos, where they presented varied patterns of Taino symbols to facilitate their popular use. Around 1955, promoted by Emile de Boyrie Moya, a modern Dominican craft inspired by Taino motifs was created. Objects made of wood, clay, stone, amber, gold and cloth, shaped what became known as "neo-Taino" art.

To this day, Antillean artisans continue to use Taino elements in their work. Three examples come to mind: the Dominican Guillen brothers, creators of a small industry of "Taino pottery"; the Puerto Ricans Héctor de León and Neftalí Maldonado Rosado, carvers in stone and wood of Taino replicas. At times, reenactments of songs, dances or Taino-inspired ceremonies take place. For example, the Concilio Taíno Guatu-Ma-cu A Borikén organizes representative events of Taino culture. The Concilio Taíno "raises awareness and promotes cultural knowledge to those who have an interest in Taino culture in Puerto Rico and abroad through education, including the revelation of the true history of the Taino, and their customs, languages, ceremonial dances, music, songs and crafts."

Taino dance. Centro Ceremonial Indígena de Caguana, Utuado, P.R.

In recent years, a number of Puerto Rican emigrants to the United States claim to be descendants of the Tainos, form civic-cultural groups, use aboriginal names, celebrate various activities, use indigenous medicinal plants or keep colorful pages on the Internet, reaffirming the indigenous personality as symbol of national identity. More recently, in July 2018, the Smithsonian's National Museum of the American Indian and the Smithsonian Latino Center opened an exhibit at George Gustav Heye Center in New York called "Taíno: Native Heritage and Identity in the Caribbean," about the indigenous peoples of the Spanish speaking Caribbean.

To a large extent, the tenacity of the indigenous theme is the result of scientific advances in the region. Modern archeology is now able to evoke the past based on scientific principles. In doing so, it promotes technical advances without losing the romantic notion. The existence of laws for the protection of historical heritage, the restoration of ceremonial plazas, the celebration of handicraft fairs, the organization of congresses, the construction of museums, and the publication of research have contributed to the dissemination of knowledge about these lost aboriginal cultures.

The Tainos and the Caribs live on as part of a hybrid Antillean culture.

Examples of artisan works with Taino inspiration.
Left column: Puerto Rico. Right column: Dominican Republic.

References and Bibliography

The original bibliography of *Taínos y caribes, las culturas aborígenes antillanas* was published in 2003. The version contained in this publication has been updated to both comport with the revisions to the book, now available in English, and to provide the reader with a comprehensive list of additional readings. While this reference list and bibliography is not intended to be comprehensive, an impossible task by definition, it is a resource summary of the most significant works on the subject of the indigenous cultures of the Antilles.

Acronyms and abbreviations used throughout and what they stand for:

>CEAPRC: Centro de Estudios Avanzados de Puerto Rico y el Caribe
>DR: Dominican Republic
>EUPR: Editorial Universidad de Puerto Rico
>FCE: Fundación Cultural Educativa
>FGA: Fundación García Arévalo
>ICP: Instituto de Cultura Puertorriqueña
>MHD: Museo del Hombre Dominicano
>PR: Puerto Rico
>SD: Santo Domingo
>SJ: San Juan
>UASD: Universidad Autónoma de Santo Domingo
>UPR: Universidad de Puerto Rico

Acosta, José de
1986   *Historia natural y moral de las Indias* (Sevilla, 1590). Madrid: Colección Crónicas de América-Historia 16. Edited by José Alcina Franch.

Acosta Saignes, Miguel
1946   Los Caribes de la costa venezolana. *Cuadernos Americanos* XXVI-2:173-184. México.
1950   *Tlacaxcipoualiztli: un complejo mesoamericano entre los Caribes.* Instituto de Antropología y Geografía, Facultad de Filosofía y Letras. Caracas: Universidad Central de Venezuela.
1954   *Estudio de etnología antigua de Venezuela.* Caracas: Universidad Central de Venezuela.

Alberti Bosch, Narciso
1912   *Apuntes para la prehistoria de Quisqueya.* La Vega (DR): El Progreso.
1922   *Clave para comprender el simbolismo de los cemíes antillanos y el sentido cifrado esotérico de los signos míticos que tienen grabados.* El Mamey, February 1ro. - May 1ro. Not published. Manuscript located in the Library of the MHD, DR.

Alcina Franch, José
1982a   *Arte y antropología.* Madrid: Alianza Editorial.
     b   Religiosidad, alucinógenos y patrones artísticos taínos. MHD, *Boletín* 17: 103- 117.

1983   La cultura taína como sociedad en transición entre los niveles tribal y de jefaturas. In: *La cultura taína* pp. 67-79. Madrid: Comisión Nacional para la Celebración del V Centenario del Descubrimiento de América.

Alegría, Ricardo E.

1971   *Descubrimiento, conquista y colonización de Puerto Rico*. SJ: Colección de Estudios Puertorriqueños.

1976   Un escudo de armas para Baltasar de Castro por su victoria contra los caribes en el Daguao en 1515. ICP, *Revista* 72: 24.

1978a *Apuntes en torno a la mitología de los indios taínos de las Antillas Mayores y sus orígenes suramericanos*. SD: CEAPRC -MHD.

    b *Las primeras representaciones gráficas del indio americano (1453-1523)*. SJ: CEAPRC - ICP.

1979a El uso de gases nocivos como arma bélica por los indios taínos y caribes de las Antillas. ICP, *Revista* 82:51-55.

    b Apuntes para el estudio de los caciques de Puerto Rico. ICP, *Revista* 85: 25-41.

1980a *Cristóbal Colón y el tesoro de los indios taínos de La Española*. SD: FGA.

    b La experiencia de Luisa de Nabarrete, puertorriqueña negra, entre los indios caribes de la Dominica (1576-1580). Universidad de Puerto Rico, *Revista del Museo de Antropología, Historia y Arte*, Vol. 1-2: 39-44. Río Piedras.

    c A Carib Chieftain in San Juan. *The San Juan Star Sunday Magazine*, October 18, pp. 2-3. SJ.

1981a Las primeras noticias sobre los indios caribes. Introduction to *Crónicas francesas de los indios caribes* (Cárdenas Ruíz, 1981). SJ: EUPR - CEAPRC.

    b *El uso de la incrustación en la escultura de los indios antillanos*. SJ: CEAPRC – FGA.

1982   "Many People of Both Nations Were Killed, Smoked and Eaten by the Caribs". Pierre Labat, 1722. *The San Juan Star*, January 10, pp. 12-13. SJ.

1983   Ball Courts and Ceremonial Plazas in the West Indies. *Yale University Publications in Anthropology* 79. New Haven: Yale University Press.

1986   Etnografía taína en el momento de la conquista de las Antillas Mayores. CEAPRC, *La Revista* 2:69-80.

1987   El ataque de los indios caribes al Daguao (1530). La captura y muerte de Cristóbal de Guzmán y la expedición punitiva contra la isla Dominica (1534). CEAPRC, *La Revista* 5:24-31.

1988   Apuntes en torno a las culturas aborígenes de Puerto Rico. See Alegría, ed. (1988: 18-53).

1995   La vestimenta y los adornos de los caciques taínos y la parafernalia asociada a sus funciones mágico-religiosas. *XV Congress of the International Association for Caribbean Archaeology* (SJ, July, 1993). See Alegría, R. E. and Miguel Rodríguez (eds.) 1995: 295-309.

1997a An introduction to Taíno Culture and History. In: Fátima Berch et al, pp. 18-32.

    b Esclavo de los caribes. *El Nuevo Día, Revista Domingo*, February 2, pp. 8-9. SJ.

Alegría, Ricardo E. (ed.)

1988   *Temas de la historia de Puerto Rico*. SJ: CEAPRC.

1993   *Índice analítico de las Actas de los Congresos de la Asociación de Arqueología del Caribe 1963- 1993*. SJ: CEAPRC.

2009   *Documentos históricos de Puerto Rico (1493-1599)*. SJ: CEAPRC- ICP. 5 vols.

Alegría, Ricardo E., and Miguel Rodríguez (eds.)

1995   *Actas, XV Congress of the International Association for Caribbean Archaeology* (San Juan, July 1993). SJ: CEAPRC.

Alegría Pons, José Francisco

1987   "El chamanismo taíno de las Antillas Mayores y sus paralelos en la América del Sur". Master's Thesis. CEAPRC. SJ.

Álvarez Nazario, Manuel
1977   *El influjo indígena en el español de Puerto Rico*. SJ: EUPR.
1996   *Arqueología lingüística*. SJ: EUPR.

Allaire, Louis
1979   On the Historicity of Carib Migration in the Lesser Antilles. *American Antiquity* 45: 238-245.
1981a   Los Caribes: ¿realidad o fábula? Critical review of J. Sued Badillo's (1978) book. UPR, *Revista de Ciencias Sociales* 23 (3-4): 737-743. Río Piedras.
      b The Saurian pineal eye in Antillean art and mythology. *Journal of Latin American Lore* 7-1: 3-22. Los Angeles.
1996   Vision of Cannibals: Distant Island and Distant Lands in Taino Image. In: R. Paquette and S, Engerman (eds.), pp. 33-49.
1997   The Caribs of the Lesser Antilles. In: Samuel Wilson (ed.), pp. 179-185.

Allsworth-Jones, P.
2008   *Pre-Columbian Jamaica*. Tuscaloosa: The University of Alabama Press.

Amodio, Emanuel
1991   El oro de los caníbales: geografía y habitantes míticos del Nuevo Mundo en los textos de Cristóbal Colón. Fundación La Salle, *Antropológica* 75-76: 93-126. Caracas.

Anglería, Pedro Mártir de
1989   *Décadas del Nuevo Mundo* (1892). SD: Sociedad Dominicana de Bibliófilos.

Anónimo de Carpentras
1990   *Un Flibustier Français dans la Mer des Antilles (1618-1620)*. Edited by Jean-Pierre Moreau. Paris: Editions Seghers. See also Moreau (1990).

Arens, William
1979   *The Man Eating Myths. Anthropology and Anthropophagy*. New York: Oxford University Press.
1998   Rethinking Anthropophagy. In: *Cannibalism and the Colonial World*, P. Barker, P. Hulme and M. Iversen (eds.), pp. 39-62. Cambridge University Press.

Armas y Céspedes, Juan Ignacio
1884   La fábula de los caribes. In: *Revista de Cuba* VIII-XV-6 (June 30), pp. 481-509. La Habana.

Arrom, José Juan
1971   El mundo mítico de los taínos: notas sobre el Ser Supremo. UASD, *Revista Dominicana de Arqueología y Antropología* Vol 1-1: 181-200. SD.
1973   Aportaciones lingüísticas al conocimiento de la cosmovisión taína. Universidad Católica Madre y Maestra, *Eme-Eme* II-8: 3-17, Santiago de los Caballeros.
1974   *Fray Ramón Pané: "Relación acerca de las antigüedades de los indios"*. México: Siglo XXI. See also Pané (c. 1498).
1975   *Mitología y artes prehispánicas de las Antillas*. México: Siglo XXI - FGA.
1986   Fray Ramón Pané o el rescate de un mundo mítico. CEAPRC, *La Revista* 3: 2-8, San Juan. Published originally in *Anales de literatura hispanoamericana*, Madrid, VIII, 1980:15-22. See also *Imaginación del Nuevo Mundo*, 1991: 36-46, México: Siglo XXI.
1989   Sobre presuntos ritos atribuidos a los naturales de Cuba, Jamaica y Puerto Rico. CEAPRC, *La Revista* 8:9-15.
1991   *Imaginación en el Nuevo Mundo*. México: Siglo XXI.
1992   Las primeras imágenes opuestas y el debate sobre la dignidad del indio. In: *De palabra y obra en el Nuevo Mundo*, M. León-Portilla et al (eds.), pp. 63-85. México: Siglo XXI.
2000   *Estudios de lexicología antillana*. SJ: EUPR.

Arrom, José Juan, and Manuel García Arévalo
1988   *El murciélago y la lechuza en la cultura taína*. Santo Domingo: FGA.

Atiles, José Gabriel and Elpidio Ortega
2001   Un sitio llamado el Manantial de La Aleta. MHD, *Boletín* 30:33-54.

Aveni, Anthony
1980   *Skywatchers of Ancient Mexico*. Austin: University of Texas Press. In Spanish: *Observadores del cielo en el México Antiguo*. México: Fondo de Cultura, 1991, 1993.
1988   *New Directions in American Archaeoastronomy*. Bar International Serie 454. Oxford: British Archaeological Reports.
2008   *People and the Sky*. New York: Thames & Hudson.
2017   *In the Shadow of the Moon: The Science, Magic, and Mystery of Solar Eclipses*. New Haven: Yale University Press.

Aveni, Anthony (ed.)
1977   *Archaeoastronomy in Pre-Columbian America*. Austin: University of Texas Press.

Aveni, Anthony and Gary Urton (eds.)
1982   *Ethnoastronomy and Archaeoastronomy in the American Tropics*. New York Academy of Sciences, Annals 385. New York.

Ayes Suárez, Carlos M.
1996   *La Cueva del Cupey*. Manatí (P.R.): Pueblo Nuevo.

Bachiller y Morales, Antonio
1883   *Cuba primitiva: origen, lenguas, tradiciones e historia de los indios de las Antillas Mayores y las Lucayas*. La Habana.

Barker, Francis, Peter Hulme, and Margaret Iversen
1998   *Cannibalism and the Colonial World*. New York: Cambridge University Press.

Baker, Patrick
1984   Ethnogenesis: The Case of the Dominican Caribs. *América Indígena* 48: 377-401.

Baker, R.J., and H. Genoways
1978   *Zoogeography of Antillean Bats*. Special Publications Academy of Natural Science of Philadelphia 13: 53-97. Philadelphia.

Ballet, J.
1875   Les Caraïbes. Compte-rendu de la prémiere sesion du *I Congrés International des Américanistes*, Nancy, 392-438. Paris: Maisonneuve.

Beckles, Hilary M.
1992   Kalinago (Carib) Resistance to European Colonization of the Caribbean. *Caribbean Quarterly* 38 (2-3): 1-14. See also: *Caribbean Slavery in the Atlantic World*, V.A. Shepherd and H.M. Beckles (eds.), 2000, pp. 117-125. Oxford: James Currey Publishers.

Benson, Elizabeth P.
1988   The Maya and the Bat. *Latin American Indian Literatures Journal*, 4-2:99-124. Geneve College, Philadelphia.
1991   Bats in South American Folklore and Ancient Art. *Bat Conservation International*, 9-1:7-10. Austin.
1997   *Birds and Beasts of Ancient Latin America*. Gainesville: University de Florida Press.

Benzoni, M. Girolamo
1992   *La historia del Nuevo Mundo*. (Venice, 1565). Translation by Marisa Vannini de Gerulewicz. Preliminary study by León Croizat. SD: Sociedad Dominicana de Bibliófilos.

Bérard, Benoit
2008   Caraïbes et Arawaks, caracterisation et identification ethnique. In: *Les Civilisations Amériediennes des Petites Antilles*, Cécile Celma (ed.), pp. 4-19. Fort-de-France: Musée Départemental d'Archéologie Précolomgienne et de Préhistoire.
2011   A la recherché des Caraïbes archéologiques. In: Grunberg (2011.)

Berch, Fátima (ed.)
1997   *Taino, Pre-columbian Art and Culture from the Caribbean*. New York: Monacelli Press - Museo del Barrio.

Bernáldez, Andrés
1875   *Historia de los Reyes Católicos Don Fernando y Doña Isabel.* Sevilla: Imprenta de D. José María Geofrin. 2 vols.

Bernand, Carmen and Serge Gruzinski
1992   *De la idolatría.* Una arqueología de las ciencias religiosas. México: Fondo de Cultura.

Biaggi, Virgilio
1983   *Las aves de Puerto Rico.* SJ: EUPR.

Biet, Antoine
1664   *Voyages de la France Équinoxiale en l'Isle de Cayenne, entrepis par les François en l'année MDCLII.* Paris: F. Clouzier.

Blasini, Antonio
1985   *El águila y el jaguar.* SJ: Publigraph.

Boas, Frank
1947   *Arte primitivo.* México: Fondo de Cultura.

Boomert, Arie
1986   The Cayo complex of St. Vincent: ethnohistorical and archaeological aspects of the Island-Carib problem. Fundación La Salle, *Antropológica* 66: 3-68. Caracas.
1987   Gifts of the Amazons: "Green Stone" Pendants and Beads as Items of Ceremonial Exchange in Amazonia and the Caribbean. Fundación La Salle, *Antropológica* 67: 33-54. Caracas.
1995   Island-Carib archaeology. In: *Wolves from the sea*, N.L. Whitehead (ed.), pp. 23-25. Leiden: Royal Institute of Linguistics and Anthropology.

Booy, Theodoor de
1915   Pottery from certain caves in Eastern Santo Domingo, West Indies. *American Anthrologist*, Vol. 17-1: 69-103.

Bosch, Juan
1935   *Indios. Apuntes históricos y leyendas.* SD, DR.

Boucher, Philip P.
1979   The Caribbean and the Caribs in the Thought of Seventeenth Century French Colonial Propagandists: The Missionaries. *Proceedings of the French Colonial Historical Society*, James Cooke (ed.), 4: 17-32. Canada.
1992   *Cannibal Encounters: Europeans and Island Caribs (1492-1763).* Baltimore: The Johns Hopkins University Press.
2000   First Impressions: Europeans and Island Caribs in the Pre-Colonial Era, 1492-1623. In: *Caribbean Slavery in the Atlantic World*, V.A. Shepherd and H.M. Beckles (eds.), pp. 100-116. Oxford: James Currey Publishers.
2008   *France and the American Tropics to 1700: Tropics of Discontent?* Baltimore: The Johns Hopkins University Press.

Bouton, Jacques
1640   *Relation de l'Establissement des François Depuis l'an 1635 en l'Isle de la Martinique.* Paris: Chez S. Cramoisy. Spanish partial translation. Cárdenas (1981:109-125).

Boyrie Moya, Emile de
1955   *Monumento megalítico y petroglifos de Chacuey, República Dominicana.* Ciudad Trujillo (SD): Universidad de Santo Domingo.

Brasselet, Patrick
2003   Remarques sur le chamanise des Caraïbes Insulaires. *XX Congress of the International Association for Caribbean Archaeology* (SD, June-29-July 6), G. Tavárez and M. García Arévalo (eds.), pp. 279-285. SD: MHD-FGA.

Breton, Raymond
1664   *Petit Catéchisme ou Sommaire des Trois Premiéres Parties de la Doctrine Chrétienne.* Auxerre: Gilles Bouquet.
1665   *Dictionnaire Caraïbe-Français Meslé de Quantité de Remarques Historiques Pour l'Esclaircissement de la Langue.* Auxerre: Gilles Bouquet. Reimpresiones: Jules Platzam, Leipzig, 1892; Karthala, Paris, 1999.
1666   *Dictionnaire Français-Caraïbe.* Auxerre: Gilles Bouquet.

1667 *Grammaire Caraïbe.* Auxerre: Gilles Bouquet.
1877 *Grammaire Caraïbe Suivie du Catéchisme Caraïbe.* Paris: L'Adam & Ch. Leclerc.
1978 *Relations de l'Ile de la Guadeloupe (1647).* Basse-Terre: Société de l'Histoire de la Guadeloupe.

Brinton, Daniel G.
1868 *The Myths of the New World.* Nueva York: Leypoldt & Holt. Reprint: Multimedia Publishing Co, New York, 1976.
1871 The Arawak Language of Guiana in its Linguistic and Ethnological Relations. *Transactions of the American Philosophical Society,* New Serie, vol. XIV-4: 427-444. Philadelphia.
1882 *American Hero-Myths.* Philadelphia: H.C. Watts & Co. Johnson Reprint Co., New York, 1970.
1899 *Races & People.* Lectures on the science of ethnography. New York.

Broda, Johanna
1982a La fiesta del Fuego Nuevo y el culto de las Pléyades. Symposium Space and Time in the Cosmovisión of Mesoamerica, *XLII International Congress of Americanists* (August 11- 17, 1979), Vancouver, Canada. Published in: *Lateinamerika Studien 10* (Franz Tichy, ed.), pp. 129-157. München: Universität Erlangen-Nürnberg.
    b Astronomy, *Cosmovisión* and Ideology in Pre-Hispanic Mesoamerica. In: *Etnoastronomy and Archaeoastronomy in the American Tropics,* Aveni y Urton (eds.), 1982, pp. 81-110.

Brown, Paula and Donald Tuzin
1983 *The Ethnography of Cannibalism.* Washington, D.C.: Society fot Psychological Anthropology.

Bry, Theodore de
1992 *América (1590-1634).* Madrid: Siruela.

Bucher, Bernadette
1981 *Icon and Conquest. A Structural Analysis of the Illustrations of de Bry's Great Voyages.* Chicago: The University of Chicago Press.

Bucher, Ira
1980 *The Organization of Social Life: The Perspective of Kinship Studies in People in Culture.* New York: Bergin Publishers.

Burke, Peter
2000 *Formas de historia cultural.* Madrid: Alianza Editorial.

Butel, Paul
1982 *Les Caraïbes au temps des flibustiers. XVIe-XVIIe siècles.* Paris: Aubier Montaigne.
2002 *Histoire des Antilles Français. XVIIe-XIX siècles.* Paris: Perrin.

Caldera Ortiz, Luis
2017 *Historia de los ciclones y huracanes tropicales en Puerto Rico.* Coamo: Editorial El Jagüey.

Callaghan, Richard T.
1985 Possible preceramic connections between Central America and the Greater Antilles. *XI Congress of the International Association for Caribbean Archaeology* (SJ).
1991 Passages to the Greater Antilles: An analysis of watercraft and the marine environment. *XIV Congress of the International Association for Caribbean Archaeology* (Martinica).
1993 Antillean cultural contacts with mainland regions as a navigation problem. *XV Congress of the International Association for Caribbean Archaeology* (SJ). Alegría & Rodríguez (eds), 1995.
1999 Computer simulations of Ancient Voyaging. *The Northern Mariner- Le Marin du nord,* IX-2:11-22.
2001 Analysis of ceramic age seafaring and interaction potential in the Antilles. *Current Anthropology,* April.
2003 Comments on the Mainland Origins of the Preceramic Cultures of the Greater Antilles. *Latin American Antiquity* 14: 323-338.
2009 Patterns of Contact Between the Islands of the Caribbean and Surrounding Mainland as a Navigation Problem. In: Curet (2009).

Callaghan, R., and Donna Fremont
1992 A computer simulation of routes of passage in the Caribbean and Gulf of México. *57th Annual Meeting of the Society for American Archaeology,* Pittsburghs, PA.

Callaghan, R., and Sthephanie J. Schwabe
1999 Watercraft of the Islands. *XVIII Congress of the International Association for Caribbean Archaeology* (Grenada).

Cameron, Catherine M.
2006 *Captives. How Stolen People Changed the World*. University of Nebraska Press.

Cárdenas Ruíz, Manuel (ed.)
1981 *Crónicas francesas de los indios caribes*. SJ: EUPR - CEAPRC.
1984 *Padre J.B. Labat: nuevo viaje a las islas de la América*. Vol.1. SJ: EUPR.

Carneiro, Robert L.
1970 A Theory of the Origin of the State. *Science* 169: 733-738.
1981 The Chiefdom: Precursor of the State. In: *The Transition in Statehood in the New World*. Jones, G.D. and R. Kaus (eds.), pp. 37-79. Cambridge University Press.
1998 What Happened at the Flashpoint? Conjectures on Chiefdom Formation at the Very Moment of Conception. In: *Chiefdoms and Chieftaincy in the Americas*, Elsa M. Redmond (ed.), pp. 18-42. University of Florida Press.

Casas, Bartolomé de Las
1951 *Historia de las Indias* (Madrid, 1875). México: Fondo de Cultura. 3 Vols. Edited by Agustín Millares Carlo.
1967 *Apologética historia sumaria* (Madrid, 1909). México: Universidad Autónoma de México, Instituto de Investigaciones Históricas. Edited by Edmundo O'Gorman.
2001 *Brevísima destrucción de las Indias* (1552). Madrid.

Cassá, Roberto
1974 *Los taínos de La Española*. SD: UASD.
1992 *Los indios de las Antillas*. Madrid: MAPFRE.

Castañeda Delgado, Paulino
1970 La política española con los caribes en el siglo XVI. Instituto Gonzalo Fernández de Oviedo, *Revista de Indias* 119-122: 73- 130. Madrid.

Castres, Caillé de
2002 *De Wilde ou Les Sauvages Caraïbe Insulaires d' Amérique* (1694). Manuscript, published by Société des Amis du Musée d'Archaéologie and the Société d' Histoire de la Martinique.

Chamberlain, Von de & John B. Carlson, and M. Jane Young (eds.)
2005 *Songs from the Sky. Indigenous Astronomical and Cosmological Traditions of the World*. Ocarina Books-The Center for Archaeoastronomy.

Chanca, Diego Álvarez
1858 "Segundo Viaje de Cristóbal Colón", *Colección de los viajes y descubrimientos que hicieron los españoles desde fines del siglo XV...* Madrid. 4 Vols. Edited by Martín Fernández de Navarrete. See also: Tió (1966).

Chanlatte Baik, Luis A.
1977 *Primer adorno corporal de oro (nariguera) en la arqueología indoantillana*. SD: FGA. valo.
1981 *La Hueca y Sorcé (Vieques, Puerto Rico): primeras migraciones agroalfareras Antillanas. Nuevo esquema para los procesos culturales de la arqueología antillana*. SD: Taller.
1986 Cultura Ostionoide: Un desarrollo agroalfarero Antillano en Puerto Rico. Universidad Interamericana, *Homines* 10-1: 11-49.
2000 Los arcaicos y el formativo antillano (6000 a.C-1492 d.C.). MHD, *Boletín* 28: 29-42.
2003 ¿Cuál fue el destino final de las poblaciones arcaicas antillanas? *XX Congress of the International Association for Caribbean Archaeology* (SD, June 29 – July 6). G. Tavárez and M. García Arévalo (eds.). SD: MHD-FGA.

Chanlatte Baik, Luis and Yvonne Narganes Stordes
1989 La nueva arqueología de Puerto Rico: su proyección en las Antillas. MHD, *Boletín* 22:9-49.
2002 "La cultura saladoide en Puerto Rico", catálogo, *Museo de Historia, Antropología y Arte*, 25 de abril. Río Piedras: UPR.

Charlevoix, Pierre François Javier de
1977   *Historia de la isla Española o de Santo Domingo* (Paris, 1790). SD: Editora de Santo Domingo, 2 vols.

Civrieux, Marc de
1974   *Religión y magia Kari'na.* Caracas: Universidad Católica Andrés Bello.
1976   *Los caribes y la conquista de la Guyana española.* Etnohistoria Kaliña. Caracas: Universidad Central Andrés Bello.

Clastres, Pierre
2001   *Investigaciones en antropología política.* Barcelona: Gedisa.

Colón, Fernando
1984   *Historia del Almirante* (Venice, 1571) Madrid: Crónicas de América-Historia 16. Edited by Luis Arranz.

Coll y Toste, Cayetano
1907   *Prehistoria de Puerto Rico.* SJ: Tipografía Boletín Mercantil.

Combes, Isabelle
1992   *La Tragédie Cannibale Chez les Anciens Tupi- Guarani.* Paris: Collection Ethnologies, Presse Universitaires de France.

Conklin, Beth A.
2001   *Consuming Grief. Compassionate Cannibalism in an Amazonian Society.* Austin: University of Texas Press.

Conzemius, Eduard
1928   Ethnographical Notes on the Black Carib (Garif). *American Anthropologist* 30:182-205.
1930   Sur les Garif ou Caraïbes Noir de l'Amérique Centrale. *Anthropos* 25: 859-877. Modling-bei-Wien.

Crespo Torres, Edwin
2002   Nuevas interpretaciones en torno a las creencias sobre la muerte y las prácticas funerarias de los indios de Boriquén. ICP, *Revista* 3-5: 83-94.
2003   Estudio paleopatológico comparativo entre dos sitios arqueológicos: Punta Candelero y Paso del Indio. *V Encuentro de Investigadores de Arqueología y Etnohistoria del* ICP (SJ, March 26-27).

Cronau, Rodolfo
1892   *América.* Barcelona: Montaner y Simon.

Crouse, Nellis Maynard
1940   *French Pioneers in the West Indies, 1624-1664.* New York: Columbia University Press. Also: New York, Octagon Books, 1977.
1943   *The French Struggle for the West Indies, 1665-1713.* New York: Columbia University Press. Reimpresión: New York, Octagon Books, 1966.

Cruces, Francisco
2001   *Las culturas musicales. Lecturas de etnomusicología.* Madrid: Trotta.

Curet Salim, L. Antonio
1992   Estructuras domésticas y cambio cultural en la prehistoria de Puerto Rico. CEAPRC, *La Revista* 14: 59-75. English version: House structure and cultural change in the Caribbean: three case studies from Puerto Rico. *Latin American Antiquity*, 3-2: 160-174, 1992.
1996   Ideology, Chiefly Power, and Material Culture: An Example from the Great Antilles. *Latin American Antiquity* 7: 114 - 131.
1997   Poder e ideología: el control del simbolismo en los cacicazgos tempranos de Puerto Rico. *Historia y Sociedad* X: 107-125. Río Piedras: UPR.
2002   The Chief is Dead, Long Live... Who? Descent and Succession in the Protohistoric Chiefdoms of the Greater Antilles. American Society for Ethnohistory, *Etnohistory* 49(2): 259-280.
2003   Issues on the Diversity and Emergence of Middle- Range Societies of the Ancient Caribbean: A Critique. *Journal of Archaeological Research* 11 -1: 1-42. The Netherlands.

2005   *Caribbean Paleodemography. Population, Cultural History, and Sociopolitical Processes in Ancient Puerto Rico.* Tuscaloosa: The University of Alabama Press.

2014   The Taíno: Phenomena, Concepts, and Terms. *Ethnohistory* 61-3: 467-495.

Curet Salim, L. A., Lee A. Newsom, and Daniel Welch

2001   Space and Time in the Civic Center of Tibes, Ponce. *XIX Congress of the International Association for Caribbean Archaeology* (Aruba).

Curet Salim, L. A., Lee A., and Lisa M. Strenger

2010   *People, Power, and Ritual at the Center for the Cosmos. Caribbean Archaeology and Ethnohistory.* Tuscaloosa: The University of Alabama Press.

Curet Salim, L. A., and Mark W. Hauser (eds.)

2011   *Islands at the Crossroads. Migration, Seafaring, and Interaction in the Caribbean.* Tuscaloosa: The University of Alabama Press.

Dacal Moure, R., and M. Rivero de la Calle

1986   *Arqueología aborigen de Cuba.* La Habana: Gente Nueva.

Dampier, Jacques de

1904   *Essai Sur les Sources de l'' Histoire des Antilles Françaises, 1492-1664.* Paris: A. Picard et Fils. Also: Martino Publishing, CT, 2003.

Dávila, Ovidio

2003   *Arqueología de la Isla de la Mona.* SJ: ICP.

Davis, Dade D., and Christopher Goodwin

1990   Island Carib Origins: Evidence and Nonevidence. *American Antiquity* 55-1: 37- 48.

Deagan, K., and J. M. Cruxent

2002   *Archaeology at La Isabela: American's First European Town.* New Haven: Yale University Press.

Deive, Carlos E.

1976   Fray Ramón Pané y el nacimiento de la etnografía americana. MHD, *Boletín* 6:133-156.

1978   Los taínos y la leyenda de las Amazonas. MHD, *Boletín 7(10):253-270.*

Delawarde, Jean-Baptiste

1938   Les Derniers Caraïbes. Leur vie dans une reserve de la Dominque. *Journal de la Société des Américanistes* 30:167-207. Paris.

1976   Essai sur la recontre et le heur de la cultura européenne et de la cultura caraibe (I). *L'Ethnographie* 72:191-207. Paris.

1977   Essai sur… (II). *L'Ethnographie* 73:99-113. Paris.

Delpuech, André

1993   *Présents Caraïbes: 500 ans d'Histoire Amérindienne.* Catalogue exposition 5 dec. 1993- 28 fev. 1994, Fort Delgres. Basse-Terre: Gaudeloupe.

2001   *Guadeloupe Amérindienne.* Guides archéologiques de la France, Editions du Patrimoine. Paris: Monum.

Delpuech, André and Corinne Hofman (eds.)

2003   *Late Ceramic Societies in the Eastern Caribbean.* Oxford: BAR.

Delpuech, André and Benoit Roux

2015   Á la recherche de la culture matérielle des Caraïbes Insulaires. In: *Á la Recherche du Caraïbe Perdu,* Bernard Grunberg (ed.), Paris: L'Harmattan.

Díaz Niese, Rafael

1945   La alfarería indígena dominicana. *Cuadernos Dominicanos de Cultura,* II-19:23-52. Ciudad Trujillo (SD).

Dickanson, Olive P.

1984   The Brazilian Connection: A Look at the Origins of French Techniques for Trading with Amerindians. *Revue Français d'Histoire d'Outre-mer* 71:129-146.

1997   *The Myth of the Savage and the Beginnings of French Colonialism in the Americas* (1984). Edmonton: University of Alberta Press.

Domínguez González, Lourdes S.
1980 Algunos aspectos sobre el arte en los grupos aborígenes agroalfareros de Cuba. *CesarAugusta* 51-52: 49-51. Zaragoza: Institución Fernando el Católico.
1994 Las comunidades aborígenes de Cuba. *Historia de Cuba*, Cap.1, pp.5-57. La Habana: Edit. Política.
2001 La mujer aborigen al inicio del siglo XVI en el Caribe. *Gabinete de Arqueología* 1-1: 88-91. La Habana: Oficina del Historiador de la Ciudad.

Dreyfus, Simone
1976 Remarques sur l'organisation socio-politique des Caraïbes insulaires au XVIIeme siecle. *VI International Congress for the Study of Pre-Columbian Cultures in the Lesser Antilles* (Guadeloupe, July 6-12, 1975), R.P. Bullen (ed.), pp. 87-97. Pointe-à- Pitre: Central University Antilles-Guayane.
1984 Historical and political anthropological inter-connections: the multilinguistic indigenous polity of the Caribbean Islands and mainland coast from the 16th to the 18th century. Fundación La Salle, *Antropológica* 59-62: 39-56. Caracas.

Dubelaar, Cornelis Nicolaas
1986 *South American and Caribbean Petroglyphs*. Holland: Foris Publications.
1991 *Bibliography of South American and Antillean Petroglyphs*. Amsterdam: Foundation for Scientific Research in the Caribbean Region: 129.
1995 *The Petroglyphs of the Lesser Antilles, the Virgin Islands and Trinidad*. Amsterdam: Foundation for Scientific Research in the Caribbean Region 135.

Dumont, Enrique D.
1876 *Investigaciones acerca de las antigüedades de la isla de Puerto Rico*. La Habana.

Durand, Gilbert
1971 *La imaginación simbólica*. Buenos Aires: Amorrottu.
1981 *Las estructuras antropológicas de lo imaginario*. Madrid: Taurus.
2002 *Mitos y sociedades. Introducción a la mitología*. Buenos Aires: Biblos.

Dutertre, Jean-Baptiste
1667-71 *Histoire Génerale des Antilles Habitées par les François*. Spanish partial traslation: Cárdenas (1981: 441-494).

Duverger, Christian
1983 *La Flor Letal, economía del sacrificio azteca*. México: Fondo de Cultura.

Eichholz, Duane W.
1976 A potencial archaeo-astronomical horizon at Las Flores. *VI International Congress for the Study of Pre-Columbian Cultures in the Lesser Antilles* (Guadeloupe, July 6-12, 1975), R.P. Bullen (ed.) p. 314. Pointe-à-Pitre: Central Universitie Antilles-Guayane.

Eliade, Mircea
1951 *El mito del eterno retorno*. Madrid: Alianza.
1955 *Imágenes y símbolos*. Madrid: Taurus.
1957 *Lo sagrado y lo profano*. Barcelona: Labor.
1963 *Mito y realidad*. Barcelona: Guardarrama.
1974 *Imágenes y símbolos*. Madrid: Taurus.
1976 *El chamanismo y las técnicas arcaicas de éxtasis*. México: Fondo de Cultura.

Escabí Agostini, Pedro C.
1981 El significado de la música en la sociedad indígena de las Antillas. UPR, *Revista de Ciencias Sociales* 23 (1-2).

Evans, Peter G. H.
1990 *Birds of the Eastern Caribbean*. London: MacMillam Educational Ltd.

Evans-Pritchard, Edward
1961 *Anthropology and History*. Manchester: Manchester University Press.
1984 *Las teorías de la religión primitiva* [Oxford, 1965]. Madrid: Siglo XXI.
1987 *Historia del pensamiento antropológico*. Madrid: Cétedra.

Fenger, Frederic A.
1917 *Alone in the Caribbean.* New York: George H. Doran Co.

Fernandes, Florestan
1952 La guerre et le sacrifice humain chez les Tupinambá. *Journal de la Société des Américanistes* XLI: 151. Paris.
1970 *A funçao social da guerra na sociedade Tupinambá.* Sao Paulo: Editora da Universidade de S. Paulo

Fernández de Navarrete, Martín
1986 *Viajes de Colón* [1825]. México: Porrúa.

Fernández Méndez, Eugenio
1969 *Crónicas de Puerto Rico (1493-1955).* SJ: EUPR.
1972 *Art and Mythology of the Taino Indians of the Greater West Indies.* SJ: El Cemí.
1979 *Arte y mitología de los indios taínos de las Antillas Mayores.* SJ: Ediciones Cemí.

Fernández Ortega, Racso and José B. González Tendero
2001 *El enigma de los petroglifos aborígenes de Cuba y el caribe insular.* La Habana: Centro de Investigación y Desarrollo de la Cultura Cubana.
2003 La mitología aborigen y el arte rupestre en la Cueva de Patana, Maisí, Cuba. *XX Congress of the International Association for Caribbean Archaeology* (Santo Domingo, June 29- July 6).

Fewkes, Jesse Walter
1907 *The Aborigines of Porto Rico and the Neighboring Islands.* Twenty-Fifth Annual Report of the U.S. Bureau of Ethnology to the Secretary of the Smithsonian Institution, Washington, D.C, Johnson Reprint Co., New York, 1970.
1922 *A Prehistoric Island Culture Area of America.* XXXIV Annual Report (1912-13). Washington: Bureau of American Ethnology.

Florescano, Enrique
2000 La visión del cosmos de los indígenas actuales. Centro de Investigación y Estudios Superiores en Antropología Social, *Desacatos*: 15-29. México.

Furst, Peter T. (ed.)
1972 *Flesh of the Gods: the Ritual use of Hallucinogens.* New York: Praeger.

Gannier, Odile
2003 *Les Derniers Indiens Caraïbe: Image, Mythe et Réalité.* Paris: Ibis Rouge Editions.

Gannon, Michael R., A. Kurta, A. Rodríguez and M. Willig
2005 *Bats of Puerto Rico.* Kingston: The University of the West Indies.

García Arévalo, Manuel A.
1977 *El arte taíno de la República Dominicana.* SD: MHD- FGA.
1983 El murciélago en la mitología y el arte taíno. In: *La cultura taína* pp. 105-114. Madrid: Comisión Nacional del V Centenario del Descubrimiento, Turner Libros.
1985 El juego de pelota taíno y su importancia comercial. *XI Congress of the International Association for Caribbean Archaeology* (SJ, July); A.G. Plantel (ed.). Curacao: Institute of Archaeology and Anthropology of the Netherlands Antilles. See also *Florida Journal of Anthropology* 16: 91-96 (1991). Florida.
1988a *Indigenismo, arqueología e identidad nacional.* SD: MHD – FGA.
    b Primeras ilustraciones arqueológicas de la isla de Santo Domingo. FGA, *Revista* 2:87-116.
1989 *Los signos en el arte taíno.* SD: FGA.
2001 Los Cigüayos: un enigma arqueológico antillano. *IV Encuentro de Investigadores ICP* (SJ, April, 26).
2002 El ayuno del behique y el simbolismo ritual del esqueleto. MHD, *Boletín* 31:83-96.
2003 Las fronteras tipológicas de la cultura taína. *XX Congress of the International Association for Caribbean Archaeology* (SD, June 29 – July 6).

García Goyco, Osvaldo
1983 "Estudio de mitología comparada entre las culturas indígenas de las Antillas, Venezuela y Mesoamérica." Master's Thesis. CEAPRC, SJ.
1984 *Influencias mayas y aztecas en los taínos de las Antillas Mayores.* SJ: Ediciones Xibalbay.
2003a Nemotecnia y mito: posibles paisajes mitológicos en el arte rupestre antillano prehispánico. *V Encuentro de Investigadores de Arqueología y Etnohistoria,* ICP (SJ, March 26-27).
b Nuevas interpretaciones en torno a la iconografía de los taínos. *XX Congress of the International Association for Caribbean Archaeology* (SD, June 29-July 6).
2011 Jácana, su probable participación en la rebelión taína de 1511. *Simposio V Centenario de la Rebelión Taína (1511-2011),* pp. 106-123. SJ: FCE-ICP.

Geertz, Clifford
2003 *La interpretación de las culturas* (1973). Barcelona: Gedisa.

Girard, René
1983 *La violencia y lo sagrado* (1972). Barcelona: Anagrama.

Glazier, Stephen D.
1980 A Note on Shamanism in the Lesser Antilles. *VIII International Congress for the Study of the Pre-Columbian Cultures of the Lesser Antilles.* S. Lowenstein (ed.), pp. 447-455. Tempe: Arizona State University.
1991 Impressions of aboriginal technology: The Caribbean canoe. *XIII International Congress for Caribbean Archaeology.* Reports of the Archaeological-Anthropological Institute of the Netherlands Antilles 9: 149-161. Curaçao.

Godelier, Maurice
1989 *Lo ideal y lo material.* Madrid: Taurus.
1998 *El enigma del don.* Barcelona: Paidós.

Godo, Pedro and Miriam Celaya
1988 Expresiones mitológicas en los burenes de Cuba. *Anuario de Arqueología,* pp. 152-184. Centro de Arqueología y Etnología, Academia de Ciencias de Cuba. La Habana: Editorial Academia.

Goeje, C. H. de
1928 *The Arawak Language of Guiana.* Amsterdam: Verhandelingen der Koninklijke Akademie van Wetenschappen ten Amsterdam, Afd. Lett. 28-2.
1946 *Études Linguistiques Caraïbes.* Amsterdam: Verhandelingen der Koninklijke Akademie van Wetenschappen ten Amsterdam, Afd. Lett. 49-2.

González Colón, Juan
1987 "Tibes: un centro ceremonial indígena". Master's Thesis. CEAPRC, SJ.

Gómez, Labor and Manuel Ballesteros
1978 *Culturas indígenas de Puerto Rico.* Río Piedras: Editorial Cultural.

González, Miriam and Pedro Godo
2000 Llora-lluvia: Expresiones mítico-artísticas en la alfarería aborigen. Casa del Caribe, *El Caribe Arqueológico* 4:70-84. Santiago de Cuba.

González, Nancie L.
1988 *Sojourners of the Caribbean: Ethnogenesis and Ethnohistory of the Garifuna.* Urbana: University of Illinois.

Gordon Wasson, R., Stella Kramrisch, Jonathan Ott, and Carl A. Ruck
1992 *La búsqueda de Perséfone. Los enteógenos y los orígenes de la religión.* México: Fondo de Cultura.

Grunberg, Bernard, E. Rouler, and B. Roux
2011 *Les Indiens des Petites Antilles. Des premieres peuplements aux débuts de la colonisation européenne.* Paris: L'Harmattan.

Grunberg, Bernard (ed.)
2015 *À la Recherche du Caraïbe Perdu. Les populations amérindiennes de Petites Antilles de l'époque précolombienne à la période coloniales.* Paris: L'Harmattan.

Grunberg, Bernard, J. Grunberg, and B. Roux
2013 *Missionnaires carmes et capucins: Pacific de Provins et Maurille de St. Michel.* Édition critique de Corpus Antilles/Sciences sur les Indiens de la Caraïbe. Paris: L'Harmattan.
2014 *Voyageurs Anonymes aux Antilles. Anonyme de Carpentras, Anonyme de Grenade, Anonyme de St. Christophe, Anonyme de St. Vincent, Anonyme edit "Gentilhomme écossais".* Éditon critique de Corpus Antilles/Sciences sur les Indiens de la Caraïbe Paris: L'Harmattan.
2015 *Missionnaires dominicains (I). Philippe de Beausmont, André Chevillard, Mathias Du Puis, Pierre Pélican.* Éditon critique de Corpus Antilles/Sciences sur les Indiens de la Caraïbe Paris: L'Harmattan.

Gruzinski, Serge
1993 *La colonización de lo imaginario.* México: Fondo de Cultura.
1994 *La guera de las imágenes.* México: Fondo de Cultura.
2007 *El pensamiento mestizo. Cultura amerindia y civilización del Renacimineto.* Barcelona: Paidós.

Guarch, José M.
1978 *El taíno de Cuba.* La Habana: Academia de Ciencias de Cuba.

Guarch, José M., and Alejandro Querejeta Barceló
1993 *Los cemíes olvidados.* La Habana: Publicigraf.

Gullick, C.J.M.R.
1978 Black Carib Origins and Early Society. *VII International Congress for the Study of Pre-Columbian Cultures of the Lesser Antilles.* Ed. Centre de Recherches Caraïbes, pp. 283-290. Caracas: Universidad Central de Caracas.
1980 Island Carib Traditions About Their Arrival in the Lesser Antilles. *VIII International Congress for the Study of Precolumbian Cultures of the Lesser Antilles*, ed. S. Lewenstein, pp. 464-72. Tempe: Arizona State University Press.
1985 Myths of a Minority. Assen, Netherlands: Van Gorcum.

Gutiérrez Calvache, Divaldo A.
2002 Sobre el simbolismo y la funcionalidad del número en el arte rupestre de la cueva de los petroglifos. Casa del Caribe, *El Caribe Arqueológico* 6: 23-34. Santiago de Cuba.

Harner, Michael J.
1973 *Hallucinogens and Shamanism.* London: Oxford University Press.

Harrington, Mark R.
1921 *Cuba Before Columbus.* New York: Museum of the American Indians, Haye Foundation. Spanish version: La Habana, 1935.

Harris, Marvin
1977 *Cannibals and Kings: The Origin of Culture.* New York: Random House.

Haslip Viera, Gabriel (ed.)
2001 *Taíno Revival: Critical Perspectives on Puerto Rican Identity and Cultural Politics.* Princeton: Markus Wiener Publishers.
2013 *Race, Identity and Indigenous Politics. Puerto Rico Neo-Tainos in the Diaspora and the Island.* New York: Latino Scholars Press.

Hayward, Michele H., Lesley-Gail Atkinson, and Michael A. Cinquine (eds.)
2009 *Rock Art of the Caribbean.* Tuscaloosa: The University of Alabama Press.

Helms, Mary W.
1987 Art styles and interaction spheres in Central America and the Caribbean: polished black wood in the Greater Antilles. *Chiefdoms in the Americas,* R.

Drennan and C.A. Uriba (eds.), pp. 67- 84. Lanham: University Press of America. See also *Journal of Latin American Lore* 12-1: 25-43, 1986, Los Angeles.

Hernández Aquino, Luis
1969   *Diccionario de voces indígenas de Puerto Rico*. SJ: Editorial Cultural.

Hernández de Lara, Odlanyer
2009   *Biblioteca de Cuba Arqueológica*. Índice bibliográfico hasta junio de 2009. www.cubaarqueologica.org

Hernández Oliva, Carlos and Lisette Roura Álvarez
2001   Reflexiones en torno al tema de la muerte en la mitología y la plástica Arahuaca. Oficina del Historiador de la Ciudad, *Gabinete de Arqueología* 1-1:36-44. La Habana.

Herrera Fritot, René
1946   *La Caleta, joya arqueológica antillana*. La Habana.
1950   Arqueotipos zoomorfos en las Antillas Mayores. *Sociedad Felipe Poey, Boletín de Historia Natural* 1-3: 140-149. La Habana.

Heyerdahl, Thor
1979   Early Man and the Ocean: A Search for the Beginning of Navigation and Seaborne Civilizations. New York: Doubleday.

Hodge, Walter H.
1942   Plants used by the Dominica Caribs. *Journal of the New York Botanical Garden* 43 (512):189-201. New York.

Hodge, Walter H., and Douglas M. Taylor
1957   Ethnobotany of the Island Caribs of Dominica. *Webbia* 12-2: 513-644. Florence. See also: Richard Schultes (1951).

Hodgen, Margaret T.
1971   *Early Anthropology of the Sixteenth and Seventeenth Centuries*. Philadelphia: University of Pennsylvania.

Hoff, Berend J.
1995   Language, Contact, War and American Historical Tradition: The Special Case of the Island Carib. In: *Wolves from the Sea*, N.L. Whitehead (ed.), p. 23-25. Leiden: Royal Institute of Linguistics and Anthropology.

Hofman, Corinne L., and Anna van Duijvenbode
2011   *Communities in Contact. Essays in Archaeology, Ethnohistory & Ethnography of Amerindian Circum-Caribbean*. Leiden: Sidestone Press.

Hofman, Corinne L., and Andrzej T. Antczak (eds.)
2019   *Early Settlers of the Insular Caribbean*. Leiden: Sidestone Press.

Hoogland, Menno L.P., and Corinne L. Hofman
1999   Expansion of the Taíno Cacicazgos Toward the Lesser Antilles. *Journal de la Société des Américanistes* 85: 93 -115. Paris.

Hoogland, Menno L. P., C.L. Hofman and A. Boomert
2011   Argyle, St. Vincent: new insights on the Island Carib occupation of the Lesser Antilles. *24th International Congress for Caribbean Archaeology*. Martinique.

Hostos, Adolfo de
1922   Notes on West Indian hydrography in its relation to prehistoric migrations. *XIX International Congress des Américanistes* (Río de Janeiro), p. 11-23.
1941   *Anthropological Papers*. SJ: Bureau of Supplies, Printing and Transportation.
1955   *Una colección arqueológica antillana*. SJ.

Huerga, Álvaro
2006   *Ataques de los Caribes a Puerto Rico en el siglo XVI*. SJ: Academia Puertorriqueña de la Historia - CEAPRC.

Hulme, Peter
1990 The Rhetoric of Description: The Amerindians of the Caribbean Within the Mode of European Discourse. *Caribbean Studies* 23. Río Piedras: Instituto del Caribe.
1992 *Colonial Encounters: Europe and the Native Caribbean 1492-1797*. New York: Methuen.
2001 *Remanants of Conquest: The Island Caribs and Their Visitors, 1877-1998*. Oxford University Press.

Hulme, Peter and Neil Whitehead (eds.)
1992 *Wild Majesty: Encounters with Caribs from Columbus to the Present Day: An Anthology*. Oxford: Clarendon.

Im Thurn, Everard F.
1883 *Among the Indians of Guianas*. New York: Dover Press.

Jara, Fabiola
1983 Constelaciones de los Arawaks. Amsterdam: Centro de Estudios y Documentación Latinoamericanos. English versión: Preliminary Catalogue of Arawak Constellation. Indigenous, Astronomical and Cosmological Traditions of the World, *Proceeding of the International Conference on Ethnoastronomy*. Washington: Smithsonian Institution.
1988 Montruosité et altérité: Le mythe des Amazones des indies Kalina et Xikrin. In: *Les Monstres dans l'imaginaire des Indiens d'Amérique Latine*. Paris: CIRCE.
2000 Arawak Constellations: In Search of the Manioc Stars in Tropical South America. *Latin Ammerican Indian Literatures Journal* Vol. 16-2: 114-149, 2000. PA.

Jiménez Lambertus, Abelardo
1978 Representación simbólica de la tortuga mítica en el arte cerámico taíno. MHD, *Boletín* 7-11:63-76.
1984 Arte rupestre sumergido. Suplemento, *Listín Diario*, 28 de enero, pp. 6-7. S.D.
1987 Mitología y genética. MHD, *Boletín* 20:13-16.
2003 Corocote: su identificación. *XX Congress of the International Association for Caribbean Archaeology* (SD, June 29- July 6).

Joyce, Thomas A.
1907 Prehistoric antiquities from the Antilles in the British Museum. *Journal of the Royal Anthropological Institute*, Vol. 31-1. London.

Jung, Carl G.
1974 *El hombre y sus símbolos*. Madrid: Aguilar.

Keegan, William F.
1992 *The People Who Discovered Columbus*. Gainesville: University Press of Florida.
2007 *Taíno Indian Myth and Practice. The arrival of the Stranger King*. Gainesville: University Press of Florida.

Keegan, William F., Corinne L. Hofman, and Reniel Rodríguez Ramos
2003 *The Oxford Handbook of Caribbean Archaeology*. New York: Oxford University Press.

Kerchache, Jacques (ed.)
1994 *L'Art des Sculpteurs Tainos: Chefs-d'Oeuvre des Grandes Antilles Precolombiennes*. Paris: Musée du Petit-Palais. (Catalog Taino Art Exhibition, February 24 - May 29).

Kirby, I. A. Earle
1980 The Carib incursion into the Greater Antilles. *VIII International Congress for the Study of Pre-Columbian Cultures of the Lesser Antilles*, S. Lewenstein (ed.), pp. 593-96. Tempe: Arizona State University Press.

Kloos, Peter
1968 Becoming a *piyei*: variability and similarity in Carib shamanism. Fundación La Salle, *Antropológica* 24: 3-25., Caracas.

Krieger, Herbert W.
1931   *Aboriginal Indian Pottery of the Dominican Republic*. United States National Museum, *Bulletin* 156. Smithsonian Institution.

Krug, Leopold
1876   Indianische Alterthüner in Porto Rico (Puerto Rico Indian Antiques). *Zeitschrift für Ethnologie* 8:428-436. Berlin.

Krupp, Edwin C.
1977   *In Search of ancient Astronomies*. New York: Doubleday & Co.
1983   *Echoes of the Ancient Skies. The Astronomy of Lost Civilizations*. New York: Harper & Row. New edition: 2004.
1997   *Skywatchers, Shamans & Kings. Astronomy and the Archaeology of Power*. New York: John Wiley & Sons.

La Borde, Monsieur
1674   *Relation de l"Origine, Moeurs, Coustumes, Religion, Guerres et Voyages des Caraïbes, Sauvages de l'Amérique*. Paris: Louis Billaine. Spanish partial translation: Cárdenas (1981:495-532).

Labat, Jean-Baptiste
1722   *Noveau Voyage aux Isles de l'Amérique*. Paris: Chez G. Cavelier. Spanish partial translantions: Cárdenas (1981: 532-611; 1984) and Francisco de Oraá (Casa de Las Américas, La Habana, 1979).

Lafitau, Joseph-François
1724   *Mœurs des Sauvages Amériquains Comparées aux Mœurs des Premiers Temps*. Paris: Chez Saugrain.

Lafleur, Gérard
1992   *Les Caraïbes des Petites Antilles*. Paris: Karthala.
1996   Contribution à l'étude du cannibalisme chez les Amériediens. *Bulletin de la Société de Histoire de la Guadeloupe* 109: 3-20. Basse Terre, Guadeloupe.

Layton, Robert
1991   *The Anthropology of Art*. Cambridge University Press.

L'Etang, Thierry
1989   Le Gibier de Chemin: les Esprits, les Sauvages, les bêtes et la mort. Contribution a una zoo-ethnologie des croyances amérindiennes des Petites Antilles. Actes du Colloque du Marin, *Civilisations Précolombiennes de la Caraïbe*, pp. 89-103. Paris: Editions l'Harmattan.
2008   Notes sur deux mythes d'origine des caraïbes insulaires / Toponymie indigéne des Antilles. *Les Civilisations Amérindiennes des Petites Antilles*, Cécile Celma (ed.), pp. 22-56. Fort-de-France: Musée Départemental d'Archéologie Précolombienne et de Préhistoire.

Le Joff, Jacques
1991   *El orden de la memoria, el tiempo como imaginario*. Barcelona: Paidós.

Le Riverend, Julio
1961   El indigenismo en la historia de las ideas cubanas. *Islas* 9: 52-62. Santa Clara-La Habana.

Lehmann-Nitsche, Robert
1922   Las constelaciones del Orión y de las Híades y su pretendida identidad de interpretación en las esferas eurasiática y sudamericana. Universidad Nacional de la Plata, *Revista del Museo de La Plata*, 26:15-68. Buenos Aires.
1924   La constelación de la Osa Mayor y su concepto como huracán o dios de la tormenta en la esfera del mar caribe. Universidad Nacional de la Plata, *Revista del Museo de La Plata*, 28:103-145. Buenos Aires.

Lestringant, Frank
1994   Le Cannibale, grandeur et décadence. Paris: Perrin.

1997a Le Brésil d'André Thevet. In: *Les Singularités de la France Antarctique (1557)*. Paris: Editions Chandeigne.
   b *Cannibals: The Discovery and Representation of the Cannibal from Columbus to Jules Verne*. Los Angeles: University of California Press.

Léry, Jean de
1994 *Histoire d'un Voyage Faict en la Terre du Brésil.* (1578). Introduction by Claude Lévi-Strauss; edited by Frank Lestringant. Paris: Biblio Classique.

Lévi-Strauss, Claude
1968 *Lo crudo y lo cocido*. México: Fondo de Cultura.
1970 *El origen de las maneras de mesa*. México: Siglo XXI.
1972 *De la miel a las cenizas*. México: Fondo de Cultura.
1974 *Estructuralismo y ecología*. Barcelona: Anagrama.
1976 *El hombre desnudo*. México: Siglo XXI.
1984 *Palabra dada*. Barcelona: Espasa-Calpe.
1986 *La alfarera celosa*. Barcelona: Paidós.

Lewis, David
1972 *We, the Navigators. The Ancient Art of Landfinding in the Pacific*. Honolulu: The University Press of Hawaii.

Liogier, Henri Alain
1990 Las plantas introducidas en las Antillas después del descubrimiento y su impacto en la ecología. Comisión Puertorriqueña para la Celebración del Quinto Centenario, *Encuentro*. SJ. Also see: *Plantas medicinales de Puerto Rico y el Caribe*. SJ: Iberoamericana de Ediciones.

Little, Elbert, F.H. Wadsworth, and J. Marrero
1977 *Árboles comunes de Puerto Rico y las Islas Vírgenes*. SJ: Editorial Universitaria.

Lizardo, Fredique
1975 *Instrumentos musicales indígenas dominicanos*. SD: Alfa y Omega.

Llamazares, Ana M., and Carlos Martínez Sarasola (eds.)
2004 *El lenguaje de los dioses. Arte, chamanismo y cosmovisión indígena en Sudamérica*. Buenos Aires: Biblos.

López Baralt, Mercedes
1976 *El mito taíno: raíz y proyecciones en el Amazonia continental*. SJ: Ed. Huracán.
1985 *El mito taíno: Lévi-Strauss en las Antillas*. SJ: Ed. Huracán.

López Baralt, Mercedes (ed.)
1990 *Iconografía política del Nuevo Mundo*. Río Piedras: EUPR.

López Belando, Adolfo J.
1993 La cueva José María: los cuadros mitológicos y la escritura jeroglífica ceremonial taína. MHD, *III Congreso Nacional de Arqueología* (SD, November 17 19).
2003 *Art in the Shadows, Pictographs and Petroglyphs in the Caves of the National Park of the East, Dominican Republic*. SD.
2018 *La memoria de la roca. Arte rupestre en la República Dominicana*. SD: FGA - Fundación Eduardo León Jimenes.
2019 *El poblado taíno de Playa Grande. Informe arqueológico*. SD: Academia de Ciencias de la República Dominicana - Shelley Foundation.

López de Gomara, Francisco
1941 *Historia general de las Indias*. (Zaragoza, 1552). Madrid: Espasa y Calpe.

López Sotomayor, Diana
1991 *Diccionario de Términos*. Catálogo de materiales arqueológicos. SJ: Museo Universidad de Puerto Rico.
2001 Un proyecto de caracterización mineralógica de cerámica precolombina. *IV Encuentro de Investigadores*, ICP (SJ, April, 26).

Lora, Silvano
1992 Construcción de una canoa monoxilica en Santo Domingo. Explicación de la ruta de Hatuey desde Santo Domingo a Baracoa, Cuba. MHD, SD.
Lothrop, S. K.
1932 Aboriginal Navigation off the West Coast of South America. *Jorunal Royal Anthropological Institution,* LXII: 229-256. London.
Loven, Sven
1935 *Origins of the Tainan Culture, West Indies.* Goeteborg: Elanders Boktryckeri Aktiebolag. Originally published: *Die Wurzeln der Tainischen Kultur,* Goeteborg, 1924.
Lumbreras, Luis G.
1984 *La arqueología como ciencia social.* La Habana: Casa de las Américas.
Luna Calderón, Fernando
1976 *Atlas de patología ósea.* SD.
1988 Enfermedades en las osamentas indígenas de la isla de Santo Domingo. MHD, *Boletín* 21:79-83.
2002 ADN Mitocondrial Taíno en la República Dominicana. *Kacike: The Journal of Caribbean Amerindian History and Anthropology.* January.
Magaña, Edmundo
1982a Hombres salvajes y razas monstruosas de los indios Kaliña (Caribes) de Surinam. *Journal of Latin American Lore* 8-1: 63-114. Los Angeles.
   b Note on Ethnoanthropological Notions of the Guiana Indians. *Anthropológica* 24: 215-233. Ottawa.
1983 Reflexiones sobre mitología. *The Journal of Intercultural Studies* 20: 142-151. Kansay University of Foreign Studies Publication.
1987 *Contribución al estudio de la mitología y astronomía de los indios de las Guayanas.* Centro de Estudios y Documentación Latinoamericanos (CEDLA) 35. Amsterdam: Foris Publications.
1988a Influencias mayas y aztecas en los indios de las Antillas Mayores. Reseña crítica al libro de O. García Goyco (1984). *Boletín de Estudios Latinoamericanos y del Caribe* 45, Amsterdam: CEDLA.
   b Historia y estructura de la Pléyades, Orión y el Can Mayor. La popa en los mitos de los indios del noreste de Sudamérica. *Mito y Ritual en América,* M. Gutiérrez Estévez (ed.), pp. 202-262. Madrid: Alhambra.
   c *Orión y la mujer Pléyades: Simbolismo astronómico de los indios kaliña de Surinam.* CEDLA 44. Amsterdam: Foris Publications.
   d Las mujeres de Luna. Pontificia Universidad Católica del Perú, *Anthropologica* 6: 363-382.
   e Orión entre los Kaliña de Surinam. *Anthropologica* 383-407.
1990a Entrevista a Claude Lévi-Strauss. Circulación privada.
   b Zarigüeya, señor de los sueños. In: Miche Perrin (ed.), 1990.
1992a La gente pecarí, el sacerdote caníbal y otras historias. Los Otros en el testimonio y la imaginación de tribus guayanesas. Fundación La Salle, Antropológica 77: 3-62. Caracas.
   b El sacerdote caníbal. Una interpretación kaliña de los misioneros. In: *De palabra y obra en el Nuevo Mundo* (M. León Portilla ed.), pp. 143 -164. Madrid: Siglo XXI.
1993 Orión y Sirio en la mitología Tarêno. *Indiana* 13: 133-150. Berlin.
1994a La palabra, el silencio y la escritura. Notas sobre algunas tribus de las Guayanas. Universidad de Chile, *Revista Chilena de Antropología* 12: 99-112. Santiago.

    b La boca del Infierno en Sudamérica: los hombres inmortales, el diablo y los sacerdotes. *Anthropologica* 11: 79-90.
2005 Tropical Tribal Astronomy: Ethnohistorical and Ethnographic Notes. In: *Songs from the Sky, Indigenous Astronomical and Cosmological Traditions of the World*, Von del Chamberlain, J.B. Carlson, and M. Jane Young (eds.), pp. 244-263. United Kingdom: Ocarina Books-Center for Archaeoastronomy.

Magaña, Edmundo (ed.)
1988 *Les Monstres dans l'Imaginaire des Indies d'Amérique Latine*. Cahiers de Recherche sur l'Imaginaire 16-19. Paris: Lettres Modernes.
1989 Latin America Ethnoastronomy Symposium. *46vo. Internatitonal Congress of Americanists* (Amsterdam, July, 1988). Published in *Scripta Etnológica* 9. Buenos Aires.

Magaña, Edmundo and Fabiola Jara
1982 The Carib Sky. *Journal de la Société des Américanistes* 68: 115-132. Paris.
1983a Astronomy of the Central Caribs of Surinam. *L'Homme* 23-1: 111-113. Paris.
      b Star Myths of the Kaliña (Carib) Indians of Surinam. *Latin American Indian Literatures Journal* 7-1: 20-37. Pittsburgh.

Magaña, Edmundo, and Peter Mason (eds.)
1986 *Myth and the Imaginary in the New World*. CEDLA 34. Amsterdam: Foris Publication.

Margery Peña, Enrique
2003 *Estudios de mitología comparada indoamericana*. San José: Editorial Universidad de Costa Rica.

Márquez Miranda, Fernando
1930 La navegación primitiva y las canoas monoxilas, contribución a su estudio. *XXIII Internatitonal Congress of Américanists*, Proceedings pp. 736-746. New York. See also: *Revista del Museo de la Plata* 33. Buenos Aires.

Martí Carvajal, Armando J.
1997 Examen de la población del Boriquén durante el período de contacto. *III Encuentro de Investigadores de Arqueología y Etnohistoria del ICP* (SJ, October 30).
2007 *Ensayos sobre las islas Boriquén y San Juan de Puerto Rico*. SJ.

Martínez Cruzado, Juan Carlos
1999 Y por un pelo somos indios. ICP, *Cultura* 3-6:77-79.
2001 The Geographic Origins of the Puerto Rico Gene Pool according to Mitochondrial DNA. *XIX Congress of the International Association for Caribbean Archaeology*. Aruba.
2002 El uso del ADN Mitocondrial para descubrir las migraciones al Caribe: Resultados para Puerto Rico y expectativas para la República Dominicana. *Kacike: The Journal of Caribbean Amerindian History and Anthropology*. January.
2003 El ADN mitocondrial revela migraciones precolombinas a Puerto Rico. *XX Congress of the International Association for Caribbean Archaeology* (SD, June 29 -July 6).
2010 The History of Amerindian Mitochondrial DNA Lineages in Puerto Rico, In: *Island Shores, Distant Pasts: Archaeological and Biological Approaches to the Pre-Columbian Settlement of the Caribbean*, S.M. Fitzpatrick and A.H. Ross (Eds.). Gainesville: University Press of Florida.

Martínez Cruzado, Juan Carlos, G. Toro Labrador, V. Ho-Fung, M. Estévez...
2001 Mitochondrial DNA Analysis Reveals Substantial Native American Ancestry in Puerto Rico. Wayne State University Press, *Human Biology* 73: 491-511.Michigan.

Martínez Cruzado, Juan Carlos, G. Toro Labrador, J. Viera Vera...
2005 Reconstructing the Population History of Puerto Rico by Means of mtDNA. *American Journal of Physical Anthropology*.

Martínez Cruzado, Juan Carlos and Marcela Díaz-Matallana
2010   Estudios sobre ADN mitocondrial sugieren un linaje predominante en la cordillera Oriental de Colombia y con vínculo suramericano para los arcaicos de Puerto Rico. *Universitas Médica* 51-3: 241-272. Editorial Pontificia Javeriana.

Martínez Planer, Carlos
2013   La representación del espíritu de los muertos entre los aborígenes del Caribe. ICP, *Revista* 12-25: 23-32.
2019   *El simbolismo del arte rupestre en el Caribe.* San Francisco: Blurb.

Martínez Torres, Roberto
1981   *Pinturas indígenas de Boriquen.* Morovis: Agrupación Paleontológica y Arqueológica Moroveña.
2018   *A Lo Sucu Sumucu. Raíces mayas del habla jíbara.* Morovis, PR.

Mason. Otis T.
1884   The Guesde Colletion of Antiquities in Point-à-Pitre, Guadeloupe. *Annual Report of the Board of Regents of the Smithsonian Institution*, 731-837. Washington, DC.

Méndez Caratini, Héctor
2016   *Petroglifos de Boriquén.* SJ.

Menzel, Donald H.
1982   *Guía de campo de las estrellas y los planetas.* Barcelona: Ediciones Omega.

Métraux, Alfred
1949   Warfare, Cannibalism and Human Trophies. In: *Handbook of South American Indians*, Bureau or American Ethnology, Bulletin 143, J. Steward (ed.), Vol. 5: 383-409. Washington, D.C.
1973   *Religión y magias indígenas de América del Sur.* Madrid: Aguilar.

Miyares González, Fernandp
1954   *Noticias particulares de la isla y plaza de San Juan Bautista de Puerto Rico* [1775]. Río Piedras: EUPR.

Montbrun, Christian
1984   *Les Petites Antilles avant Christophe Colomb.* Paris: Karthala.

Montenegro, Ernesto P.
2003   Los Karibes: el fantasma del Medioevo que ronda por la arqueología moderna. *XX Congreso Internacional de Arqueología del Caribe* (Santo Domingo, June 29-July 6), G. Tavárez y M. García Arévalo (eds.), pp. 477- 486. SD: MHD-FGA.
2004   Los Karibes y los fantasmas medievales. Fundación Fernando Ortiz, *Catauro* 5-9: 63-81. La Habana.

Moore, Richard B.
1973   Carib Cannibalism: A Study in Anthropological Stereotyping. *Caribbean Studies* 13 - 3: 117-135. Río Piedras: Instituto del Caribe.

Morales Cabrera, Pablo
1932   *Puerto Rico indígena. Prehistoria y protohistoria de Puerto Rico.* SJ: Imprenta Venezuela.

Morales Patiño, Osvaldo
1943   La religión de los indígenas antillanos. *Primer Congreso Nacional de Historia* (October 8-12, 1942); Vol. II: 164-166. La Habana.

Morbán Laucer, Fernando
1970   *Pintura rupestre y petroglifos en Santo Domingo.* SD: UASD.
1978   *El arte rupestre de la República Dominicana.* SD: FGA.
1979   *Ritos funerarios: acción del fuego y medio ambiente en las osamentas precolombinas.* SD- Academia de Ciencias.
1988   El murciélago, sus representaciones en el arte y la mitología precolombina. MHD, *Boletín* 21: 37-57.
1994   *El arte rupestre de la Sierra de Bahoruco.* SD: Taller.

Moreau, Jean-Pierre
1985 "Navigation européenne dans les Petites Antilles au XVIe siécle et debut du XVIIe siécle, sources documentaires, approche archéologique". Thése IIIe cycle, Université de Paris I.
1987 *Un Flibustier Français dans la Mer des Antilles (1618-1620)*. Paris: Clamart. Paris, Seghers, 1990. See also: Anónimo de Carpentras.
1988 Le jeu de balles chez les Caraïbes Insulaires. *XLVI Internatitonal Congress of Américanists* (Amsterdam, July 4-8).
1989 Les Caraïbes Insulaires et la mer aux XVIeme siécle. In: *Civilizations Précolombiennes de la Caraïbe*. Actes du Colloque du Marin, pp. 104-128. Paris: Editions l'Harmattan.
1991a Nouvelles donnees sur les indiens Caraïbes recueillies par un filibustier français ayant sejourne onze mois à la Martinique en 1619. *XII Congress of the International Association for Caribbean Archaeology*, L. S. Robinson (ed.), pp. 271-283. Martinique: A.I.A.C.
   b Caraïbes Insulaires et la Mer aux XVIe et XVII siécles d'Aprés les Sources Ethnohistoriques. *Journal de la Société des Américanistes* LXXVII: 63-75. Paris.
1992a Les Petites Antilles de Christophe Colomb à Richelieu (1493-1635). Paris: Karthala.
   b Les Caraïbes vus par les Français aux XVI et XVII siécles. In: *Voyages aux Iles d'Amérique*, Jean Favier (ed.), pp. 123-7. Paris: Archives Nationales.
2006 Quelques exemples de traite sur les Amériens des Antilles françaises du XVIe au XVIIIe siècle. *Généalogie et histoire de la Caraïbe*, 197: 5002-5003.

Moscoso, Francisco
1986 *Tribu y clase en el Caribe antiguo*. Serie Científica 23, Vol. LXII. San Pedro de Macorís (DR): Universidad Central del Este.
1991 *Los cacicazgos de Nicaragua antigua*. Cuadernos de Estudio 10. SJ: Instituto de Estudios del Caribe.
1999 *Sociedad y economía de los taínos*. SJ: Edil.
2008 *Caciques, aldeas y población taína de Boriquén*. SJ: Academia Puertorriqueña de la Historia.
2016 *Caguas en la conquista española del siglo 16*. SJ: Publicaciones Gaviota.
2018 *Cacicazgos en el Caribe y continente americano*. SJ: Ediciones Puerto.

Moscoso Puello, Rafael M.
1955 *Anotaciones a las "Palabras Indígenas" de Emiliano Tejera*. Ciudad Trujillo (SD): Editora del Caribe.

Moya Pons, Frank
1978 *La Espanola en el siglo XVI*. Santiago (DR): Universidad Católica Madre y Maestra.

Moya Pons, F., and Rosario Flores Paz (eds.)
2013 *Los taínos en 1492. El debate demográfico*. SD: Academia Dominicana de la Historia.

Mundkur, Balaji
1983 *The Cult of the Serpent. An Interdisciplinary Survey of Its Manifestations and Origins*. Albany: University of New York Press.

Murga, Vicente
1960 *Puerto Rico en los manuscritos de Juan Bautista Muñoz*. Río Piedras: EUPR.
1961- *Cedulario Puertorriqueño I (1505-1517); II (1518-1525); III (1526-1528)*.
1986 Río Piedras: EUPR.

Myers, Robert
1978 Ethnohistorical vs. Ecological Considerations: The Case of Dominica's Amerindians. *VII International Congress for the Study of Pre-Columbian Cultures of the Lesser Antilles*, Centre de Recherches Caraïbes, pp. 325-341. Caracas: Universidad Central de Caracas.

1981 *Amerindians of the Lesser Antilles: A Bibliography*. New Haven: Human Resources Area File.
Narganes Storbe, Yvonne
1993 Fauna y cultura indígena de Puerto Rico. *Museo de Historia, Antropología y Arte*. UPR.
1995 La lapidaria de Sorcé (Vieques) y Tecla (Guayanilla), P.R. *XVI Congress of the International Association for Caribbean Archaeology*, (Guadeloupe, July 24-28).
2003 Pendientes antillanos, animales suramericanos. *XX Congress of the International Association for Caribbean Archaeology,* (SD, June 26-July 6).
2015 "Sorcé, historia de una aldea de pescadores". Ph. D. Thesis, CEAPRC, SJ.
Nau, Emile
1982 *Historia de los caciques de Haití* [1854, in French]. SD: Editora de Santo Domingo.
Nazario Cancel, José María
2010 *Guayanilla y la historia de Puerto Rico* [Ponce, 1893]. Irving Sepúlveda Pacheco (ed.), Guayanilla: Centro Cultural Marina Arzola.
Newson, Lee Ann and Barbara Purdy
1990 Florida Canoes: A Maritime Heritage from the Past. *The Florida Anthropologist* 43-3: 164-180.
Nicholson, Desmond V.
1975 Precolumbian Seafaring Capabilities in the Lesser Antilles. *VI International Congress of Precolumbian Cultures of the Lesser Antilles*. Guadeloupe.
1979 Some aspects of Ethnobotany in the Lesser Antilles as Represented in Antigua and Barbuda. *VIII International Congress of Precolumbian Cultures of the Lesser Antilles* (St. Kitts, July 30 - 4 Aug. 30).
Núñez Jiménez, Antonio
1975 *Cuba: dibujos rupestres*. La Habana: Instituto Cubano del Libro, Editorial de Ciencias Sociales.
1992 *En canoa del Amazonas al Caribe*. SD.
1994 *En canoa por el Mar de las Antillas*. SD: Patronato de la Ciudad.
Ober, Frederick A.
1880 *Camps in the Caribbees. The Adventure of a Naturalist in the Lesser Antilles*. Boston.
1893 *In the Wake of Columbus*. Boston: Lothrop Co.
1895 The Aborigines of the West Indies. Proceeding of the *American Antiquarian Society*. Worcester, Mass.
Oberg, Kalervo
1955 Types of Social Structure among the Lowland Tribes of South & Central America. *American Anthropologist* 57-3: 472-487.
Olazagasti Colón, Ignacio
1988 "La utilización de los moluscos costaneros en la manufactura de artefactos prehistóricos en Puerto Rico". Master's Thesis. CEAPRC, SJ.
Oldfield Howey, M.
1955 *The Encircled Serpent. A study of serpent symbolism in all countries and ages*. New York: Arthur Richmond Company.
Oliver, José R.
1992 The Caguana Ceremonial Center: A cosmic journey through taíno spatial & iconographic symbolism. *X Symposium Internacional de las Asociación de Literatura Indígena Latinoamericana* (SJ, January 7- 11).
2009 *Caciques and Cemí Idols. The web spun by Taíno rulers between Hispaniola and Puerto Rico*. Tuscaloosa: The University of Alabama Press.
Oliver, José R., Colin McEwan and Anna Casas Gilberga (eds.)
2008 *El Caribe precolombino. Fray Ramón Pané y el universo taíno*. Barcelona: Museu Barbier-Mueller d'Art Precolombi.

Olsen, Fred
1974 *On the trail of the Arawaks.* Oklahoma: University of Oklahoma Press.
1980 The Arawaks, their Art, Religion and Science. *VIII International Congress for the Study of Pre-Columbian Cultures in the Lesser Antilles* (St.Kitts, July 30 – Aug. 4, 1979), S.M. Lewenstein (ed.), pp. 1-41. Tempe: Arizona State University.

Ortega, Elpidio and Gabriel Atiles
2003 *Manantial de la Aleta y la arqueología en el Parque Nacional del Este.* SD: Academia de Ciencias de la República Dominicana.

Ortiz Aguilú, Juan J.
2001 Cronometría, cronología y los problemas de las secuencias arqueológicas en Puerto Rico. *IV Encuentro de Investigadores de Arqueología y Etnohistoria del ICP* (SJ, April, 26l).

Ortiz, Fernando
1943 *Las cuatro culturas indias de Cuba.* Biblioteca de Estudios Cubanos I. La Habana: Arellano y Cía.
1947 *El huracán, su mitología y sus símbolos.* México: Fondo de Cultura.
2002 *Contrapunteo cubano del tabaco y el azúcar* [La Habana, 1940]. Madrid: Cátedra.

Ouellet, Réal
2001 The Representation of the Antilles at the XVII Century in the Correspondence of the Missionaries. *Letters et Images d'ailleurs*, (Grignan, October 19-20). Centre de Recherche sur la Litérature des Voyages.

Oviedo y Valdés, Gonzalo Fernández de
1959 *Historia general y natural de las Indias* [Sevilla, 1535]. Madrid: Biblioteca de Autores Españoles.
1969 *De la natural historia de las Indias* [1526]. Chapel Hill: University of North Carolina Press.
1986 *Sumario de la natural historia de las Indias* [Toledo, 1526]. Madrid: Crónicas de América-Historia 16. Edited by Manuel Ballesteros.

Pagán Jiménez, Jaime
2007a *De antiguos pueblos y culturas botánicas en el Puerto Rico indígena: El archipiélago borincano y la llegada de los primeros pobladores agroceramistas.* BAR International Serie 1687. Oxford.
    b Sobre los orígenes de la agricultura en las Antillas. *21st International Congress for Caribbean Archaeology*, B. Reid, H. Petitjean Roget, and A. Curet (eds.), pp. 252-259. University of the West Indies.

Pagán Perdomo, Dato
1978a *El arte rupestre en el área del Caribe.* SD: FGA.
    b *Nuevas pictografías en la isla de Santo Domingo: las cuevas de Borbón.* SD: MHD.
1985 *Sir Robert H. Schomburgk. Notas críticas a su obra etnológica en Santo Domingo.* SD: MHD - Academia de Ciencias.

Pané, Ramón
c.1498 *Relación acerca de las antigüedades de los indios.* See the annotated version by José Juan Arrom (1974).

Paquette, Robert and Stanley Engerman (eds.)
1996 *The Lesser Antilles in the Age of European Expansion.* Gainesville: University of Florida Press.

Peguero Guzmán, Luis A.
2001 Las plazas ceremoniales como espacio ritual de las culturas prehistóricas del Caribe. MHD, *Boletín* 29:29-62.

Pelleprat, Pierre de
1965 *Relato de las misiones de los padres de la Compañía de Jesús en las islas y en Tierra Firme de América Meridional* [Paris, 1655]. Caracas: Biblioteca de la Academia Nacional de la Historia, No. 77.

Peña Franjul, Marcos
1986 El agrosistema de la yuca: una tecnología apropiada en el ambiente precolombino de la Hispaniola. Academia de Ciencias de la República Dominicana, *Anuario* 10: 123-156. SD.

Perea, Juan Augusto and Salvador
1941 *Glosario etimológico taíno-español, histórico y etnográfico*. Mayagüez: Tip. Mayagüez Printing.

Pérez Merced, Carlos
1996 "Los petroglifos de la colección del Instituto de Cultura Puertorriqueña". Master's Thesis. CEAPRC, SJ.

Pérez Reyes, Roberto
2017 *El secreto mejor perdido: Las ciencias escondidas en el "arte taíno" y otros antiguos "artes" alrededor del mundo*. SJ.

Pérez Silva, Matilde and Adolfo de Hostos
1981 *Aplicaciones industriales del diseño indígena de Puerto Rico*. SJ: ICP.

Perrin, Michel (ed.)
1990 *Antropología y experiencias del sueño*. Ecuador: MLAL-Ediciones Abya-Yala.

Petitjean-Roget, Henri
1975 *Contribution à l'Étude de la Préhistoire des Petites Antilles*. Paris: École Practique des Hautes Études. 2 vols.
1976a Le Théme de la Chauve-Souris Frugivore dans l'Art Arawak des Petites Antilles. *VI Congrès International d'Études des Civilisationes Précolombiennes des Petites Antilles* (Pointe-à-Pitre, July 6-12, 1975), R.P. Bullen (ed.), pp. 182-186. Guadeloupe: Central University Antilles-Guayane.
    b Note Sur le Motif de la Grenouille dans l'Art Arawak des Petites Antilles. *VI Congrès International d'Etudes des Civilisationes Précolombiennes des Petites Antilles* R.P. Bullen (ed.), pp. 177-182. Guadeloupe: Central University Antilles-Guayane.
1978 *L'Art des Arawak et des Caraïbes des Petites Antilles. Analyse de la Décoration des Céramiques*. Fort-de-France: Centre d'Études Regionales Antilles-Guyane.
1980 Faragunaol: Zemi du Miel Chez les Tainos des Grandes Antilles. *VIII International Congress for the Study of the Pre-Columbian Cultures of the Lesser Antilles*, S. Lewenstein (ed.), pp. 195-205. Tempe: Arizona State University.
1984a De l'Origine de la Famille Humaine ou Contribution a l'Étude des Pierres a Trois-pointes des Antilles. *IX International Congress for the Study of Pre-Columbian Cultures in the Lesser Antilles* (SD, August 2-8, 1981), pp. 511-525. Centre de Recherches Caraïbes, Université de Montréal.
    b Les Caraïbes et la Mer. Les Cahiers du Patrimoine. *Revue du Bureau du Patrimoine du Conseil Régional de la Martinique*. La Mer II-3: 58-65. Fort-de-France.
1985 Mythes et Origine des Maladies Chez Tainos. Les Zémis Bugia at Aiba (Badraima) et Corocote. *X Congrès International d'Etudes des Civilisationes Précolombiennes des Petites Antilles* (Fort-de-France, 1983), Centre de Recherches Caraïbes, Université de Montréal. pp. 159-172.
1990 Archéologie de l'Imaginaire: 12 Oct 1492- 16 Janvier 1493. Les Tainos, les Espagnols et les Caraïbes. *Bulletin de la Société de Histoire de la Guadeloupe* 83-86: 53-69. Basse Terre.
1993 L'Anthropophagie des Caraïbes: Mythe ou Réalité? In: *La Découverte et la Conquêtede la Guadeloupe*, A. Yacou et J. Adélaïde-Merlande (eds.), pp. 271-279. Paris: Editions Karthala-CERC.
1994 Eléments Pour une Étude Comparée des Mythologies Tainos et Caraïbes Insulaires (Kalinas) des Antilles. Centre d'Études et de Recherches Caribéennes, Université des Antilles et de la Guyane, *Espace Caraïbe* 2: 91-107.

1996 Les Femmes Caraïbes Insulaires: Lecture Comparée des Chroniques Françaises du XVIIe et du XVIIIe Sur les Petites Antilles. *Bulletin de la Société de Histoire de la Guadeloupe* 109: 45-69. Basse Terre.

2003 Les Petroglyphes des Antilles: Des Gravures Contre la Peur de Voir l'Eau Douce Disparaître à Jamais. *XX Congress of the International Association for Caribbean Archaeology* (SD, June 29- July 6), G. Tavárez and M. García Arévalo (eds.), pp. 587-591. MHD-FGA.

2015a *Les Tainos, les Callinas des Antilles.* Guadeloupe: Association Internacionale d'Archaéologie de la Caraïbe.

b *Archéologie des Petites Antilles. Chronologies, Art Céramique, Art Rupestre.* Guadeloupe: Association Internacionale d'Archaeologie de la Caraïbe.

Petitjean-Roget, Jacques

1961 Les Caraïbes Vus a Travers le Dictionnaire du R.P. Breton. *Premier Congrès International d'Études des Civilisations Précolombiennes des Petites Antilles* (Fort-de-France, July 3-7). Societé d'Histoire de la Martinique, Fort-de-France.

Petitjean-Roget, Jacques and Ady

1991 Regards sur le Cannibalism. *XII Congress of the International Association for Caribbean Archaeology*, L.S. Robinson (ed.), pp. 285-295. Martinique: AIAC.

Piazzini, Carlos Emilio

2011 *La arqueología entre la historia y la prehistoria. Estudios de una frontera conceptual.* Bogotá: Universidad de los Andes.

Picard, Bernard

1723 "Manière dont les prêtres Caraïbes soufflent le courage" In: *Cérémonies et coutumes religieuses de tous le peoples du monde* [...]. Amsterdam: J.F. Bernard. Bibliothèque Nationale de France.

Pichardo Moya, Felipe

1956 *Los aborígenes de las Antillas.* México.

Plumier, Charles

1688 *Plantes de la Martinique et de la Guadeloupe (...) dessinés, coloriés et décrits par le Père Plumier.* Paris: Bibliothèque Nationale de France.

Pons Alegría, Mela

1980 Taino Indian Art. *Archaeology* 33-4: 8-15.
1987 El impulso mágico y el arte aborigen antillano. CEAPRC, *Revista* 4. SJ.
1993 *El diseño pintado de la cerámica saladoide de Puerto Rico.* SJ.

Portorreal, Fátima

2000 La resistencia indígena en Santo Domingo frente a la conquista. MHD, *Boletín* 27-28: 97-107. SD.

Preuss, Mary H. (ed.)

1990 *LAIL Speaks!* California: Labyrinthos.

Pury-Toumi, Sybille de

1999 Le Père Breton par Lui-même. In: *Dictionnaire Caraïbe-Français, Reverand Pere Raymond Breton, 1665*, pp. XV-XLV. Paris: IRD-Kathala.

Ramírez Alvarado, María del Mar

2001 *Construir una imagen: visión europea del indígena americano.* Sevilla: Consejo Superior de Investigaciones Científicas.

Ramos Pérez, Demetrio

1975 Actitudes ante los caribes desde su conocimiento indirecto hasta la capitulación de Valladolid de 1520. *Tercera Jornada Americanista de la Universidad de Valladolid*, pp. 1-30. Valladolid.

1982 *El descubrimiento humano de América: las suposiciones colombinas sobre los caribes y su importancia como guía conductora.* Granada: Exma. Diputación Provincial.

Real Díaz, José J. (ed.)
1968 *Catálogo de las cartas y peticiones del Cabildo de San Juan Bautista de Puerto Rico en el Archivo General de Indias (siglos XVI-XVIII)*. SJ: Municipio de San Juan- ICP.

Redmond, Elsa M. (ed.)
1998 *Chiefdoms and Chieftaincy in the Americas*. University Press of Florida.

Reichel-Dolmatoff, Gerardo
1971 *Amazonia Cosmos*. Chicago: The University of Chicago Press.
1978 *Beyond the Milky Way, the Hallucinatory Imagery of the Tukano Indians*. Los Ángeles: University of California.

Reid, Basil A.
2018 *The Archaeology of Caribbean and Circum-Caribbean Farmers (6000 BC-AD1500)*. New York: Routledge.

Reid, Basil A. and Grant Gilmore (eds.)
2014 *Encyclopedia of Caribbean Archaeology*. Gainesville: University Press of Florida.

Renault-Lescure, Odile
1999 Le Caraïbe Insulaire. Langue Arawak: un Imbroglio Linguistique, Glossaire Français d'Origine Amérindienne et Glossaire Ethnolinguistique. In: *Dictionnaire Caraïbe-Français*, Révérend Père Raymond Breton, 1665, pp. XLVII-LXIV, and 257-303. Paris: IRD-Karthala.

Rennard, Joseph
1929 *Les Caraïbes - La Guadeloupe, 1635-1656. Histoire des Vingt Premières Annés de la Colonisation de la Guadeloupe d'Après les Relations du R. P. Breton*. Paris: G. Ficker.

Riley, Carrol and C. Kelly, C. Pennington, R. Rands
1971 *Man Across the Sea. Problems of Pre-Columbian Contacts*. Austin: University of Texas Press.

Ripley, Geo
2002 *Imágenes de posesión: vudú dominicano*. SD: Cocolo Editorial.

Rivera Calderón, Viginia
2003 Revisión al sitio Lujuán I, primer yucayeque en Vieques. *V Encuentro de Investigadores de Arqueología y Etnohistoria del ICP* (March 26-27). SJ.

Rivero, Juan A.
1978 *Los anfibios y reptiles de Puerto Rico*. SJ: EUPR.

Rivero de la Calle, Manuel
1966 *Las culturas aborígenes de Cuba*. La Habana.
1987 La cueva número uno de Punta del Este, joya arqueológica del arte rupestre antillano. *VIII Simposio Internacional de Arte Rupestre Americano* (MHD, June 8-13), pp. 471-477.

Rivet, Paul
1923 L'Orfévrerie Précolombienne des Antilles, des Guyanes et du Venezuela, sans ses Rapports avec l'Orfévrerie et la Métallurgie des Autres Régions Américanines. *Journal de la Société des Américanistes* XV, Paris.

Robiou Lamarche, Sebastián
See "Author Bibliography"

Rochefort, César de
1658 *Histoire Naturelle et Morale des Iles Antilles de l'Amérique*. Rótterdam: Chez Arnout Leers. Spanish partial translation: Cárdenas (1981:281-436).

Rodríguez Álvarez, Ángel
1997 La piedra de Krug. *XVII Congress of the International Association for Caribbean Archaeology* (Nassau, July 20-25).
2001 *Prehistory Astronomy in Puerto Rico*. SJ.

Rodríguez Beauchamp, Sandra
2001 La Cueva Lucero: arte, mito y rito de los taínos. Private circulation, SJ.

Rodríguez Demorizi, Emilio
1971 *Los dominicos y las encomiendas de indios de la isla Española*. SD: Academia Dominicana de la Historia.

Rodríguez Durán, Armando
2002 Los murciélagos en las culturas pre-colombinas de Puerto Rico. *Focus* 1:15-18.

Rodríguez Olleros, Ángel
1974 *Canto a la raza: composición sanguínea de estudiantes de la Universidad de Puerto Rico*. SJ: Ediciones del Colegio de Farmacia.

Rodríguez Ramos, Reniel
2001 Dinámicas de intercambio en el Puerto Rico prehispánico. *IV Encuentro de Investigadores, Instituto de Cultura Puertorriqueña* (April, 26). SJ. See also: Casa del Caribe, *El Caribe Arqueológico* 6: 16-22, 2002. Santiago de Cuba.
2003 La continuidad tecnológicas del Arcaico al post- saladoide en Puerto Rico. *XX Congress of the International Association for Caribbean Archaeology* (SD, June 29-July 6).
2010 *Rethinking Puerto Rican Precolonial History*. Tuscaloosa: The University of Alabama Press.

Rodríguez Ramos, R., Jeff Walker, and Eduardo Questell
2003 La explotación de pedernal en el noroeste de Puerto Rico: fuentes, técnicas e implicaciones. *V Encuentro de Investigadores de Arqueología y Etnohistoria del ICP* (26-27 de marzo). SJ.

Rodríguez López, Miguel
1989 La colección arqueológica de Puerto Rico en el Museo Peabody de la Universidad de Yale. CEAPRC, *Revista*.
1991 Arqueología de Punta Candelero, Puerto Rico. *XII Congress of the International Association for Caribbean Archaeology* (Curaçao, July 24-29), pp. 605-627. Willemstad: Archaeological-Anthropological Institute of the Netherlands Antilles.
1992 El jaguar domesticado: simbolismo del perro en las culturas precolombinas de Puerto Rico y el Caribe. *X Simposio Internacional de Literaturas Indígenas Latinoamericanas* (SJ, January 7-11).
1996 Maruca, Ponce. *II Encuentro de Investigadores Instituto de Cultura Puertorriqueña* (October 4), SJ.
2001 Arqueología de los perros. *XIX Congress of the International Association for Caribbean Archaeology*. Aruba.
2003 Arqueología de los "sin burenes". *XX Congress of the International Association for Caribbean Archaeology* (SD, June 29-July 6).
2017 *La arqueología de la isla de Culebra*. SJ: Editorial Tiempo Nuevo.

Roe, Peter
1982 *The Cosmic Zygote: Cosmology in the Amazon Basin*. New Brunswick: Rutgers University Press.
1990 The Pleiades in Comparative Perspective: The Waiwai Shirkoimo and Shipibo Huishmabo. *Oxford 3: The Third International Conference on Archaeoastronomy* (St. Andrews, Scotland, September, 10-14).
1991 Cross-Media Isomorphisms in Taino Ceramics and Petroglyphs from Puerto Rico. *XIV Congress of the International Association for Caribbean Archaeology* (Barbados, July 21-27).
1993 Advances in the Study os Lowland South American and Caribbean Rock Art. *Journal of the Virgin Islands Archaeological Society* 11.
1995 *Arts of the Amazon*. Barbara Braun (ed.). London: Thames and Hudson.
1997 Just Wasting Away: Taíno Shamanism and Concepts of Fertility. In: Fátima Bercht et al, pp. 124-157. New York.

Román, Juan Carlos
2016   Dos arquetipos culturales milenarios de la selva tropical americana, como compañeros de viaje en la Ruta de la Cojoba. MHD, *Boletín* 47: 189- 213.

Rosa Corzo, Gabino la
2002   La selección del espacio fúnebre aborigen y el culto solar. Casa del Caribe, *El Caribe Arqueológico* 6: 77-85. Santiago de Cuba.

Rostain, Stéphen
1992   La Céramique Améridienne de Guyane Française. Société Suisse des Américanistes, *Bull.* 55-56:93-127.

1994   Archéologie du Litoral de Guyane, une Region Entre des Influences Culturelles de l'Orénoque et de l'Amazone. *Journal de la Société des Américanistes* 80:9-46.

2014   *Islands in the Rainforest: Landscape Managament in Pre-Columbian Amazonia*. New York: Routledge.

Roth, Henry Ling
1887   The aborigines of Hispaniola. *Journal of the Royal Anthropological Institute of Great Britain and Ireland* 16:247-286. London.

Roth, Walter E.
1915   *An Inquiry into the Animism and Folk-lore of the Guiana Indians*. Thirtieth Annual Report (1908-09) of the U.S. Bureau of American Ethnology to the Secretary of the Smithsonian Institution. Johson Reprint Corp., New York, 1970.

1924   *An Introductory Study of the Arts, Crafts, and Customs of the Guiana Indians*. Thirty-Eighth Annual Report (1916-17) of the U.S. Bureau of American Ethnology to the Secretary of the Smithsonian Institution. Johnson Reprint Corp., New York, 1970.

Roumain, Jacques
1942   Contribution a l'Étude de l'Ethnobotanique Précolombienne des Grandes Antilles. *Bulletin du Bureau d'Ethnologie de la Républic d'Haiti* 1. Port-au-Prince: Imprimerie de l'État.

Rouse, Irving
1948   "The Arawak" and "The Carib", in *Handbook of South American Indians*, Julian H. Steward (ed.). IV: 507-565. Washington: Smithsonian Institution. Reprint: Cooper Square, New York, 1963.

1952   Porto Rican Prehistory. *Scientific Survey of Porto Rico and the Virgin Islands*, vol. 18:3-4. New York: New York Academy of Sciences.

1964   Prehistory of the West Indies. *Science* 144: 499-513.

1970   The Entry of Man into West Indies. *Yale University Publications in Anthropology* 61:3-26. New Haven.

1986   *Migration in Prehistory. Inferring Population Movement from Cultural Remains*. New Haven: Yale University Press.

1992   *The Tainos: Rise and Decline of the People who Greeted Columbus*. New Haven: Yale University Press.

Rouse, Irving and Ricardo E. Alegría
1990   Excavations at María de la Cruz Cave and Hacienda Grande Village Site, Loiza, Puerto Rico. *Yale University Publications in Anthropology* 80. New Haven: Dept. of Anthropology and the Peabody Museum Yale University.

Rubin, Jane G., and Ariana Donalds
2003   *Bread Made from Yuca. Selected Chronicles of Indo-Antillean Cultivation and Use of Cassava, 1526-2002*. New York: InterAmericas.

Saffor, William E.
1916   Identity of Cohoba, the Narcotic Snuff of Ancient Hayti. *Washington Academy of Science, Journal* 6: 547-562. Washington, D.C.

Salas, Julio César
1920 *Los indios caribes: estudio sobre el mito de la antropofagia.* Madrid: Editorial América. Reprint: Talleres Gráficos Lux, Barcelona, 1921.

Salivia, Luis A.
1972 *Historia de los temporales de Puerto Rico y las Antillas (1492-1970).* SJ: Editorial Edil.

Samson, Alice V. M.
2009 House Trajectories in El Cabo, Dominican Republic: The Building Block of Late Ceramic Age Culture. *XIII Congress of the International Association for Caribbean Archaeology* (Antigua, June 29-July 3).
2010 *Renewing the House.* Trajectories of Social Life in the Yucayaque of El Cabo, Higüey, Dominican Republic, AD 800 to 1504. Leiden: Sidestone Press.

Samson, Alice V. M., and Jago Cooper
2015 La historia de dos islas en un mar compartido: Investigaciones pasadas y futuras en el pasaje de La Mona. MHD, *Boletín* 46: 23-48.

Sánchez, Domingo
2000 El concepto del tiempo en las etnias Caribes de Venezuela. 50vo. *International Congress of Américanists* (Warsaw, July).

Sanday, Peggy Reeves
1986 *Divine Hunger: Cannibalism as a Cultural System.* Cambridge University Press.

Sanders, William T. y D. Webster
1978 Unilinealism, Multilinealism and the Evolution of Complex Societies. In: *Social Archaeology beyond Subsistence and Dating,* C.I. Redman (ed.). New York: Academy Press.

Santiago Capetillo, Nancy R.
2018 *Historiografía arqueológica: teorías aplicadas al Nuevo Mundo.* SJ: Caballero Editores.

Schiappacasse Rubio, Paola A.
1994 "Colecciones arqueológicas de Puerto Rico en cuatro museos del este de los Estados Unidos". Master's Thesis. CEAPRC, SJ.
2001 Apuntes sobre dos colecciones arqueológicas de Puerto Rico. *IV Encuentro de Investigadores de Arqueología y Etnohistoria del ICP* (April, 26), SJ.

Schiffino, José
1949 *Árboles de la flora dominicana.* Ciudad Trujillo (SD): Pol Hermanos.

Schwerin, Karl H.
2003 Carib Warfare and Slaving. Fundación La Salle, *Antropológica* 99-100: 45-72. Caracas.

Schultes, Richard E., and Albert Hofmann
1992 *Plants of the Gods. Their Sacred, Healing and Hallucinogenic Powers.* Rochester. Healing Arts Press.

Schultes, Richard E. (ed.)
1951 *Recent Advances in American Ethnobotany,* Waltham, Mass.

Schuller, Rudolph
1929 El "Huracán", Dios de la Tormenta y el Popol-Vuh. *Archivos del Folklor Cubano* IV-2: 113-118. La Habana.

Sellon, Michael
1973 The Janus Mode in Tainan Imagery. Museum of the American Indian, Heye Foundation, *Indian Notes* IX-4: 119-127. New York.

Service, Elman R.
1962 *Primitive Social Organization.* New York: Random House.

Shankman, Paul
1969 Le Roti et le Bouilli: Lévi-Strauss Theory of Cannibalism. American Anthropologist 71:54-69.

Shelley, Daniel W.
2013 The Meaning and Location of the Taino Places of Origin in the Prehistoric Caribbean. XXV *Congress of the International Association for Caribbean Archaeology* (SJ).
2016 Los lugares sagrados taínos: paisajes mitológicos y/o lugares geográficos. MHD, *Boletín* 47: 135-154.

Siegel, Peter E.
1996 Ideology and Cultural Change in Prehistoric Puerto Rico: a View from the Community. *Journal of Field Archaeology*, Vol. 23-3: 313-333. Boston: Boston University.
1997 Ancestor Worship and Cosmology Among the Taíno. In: Fátima Bercht et al., pp. 106-111.
1999 Contested Places and Places of Contest: The Evolution of Social Power and Ceremonial Space in Prehistoric Puerto Rico. Society for American Archaeology, *Latin American Antiquity* 10-3:209-238.

Siegel, Peter E. (ed.)
2005 *Ancient Boriquen. Archaeology and Ethnohistory of Native Puerto Rico*. Tuscaloosa: The University of Alabama Press.

Staden, Hans
1944 *Vera Historia* [1557, in German]. Buenos Aires: Universidad de Buenos Aires.

Stahl, Agustín
1889 *Los indios borinqueños: estudios etnográficos*. SJ: Imprenta y librería de Acosta.
1903 La medicina entre los indios. Asociación Médica de Puerto Rico, *Boletín* I-11: 166; II-21: 321. SJ.

Stevens Arroyo, Antonio M.
1981 "The Indigenous Elements in the Popular Religion of Puerto Ricans". Ph.D. Thesis. Fordham University.
1988 *Cave of the Jagua: The Mythological World of the Tainos*. Albuquerque: University of New Mexico Press.
1993 Praxis y persistencia de la religión taína. Casa de las Américas, *Anales del Caribe* 13: 129-143. La Habana.

Steward, Julian H. (ed.)
1946 *Handbook of South American Indians*. Bureau of American Ethnology, Bulletin 143. Washington, D.C.: Smithsonian Institution.

Stockton de Dod, Annabelle
1987 *Aves de la República Dominicana*. Santo Domingo: Museo de Historia Natural.

Sued Badillo, Jalil
1977 *Bibliografía antropológica para el estudio de los pueblos indígenas del Caribe*. SD: FGA.
1978 *Los Caribes: realidad o fábula*. SJ: Editorial Antillana.
1979 *La mujer indígena y su sociedad*. Río Piedras: Editorial Antillana.
1981 The Maligned Caribs. *The San Juan Star Sunday Magazine*, November 8, pp.12-13.
1983 Another Version of the Carib Affair-Bartolomé de las Casas, the Caribs and the Problem of Ethnic Identification. Universidad Interamericana, *Hommines* 6 - 2: 199-208. SJ.
1984 Los conquistadores caníbales. Universidad Interamericana, *Homines* 8 – 2: 68-80. SJ.
1985 Las cacicas indoantillanas. ICP, *Revista* 87: 17-26. SJ.
1986 *The Caribs: a Proper Perspective*. SJ: Fundación Arqueológica, Antropológica e Histórica de Puerto Rico.
1992 Facing up to Caribbean History. *American Antiquity* 57-4: 599-607.
1995 The Island Caribs: New Approaches to the Question of Ethnicity in the Early Colonial Caribbean. In: *Wolves from the Sea*, N.L. Whitehead (ed.), pp. 23-25. The Netherlands: Royal Institute of Linguistics and Anthropology.

2001   *El Dorado borincano: la economía de la conquista (1510-1550)*. SJ: Editorial Puerto.
2003   Ethnohistorical Research in the Hispanic Caribbean: The Indigenous Societies at the Time of Conquest. In: *General History of the Caribbean*, Vol.1. Jalil Sued Badillo (ed.), pp. 8-29. Paris: UNESCO Publishing.
2007   Guadalupe: ¿Caribe o Taína? La isla de Gudalupe y su cuestionable identidad Caribe en la época precolombina: una revisión etnohistórica y arqueológica. *Caribbean Studies* 35-1: 37-85. SJ.
2008   *Agüeybaná El Bravo*. SJ: Ediciones Puerto.

Suro, Darío
1952   Arte Taíno. Instituto de Cultura Hispánica, *Cuadernos Hispanoamericanos* 35:21-26. Madrid.

Szaszdi Nagy, Adam
1984   *Un mundo que descubrió Colón: las rutas del comercio prehispánico de los metales*. Cuadernos Colombinos XII. Valladolid: Casa-Museo de Colón y Seminario Americanista de la Universidad de Valladolid.

Tabío, Ernesto and Estrella Rey
1966   *Prehistoria de Cuba*. La Habana: Academia de Ciencias de Cuba.

Taylor, Douglas MacRae
1935   The Island Caribs of Dominica, B.W.I. *American Anthropologist* 37(2): 265-272.
1936   Additional Notes on the Island Carib of Dominica, B.W.I. *American Anthropologist* 38: 462468. Washington, D.C.
1938   The Caribs of Dominica. Anthropological Papers 3. Bureau of American Ethnology, *Bulletin* 119: 103-171. Smithsonian Institution.
1945   Carib Folk-Beliefs and Customs from Dominica, B.W.I. *Southwestern Journal of Anthropology* 1-4: 507-550. Albuquerque.
1946a   Notes on the Star Lore of the Caribbees. *American Anthropologist*. New Series, Vol. 48: 215-222. Kraus Reprint Co., New York, 1962.
      b   Kinship and Social Structure of the Island Carib. *Southwestern Journal of Anthropology* Vol. 2: 180-212. Albuquerque.
1949   The Interpretation of Some Documentary Evidence on Carib Culture. *Southwestern Journal of Anthropology* 5: 379-392. Albuquerque.
1950   The Meaning of Dietary and Occupational Restrictions among the Island Carib. *American Anthropology* 52: 343-349
1951   *The Black Carib of British Honduras*. Viking Fund Publications in Anthropology 17. New York: Wenner-Gren Foundation for Anthropological Research.
1952   Tales and Legends of the Dominica Caribs. *Journal of American Folklore* 65(257): 267-279.
1954   Diachronic Note on the Carib Contribution to Island Carib. *International Journal of American Linguistics* 20: 28-33.
1957   The Ethnobotany of the Island Caribs of Dominica. *Webbia* XII-2:513-644. Florence. See. Hodge (1957).
1958   Carib, Caliban, Cannibal. *International Journal of American Linguistics* 24: 56-57.
1961   El Taíno en relación con el caribe insular y el lokono. ICP, *Revista* 11: 22-25.
1977   *Languages of the West Indies*. Baltimore: Johns Hopkins University Press.

Tejera, Emilio
1977   *Indigenísmos*. SD: Editora de Santo Domingo. 2 vols.

Thevet, André
1997   *La Singularités de la France Antarctique* [1557]. Frank Lestringant (ed.). Paris: Editions Chandeigne.

Thompson, J. Eric S.
1951   Canoes and Navigation of the Maya and Their Neighbours. *Journal of the Royal Anthropological Institute* 79: 69-78. London.

Tió Nazario, Aurelio
1961   *Nuevas fuentes para la historia de Puerto Rico.* Barcelona.
1966   *Dr. Diego Álvarez Chanca: estudio biográfico.* SJ: ICP- Universidad Interamericana.
1975   Los cálculos astronómicos de D. Juan Ponce de León. Academia Puertorriqueña de la Historia, *Boletín* IV-14: 11-48. SJ.
1980   Un hallazgo arqueológico transcendental. Los monumentos del padre Nazario, un enigma de la prehistoria de Puerto Rico. Academia Puertorriqueña de la Historia, *Boletín* VI-24: 17-336. SJ.

Todorov, Tzvetan
1993   *Las morales de la historia.* Barcelona: Paidós.
2003a   *Nosotros y los Otros.* México: Siglo XXI.
    b   *La conquista de América, el problema del Otro.* Buenos Aires: Siglo XXI.

Troiani, Duna
2001   El caribe insular del siglo XVII. Tratado sobre la lengua y la cultura de los Callínagos. Traducción al español del *Dictionnaire Caraïbe-Français* de R. Breton (1665). Paris: CELIA-CNRS.
2003   Las estrategias del Padre Breton para presentar el caribe isleño del siglo XVII. *XXV International Congress of Américanists* (Xalapa, Octuber 21-24). Quaderni di Thule III: 2, pp. 265-272.

Tyrrell, Esther Q. y Robert A.
1990   *Hummingbirds of the Caribbean.* New York: Crown Publishers, Inc.

Ulloa Hung, Jorge
2005   *Una mirada al Caribe precolombino.* SD: Instituto Tecnológico de Santo Domingo.

Ulloa Hung, J., and R. Valcárcel Rojas (eds.)
2016   *Indígenas e indios en el Caribe. Presencia, legado y estudio.* SD: Instituto Tecnológico.
2018   *De la desaparición a la permanencia. Indígenas e indios en la reinvención del Caribe.* SD: Instituto Tecnológico de Santo Domingo.

Urton, Gary
1981   *At the Crossroads of the Earth and the Sky. An Andean Cosmology.* Austin: University of Texas Press.

Valcárcel Rojas, Roberto
2000   Seres de barro. Un espacio simbólico femenino. Casa del Caribe, *El Caribe Arqueológico* 4:20-34. Santiago de Cuba.
2016   El mundo colonial y los indios en las Antillas Mayores. MHD, *Boletín* 47:359-376.

Vega, Bernardo
1979   *Los metales y los aborígenes de la Hispaniola.* SD: MHD.
1980   *Los cacicazgos de la Hispaniola.* SD: MHD.
1981   La herencia indígena en la cultura dominicana de hoy. In: *Ensayos sobre cultura dominicana.* SD: MHD.
1987a   *Santos, shamanes y zemíes.* SD: Fundación Cultural Dominicana.
    b   *Arte neotaíno.* SD: Fundación Cultural Dominicana.
1995   Frutas en la dieta precolombina en la Isla Española. Academia Dominicana de la Historia, *Clío* LXIV-153: 11-90. SD.
2014   *El zemí de algodón taíno.* SD: Academia Dominicana de la Historia.
2015   Los Paredones: ¿Arte precolombino o falsificaciones contemporáneas? MHD, *Boletín* 46: 49-60.

Veloz Maggiolo, Marcio
1972   *Arqueología prehistórica de Santo Domingo.* New York: McGraw-Hill Far Eastern Publishers.
1976-7 *Medioambiente y adaptación humana en la prehistoria de Santo Domingo.* Tomo I y II. Colección Historia y Sociedad No. 30. SD: UASD.

1988 Distribución de espacios en los asentamientos pre-urbanos en las Antillas precolombinas. CEAPRC, *La Revista* 6: 117-123. SJ.
1991 *Panorama histórico del Caribe precolombino.* SD: Banco Central de la República Dominicana (BCRD).
1992 *La Isla de Santo Domingo antes de Colón.* SD: BCRD.
2001 *Antropología portátil.* SD: BCRD.

Verin, Pierre
1966 L'Ancienne Culture Caraïbe à l'Époque Coloniale. *Bulletin de la Société de Histoire de la Guadeloupe* 5-6:16-27. Basse Terre.

Verrand, Laurence
2001 *La Vie Quotidienne des Indiens Caraïbes aux Petites Antilles (XVII).* Paris: Karthala.

Vié-Wohrer, Anne-Marie
2008 Hypothèses Sur l'Origine et la Diffusion du Complexe Rituel du Tlacaxipehualiztli. *Journal de la Société des Américanistes* 94-2: 143-178. Paris.

Waldron, Lawrence
2016 *Handbook of Ceramic Animal Symbols in the Ancient Lesser Antilles.* University Press of Florida.

Warmke, Germaine L. and R. Tucker Abbott
1961 *Caribbean Seashells.* Narberth (Pennsylvania): Livingston Publishing Company.

Weeks, John M. and Peter J. Ferbel
1994 *Ancient Caribbean.* Research Guides to Ancient Civilizations. New York & London: Garland Publishing.

Whitehead, Neil L.
1984 Carib Cannibalism. The Historical Evidence. *Journal of the Société des Américanistes* 70: 69-87. Paris.
1988 *Lords of the Tiger Spirit. A history of the Caribs in colonial Venezuela and Guyana.* Dordrecht (Holanda): Foris Publications.
1990 Carib Ethnic Soldiering in Venezuela, the Guianas and Antilles, 1492-1820. *Ethnohistory* 37-4: 357-385.

Whitehead, Neil L.(ed.)
1995 *Wolves from the Sea. Reading in the Archaeology and Anthropology of the Island Carib.* Leiden: Royal Institute of Linguistics and Anthropology, KITLV Press.

Wilbert, Johannes
1976 To Become a Maker of Canoes: An Essay in Warao Enculturation. In: Enculturation in Latin America: An Anthology. J. Wilbert (ed.), *Latin America Studies* 33: 303-358. Los Angeles: University of California.
1977 Navigators of the Winter Sun. In. *The Sea in the Pre-Columbian World*, E. Benson (ed.), pp. 16-46. Washington, D.C.: Dumbarton Oaks Research Library and Collection.
1981 Warao Cosmology and Yekuana Roundhouse Symbolism. *Journal of Latin American Lore* 7-1: 37-72. Los Angeles.

Williamson, Ray
1984 *Living the Sky: the Cosmos of the American Indian.* Boston: Houghton Mifflin Co.

Wilson, Samuel M.
1990 *Hispaniola: Caribbean Chiefdoms in the Age of Columbus.* Tuscaloosa: The University of Alabama Press.
1998 Preceramic Connections between Yucatán and the Caribbean. *Latin American Antiquity*, Vol. 9-4:342-352. Washington: Society for American Archaeology.
2007 *The Archaeology of the Caribbean.* New York: Cambridge University Press.

Wilson, Samuel M. (ed.)
1999 *Indigenous People of the Caribbean.* Florida: University Press of Florida.

Yacou, Alain y Jacques Adélaide-Merlande (eds.)
1993   *La Découverte et la Conquête de la Guadeloupe.* Paris: Karthala.
Zamora Munné, Juan Clemente
1976   *Indigenismos en la lengua de los conquistadores.* SJ: EUPR.

Author Bibliography

1979   La plaza ceremonial en la Bajura de los Cerezos, Isla de Mona, P.R. Not published.
1980   Arqueoastronomía en Chacuey. Suplemento *Listín Diario*, December 27, pp. 13-15. SD.
1981   El Corral de los Astros. Suplemento *Listín Diario*, June 11, pp. 8- 9. SD.
1983   Del mito al tiempo sagrado: un probable calendario agrícola-ceremonial taíno. MHD, *Boletín* 11(18): 117-140.
1984a Astronomy in Taíno Mythology. Journal of the Center for Archaeoastronomy, *Archaeoastronomy* 7 (1-4): 110-115. Maryland.
     b Eclipses en la prehistoria antillana. *Listín Diario*, December 15, pp. 4-6. S. D.
1985   Panorama de la Arqueoastronomía en las Antillas. *I Congreso Nacional de Arqueología* (September, MHD). Published as "Panorama de la Astronomía Indígena en las Antillas", MHD, *Boletín* 14-20: 83-95, 1987.
1986   Ida y vuelta a Guanín: un ensayo sobre la cosmovisión taína. In: *Myth and the Imaginary in the New World,* CEDLA 34, E. Magaña & P. Mason (eds.). Amsterdam: Foris Publication.
1988a Astronomía primitiva entre los taínos y caribes de las Antillas. *46 International Congress of Américanists* (Amsterdam, July 4-8). Published in A.F. Aveni (ed.) 1988: 121-141.
     b Posibles símbolos astronómico-meteorológicos en al arte rupestre antillano. *Actas del VIII Simposio Internacional de Arte Rupestre Americano* (SD, June 8-13), Dato Pagán Perdomo (ed.), pp. 405-429. SD: MHD.
     c Mitología y astronomía caribe según los cronistas franceses y el *Dictionaire Caraibe-Français* del padre Raymond Breton (1665). *II Congreso Nacional de Arqueología* (SD, November 17-19). Published in MHD, *Boletín* 16(22):199-222, 1989. English version: Island Carib Mythology and Astronomy. *Latin American Indian Literatures Journal* 6-1: 36-54, 1990. McKeesport, Pennsylvania.
1990a El huracán y la Osa Mayor en Mesoamérica y las Antillas. *VII Symposium Latin American Indian Literatures Journal* (Albuquerque, June 10-18). Published in Mary Preuss (ed.) *Lail Speaks!* pp. 81-87, 1990. California: Labyrinthos.
     b Astronomía primitiva entre los taínos y los caribes de las Antillas. CEAPRC, *La Revista* 7:15-25. See also XI *Congress of the International Association for Caribbean Archaeology* (SJ, 1985), A.G. Plantel (ed.), pp. 162-169. SJ: Fundación Arqueológica, Antropológica e Histórica de Puerto Rico - UPR.
1991   Aportación indígena a la cultura puertorriqueña. First Prize, Comisión Puertorriqueña para la Celebración del Quinto Centenario del Descubrimiento de América y Puerto Rico, *Encuentro* 4: 4-7. SJ.
1992a Chemin la Tortue: la Vía Láctea entre los caribes- insulares. *X Symposium Latin American Indian Literatures Journal* (SJ, January 6-11), CEAPRC. Not published.
     b *Encuentro con la mitología taína.* Foreword by José J. Arrom. SJ: Editorial Punto y Coma.

1993a Iconografía del murciélago en la prehistoria antillana. *III Congreso Nacional de Arqueología* (Santo Domingo, November, 17-19). Published in MHD, *Boletín* 20- 26: 93- 111, 1995. See also Robiou (2016).
b La navegación indígena antillana. MHD, *Boletín* 19-25: 69-115. See also Robiou (2016).
c Coulúmon: el langostino celeste de los caribes-insulares. *XV Congress of the International Association for Caribbean Archaeology* (SJ, July 26-31). Published in R. Alegría and M. Rodríguez (eds.), pp. 343-350, 1995. SJ.
d Aportación de la farmacopea taína a la cultura puertorriqueña. First Prize, Comisión Puertorriqueña para la Celebración del Quinto Centenario del Descubrimiento de América y Puerto Rico (1992). Universidad de América, *Revista* 5 (2): 44-48. Bayamón.
1995a ¿Eran caníbales los caribes? Magacín, *El Nuevo Día*, September 24, pp. 16-17.
b Vía Láctea, Osa Mayor y Pegaso: su relación simbólica con las expediciones guerreras y los rituales antropofágicos de los caribes-insulares. Send to *XVI Congress of the International Association for Caribbean Archaeology* (Guadeloupe, July 24-28).
1997a "Cosmología taína y caribe-insular: sus orígenes suramericanos y sus transformaciones antillanas", Master's Thesis. CEAPRC, SJ.
b Herencia de la farmacopea taína en la medicina popular puertorriqueña Museo del Barrio, *Taino: Pre-Columbian Art and Culture from Caribbean Exhibition* (Sept. 25, 1997-March 29, 1998). Conference, November 1, 1997. New York. Published in Robiou (2016).
1998a El antropólogo Gerardo Reichel-Dolmatoff (1912-1994). CEAPRC, *La Revista* 18:105-106. SJ.
b La cerámica indigenista de Daniel Silva Pagán. *Simposio Incidencias de la Cultura Precolombina en el Arte Contemporáneo del Caribe* (SD, January 15-17). Published by Mildred Canahuate (ed.), pp. 61-67, 2000. SD.
c Comparación entre la cosmología de los taínos y los caribes insulares. Federación Internacional de Sociedades Científicas, *Seminario Regional de Culturas Aborígenes del Caribe* (SD, November 12-13). Published in *Culturas aborígenes del Caribe*, FISC-FISS (ed.), pp. 137-144, 2001. SD: Banco Central de la República Domincana. See also Robiou (2016).
1999 Acáyouman: el sistema de parentesco astronómico caribe-insular. MHD, *Boletín* 27: 73-93. Published also in *Latin American Indian Literatures Journal* 15 -2: 117-136, 2000. McKeesport, PA., and Robiou (2016).
2000a Espacio y tiempo entre los taínos. MHD, *Boletín* 28: 163-171.
b La Gran Serpiente entre los taínos y caribes de las Antillas. *XV Symposium Latin American Indian Literatures* (Washington, DC July 15). Published in *Latin American Indian Literatures Journal*, pp. 21-41, 2002. McKeesport, PA. See also Robiou (2016).
c Anotaciones sobre la cosmología taína y caribe- insular. ICP, *Cultura* 4-9: 11-16. SJ.
2001 La cerámica caribe-insular según los cronistas franceses. CEAPRC, *La Revista* 20:18-25. SJ. See also Robiou (2016).
2002 Osa Mayor: la idealización del huracán de Mesoamérica a las Antillas. Casa del Caribe, *El Caribe Arqueológico* 6: 86-93. Santiago de Cuba. See also MHD, *Boletín* 30-33: 123-140, 2003 and Robiou (2016).
2003a *Taínos y Caribes, las culturas aborígenes antillanas*. Foreword by Ricardo E. Alegría. SJ: Editorial Punto y Coma.
b El simbolismo cosmológico del viaje mítico de Guahayona. *XX Congress of the International Association for Caribbean Archaeology* (SD, June 29 - July 6). G. Tavárez

and M. García Arévalo (eds.), Vol. II: 613-615, 2005. SD: MHD-FGA. See also Robiou (2016).

2004 La Gran Serpiente en la mitología taína. Gabinete de Arqueología del Historiador de la Ciudad de La Habana, *Boletín* 3-3: 51-58. La Habana.

2005 De Caribes a Garífunas: historia y creencias de la primera transculturación afro-antillana. *La continuidad de las culturas indígenas en las Antillas*, Museo de Las Américas-Smithsonian National Museum of the American Indian (CEAPRC, September 7), SJ.

2006a *Mitología y religión de los taínos*. Foreword by José Juan Arrom. SJ: Editorial Punto y Coma.

    b El símbolo del Centro entre los taínos. *Congreso Internacional de Antropología y Arqueología Fernando Luna Calderón* (SD, October 10-14). Published in MHD, *Boletín* 42:103-113, 2008. See also Robiou (2016).

2007a Apuntes para el simbolismo de las aves entre los indios caribes-insulares. *Congreso Sociedad para la Conservación y el Estudio de las Aves del Caribe* (CEAPRC, July 19), CEAPRC. Published in Robiou (2016).

    b Historia y folclor de los huracanes. Revista Domingo, *El Nuevo Día* pp. 8-9. SJ. See also Robiou (2016).

2008a "El imaginario del indio Caribe de las Antillas Menores, según los cronistas franceses del siglo XVII", Ph. D. Thesis. Centro de Estudios Avanzados de Puerto Rico y el Caribe, SJ.

    b La trayectoria de un imaginario. La representación gráfica del indio taíno, siglo XV-XVII. *Simposio Conmemorativo del V Centenario del Nacimiento de la Sociedad Puertorriqueña, 1508-2008*, (SJ, September 19). Universidad Sagrado Corazón. Published in Robiou (2016).

2009a *Caribes, creencias y rituales. La verdadera historia de los Caribes*. SJ: Editorial Punto y Coma.

    b Astronomía y Cosmovisión de los Caribes. *Le Ciel des Améridienns et Croyances*, Musée Département d'Archéologie et de Préhistoire (Fort-de-France, June 9-11), Martinique.

    c Etnohistoria y cosmología Caribe: los cronistas franceses del siglo XVII. *VII Encuentro de Investigadores de Arqueología y Etnohistoria del ICP* (SJ, November 5-6). Published by Laura del Olmo (ed.), pp. 26-37, 2010. SJ: ICP.

2010 Introduction. Fundación Cultural Educativa, *Simposio Encuentro con el Caribe Francés* (SJ, March 10-14), CEAPRC. Published by Laura del Olmo (ed.), pp. 8-11, 2010. SJ: ICP.

2011a Mitología taína y cosmología Caribe. *Symposium Civilisations Précolombiennes et Arts Contemporains* (Marin, November 25-27). Martinique.

    b Teodoro de Bry, la imagen gráfica del taíno y la crítica a la conquista española. Fundación Cultural Educativa, *Simposio V Centenario de la Rebelión Taína, 1511-2011* (SJ, February 18-19), CEAPRC. Published by Laura del Olmo (ed.), pp. 30-35, 2012. SJ: ICP.

    c Visión comparativa del Caribe-insular según las crónicas españolas y francesas, siglo XVI-XVII. *IX Encuentro de Investigadores de Arqueología y Etnohistoria del ICP* (SJ, April 7-8). Published by Laura del Olmo (ed.), pp. 54 - 64, 2012. SJ: ICP. See also Robiou (2016).

2013a La arqueología del imaginario. Los cronistas españoles frente al arte taíno. ICP, *Cultura* pp. 24-47. SJ. See also Robiou (2016).

    b El rito de la *Cohoba*: la comunicación de los taínos con el más allá. *II Encuentro de Diálogo sobre el Espiritismo y la Cultura* (Carolina, February 9) Simposio del Círculo de Investigaciones y Documentación Espiritismo y Cultura (CIDEC)-Universidad del Este, Carolina. P.R. Published in Robiou (2016).

c Cosmología de los Caribes en las Antillas Menores. *IV Congreso Internacional de Antropología y Arqueología Ing. Elpidio Ortega* (SD, October 12-14, 2010), MHD. Published in MHD, *Boletín* 45:19-28 and Robiou (2016).

2014 Las versiones de la *Relación* de fray Ramón Pané (1571-1974). *Symposio Siglo XVI: Período de Transición* (SJ, April 12), CEAPRC. Published in Robiou (2016).

2015 Garífunas, la transculturación entre los indios caribes y los negros esclavos en las Antillas Menores. *VII Congreso Internacional de Antropología y Arqueología Carlos E. Deive* (SD, October 20-22), MHD. Published in Robiou (2016).

2016a El chamanismo taíno y caribe, según las crónicas españolas y francesas, siglos 16-17. *III Encuentro de Diálogo sobre el Espiritismo y la Cultura: Chamanismo y mediunidad, convergencias y contrastes* (Río Piedras, May 22). Simposio del CIDEC – Centro Universitario Católico. Not published.

b *De aquí y de allá. Antología de escritos en el tiempo y el espacio (1980-2016)*. Foreword by Marcio Veloz Maggiolo. SJ: Editorial Punto y Coma.

2018 La esclavitud entre los Caribes-Insulares según la documentación del siglo 16 *I Simposio de Investigadores de Arqueología y Etnohistoria* (SJ, May 18). ICP.

Made in the USA
Columbia, SC
11 February 2023